*American Opinion
and the Russian Alliance,
1939–1945*

American Opinion and the Russian Alliance, 1939–1945

By Ralph B. Levering

The University of North Carolina Press
Chapel Hill

Library of Congress Cataloging in Publication Data

Levering, Ralph B
   American opinion and the Russian alliance, 1939–1945.

   Bibliography: p.
   Includes index.
   1.   United States—Foreign relations—Russia.
2.   Russia—Foreign relations—United States.
3.   Russia—Foreign opinion, American.   I.   Title.
E183.8.R9L47   327.73'O47   76–1996
ISBN 0–8078–1260–9

To Patty

Contents

Illustrations

Figures

~~~~Preface

Although this study obviously must consider the role of American attitudes in the coming of the Cold War, it is not intended to be another in the long list of monographs which focus on the "origins of the Cold War." Nor does it seek to offer an overarching theory of why the major wartime allies became such bitter enemies in the early postwar years. Its more modest objective is to assist in understanding the ever-shifting wartime climate of opinion toward Russia in the United States, a climate of opinion characterized generally by greatly increased friendliness toward Russia coupled with continuing fear of communism. Despite some persistent areas of disagreement, American-Russian attitudes and diplomatic relations during World War II marked the first period of détente with Communist Russia.

Most studies that have considered wartime public opinion toward Russia at all have treated the period analyzed in this study largely as background for the Cold War attitudes that began to predominate soon after the end of the fighting. I am convinced that American attitudes toward Russia during World War II are in themselves a worthy object of study, and that they should be approached on their own terms, not as background. Indeed, to approach wartime American attitudes toward Russia largely as antecedents of Cold War attitudes would involve wrenching them out of their historical context; for the overwhelming majority of Americans in 1941, 1943, or even early 1945 had no idea that intense animosity would develop toward any of the allies after the war.

Assuming, then, that the wartime climate of opinion toward Russia provides a proper focus, the chronological boundaries of the study logically become September 1939 to May 1945. Beginning about the time of the onset of war in Europe in 1939 should provide sufficient background to comprehend the remarkable shift to positive attitudes toward Russia which occurred from 1941 to 1943. And just as the alliance against Nazi Germany beginning in 1941 provided much of the impetus for the development of positive attitudes toward Russia, so Germany's utter collapse in the spring of 1945 ended the necessity for full-scale collaboration among the allies. In fact, allied victory in Europe was the crucial precondition for the coming of the Cold War in both its diplomatic and its attitudinal aspects. Only after V-E Day was diplomatic stalemate such as occurred at Potsdam and London in the summer and fall of 1945 thinkable; only after V-E Day was it possible for "respectable" congressmen and commentators to suggest that Russia was America's new adversary—or for Russian spokesmen to suggest the reverse.

In my writing I have tried to combine the historian's traditional effort to consider as much primary evidence as possible with the social scientist's interest in methodology. Except for portions of the introductory and concluding chapters in which I concentrate on public-opinion research and theory, I have tried to allow methodology to inform but not to intrude into the narrative. I also consider it essential in a study of public attitudes—even more than in most historical studies—to allow those expressing opinions to speak for themselves as much as possible in order to convey the nuances of thought and expression which can be lost so easily in paraphrasing. Using both direct quotation and textual analysis, I have tried above all else to convey the full range and relative significance of opinion toward Russia expressed during the war in speeches, on the radio, in the print media, in public-opinion polls, and in diaries and other private sources.

Dozens of thoughtful persons contributed to the community of scholarship upon which this study is based. Librarians at Princeton University Library; the Princeton Theological Seminary; the Franklin D. Roosevelt Library; the New York, Trenton, and Washington public libraries; the University of Washington; Columbia University; Rutgers University; Western Maryland College; the University of Maryland; the Johns Hopkins University; and the Library of Congress have been helpful, as have archivists at the National Archives, the State Department, the Roper Public Opinion Research Center of Williams College, the Gallup organization, the National Broadcasting Company, and the Phonoarchive of the University of Washington. Professor Milo Ryan, the archivist of the Phonoarchive, a virtually untapped source of information about modern American history, must be specially mentioned, for he extended every kindness to me during my visit to Seattle in the winter of 1970.

I would also like to thank George F. Kennan, Corliss Lamont, and Robert Mumford for granting interviews which lasted well over an hour in each case, and for allowing me to tape-record their comments. Wallace Carroll kindly wrote me a detailed letter in response to the questions I posed to him. Elizabeth Levering Morgan suggested the book's title,

Rhonda Kiler helped with typing, and Margaret and Al Woltz checked references.

I especially wish to thank all those who read and commented on drafts of this manuscript. These include Sheldon Avery, Richard D. Challener, Harwood L. Childs, Wayne S. Cole, Cornelius Darcy, Ronald Hoffman, Helen Levering Kern, Keith Olsen, and Arthur S. Link. Professor Link, who supervised the manuscript as a dissertation at Princeton University, helped me immeasurably. His broad knowledge and sure judgment, his interest in his own work in relationships between domestic and foreign sources of international behavior, and his open-mindedness toward possible contributions from the other human sciences to historical scholarship all obviously helped to guide my choice of a subject and to structure my approach to it.

With the possible exception of Professor Link, no one has been more helpful than my wife, Patricia Webb Levering, to whom this study is dedicated. In their prefaces many scholars thank their wives for "enduring" the ordeals which all writers experience. My wife *shared* the ordeals and contributed substantially at every stage from selection of sources to final revision, and I am grateful for her help from the bottom of my heart.

*American Opinion
and the Russian Alliance,
1939–1945*

Introduction
Of Matter and Method

At the beginning of 1970, most Americans disliked and distrusted Red China. Ever since the successful Communist revolution in China slightly over two decades before, the United States had refused to recognize the Peking government, and both American officials and the vast majority of newspapers, magazines, books, and electronic media had been consistently hostile toward the mainland Chinese, a hostility reflected in American public-opinion polls.[1] Yet two years later, in February 1972, Richard M. Nixon became the first American president to visit mainland China. The American media lavished praise on the People's Republic of China and its leaders, and widespread and sincere friendship was the dominant trend in American opinion.

A generation before, at the beginning of 1940, American attitudes toward "godless" Russia hit rock bottom. The Russian army had just invaded "poor little" Finland, a move which appeared to infuriate Americans even more than the German invasion of Poland in September 1939. Stalin was considered to be Hitler's partner in evil, and many Americans believed that the two dictators were determined to destroy European civilization. By the beginning of 1942, however, Russian soldiers were fighting valiantly to repulse the German attack begun the previous June, and Americans of all backgrounds were expressing their gratitude for and admiration of Soviet tenacity against the common enemy. And in February 1945 Franklin D. Roosevelt attended the big-three conference at Yalta; thus he became the first president to visit Russia.

The recent shift in attitudes toward China is cited not to suggest that the two cases are parallel in all respects but rather to illustrate how rapidly and unpredictably attitudes toward other nations can shift. To my knowledge no American in early 1940 or early 1970 predicted anything resembling the extent of the changes which occurred in less than two years. Nor did anyone predict the extent of change during the postwar years in American relations and attitudes toward our common enemies of World War II, Germany and Japan, and toward our most powerful ally, the Soviet Union.

In this study I deal with American attitudes toward Russia during the period of this century's second great European war, which began with the German advance into Poland on 1 September 1939 and ended with the German surrender on 8 May 1945. The scope of this book is limited to the period of the European war because the final defeat of Nazi Germany signaled a new period in Russian-American relations. The nation against whose policies the Grand Alliance had been constructed lay in ruins, a new diplomatic and strategic situation had come into being, and American attitudes toward Russia began their dramatic descent which characterized the Cold War.[2]

Within the five years and eight months between Germany's success in Poland and her unconditional surrender to the Allies occurred the greatest shifts in the international balance of power in the twentieth century, if not in modern times. In 1939 and 1940 Germany, the world's leading land power since the 1870s, demonstrated her continued superiority with decisive victories over Poland, France, and other European nations. At the same time England remained the preeminent sea power, a position she had held since the defeat of the Spanish Armada in 1588. Other "great powers" at the start of the war included China, France, Italy, Japan, Russia, and the United States. By May 1945 such startling and decisive changes had occurred that only the United States and Russia could be considered "great powers" in the traditional sense, and simultaneous changes had shaken dozens of smaller countries and colonies in Europe, Africa, and Asia.

Americans from President Roosevelt down to the poorest sharecropper naturally found it difficult to comprehend the changes in the international order taking place almost continuously throughout the war. No one could foretell it, but many Americans of diverse backgrounds speculated about and tried to influence the shape of the postwar international order and America's role in it.[3] The only certainty was that the fragile structures of the interwar period could not and would not be restored.

This period of transition leading to the status of the United States and the Soviet Union as superpowers has been studied assiduously by diplomatic and military historians. Even the narrower topic of American-Soviet relations during the war has attracted dozens of historians, and many valuable studies of what John R. Deane called "the strange alliance" have been produced.[4]

Despite the very substantial scholarship on wartime Russian-American relations, no other work has concentrated on the domestic context of American policy toward Russia during the war.[5] In fact, the only full-length studies which deal with the attitudes of nonintellectuals toward Russia are an early study by Meno Lovenstein and an excellent recent work by Peter G. Filene, both of which deal with the interwar years.[6] Considering the absence before the mid-1930s of public-opinion polls, Filene's achievement is especially impressive.

My intent in this study is not only to describe as accurately as possible the shape of American attitudes toward Russia during World War II. I seek to offer some insight into the process by which attitudes toward Russia were formed at that time, to make some contribution to understanding the role of national leadership in helping to shape wartime public attitudes toward foreign policy, and to elucidate wartime thinking about American and Russian roles in the postwar world that would assist in explaining why the Cold War with Russia could develop so soon after the Axis collapse.

I must emphasize that in this study I do not explore the particular diplomatic issues involved in understanding relations between the American and Soviet governments during World War II. The major reason for avoiding diplomacy as such here is that public attitudes cannot be approached in this manner—at least not so long as many elements of diplomacy are characterized by secrecy. Officials provide the public with possible sources of insight into international relations (speeches and treaties, for example), but the public must judge, on the basis of very limited information, how accurately these sources reflect the realities of foreign policy at any given time. In a study of attitudes, therefore, it is what various people believe to have happened rather than what actually happened which forms the primary object of study.

I must also emphasize that the scope of this study includes neither a systematic attempt to analyze Russians' attitudes toward the United States nor a comprehensive analysis of the merits of Russian behavior during the war. My more limited objective is to shed some light on wartime American attitudes toward issues of foreign policy generally and toward Russia specifically. Understanding the wartime climate of opinion— how it was changed and in what ways it remained the same—is necessary for understanding the hostility toward Russia which began to develop in the aftermath of the Yalta Conference and then continued to intensify during the early postwar period. I hope that this study of how Americans reacted to Russia during the war will be helpful in understanding how the attitudes present in the early Cold-War period came into being.

ᏝᎧᎧᎧᎧᎧᏝ My first objective, describing American attitudes toward Russia during World War II, is not so simple as it might appear. For one thing, attitudes as mental constructs are more abstract and therefore more difficult to describe than many other historical phenomena. Even social psychologists and other social scientists have not been able to agree on a single definition of the term attitudes. But, as political scientist James F. Best noted recently, "they are most frequently defined as more or less enduring orientations toward an object or situation and predispositions to respond positively or negatively toward that object or situation."[7] Sociologist Bernard Berelson and psychologist Gary A. Steiner described the nebulous relationship between attitude and related concepts: "Usually the term 'opinion' refers to more superficial and transitory issues, the term 'attitude' to somewhat deeper and longer-lasting convictions, and the term 'value' or 'belief' to the deepest of all."[8] To simplify, opinions reflect and develop from attitudes, which in turn reflect and develop from beliefs, or belief systems.[9]

Another difficulty in studying attitudes is the selection of materials—what to examine, and how much is enough.[10] I examined more than forty newspapers on a systematic basis, including leading circulation dailies in major cities in every region, dailies in the smaller cities of Trenton, New Jersey; Asheville, North Carolina; and Casper, Wyoming; and student newspapers at Rutgers University and the University of Washington. I listened to many hours of radio recordings from the two leading networks, CBS and NBC; viewed dozens of newsreels and films; consulted private manuscripts and public archives; and read many hundreds of books, magazine articles, and public-opinion polls and government releases dealing with Russia, not all of which merited inclusion in the bibliography. I also interviewed a few ordinary citizens and several people who helped to shape attitudes during the war.[11] I consider these materials representative of the kinds of information and ideas circulated among the American public, which it could use to develop the attitudes that were represented in the polls and other sources.

Despite the abundance of materials, some important weaknesses exist in the record. For example, no detailed scholarly studies of specific individuals' attitudes toward Russia were done until 1947, by which time favorable wartime attitudes had been largely reversed.[12] Moreover, even granting that several hundred thousand Americans were interviewed by pollsters on issues relating to Russia, and several thousand more left written or spoken comments about Russia, this group is still less than 1 percent of the population. The exact opinions of the other 99 percent are lost to history. Finally, public-opinion polls provide no panacea for getting at public opinions, much less for understanding the attitudes and belief systems which underlie them.

In the first place, public-opinion polls do not enable one to distinguish between the thinking of the mass and attentive publics, and they reveal nothing about what opinion makers, opinion submitters, and decision makers are thinking. Second, as in the case of other materials available to the student of past behavior, polls are not pliable instruments of understanding. The researcher is bequeathed only those questions (and responses) on which the leaders of opinion measurement decide to poll the public, and the timing of the polls as well as their nature are dictated by contemporary considerations of interest, profit, and feasibility. Finally, the answers to most questions provide a bare minimum of information, and even that is potentially misleading.

The knowledge to be gained from poll data is potentially misleading precisely because it is so meager. In almost all polls the respondent may answer yes, no, or no opinion. Such choices may be required for quick and inexpensive data processing, but what do the responses mean? Was the yes of an Oshkosh resident heartfelt or hesitant? How much did it depend on the way the question was worded, on the interviewer's intonation, or even on the answers to previous questions? Did no opinion mean that the respondent failed to understand the question, that the yes-no dichotomy would not express his opinion adequately, or that the question simply did not arouse his interest? Or did it mean, as pollsters tend to assume, that the respondent lacked the information to answer honestly either way? The answer to these and other questions about past public opinion will never be known.[13]

This being the case, it is apparent that poll data, like all other historical sources, must be approached with extreme caution. The statement "Fifty-five percent of the public believes . . . " is perhaps acceptable as intellectual shorthand if a score of qualifications is kept in mind; at worst it is stark credulity.

Even so, without public-opinion polls a useful study of the opinion-making process under modern conditions would be virtually unimaginable. There would not be enough feedback to judge which opinions were taking hold with the public and which were not. Polls clearly have superseded journalists and other observers as the premier guides to mass thinking. Now that these other observers have assumed supplementary rather than primary roles, their biases are easier to consider intelligently, and their potential contributions to understanding have thus increased. A single poll, examined without other knowledge about a historical period, has little value. But as other sources are studied, and as the number of relevant polls jumps into the hundreds and even thousands—as happened during the period of this study—their value increases enormously. Whatever their faults, opinion polls cannot be slighted by students of the recent past.

My second objective is to analyze the process by which wartime attitudes toward Russia were formed. In his influential book, *Public Opinion and Foreign Policy*, political scientist James N. Rosenau delineated the three processes which form the relationship between public opinion and foreign policy.

One is the *governmental decision-making process* through which foreign policy is formulated and into which existing public opinion is integrated by the officials responsible for the conduct of policy (henceforth designated as the decision-makers or policy-makers). Another is the *opinion-submitting process* that occurs whenever opinions are conveyed to or impressed upon decision-makers by individual members or segments of the public (hereafter called the opinion-submitters). And thirdly, there is the *opinion-making process* whereby ideas about foreign-policy issues are formed and circulated in American society (through the interaction of what shall be referred to as opinion-holders and opinion-makers, the former being the entire citizenry and the latter those citizens who introduce opinions into the impersonal channels of the communications system) [Rosenau's italics].[14]

And what are the basic relationships among these three processes? The first and third, Rosenau argues, "are independent systems of interaction, which is to say that both can occur irrespective of any linkage with the other." This means simply that opinions on foreign policy can be circulated without coming to the attention of decision makers and, conversely, that decision makers "can arrive at foreign-policy decisions without knowledge of the existing state of public opinion." Understanding that these two processes can be independent is crucial, because the "opinion-policy relationship is defined in terms of a linkage between these two processes." If there were no linkage, as might result under a "pure" dictatorship, any similarity between opinion and policy would be entirely accidental; but if the linkage were total, as in a "pure" democracy, one would always find exact correlation between the two. Finally, the opinion-submitting process "derives from the other two processes. If the decision-making process is inaccessible, or if the opinion-making process is quiescent or not governmentally oriented, there can be no opinion-submitting process."[15]

In this study I focus on the opinion-making process for three major reasons. In the first place, it would be impossible to do justice to all three processes and the relationships among them in a single study covering nearly six years, as this one does. Second, the opinion-making process is still the least understood of the three. Historians and other scholars have made many studies of lobbyists and other opinion submitters and of decision makers and the forces which act upon them, but there has been very little sustained study of the opinion-making process.[16] Third and most important, concentration on the opinion-making process will certainly permit maximum insight into American attitudes toward Russia.

In respect to the opinion-making process the public is "stratified" according to the extent of participation available to each person and to the manner in which each person participates. In regard to extent of participation, there are two basic types of persons. At least 99 percent of the adult population is composed of *opinion holders*, whom Rosenau defines as "those persons in the society who, on a given issue or in general, cannot circulate opinions to persons with whom they are not acquainted."[17] These people might have an occasional letter to the editor published or might even be interviewed by a roving reporter, but still they have no regular access to the society's impersonal channels of communication, which are basically the mass media. The others, the *opinion makers*, do. They are "those who by virtue of their position of leadership in the society, have access to the impersonal channels."[18]

"Differences in the *manner* of participation," Rosenau says, "can be traced along a motivation-information scale ranging from opinion holders who are totally unconcerned and uninformed about world affairs to those who are greatly concerned and well-informed about such matters." These two broad groupings are usually called the mass public, whose size is usually estimated at between 75 and 90 percent of the adult population, and the attentive public, which is composed of the remainder of adult Americans. The mood of the mass public is normally characterized by indifference, passivity, instability, and irrationality. The attentive public is likely to have opposite traits, though the complexity of the composition of each group and the fact that different people may be alert or impassive on different issues rule out simple dichotomies. But the attentive public does tend "to offset the irrational impact of mass moods and to fill the vacuum which exists when indifference is the prevailing mood." Functionally, the mass public essentially "sets the outer limits beyond which policy choices cannot be made," whereas the attentive public "can be said to determine the inner limits within which the opinion-policy relationship operates."[19]

The functions of the mass and attentive publics are impressive, but those of the opinion makers are even more so, because they largely shape the society's opinions about foreign affairs. As Rosenau argues throughout his book, basic opinions about foreign policy simply are not "made" at the local level by people with no access to impersonal channels. These people may have an important function in circulating opinions at the final stage to their friends and relatives, but their opinions are almost always derived from the thinking of the national opinion makers whom they or their friends trust. In this study, they may trust Franklin Roosevelt, Herbert Hoover, Walter Lippmann, or Westbrook Pegler; but the point is that they receive their basic ideas from one or from many respected opinion makers.

Who are the opinion makers at any given time? Rosenau contends that there are four major occupational types of opinion makers: governmental, associational, institutional, and individual. Within each of these groups there are four other types: national multiissue, national single-issue, local multiissue, and local single-issue. Among governmental opinion makers a senator would be a national multiissue opinion maker, an assistant secretary of state for European affairs would be a national single-issue opinion maker, a mayor would be a local multiissue opinion maker, and the chief customs officer at a port city would be a local single-issue opinion maker. Respective examples of associational opinion makers would be the national commander of the American Legion, the president of the Foreign Policy Association, the commander of a city's Veterans of Foreign Wars, and the head of a county's refugee organization. Respective examples of institutional opinion makers would be the president of Ford Motor Company, the head of a missile manufacturing company, the president of a city's leading bank, and a partner in a coffee-importing firm. Finally, respective examples of individual opinion makers would be a syndicated columnist, the nation's leading demographer, a prominent author in the community, and the professor of Asiatic affairs at a nearby college.[20] Obviously, the national opinion makers are usually better able to circulate their opinions to large numbers of people, and the national multiissue opinion maker would generally be better able to have his views circulated regularly than would the national single-issue opinion maker. Essentially the same distinctions apply within each of the other groups.

Rosenau argues that most opinion makers acquire access to impersonal channels by ascription. Some, especially those among individual opinion makers, do so by achievement, but these are in the minority.[21] To say that most opinion makers acquire access by ascription is not to imply that most are not also high achievers. It is to say, rather, that the position which typically commands respect itself permits access to the impersonal channels of communication rather than the personal merits of the position's occupant. Thus, the president of General Motors probably would be able to have his strongly held views about foreign affairs circulated even though he might lack both general intelligence and specific knowledge of what he was talking about, as compared to any of a number of professors at the University of Michigan whose views might never be circulated through the mass media. When John Nance Garner was vice-president of the United States, he had no difficulty circulating any opinions which reporters considered at all controversial. But after Garner left office and returned to his small hometown in Texas, his views were usually ignored.

During the years of this study, neither the president of General Motors nor Garner had direct access to the impersonal channels of communication; reporters and commentators had to decide whether their views on any subject deserved to be circulated or discarded. One source of Franklin Roosevelt's power, which was probably unprecedented in American history, was that he was able to bypass the judgments of the press and speak to the people directly on radio whenever he chose. Other national politicians of the era liked to do the same thing, but they either had to buy their time or be invited to appear. Essentially these leaders had to rely on the judgment and goodwill of reporters, editors, and commentators to decide when their views deserved to be circulated widely and when they did not.

All successful politicians seem to realize that the media form the very heart of the system through which opinions are circulated to local leaders of opinion and to the public. The manner in which the press, radio, periodicals, pamphlets, books, movies, and newsreels presented Russia and the ideas about Russia which prominent Americans were attempting to circulate through them is a central concern of this study.[22]

My third objective in this study is to examine the role of leadership in helping to shape wartime attitudes toward Russia. Much more than is the case for domestic affairs, public attitudes toward foreign affairs are shaped by political leaders—especially the president—and by the media. As Bernard C. Cohen noted recently,

Contemporary scholarship on public opinion and foreign policy underlines the capacity of leaders to shape the public opinion to which they are supposedly responsive, and to interpret the opinions they hear in ways that support their own views.

The President is especially powerful as a shaper of public opinion, since he is the acknowledged symbol of and spokesman for the country in foreign affairs. He commands attention from the media whenever he wants it, he formulates policy alternatives with an authority no one else possesses, and he has a substantial and more or less natural base of sympathy and identification on which he can draw and which he can dissipate only with the greatest difficulty.[23]

A basic reason why attitudes toward foreign policy are more amenable to governmental and media leadership than are attitudes toward domestic affairs is because very few people have personal knowledge of other nations or their foreign policies. Whereas many people have personal knowledge of such domestic concerns as labor-management disputes and race relations, a minute percentage of the population has visited Russia and studied in depth its history, institutions, and policies. Only those at the highest levels of government expect to have access to state secrets; thus, almost everyone is dependent upon public officials and other "experts" for information about foreign affairs. And because most ideas about foreign policy reach local communities through the media, knowledge is circumscribed by interest, effort, and the sources of information which are available locally. It is not surprising that "dark areas of ignorance" limited many Americans' understanding of foreign affairs throughout the 1940s—or that they still do today.[24]

The question of leadership in foreign affairs relates directly to the study's fourth objective: some elucidation of the wartime preconditions of the bitter hostility toward Russia which emerged so rapidly after the end of the fighting. The wartime origins of the Cold War clearly involved diplomacy and decision making, as has been emphasized in most previous studies. But the Cold War also involved the mobilization of the people of the United States to warlike animosity. I hope that concentration on the domestic context of American relations with Russia during the war will provide some new perspectives on the emergence of the Cold War.

Did Americans accept the wartime alliance with Russia and believe that it would last? Was *Russia* synonymous with *communism* in American thought? What conceptions of the postwar world, and of American and Russian roles in it, were preponderant? How did President Roosevelt and other opinion makers seek to shape attitudes toward Russia at various times? Did wartime opinion makers foresee a bitter rivalry with Russia after the war? If so, did they believe it could be averted? Was their leadership of the public equal to the requirements of the time? These and other issues bearing upon the background of the Cold War receive implicit and explicit consideration throughout this study.

Some of the ideas of two other scholars—sociologist Robert K. Merton and historian Arno J. Mayer—also form a backdrop to the entire study. Their insights concern two of the most basic divisions in the modern American social order, divisions which were reflected in wartime attitudes toward foreign policy generally and toward Russia specifically.

The first of these ideas is the distinction between *cosmopolitans* and *locals* in modern American society first made by Merton in the 1940s. Merton's basic argument is that there are two types of "influentials" in American communities: "cosmopolitans" and "locals." He observed the major differences between the two types in 1943 in a study of "Rovere," a town of 11,000 in the Northeast. "The chief criterion for distinguishing the two," Merton wrote,

is found in their *orientation* toward Rovere. The localite largely confines his interests to this community. Rovere is essentially his world. Devoting little thought or energy to the Great Society, he is preoccupied with local problems, to the virtual exclusion of the national and international scene. He is, strictly speaking, parochial. Contrariwise with the cosmopolitan type. He has some interest in Rovere and must of course maintain a minimum of relations within the community since he, too, exerts influence there. But he is also oriented significantly to the world outside Rovere, and regards himself as an integral part of that world. He resides in Rovere but lives in the Great Society. If the local type is parochial, the cosmopolitan is ecumenical.[25]

The difference between the two types of influentials were many and profound, extending far beyond the focal points of their interests. The local was more tied to the community and in fact had customarily lived there all of his life; the cosmopolitan was much more mobile. The locals wanted to know as many people as possible in their town; the cosmopolitans wanted their contact to be largely limited to people "with whom they could really talk." The locals belonged to general service organizations such as the Masons and Kiwanis; the cosmopolitans belonged to those organizations in which they could "exercise their special skills and knowledge." The influence of the locals tended to depend on "who they know," the cosmopolitans' on "what they know."[26]

These and other contrasts were reflected in the communications behavior of the two groups. The cosmopolitans subscribed to four or five magazines, the locals to two or three. The former read *Time* and other relatively sophisticated magazines such as *Harper's* and *National Geographic*, whereas the latter tended to follow the mass public in reading *Reader's Digest*, *Life*, and the *Saturday Evening Post*. All of the cosmopolitans read the *New York Times* or the *New York Herald Tribune*, or both, whereas about half of the locals read New York's tabloid newspaper.[27]

"Gratifications derived from mass communications," Merton concluded, "are not merely psychological in nature; they are also a product of the distinctive social roles of those who make use of these communications. It is not that the newsmagazine is one man's meat and another man's poison. It is, rather, that the newsmagazine is meat for one social type and poison for another social type."[28]

Since the 1940s, many scholars have arrived at observations similar to Merton's. Urban sociologists Herbert Gans and Scott Greer, for example, have pointed toward the conclusion that locals and cosmopolitans coexist in America's most urban areas. Greer noted that farmers in large-scale societies may become "urbane," and that "citizens of Boston may be comfortable in the role of urban peasant."[29] Alfred Hero reached similar conclusions about the South. Within leadership groups and the mass public alike, Hero found significant and persistent differences between those who attempt to remain attuned to national and international trends and those whose interests are confined largely to their communities. Moreover, these differences are reflected very markedly in diverging outlooks on foreign policy.[30] That these differences emerge on issues of foreign policy as well as in domestic attitudes and opinions is yet another evidence of the existence in American society of profound and pervasive domestic sources of foreign policy.

The second essential idea has been offered and defended in two detailed studies of World War I and its aftermath by Professor Mayer.[31] His basic argument is that the diplomacy of that era must be approached in terms of the sweeping division in the world between the "forces of order" and the "forces of movement." The forces of order consisted of conservatives and their allies who, in defense of their interests and ideals, were committed to undoing, or at least to containing, the Russian Revolution. The forces of movement, in contrast, were committed in varying degrees to furthering the assault on liberal, bourgeois society that was so successfully initiated in Russia. Mayer suggests that much of the history of the half-century since the Russian Revolution might well be approached in terms of this division.

After the relative placidity of American politics in the 1920s, the latent division between Left and Right burst into the open with the advent of the New Deal. No one knew precisely how far Franklin Delano Roosevelt proposed to carry the drive to the Left which began with the defeat of Herbert Hoover in 1932, and most businessmen and many others had no desire to find out. When they did find out—in the form of the Wagner Act and similar legislation and the administration's assault upon the Supreme Court—they were distinctly displeased. They longed for the good old days less than half a decade before when none of this "wild radicalism" would have merited even a hearing. Meanwhile, militant labor leaders and their many supporters among intellectuals and the disadvantaged were committed to the perpetuation and expansion of the New Deal.

Those with fresh memories dating to only the 1950s could easily overlook the intensity of the struggle between the forces of order and forces of movement in America in the 1930s. The fervor with which much of the Left looked to Russia as the epitome of the good and the beautiful, and the corresponding distaste with which the Right reacted to everything emanating from Moscow, also seem to be part of a remote past.[32] But just as they were live issues throughout the industrialized nations when they emerged from World War I, so were they vibrant questions for Americans as the advanced nations of Europe again resorted to force on 1 September 1939. And they still seemed unsettled when Roosevelt died in Warm Springs, Georgia, on a sunny April day in 1945 less than three weeks before humble American and Russian infantrymen met and embraced in the heart of defeated Germany.

Chapter 2

Friend of Fascism,
1939–1941

In the autumn of 1938 there had been a flurry of American interest in the deepening European crisis. The question of whether or not peace would last had been brought to the forefront of American concerns that autumn by the frequent commentaries of H. V. Kaltenborn and other radio analysts who had been developing on-the-scene assistants in Europe for several years as if in preparation for crises. But after the meetings near Munich, which admittedly did avert war for a time, most Americans returned to their normally dominant domestic preoccupations.

The economic crisis, though no longer so intense as before, was still a dark reality for perhaps ten million American families. Economic insecurity was the condition of tens of millions more, some of whom could count on returning to the bread lines should another severe recession occur. And even those who were relatively secure could read the financial pages without tangible evidence that values would ever return to even the level of ten years before.

Reviewing the situation at the end of the decade, Raoul de Roussy de Sales, the American correspondent for the newspapers *Paris Soir* and *Paris Midi*, observed in his diary that the "predominating impression is that America has passed through a tremendous crisis . . . , a crisis that has left a legacy of bitterness and uneasiness." To him, the preceding decade seemed "definitely retrogressive from the American conception of 'civilization.' Figures have not attained the 1929 level; to a good many Americans, perhaps to the majority, this represents ten years of loss."[1]

To those who supported it, the New Deal had provided a spark of hope; to those who did not, it seemed a threat to the ethic of success and status through individual effort and business hegemony which they thought had made America great. Although many New Deal programs were being carried forward in 1938 and 1939, the overall movement seemed to have lost its punch. Having fulfilled neither the fears of its critics that it would result in communism for America nor the hopes of its prophets that it would end unemployment and ease social and economic inequalities, it had somehow become stalemated. The major question of the day no longer concerned the New Deal's substance. It was whether its seemingly indispensable champion, Roosevelt, would dare to run for a third term; and, further, if he did so dare, whether he would be defeated.

Confronted with an uneasy domestic situation and habituated through most of their history to the belief that foreign affairs were basically the business of foreigners, most Americans did not face fondly the growing turmoil in international relations touched off by expansionist, relatively underprivileged nations in Europe and Asia. What they did observe, of course, they did not like. But they were not really surprised to find their moral inferiors abroad going at it again, as they had done so often in the past. Whatever her domestic difficulties might be at the moment, America was still the citadel of reason and virtue in an unreasonable and immoral world, and most Americans wanted to keep it that way by not getting very deeply involved in foreign affairs.

The books they were buying and reading in 1939 illustrated that the minds of the mass and attentive publics were still largely concerned with domestic interests. John Steinbeck's novel *The Grapes of Wrath*, the number-one best seller that year, showed that Americans still had at least one eye on the depression. Lloyd Douglas's *Disputed Passage* and Marjorie Rawlings's *The Yearling* also were unlikely to direct attention to global developments. As usual, nonfiction best sellers more closely reflected current events, but even those who read all of the top ten would have been poorly informed about the Europe of 1939. Pierre van Paassen's reminiscences, *Days of Our Years*, topped the list. It was joined by four other autobiographies: William Lyon Phelps's *Autobiography with Letters*; Bellamy Partridge's *Country Lawyer*; Edna Ferber's *A Peculiar Treasure*; and Adolf Hitler's *Mein Kampf*, published in full in America for the first time. John Gunther's *Inside Asia* was third on the list, but the other two works which might have passed for commentaries on contemporary affairs, Vincent Sheean's *Not Peace But a Sword* and Anne Morrow Lindbergh's *Listen! The Wind*, were only ninth and tenth.[2]

By the late 1930s, most Americans had decided that the man who had written *Mein Kampf* more than a decade before was the worst villain on the horizon. He, more than anyone else, seemed to threaten the continuance of their domestic preoccupations. Joseph Stalin may well have stood for equally bad or even worse things, but he was a kitten compared to the German tiger in his ability as well as his apparent aspiration to upset the international status quo.

Germany's unenviable position in America—heightened daily by editorialists, commentators, politicians, and other opinion makers—was reflected in the polls. In November 1938, George Gallup's pollsters asked their customary sample of three thousand adult Americans this question: "If there was a war between Germany and Russia, which side would you rather see win?" Eighty-two percent of those who responded answered Russia, while only 18 percent replied Germany.[3] It was obvious from this and dozens of other indicators of opinion that most Americans were very likely to consider Germany the culprit if war erupted in Europe.

The tremendous intensity of their fear and hatred of Germany is further underscored by the fact that most Americans considered Russia worse than Germany in two important respects. To the question, "If you HAD TO CHOOSE, which kind of government would you prefer to live under—the kind in Germany or the kind in Russia?" 59 percent of those with opinions chose Germany, while only 41 percent favored Russia.[4] As in their judgment of these two foreign societies, Americans in February 1939 responded to another Gallup question, by a margin of 55 percent to 45 percent, that American Communists were a greater danger than Nazis living in the United States.[5]

It must not be inferred from this presentation of poll data that the average interviewee was deeply concerned about the problems posed by the questions. In this case, most people surely were not. Each of the three above questions, after all, dealt with seemingly distant possibilities rather than with facts that had to be faced immediately. A Russo-German war, the choice of having to live under nazism or communism, and the danger these movements posed to America must have seemed quite remote to most Americans when the questions were asked. But the responses do aid in understanding general American attitudes toward the major European powers before Hitler's Polish gamble touched off a general war in Europe. After World War II Americans feared Russia more than they feared all other foreign powers. Before and during the war the simple but extremely significant fact was that Germany occupied this role of master culprit.

In the summer of 1939, attitudes toward Russia's ideology and international position as it related to Germany's assumed three basic forms. As usual, the most common attitude probably was apathy. For most, the problems posed by aggressive nazism coupled with pacific communism simply did not exist. The second view, presented mainly by conservative spokesmen, suggested that nazism was somehow an ominous offshoot of that great devil of the modern age, communism. Differing as always with their conservative domestic opponents, liberals and radicals tended to believe that communism and nazism were so antithetical that rapprochement between them was unthinkable. The general grounds for apathy were considered in the first several paragraphs of this chapter; the other two views require elucidation.

The foundations of the conservative position were established by the journalist Eugene Lyons in his book published in 1937, *Assignment in Utopia*, which enjoyed a lengthy sojourn on the best-seller lists. Coming at a time when the American Left was heady with success, the work apparently aroused wide interest among conservatives eager to hear that communism was not the wave of the future. Lyons had gone to Soviet Russia in the 1920s in search of utopia. Disillusioned, he returned to America with a mission which occupied the rest of his life: to warn his compatriots of the weaknesses of the utopia he had sought in vain.

"The 'coming struggle'—and it is not coming, it is already here," Lyons wrote, "is not between communism and fascism. It is the struggle for the moral and ethical ideals which have been renounced by both these movements."[6] Such was the eloquent epitome of the conservative position. Ironically Lyons—like another stalwart anticommunist, the Socialist Norman Thomas—was not a conservative. On the contrary, he criticized Stalinist Russia for becoming "one of the great forces for conservatism in the modern world" because of "the intense entrenchment of the new ruling political and economic groups on a basis of thoroughgoing conservatism."[7]

Despite his total rejection of Russia as it had developed in the late 1920s and early 1930s, Lyons still saw the Russian Revolution as a landmark of modern times: "The original ideals of the Russian revolution are in the stream of human thought: not a million Stalin's and G.P.U.'s can change that. . . . What happened in Russia twenty years ago will remain a frontier in time, token of the deepening twilight of the capitalist era."[8]

Understandably, the conservative writers who proceeded from Lyons's link between the present practice of communism and fascism did not dwell upon the suggestion that the capitalist era might be receding. But they were the only ones ever to mention the possibility that Hitler and Stalin might decide to join hands. The most famous but by no means the only prediction of rapprochement was offered by W. G. Krivitsky in the *Saturday Evening Post* at the end of April 1939.[9] "There is probably no more widespread myth in the world today," Krivitsky asserted, "than the one which presents Hitler and Stalin as mortal and irreconcilable enemies. The true picture is that of a persistent suitor who will not be discouraged by rebuffs. Stalin is that suitor."[10]

Perhaps the leading purveyor of the conservative position at this time and later was the nation's most devout and widely read adversary of organized labor and communism, the columnist Westbrook Pegler. Pegler's great simplification in 1939 was that communism and "nazi-fascism" were one and the same thing. "These two are, in fact, only one ism, to wit, bolshevism," Pegler wrote in the April issue of the *American Legion Magazine*. "The pretentious intellectual opposition between them is no more real than the ear-splitting, if not side-splitting, mock feuds between radio comics. It is just an act."[11]

Having tarred Hitler with the communist brush, Pegler could proceed to inform his readers that "Hitler bolshevism" was "the more dangerous to American freedom and internal peace at the moment and to the political and economic system under which we were born."[12] Pegler concluded with an oblique reference to the view, which he apparently was not yet ready to share with his readers, that communism had become more conservative in Russia and less threatening to the United States than dynamic nazism: "Hitler's bolshevism and Stalin's are practically identical now but Hitler is still innovating and may yet exceed the Russian kind."[13]

The Left featured equally outspoken leaders. The man most ready to jump at the Right on any occasion was the brash midwesterner, Earl Browder, secretary of the American Communist Party. Browder, like other American Communists, had an extraordinary gift for making a fool of himself and his party. In the summer of 1939, for example, he spent much of his time assuring the American people that a German-Soviet pact was unthinkable. "Reactionaries openly speculate," Browder said with characteristic derision, "that the Soviet Union may try to beat Chamberlain at his game by joining hands with Hitler." On another occasion, in a speech in July in Charlottesville, Virginia, Browder asserted, "There is as much chance of Russo–German agreement as of Earl Browder being elected President of the Chamber of Commerce."[14]

There was dual irony in Browder's assertions. In the first place, no real need existed for Browder to say anything on this subject. If they thought about it at all, most Americans surely would have agreed with Browder's view; or at least they would have agreed with it until they heard Browder voice it! Considering that he was the head of an aspiring political party, Browder had an amazingly weak sense of what needed to be said and when, and what was better left unsaid. By vociferously denying the scattered predictions of rapprochement Browder only directed attention to the issue. Secondly, for a leader who was widely believed to be under Moscow's direct control, Browder knew very little about developments in Soviet foreign policy. This meant in practice that the American Communist Party was embarrassed by nearly every change in Russia's international position before and during the war. That Browder would soon be put into federal prison for illegally obtaining a passport was probably a boon to the party as well as to American attitudes toward Russia.

Browder was by no means the only leftist soon to be embarrassed by the Nazi-Soviet Pact. In the 26 August issue of the *Nation*, a leading liberal journal,[15] there appeared a letter signed by more than four hundred prominent American liberals and radicals, including Matthew Josephson, Waldo Frank, Granville Hicks, Max Lerner, Vincent Sheean, and I. F. Stone. The following is the key paragraph of this pro-Russian piece which appeared on the newsstands just before the pact was announced and which provided an excellent summation of American leftist thought at this time.

On the international scene the fascists and their friends have tried to prevent a united anti-aggression front by sowing suspicion between the Soviet Union and other nations interested in maintaining peace. On the domestic scene the reactionaries are attempting to split the democratic front by similar tactics. Realizing that here in America they cannot get far with a definitely pro-fascist appeal, they strive to pervert American anti-fascist sentiment to their own ends. With the aim of turning anti-fascist feeling against the Soviet Union they have encouraged the fantastic falsehood that the U.S.S.R. and the totalitarian states are basically alike. By this strategy they hope to create dissension among the progressive forces whose united strength is a first necessity for the defeat of fascism.[16]

The signing of the Nazi-Soviet Pact had many repercussions for the American Left, not the least of which was its development of a sober approach to the realities of international relations and the possibilities for domestic reform. Things were not so simple as they seemed, and many on the Left learned that, despite their high levels of sophistication and educational attainment, they and everyone else knew much less about the contemporary world than they had thought. For attentive as well as mass opinion to be in a state of flux much of the time is perhaps a more natural and healthy situation, given the ubiquity of complexity and change in the modern world, than excessive consistency of attitudes and opinions.

Americans of all political persuasions and degrees of interest in world affairs were deeply concerned at this time about the rising threat which the spread of totalitarianism abroad seemed to pose to American institutions. Since World War I not only had Russian Communism proved to be totalitarian, but also Germany and Italy in Europe and several countries in Latin America and Asia had embraced totalitarian concepts of social and political organization. To liberals, the most crushing blow of all had come when the totalitarian Right had systematically crushed populist hopes in Spain within the previous two years. To many American Catholics and some conservative Protestants the victory of Franco was not unwelcome, but to anyone left of center the Franco regime was anathema. Although these sharply different outlooks toward Spain were usually left unspoken during the war, they constituted one of the bulwarks of conflicting perspective on foreign affairs.

The more specific concern in 1939 and 1940, however, was that the upsurge of totalitarianism might engulf America as it had so many other countries. This view was widely reflected in leading organs of opinion circulation such as *Life* and the *New York Times*, but in retrospect it seems most striking in publications of civic and church groups. In a collection of speeches and writings published by the National Municipal League, for example, Clarence A. Dykstra, the league's president, asked, "Is it not time for all of our educational enterprises in the United States to recognize how widespread is teaching throughout the world which by precept and implication throws overboard the whole theory and method of democracy? Is it not time for us to find out why it has been so easy for the dictators to get rid of democratic processes?"[17] The editor of the journal of the Federal Council of Churches was concerned about who was communicating with youth: "In Russia it is youth to whom Communism makes its strongest appeal. The Communist leader tells the young people that theirs is the opportunity to 'make a new world.' In Germany National Socialism makes its strongest bid to the youth. . . . The Communists and the Nazis know where their largest opportunity lies."[18]

The most coherent proposal in 1939 for bolstering democracy against totalitarianism was offered by an obscure European correspondent of the *New York Times*, Clarence K. Streit.[19] His book, *Union Now, A Proposal for Federal Union of the Democracies of the North Atlantic*, was read and discussed widely and went through several editions during the war. The book's content was a thoughtful elaboration on its title. The limitation of the "union" to the North Atlantic, Streit argued, was dictated by existing facts: it was hard to find democracy anywhere but in America, the British Commonwealth, and some isolated European countries. Germany and Italy certainly did not qualify at that time, nor did Russia, though it was much closer to membership than those two nations. "We need more time," Streit wrote, "to answer definitely whether Soviet departures from the basic principles of democracy have been matters of expediency or principle."[20] He continued:

> I would favor admitting Soviet Russia to the nucleus as soon as it guaranteed freedom of the press and the other Rights of Man to the minimum degree common to the peoples in the nucleus. A world government whose principle of freedom not only allows but encourages the United States to retain its republic and Great Britain its monarchy could not refuse Russia its soviet.[21]

Most Americans on 21 August 1939 were not pondering Streit's proposals. In fact, more than two-thirds of them probably would not have understood three or four of the words he used in the portions just quoted. But most would have shared his mixed appraisal of Russia.

According to the prevailing view, Russia had a bad form of government and a wicked leader who had conducted the purges but who had also brought economic development to this backward nation. Russia had a record of trying to spread communism abroad but had done well in attempting to unite the forces that opposed Hitler. During the next six months, the goodwill that existed on this day would almost totally disappear.

☙ Despite the apathy that since 1937 had become typical of American attitudes toward supposedly earthshaking international events, many Americans were shocked by the announcement of the Russo-German Non-Aggression Pact. They were like spectators at a circus shaken by a performer's fatal fall from a flying trapeze. In a world where almost anything was possible, this simply was not supposed to have happened. Even the Right, which had been trying to discredit both Germany and Russia by linking them with each other, found it hard to believe that these sworn enemies had joined hands. The noncommunist Left, which had been shaken by the Soviet purges, but which recovered when Russia gave the only significant support to the Spanish revolutionaries, was bewildered and then infuriated. Only true believers such as Earl Browder could accept this move with a semblance of equanimity.

Even Browder was almost speechless when reporters hounded him with texts of his Charlottesville speech. When he finally agreed to be interviewed, the best he could offer were the observation that every nation should sign a nonagression pact with Russia and the contention that this was Stalin's "master stroke" for peace.[22] When the *Daily Worker* argued that this step "unquestionably strengthens the leading role of the Soviet Union in its inspiring fight against fascist aggression,"[23] its editors must have known that anyone with a semblance of intellectual independence would stop believing a word they wrote.

Unlike the editors of the *Daily Worker*, most other American editors did not experience intellectual and emotional crisis in the wake of the announcement from Berlin. But virtually all of them did feel compelled to comment on this seemingly momentous event whose announcement glared from the front pages of their papers. As usual, they uttered thoughts on this subject that were more consistent with their thoughts on other subjects than with the apparent facts of the case. Their editorials illustrate the diversity of opinions that can circulate after only a single event, especially when the causes and consequences of that event are far from clear. The presentation of opinion on this issue from the major local and regional journalistic opinion makers around the country will provide an introduction to the general attitudes and intellectual level of newspapers which will reappear frequently throughout this study.

Then as now the preeminent American newspaper was the *New York Times*, which sometimes endorsed ideas originating from the Left or the Right but usually tried to steer a moderate course. While officially eschewing ideology, it nevertheless propagated a pragmatic ideology grounded on respect for the perquisites of position and power but modified by the belief that gradual change was sometimes desirable as well as necessary.

On the very day of the announcement, the ever-poised pens of the *Times*'s editors prepared for publication the next morning perhaps the most perceptive editorial written about the pact. Reflecting the regnant belief that Germany was the truly great power in Europe, they entitled the editorial "German Bomb." But while they argued that this was primarily Hitler's handiwork, they also noted Stalin's apparent shrewdness in agreeing to it: "It is easy to imagine Stalin, as he surveys the sharpening struggle between the Fascist and the democratic powers, resolving to let them fight it out." They continued with an appraisal—so common at this time—of the effects the pact might have on the capitalistic democracies:[24] "A weakened, perhaps exhausted Europe would hasten the end of the capitalist system and offer fertile ground for the spread of the proletarian revolution."[25]

After reflecting on the pact for two days, the *Times*'s editors saw a further implication in it, one that was echoed by William Allen White, the noted national opinion maker from Emporia, Kansas, and other budding interventionists. "At last," the *Times* of 24 August observed, "there is a democratic front. The sham fronts are down and the anti-democratic systems are on one side and the democracies on the other. Inevitably we are more deeply engaged in the conflict."[26]

The *Times*'s opponent and opposite, the *New York Daily News*, thought otherwise. "It's the old game of power politics all over again," the *Daily News* moralized. "The whole thing should teach us once more that we have no business in Europe." People and journals who wished to forget about Europe sometimes had glaring difficulties in analyzing its affairs. "The projected pact," the *Daily News* said in the same editorial, "may lessen the chances of a general war."[27]

The remaining New York dailies of mass circulation, all of which were ideologically on the Right (the leftist *New York PM* had not yet appeared), wasted no time in stuffing the pact down the throats of the Left both at home and abroad. That paragon of Republican respectability, the *New York Herald Tribune*, was pleased that the leftists' " 'popular front' strategy is doomed, and they stand forth for what they have always been, the tools of a dictator whose principles and objectives differ only in nomenclature from those of the gentleman at Berchtesgaden."[28] The *Herald Tribune* also was happy because "the world as a whole sees now beyond any possible doubt that the cleavage between the totalitarian states and those other nations which are usually referred to as the 'democracies' is complete."[29]

The *New York Mirror*, a tabloid like the *Daily News* which also mixed news and entertainment liberally throughout, agreed with the *Daily News* that the "probabilities of peace in Europe were increased. . . . In one stunning blow [the *Mirror* continued] this fact has been demonstrated to the world: NOBODY can trust ANYBODY in Europe today. That fact is a bulwark of peace. To wage war in Europe today, a nation must be able to trust its allies."[30]

Naturally, the nation's journalistic center had entries from the seemingly ubiquitous Scripps-Howard and Hearst chains. The Scripps-Howard paper, the *New York World-Telegram*, astutely observed on 23 August that "Soviet Russia has sold out to the highest bidder." The *World-Telegram*'s editorialist went on, "It is cold comfort for Britain and France to discover that Russia undoubtedly would have been an undependable ally, as she has been a treacherous friend."[31] "As one American said after observing them both," the popular columnist Raymond Clapper noted that same day in the several hundred newspapers in which his column appeared, including the *World-Telegram*, " 'the chief difference between Moscow and Berlin is that in Moscow the winters are colder.' "[32] The *Journal-American*, which faithfully propagated the philosophy passed down by the lord of San Simeon, William Randolph Hearst, was inclined to blame the pact on England, France, and communists. "Why did Germany make a peace compact with Russia, its social and political enemy?" the *Journal-American* asked in a large-type editorial on the front page. "Because Germany was unable to make a peace alliance with France and England, its natural locational and political associates." With characteristic gusto the *Journal-American* blamed the pact on "the radicals in England, the Communists and pseudo-Communists, the Reds, the pinks and the punks."[33]

Except for scattered outposts of the Scripps-Howard, Hearst, and Patterson-McCormick publishing empires, newspaper comment in the East was reasonably restrained. The *Christian Science Monitor*, New England's most important voice, argued with typical thoughtfulness that "too much meaning should not be read into the Berlin announcement. Certainly it should not be assumed that this is the prelude to a much-dreaded offensive alliance by which they would divide Eastern Europe between them and then tackle the West."[34] Observing that the public was anticipating the outbreak of war, the *Trenton Times* said on 25 August that the "conversation on the street today is about the war."[35] The *Philadelphia Inquirer* featured Westbrook Pegler's triumphant column, "Communism at Last Seen in True Light."[36] And the cautious *Baltimore Sun* agreed with the *Christian Science Monitor* that the pact was "not necessarily as overwhelmingly important as many of the commentators seem to think."[37]

Washington is uniquely important not only because it is the nation's capital, but also because it is the meeting ground of northeastern and southeastern America. Its press is read by the nation's political leaders, the many other opinion makers living in Washington, and by other opinion makers in both the North and the South. These facts have given Washington's newspapers an eminence which, until recently, they probably did not deserve, as is illustrated by their undistinguished comments on the Russo–German pact.

The capital's respectable morning paper, the *Washington Post*, was sure that Russia, "for reasons of her own, has capitulated to German pressure"; and that the "onward march of party dictatorships [is] a challenge to the very concept of democracy."[38] The *Washington Star* pointed out that "the German position has been greatly strengthened."[39] The *Washington Times-Herald*, the weakest link in the McCormick–Patterson chain that consisted also of the *Chicago Tribune* and the *New York Daily News*, thought the "whole thing ought to teach us once more that we have no business in Europe."[40] Not surprisingly, these were, as we have seen, the exact words which the *Daily News* used to describe the pact on the very same day.

The South was much less advanced economically relative to the rest of the nation then than it is now, but its newspapers generally were not less perceptive than those of other regions. The *Asheville Citizen* hinted that the democracies might have received their due after Russia's exclusion from Munich. This "sad blow for the democracies," the *Citizen* suggested, "was no more perhaps than could be expected following the way the Soviets were cold shouldered during the 'final' settlement of European affairs at the Munich council table last September."[41] "It is a great game of power politics," the *Atlanta Constitution* contended, "and it appears to be the ninth inning with the bases full, two out and the count three and two on the batter. But one cannot be exactly sure just who is at bat."[42]

The *New Orleans Times-Picayune* did not believe that power politics had led to the pact. Instead, it agreed with Pegler that the two nations' "identical views and practices [had] supplied the basis for the partnership."[43] The *Houston Post*, in contrast, did not seem concerned about the bolshevizing of Europe. From Houston's vantage point, it appeared that this fear had already been realized, thus leading to the aberration of behavior in Germany and Italy from democratic standards. "Nazism," the *Post* said, "is the peculiar German type of Communism, which was given birth to keep Russian Communism out of Germany. Fascism is the Italian brand of Communism which rose to power for the same reason."[44]

In the Midwest there were nearly as many views of the pact as there were newspapers. The liberal *Cincinnati Enquirer* expressed the belief that the treaty resulted from "the snubs adminstered to Russia at Munich and before."[45] The *St. Louis Post-Dispatch*, which was one of the nation's few outstanding newspapers at this time, agreed that "the Chamberlain choice was Hitler on the Rhine rather than the risk of Communism."[46] This argument was the exact opposite of Hearst's in that it held British conservatives rather than British liberals responsible for the Russo-German treaty.

The *Cleveland Plain Dealer* thought that democracy had been "kicked in the teeth."[47] The *Detroit News*, another excellent newspaper, judged that the air had been cleared, that "democracy can afford no ally in its battle for human freedom."[48] And the *Milwaukee Journal* thought the pact's cardinal message was domestic: "The hollowness of all this, its essential falsity, ought to make our citizens realize that they had better turn their attention back to America and its institutions."[49]

Chicago, the hub of the midwest, was the center of the nation's conservative and isolationist sentiment just as New York was the center of liberal and internationalist thought. As New York's great financial houses and cultural centers balanced Chicago's mighty industries and slaughterhouses, so New York's Communist and Socialist elements offset the effects of Chicago's Bundist and anti-Semitic groups. One source of America's internal strength has been the remarkable ability of antagonistic groups to retain their autonomy. Perhaps it was only fitting, therefore, that the nation's two greatest cities seemed to be dominated respectively by Jews and anti-Semites. And it was also characteristic of the nation's diversity that neither of these groups represented the mainstream of American life.

The *Chicago Tribune*'s circulation of nearly one million, the greatest of all but the New York tabloids, demonstrated that conservatism had broad appeal along the southern shores of Lake Michigan. Until Marshall Field dared to invest part of his fortune in the *Chicago Sun* in 1941, the *Tribune* was Chicago's only morning paper, having driven off a dozen would-be competitors since 1920. The *Chicago Daily News*, the leading afternoon paper, was also conservative and isolationist.

"That the blood brothers followed natural inclinations must be beyond doubt," Colonel Robert R. McCormick's *Chicago Tribune* exulted on 23 August. "Stalin recognized a man of his own heart when Hitler personally led his gun men in the purge of June 30, 1934, when generals, storm troopers, and high Nazi officials were shot down in their homes." Having credited Hitler with courage he never possessed and Stalin with thoughts his biographers have never discerned, the colonel turned to the domestic implications of the pact. "Mr. Roosevelt's great Russian liberal democratic friend has turned despot," the editorial gleefully went on. "The New Deal gets the busy signal on the Moscow line."[50] The *Chicago Daily News* chimed in with the pleasing prospect that the pact "promises to make things rather awkward for many of our own commies, pinkos and intellectuals."[51]

Farther west, the *Denver Post* pronounced the pact to be "Hitler's greatest diplomatic triumph."[52] The *Casper Tribune-Herald* doubted that the pact would last. As it put it, "Russia will hardly forget that there is room for only one great power in Europe."[53] The *Los Angeles Times*, the premier paper in the West's largest city, said on the same theme that "alliance between gangsters is of notoriously short duration."[54] The *San Francisco Examiner*, Hearst's most successful journal, naturally expressed the very same thoughts as the *New York Journal-American* and other Hearst papers. Finally, the *Seattle Times*, like so many others, was interested primarily in the domestic implications of the pact. "With Hitler and Stalin all buddied up," the *Times* said only half-jokingly, "there seems to us no reason to delay consolidation of the American Communist Party and Herr Kuhn's bund. Investigating committees may then lay off, unless they, too, wish to consolidate."[55] The final references were to the Dies and LaFollette committees which were receiving considerable publicity, much praise, and some criticism for their investigations of Communist and Nazi activities, respectively. So divided was the nation into forces of order and forces of movement that few opinion makers criticized both committees, while most criticized at least one.

This tour of the major American cities and their leading newspapers at the end of the 1930s must not lead to the assumption that the press was the only important medium of opinion circulation at this time. On the contrary, developments during the 1930s, cemented during the war into the modern pattern, resulted in three seemingly coequal, if functionally distinct, branches of the mass media.

The reference to coequal branches, which brings to mind an imperfect analogy to the structure of the federal government, is intentional. The press may be compared with the legislative branch, with its cacophony of local voices and concerns and declining relative position throughout the present century. Just as legislators tend to represent the dominant attitudes of their constituents, so newspapers must cater effectively to the desires of local readers or collapse. In the press there is a greater body of parochial viewpoints than in the other two media, and it is the exceptional newspaper (or legislator) which has a national following.

Radio, the essential power of which has always been concentrated in a very small number of national networks, may be likened to the executive branch. Like the president, its opinions can reach tens of millions of Americans quickly and intimately; and, like the president relative to Congress, it usually has stood higher in public esteem than the press.[56] It is noteworthy but not surprising that the mighty national leaders of that era—Roosevelt, Churchill, Hitler, Mussolini, and Stalin—were gifted in the use of radio to bolster public support for their leadership. If Roosevelt, like Wilson, had been forced to rely primarily on a hostile Republican press for the propagation of his views, it is hard to believe that he would have been able to maintain his extraordinary popular position for nearly so long as he did.

Finally, periodicals merit comparison with the judicial branch. Like judicial opinions handed down from the bench, periodical articles generally require a more informed and sophisticated audience than do the contents of the other media. In fact, it was only the development of the picture magazine in the 1930s that allowed the periodical branch of the media to reach a truly mass audience. In 1939 most periodicals continued to be aimed at fairly discrete segments of the population: *Fortune* at sophisticated businessmen, *Women's Home Companion* at middle-class women, *Farm Journal and Farmer's Wife* at farmers, and *Foreign Affairs* at the very attentive segment of the public which was concerned with or involved in foreign policy. The very broadly aimed, successful periodicals numbered fewer than ten. The three most important of these were *Life*, *Saturday Evening Post*, and *Reader's Digest*. They and a very few others were extremely important to the millions who read them devoutly every week or month.

The precise response of radio to the Nazi-Soviet pact will not concern us here, for we will have ample opportunity throughout the war to examine radio's role closely. Suffice it to say that crisis was the key to radio's swift development during the late 1930s as a major news medium.[57] Newspaper owners, aware of radio's potential, had fought bitterly against radio news during the early thirties. But when they realized that they could not stop its development, they bought stations as a hedge against possible declines in newspaper sales. As it happened, radio and the press soon proved to be complementary media: those who heard about a news development on the radio sought to learn more about it from their newspapers, just as those who attend political rallies or sporting events are most likely to read about them in detail the next morning. By the autumn of 1939, the two national radio networks, CBS and NBC, had well-trained corps of foreign correspondents in the major European capitals ready to report every development in the onrushing crisis to anxious Americans back home.

In periodicals as in the press, the announcement of the Nazi-Soviet pact and the subsequent outbreak of war, with Germany and Russia as partners in the plunder of eastern Europe, provided abundant ammunition for an assault on the American Left. It was naturally led by conservative periodicals, but center and even liberal journals were quick to join the attack.

From September through November 1939, scarcely a week passed without a fresh barrage from the *Saturday Evening Post*, which obviously was pleased to take the offensive after the tribulations which had befallen American conservatives in the mid-1930s. Even the *Reader's Digest*, its great ideological partner among mass periodicals, could not maintain the *Post's* pace. On 2 September, the *Post* featured an article on the American labor movement by Benjamin Stolberg which contended that communist influence was the "one basic reason for the disintegration of the C.I.O." Unlike Pegler, who thought that Germany's problem was that it was communist, Stolberg argued that Russia's ailment was fascism. The American Communist Party, Stolberg wrote, is "merely an agent of the Stalin dictatorship. The Stalin dictatorship is, of course, neither Communist nor a democracy. It is a police state, based on the bureaucratic ownership not only of wealth but of the people itself. It is, in short, a highly developed Fascist regime."[58] Though Stolberg did not say so, this equating Russia with Germany naturally implied that the CIO's troubles stemmed from an overdose of fascism!

On 30 September, W. G. Krivitsky, one of the *Post's* regular contributors, accused Stalin of resorting to "methods of common crime" when he, according to Krivitsky, counterfeited dollars during his Five-Year Plans.[59] Two weeks later the *Post* complained editorially that the Roosevelt administration "took Communists, fellow travelers and intellectual revolutionaries to its bureaucratic bosom and has not yet purged them entirely away."[60] In that same issue, another of the *Post's* regulars, Demaree Bess, said that Stalin "shares equal responsibility with Hitler for plunging Europe into war." More nearly correct was Bess's further contention that through the pact with Germany "Stalin completely wrecked the Communist movement in all countries except his own. He finally made it clear, even to the most muddleheaded liberals, that there is little or nothing to choose between Stalin and Hitler, between Bolshevism and Nazism. He deliberately threw away any prospect of world leadership which he might have possessed."[61]

Less than a month later, on 8 November, the *Post* laid bare one of the roots of its persistent isolationism. The reason, however subtly stated, was that even a Germany at war with France and England was a bulwark against communism. That this argument shattered their contention that Russia and Germany were the same did not seem to trouble the *Post*'s editors. "Imagine," the *Post* argued, "that between Hitler and Stalin it should come to a stalemate, with a powerful Russian army still in being and beyond reach, and that then, in time, Germany should collapse, not in the face of an Anglo-American army but from internal strain and attrition." That did require considerable imagination, especially since Hitler and Stalin were then allies rather than adversaries. "Soviet Russia, in that case," the *Post* continued, "would be the paramount land power of Europe. What should we do about that? Having saved the world from Nazism, should we not be morally obliged to go on and save it from Bolshevism?"[62]

Reader's Digest and *American Mercury*, two conservative journals in compact digest form, also could hardly wait to lash out against the Left. Instead of waiting for a suitable article to appear in another magazine to be reproduced in the *Digest*, that journal yanked an article by Mark Sullivan from the *New York Herald Tribune* to meet the deadline for its October issue. After noting his own perspicacity in having already written "scores of times" that communism and nazism were the same, Sullivan applied his now acceptable formula in what must have been his thousandth attack on the New Deal: "Some of the New Deal is identical in principle with, or is parallel to, or has precedent in, or takes inspiration from, the Nazi-Fascist-Communist conception of society and government in Europe."[63] *American Mercury*, meanwhile, was content to point out discrepancies in the radicals' letter which appeared in the *Nation* in August[64] and to assert that the communist front organization, the League for Peace and Democracy, was the "biggest political hoax ever put over in America by a foreign power."[65]

While the conservatives were launching virulent attacks, the liberal journals' flirtation with Russia also cooled quickly during August and September. The *Saturday Review of Literature* thought that the League of American Writers should renounce its August assertion of the "value of the Soviet Union as a factor for peace.... To let it stand [the *Saturday Review* editorialized in early September] is to impress upon those of us who have never shared the League's touching faith the conviction that its eminent members take pleasure in being played for suckers."[66]

"Who will be foolish enough to continue to defend the Russo-German 'non-aggression' pact?" Louis Fischer inquired in the *Nation* later that month. "On March 10 Stalin promised that he would support states fighting for their independence. He has broken that promise. On August 31 Molotov declared 'We have a non-aggression pact with Poland.' Today he says there is no Poland.'"[67] Such soul-searching went on also in the *New Republic* and indeed everywhere on the Left except among the most devout Communists.

A scholarly expert on Russia of this era, Samuel N. Harper, wrote later that heavy pressure was applied in the fall of 1939 by "university colleagues and Washington politicians alike" to "join in the emotional upsurge" against both Stalin and Hitler. To Harper, the apparent reason for the emotional upsurge of these months was to "secure our national unity" through the argument that Stalin and Hitler had truly joined hands against the world. The means of securing unity, Harper contended, was to "rally the liberals against Stalin and the conservatives against Hitler."[68] In Harper's case, the pressure on him to conform to the idea of total Nazi-Soviet rapprochement lest he be considered a Nazi-Soviet agent was so intense that it resulted in a severe nervous breakdown.

Harper was neither a Communist nor a fellow traveler. The former as true believers could take anything, but most of the latter avoided catharsis by departing en masse from popular-front organizations such as the League for Peace and Democracy. Being completely disgusted with Russia's actions and the *Daily Worker*'s intellectual gyrations, they turned their backs on the popular front of the thirties.[69] Much of the explanation for the abrupt collapse of the front rests on the fact that Jewish intellectuals who formed its backbone simply could not tolerate the idea of "progressive" Russia allying herself with the open oppressor of Judaism.

Fervent Communists aside, the American response to the nonaggression pact was characterized, as we have seen, by concern and reflection. The general American response to the Soviet attack on Finland beginning on 30 November 1939 was, in contrast, marked by outrage and contempt. For conservatives, the pact had served a domestic purpose: it had aided their assault on the Left generally and the Roosevelt administration specifically. But the Soviet attack on "poor little Finland" came after that assault had been largely successful. And when the Finnish government asked for aid, conservatives and isolationists were presented with a disturbing challenge to their faith in American isolationism. In practice, their faith proved so strong that the aid which was eventually extended to the Finns was very little and very late.

At the end of October, just after Earl Browder was indicted on the charge of using a false American passport, Russian Foreign Secretary Molotov berated the American government for attempting to intervene in negotiations between Russia and Finland. From then until war broke out a month later, Americans knew that all was not well in Russo-Finnish relations. But they did not really think that war would ensue, for Russia did not yet seem to be so overbearing as Germany.

If Stalin and Molotov had stayed up nights during the fall of 1939 thinking of ways to antagonize Americans, they could hardly have found a more successful one than the attack on Finland. Many Americans thought that Finland was a noble outpost of democracy in Europe; they did not realize that in recent years many of its leaders had developed pronounced profascist tendencies. They also did not know that Russia's actual aim was not to subjugate the Finnish people or to overthrow their government but to gain strategic positions for the defense of Leningrad in case of German attack, positions which the Finnish government had been totally unwilling to yield through negotiation. As a "friend" of Germany, Russia could hardly make this point herself.

Informed Americans did know, however, that Finland had been the only European country which had always met its payments on loans from the United States during World War I and in fact was still meeting them punctually when the war with Russia broke out. If there was anything which isolationist and conservative Americans particularly liked, it was a foreign country which did not try to take advantage of America's wealth and generosity. Finally, Finland was a small country; and after what had happened to small countries such as Austria, Czechoslovakia, and Poland in recent years, it was axiomatic that small countries in Europe were always in the right in disputes with large neighbors.

Except for the *Daily Worker*, probably every newspaper in America denounced Russia's attack. The *New York Times* set the pattern for other relatively liberal papers like the *Atlanta Constitution* and the *St. Louis Post-Dispatch*. "In the smoking ruins of the damage wrought in Finland lies what remained of the world's respect for the Government of Russia," the *Times* editorialized on 1 December. "When the test came the Soviets were prepared to show how highly they hold the common decencies of life, how little they care for the plight of their desperate apologists abroad, how willingly they sacrifice socialist ideology on the altar of expediency."[70] Another liberal daily, the *New York Post*, was sure that the Russian attack "springs solely from lust for empire."[71]

Across the nation, in Seattle, the editor of the student newspaper at the University of Washington was particularly crestfallen. "It was not merely the fact that thousands are dying that is disturbing," he wrote in the *University of Washington Daily*, "it was more that Russia had set herself up as a political idealist, a nation bent on preserving the rights of small nations. . . . We shall never be able to look on Russia in the same light again."[72]

"Not even the invasion of Poland aroused as much indignation in the United States as has the Russian attack on Finland," the editors of the *Christian Century*, a leading Protestant periodical, observed in its review of newspaper opinion on the subject on 13 December.[73] The reasons for this stemmed not only from respect for Finland, but also from the latent fear of Russia and communism that became manifest in the nation during the last few months of 1939. "The invasion of Finland may present the greatest menace of this uncertain war," the *Chicago Tribune* argued. "It may contain the beginning of the greatest catastrophe with which Europe has been threatened since the Hunnish invasion. Asiatic hordes are again crowding up on Europe's frontiers, under a leader whose personal history accepts no competition from any other terror that ever came out of the east."[74]

Other conservative journals called for the severing of diplomatic relations with Russia and a "cleanup campaign" to rid the Roosevelt administration and the nation of Communists and fellow travelers. "The time has come . . . ," the *Trenton Times* thought, "to take stock of our diplomatic relations with the Soviet government and to decide coldly whether they are worth keeping."[75] "We trust," the *Pittsburgh Press* observed smugly, "that the ill wind will blow forever out of our country the last admirers of the Third International."[76] The *Detroit Free Press*, aware that the presidential election was only eleven months away and not averse to using some of Stalin's own methods, called for a "purge in Washington." "Unquestionably he intended nothing of the sort," said the *Free Press* with journalistic tongue in cheek, "but President Roosevelt himself opened the gates of the nation to the Red agents and propagandists now crawling about almost everywhere when he let himself be tempted by false promises of trade and good behavior, and insisted upon giving Russia diplomatic recognition."[77]

Most of the nation's political leaders did not waste this opportunity to speak out on a noncontroversial subject. "It is tragic to see the policy of force spreading," President Roosevelt said, "and to realize that wanton disregard for law is still on the march."[78] "Civilization struck a new low with the communists' attack on peaceful Finland," former President Hoover added. "It is a sad day to every decent and righteous man and woman in the world."[79] In calling for the severance of diplomatic relations with Russia, Senator William H. King of Utah said that he hoped "my country will no longer grasp the bloody hands of Stalin."[80] "We are opposed to war," the as yet little-known Wendell Willkie said during the debate on aid to Finland. "But we do not intend to relinquish our right to sell whatever we want to those defending themselves from aggression."[81]

An extremely useful guide to shifts in the circulation of information and opinion in the press is provided for the years covered by this study by James O. Twohey's "Analysis of Newspaper Opinion." Twohey's weekly mimeographed report was based on a sample of the front and editorial pages from across the country representing more than 20 percent of the nations's newspaper circulation.[82]

Immediately after the Russian attack, 27 percent of Twohey's sample called for the severance of diplomatic relations with Russia, 21 percent thought that Roosevelt properly expressed the sympathy of Americans for Finland, 20 percent believed that the United States had done what it could, 13 percent argued that this country should give all possible aid to Finland, 13 percent were especially concerned that Communists now be rooted out of the United States, and the final 6 percent offered miscellaneous comments. Before the attack on Finland, most newspapers had judged Hitler to be the worst influence in Europe. But after the Russo-Finnish war began, 33 percent thought that Stalin was a greater threat because of the danger of communism to Western civilization, 30 percent found Hitler and Stalin equally evil, and 16 percent thought that Hitler should be uneasy now that Stalin had copied his method.[83] For the first two weeks of December the Russo-Finnish War occupied nearly 50 percent of the space on the front pages of Twohey's sample of American newspapers, and it continued to occupy more than 20 percent on into 1940.

Throughout December, Twohey also noticed a strong trend in the press toward a witch-hunt of American Communists coupled with majority support for a German-Allied alliance against Russia leading quite possibly to a holy war against communism. "Opinion has been oscillating for months between a counsel of restraint and a build-up to a witch-hunt," Twohey observed on 9 December. "The present swing is toward the latter course, but does not appear to have gained decisive impetus as yet."[84] The next week Twohey reported that the swing toward a witch-hunt had gained "further momentum." As the respected *Philadelphia Inquirer* said about the arrest of the Communist Nicholas Dozenberg, "It is not what you get them for that counts so much; it's getting them."[85] But as Finnish resistance stiffened and the season of goodwill approached, the witch-hunt atmosphere largely disappeared.

George Gallup was also finding overwhelming animosity toward Russians and their American friends. Of the 89 percent of Americans with opinions, 99 percent favored Finland in the war, and only 1 percent favored Russia in Gallup's December 1939 poll.[86] But isolationist sentiment was still so strong that only 39 percent believed, at the height of the campaign to aid Finland in early February, that the United States should lend money to Finland for "airplanes, arms and other war materials."[87]

On the other hand, Russia's international activities and the domestic efforts of her supporters had spurred public support for the Dies Committee on Un-American Activities to an all-time high. Despite the open opposition of President and Mrs. Roosevelt and other liberals, 75 percent of the sample polled in December 1939 wanted the committee continued for another year, and 70 percent thought it was more important for the committee to concentrate on Communist rather than on Nazi activities in this country.[88]

At the end of 1939, therefore, the words *Russia*, *Stalin*, and *communist* were obviously anathema to almost all Americans familiar with them. *Time* named Stalin its man of the year, but that was clearly because it seemed to be one of those years when evil triumphed over good. In *Time*'s opinion, Stalin had "matched himself with Adolf Hitler as the world's most hated man." It did point out parenthetically that the "nightmare of a combination of capitalist nations that would turn against her" might have led Stalin "to take measures to insure the Soviet Union against easy attack."[89]

But most American opinion makers, *Time* included, simply were unwilling to give Russia the possible benefits of any doubts, and it is quite easy to understand their position. The Soviet Union, which had enraged Americans by outlawing religion and private property, had now plunged Europe into war by signing on Hitler's dotted line, joined with him in plundering eastern Europe, and even preceded him in extending the war to Scandinavia. Consequently, for almost all Americans the fall of the Soviet Union's esteem in 1939 had been meteoric. Never again, many vowed, would that godless state of the East merit their respect and admiration.

🐚 🎀 ❧ During the eighteen months from the end of 1939 to the German attack on Russia in June 1941 there was little change in American attitudes toward Russia. The changes that occurred were largely favorable. But even these resulted not from any friendly overtures by either Russia or the United States, but rather from the fact that Russia largely disappeared from the public spotlight as well as for the obvious reason that attitudes could hardly have become more unfavorable than they were at the end of 1939. Given this lack of change and the insignificance of Russia in American thinking during these months, consideration of this period will be brief.

Before the end of the Russo-Finnish War, President Roosevelt shrewdly protected himself against possible charges of friendliness to Russia in the upcoming presidential campaign with a scathing and well-publicized attack on that country before a hostile audience at the Communist-front American Youth Congress in February 1940. "The Soviet Union, as everybody who has the courage to face the facts knows," Roosevelt asserted, "is run by a dictatorship as absolute as any other dictatorship in the world." Roosevelt also told the jeering delegates that he "disliked the regimentation," "abhorred the indiscriminate killing," and "heartily deprecated the banishment of religion" in Russia.[90]

Russia's defeat of Finland in March and her blunt takeovers of Latvia, Lithuania, and Estonia that summer confirmed Americans in their attitudes. After July 1940, however, the presidential election and the exciting Battle of Britain tended to remove Russia from the front pages of the newspapers, the lead articles in periodicals, and the radio newscasts. The major issue of foreign policy in the campaign was the American posture toward the European war. Russia, as a nonbelligerent, was seldom mentioned during the campaign. When she was mentioned, she was often lumped together, as in 1939, with other despised dictatorships.[91]

By early 1941, after administration policies toward Russia could no longer become campaign issues, there were signs of increasing rapprochement between the two nations. By this time, the State Department was lifting the "moral embargo" against Russia on some war material and even warning the Russians of rumors that they were next on Hitler's attack list.[92]

Despite these ill-publicized changes in the government's approach, most Americans were still deeply suspicious of Russia in the spring of 1941. This was especially true of Roman Catholics, whose hostility toward Russia had been unrelenting ever since the Revolution. "Now that the policy seems to point to the appeasement of Russia, since trial balloons are already in the air," the president of Fordham University told a New York City audience on 2 February 1941, "the time has come to insist that Russia is still our principal enemy."[93]

Columnist Walter Lippmann implied, a month later, that Hitler should attack Russia, "which is easy to conquer and well worth conquering."[94] "Our diplomacy does not need to go out of its way to attack him," the *New York Times* editorialized in April, "but we certainly ought to stop sending any potential war supplies to Russia that could either be transhipped to Germany or that could take the place of Russian supplies shipped to Germany."[95] And former Democratic presidential candidate Alfred E. Smith, to cite yet another of many possible examples, implied strongly that concern about communism was one reason for the nation's defense program. "Our program is designed and intended solely for our own security," Smith said in a nationwide radio address on 28 May. "That security is threatened by one man. That security is threatened by three systems," Smith continued in measured tones. "Hitler is that man, aided and abetted by Mussolini and Stalin. The systems, of course, are Nazism, Fascism, and Communism."[96]

Finally, books dealing with Russia during this period were over-whelmingly anti-Russian.[97] The only balanced work on the subject in 1940 was Cambridge professor Bernard Pares's *Russia*, which was widely read in America in its Penguin paperback edition after Russia became a partner of the United States. The only work of significance that appeared in America by a spokesman of the Left was *The Soviet Power* by Hewlett Johnson, the dean of Canterbury. "If I am asked what is my view of Soviet policy today," Johnson wrote to summarize his analysis of Soviet foreign policy at the time, "I would summarize it in two words: self-preservation and peace, and where the two may clash, self-preservation comes first."[98] But Johnson was forced to rely on an obscure leftist publisher, Modern Age Books, to transmit his ideas to the American public.

Probably the most widely read work on Russia in 1940 was Eugene Lyons's *Stalin, Czar of All the Russians*. In this new book, Lyons, now the editor of *American Mercury*, picked up where he had left off in *Assignment in Utopia*. The main difference was that Lyons's greatly increased animosity toward Russia undermined the usefulness of his analysis. The earlier best seller often had shown considerable depth of insight in presenting the ambiguities of the Soviet experiment; the newer work was primarily vituperative. As such, perhaps it was what Americans wanted after the Russo-German pact and the attack on Finland. "A dark-visaged, pock-marked, slow-moving Asiatic dominates the landscape of world affairs today," Lyons wrote near the book's beginning in obvious if perhaps unintentional disagreement with the great majority of opinion makers, who surely would have accorded Hitler the dominant role. Near the end of the book he summarized his presentation: "Stalin's cruelty is not angry and impulsive, like Hitler's or Mussolini's, but far more terrible: quiet, patient, carefully planned."[99]

In *Stalin's Russia and the Crisis in Socialism*, Max Eastman, another former seeker of utopia in Russia, held that "Stalin is a super-fascist."[100] "Seen from Stalin's Russia," Freda Utley argued in *The Dream We Lost, Soviet Russia Then and Now*, "Nazi Germany appears rather less horrible than as observed from the democratic states of western Europe and America." She continued: "The very fact that so many Germans and German Jews have been allowed to leave the country and tell the world about it, instead of being shot or immured for life in concentration camps, proves the *comparative* mildness of the Nazi regime" (Utley's italics).[101] And T. A. Taracouzio, in his scholarly *War and Peace in Soviet*

Diplomacy, sought to "emphasize the fundamental differences in the concept of war and peace held by the non-communist democracies and the Soviet Union."[102] The basic difference, in Taracouzio's view, was that the Soviet Union went to war to spread its power, whereas the democracies resorted to war only in self-defense.

Such were the reigning attitudes when Hitler's massive attack against Russia on 22 June 1941 made it clear that Soviet Russia was no longer—if indeed it ever was—a friend of fascism. For Americans, the job of making Russia a friend of the democracies was much more difficult than linking her with fascism had ever been. This was partly because the link with fascism had come first, but more because American opinion makers had been linking Soviet Russia with the entire spectrum of evil for nearly a quarter of a century when Hitler commenced his "holy war against communism."

chapter 3

Is Russia Our Ally?

On 22 June 1941, only a few hours after the Germans and their allies invaded Russia, British Prime Minister Winston S. Churchill went on radio to state his government's policy in this new phase of the war. It was one of the most powerful speeches the prime minister made in his remarkable oratorial career. Before they had had time to form opinions on this startling subject, Americans by the millions heard the NBC broadcast of Churchill's speech. In a very real sense, the American response to Hitler's latest move toward apparent world conquest was formed as soon as—or even before—the British leader had finished speaking.

Like all great orators, Churchill went from vivid description to incisive analysis. After describing the attack, the prime minister depicted its author, Adolf Hitler, as "the monster of wickedness, insatiable in his lust for blood and plunder." "It is not too much to say here this summer evening," Churchill added, "that the lives and the happiness of a thousand million additional human beings are now menaced with brutal Nazi violence. This is enough to make us hold our breath."[1]

The stage now set, Churchill launched forth into one of the most compelling antitheses in the history of spoken English. First came the denial of any kinship with communism: "No one has been a more consistent opponent of Communism than I have for the last twenty-five years. I will unsay no words that I have spoken about it. But all this fades away before the spectacle which is now unfolding. The past with its crimes, its follies and its tragedies flashes away."[2]

And what of the present? The prime minister's vision was vivid:

I see Russian soldiers standing on the threshold of their native land guarding the fields which their fathers have tilled from time immemorial. I see them guarding their homes, where mothers and wives pray. Ah, yes, for there are times when all pray for the safety of their loved ones, for the return of the bread winner, of the champion, of their protector. I see the 10,000 villages in Russia where the means of existence is wrung so hardly from the soil, but where there are still primordial human joys, where maidens laugh and children play. I see advancing

39

upon all this the invidious onslaught of the Nazi war machine, with its clanging, heel-clicking, dandified Prussian officers, its crafty expert agents, fresh from the cutting and cowing down of a dozen countries. I see also the dull, drilled, docile, brutish masses of the Hun soldiery coming on like a swarm of crawling locusts. I see the German bombers and fighters in the sky, still smarting from many a British whipping, and they are likely to find, they believe, an easier and safer prey.

Behind all this storm, I see that small group of venomous men who planned, organized and launched this cataract of horrors upon mankind. Then my mind goes back across the years to the days when Russian armies were our allies against the same deadly foe, when they fought with so much valor and constancy and helped to gain a victory, from a share of which, alas, they were, from no fault of ours, utterly cut out.[3]

Even after this striking comparison of the Russian people and the German leaders, Churchill was not finished. He still had pointed words for appeasers and isolationists in Britain and America. The German invasion of Russia, he warned, was not a respite, but a "prelude to an attempted invasion of the British Isles." Hitler hoped, Churchill said,

that all this may be accomplished before the winter comes, and if he can overwhelm Great Britain before the fleets and air power of the United States might intervene, he hopes that he may once again repeat upon a greater scale than ever before that process of destroying his enemies one by one, by which he has so long thrived and prospered, and that then the scene will be clear for the final act without which all conquest would be in vain; namely the subjugation of the Western Hemisphere to his will and his system.[4]

"The Russian danger is therefore our danger and the danger of the United States," Churchill concluded in an implicit plea for recognition of the existence of an interrelated world, "just as the cause of any Russian fighting for his hearth and home is the cause of free men and free people in every quarter of the globe. Let us redouble our exertions and strike with united strength while life and power remain."[5]

Most Americans were still unwilling to heed Churchill's plea to jump into the battle against Hitler, but undoubtedly they were moved by his words, the complete text of which appeared the next morning in many American newspapers. Except for those associated with the isolationist press, who withheld comment, the response of American editors was all favorable. Ralph Ingersoll, the crusading editor of New York's newly founded liberal daily, *New York PM*, wrote on 23 June, "For so many Churchill said it and said it so beautifully—so forcibly and clearly—there's no need for any man to say it again, just to use other words."[6] "There are those who will say we are now allied with communism," the *New York Post* observed. "Our answer is the Prime Minister's speech."[7]

Many other dailies shared these sentiments. The *Baltimore Sun* entitled its lead editorial of 23 June, "Mr. Churchill Knows Who Is Europe's

Worst Enemy."[8] "As Prime Minister Churchill states," the *Casper Tribune-Herald* argued the same day, "the Russians are also fighting for their way of life against a scourge that threatens all but the Nazis and Fascists."[9] An NBC roundup of newspaper opinion just after Churchill's speech showed overwhelming support for aid to Russia. Among the newspapers strongly advocating aid were the *Birmingham Herald*, the *Des Moines Register*, and the *Chicago Times*.[10] Whether or not it was Churchill's primary goal, a redoubling of aid to Britain was, James Twohey reported, the major response of the American press to Germany's invasion of Russia.[11]

Churchill's speech was effective not only because of its timing and power, but also because of the prime minister's enormous prestige with the American people. To the British people, President Roosevelt probably was the noblest political leader in the world. But to Americans, who were divided sharply in regard to their president's merits, Churchill would almost certainly have won this distinction. He was, after all, the epitome of principled opposition to Nazism as well as the courageous leader of the first successful rebuke to German arms. He heartened liberals with his resistance to Hitler and pleased conservatives with his basic political philosophy. Until the questions of Indian independence and the second front erupted on the front pages in the summer of 1942, Churchill was above criticism in America. If his response to the German invasion of Russia had been different, it is probable that the general American response would have differed virtually to the same degree. As it happened, Churchill got two strikes on the isolationists even before they came to bat.

Because the German invasion was a discrete and generally unexpected event,[12] its impact in the United States provides excellent material for thorough studies of all three aspects of the formulation of foreign policy, including the opinion-making process emphasized in this study. Careful analysis of the opinion-making process in the aftermath of the German invasion not only should clarify the structure of American attitudes toward Russia in the summer of 1941; it also should suggest how opinions about events and the issues they raised throughout the war tended to circulate.

I have already implied that Churchill's speech was second only to the invasion itself as an impetus to and an item of circulation of opinion on this issue. The cautious response of President Roosevelt and the State Department did not provoke much controversy or result in much circulation of opinion. This was probably their intent, and it was almost certainly wise whether or not it was their explicit intent. Roosevelt's great skill as a democratic political leader was based largely on his extraordinary judgment of when to lead and when to appear to follow, and in this case he chose the second course. Apart from saying in effect in his press conference of 24 June that another enemy of fascism was always welcome,[13] the president permitted other opinion makers to take the lead in circulating opinions on this issue.

In structure, the circulatory system for opinions consisted, on this issue as on others, of well-placed persons in society transmitting their opinions through the three branches of the mass media. Like boards of directors deciding how their stockholders' money should be used, the leaders of the media decided whose opinions were "newsworthy," and hence which opinions deserved to be circulated and which would be deposited in newsroom trash cans. Also like the board of directors' financial resources, some of the opinions that would be circulated originated with them, but most came from other national leaders whose opinions "deserved" to be circulated. Obviously, the leaders of the media held crucial positions in the process of circulating opinion.

Opinions on foreign policy at this time may well be discussed in terms of James MacGregor Burns's division of the nonapathetic American public, which is a departure from the isolationist-interventionist dichotomy employed by most previous scholars of the early part of World War II.[14] Burns argues that there were four basic political constituencies in the United States in the late 1930s and early 1940s: two Democratic and two Republican "parties," with one of each centered in the presidency and the other in Congress.[15] The "presidential Democrats," based in the Northeast and industrial Midwest, were generally liberal in regard to domestic issues and interventionist in foreign policy. The "congressional Democrats," in the South, were generally both more conservative and more interventionist. The "presidential Republicans," located primarily in the Northeast, tended to support the president's foreign policies and demur on his domestic programs. The "congressional Republicans," whose power base was the midwestern and mountain states, were divided in their opinions on domestic issues but were basically united in their aversion to possible American participation in foreign wars.

From the standpoint of opinion circulation, by far the most important of these groups were the presidential Republicans and the presidential Democrats. The presidential Republicans owned or at least controlled, by conservative estimate, three-fourths of the media's circulatory capacity. They dominated the radio networks, large periodicals, and eastern press. Supporters of congressional Republicans controlled some newspapers and newspaper chains, but their power was nothing like the three-pronged strength of the eastern Republicans. Taken together, the presidential and congressional Democrats probably did not account for 10 percent of the media's total appeal. But control of the administration assured the Democrats that their views usually would be news.

It was very fortunate for the president that Republicans with the firmest grasp on the media tended to support his cautiously interventionist policies. More to the point, they supported his cautious approach toward assistance to Russia in its struggle against Nazism. The leading commentators on CBS, Elmer Davis and Edward R. Murrow, were unabashedly interventionist. Though they never asserted their interventionism indiscreetly, their tone and selection of news made their position unmistakable. The same approach also was evident at NBC, where H. V. Kaltenborn and Robert St. John, among others, held forth.

The entire group of Luce periodicals, then at the height of their prestige, were also interventionist, as were such eminent newspapers as the *Christian Science Monitor,* the *New York Times,* the *Washington Post,* and the *Atlanta Constitution.* Against this array of powers, the congressional Republicans had to count on scattered citadels of influence like the Hearst and Patterson-McCormick papers, the *Saturday Evening Post,* and some religious periodicals. With the British prime minister, the American president, the congressional Democrats, and the bulk of the media lined up against them, the congressional Republicans and their journalistic supporters were unlikely to win the battle for public opinion on the question of aid to Russia.

Because Roosevelt did not ask at this time for material assistance to Russia, the battle lines could be drawn only on the question of Russia's fitness as an enemy of fascism. Not surprisingly, the great interventionist media and their allies carried the day. When Gallup interviewers polled a cross-section of adult Americans early in July on the question, "In the present war between Germany and Russia, which side would you like to see win?" 72 percent said Russia, 4 percent answered Germany, 17 percent thought it made no difference, and 7 percent did not offer an opinion (see figure 1). Dr. Gallup summarized the typical response of the members of the sample as follows: "'Russia is not imperialistic, but Germany is. Russia, even if she won, would not invade the United States, whereas Germany probably would.'"[16]

One source of support for Russia apparently stemmed from expectations that Germany would win. To the question, "Which side do you think will win the war?" 47 percent said Germany, 22 percent said Russia, 8 percent expected a stalemate, and 23 percent offered no opinion (see figure 1). Americans generally favor an underdog, and they specifically abhorred the possibility that Hitler might soon add yet another victim to his collection of conquered nations. Finally, Gallup found that fewer Americans favored entering the war immediately than had favored such a course before Germany attacked Russia. To the question, "Should the United States enter the war now?" those replying in the affirmative dropped from 24 to 21 percent.[17] Here, if not elsewhere, the isolationist argument that the pressure was off Britain appeared to be having an effect.

The exact degree to which the media directly influence individual opinions can be estimated scientifically only on the basis of thorough studies of numerous individuals in the wake of particular events, something a historian could never attempt. It does seem significant, however, that all of the above-noted distributions of opinion correlate very closely with the opinions which Twohey and I observed the media to have circulated during the two weeks before these polls were taken.[18]

The less the public is divided on an issue, as a rule, the less will be the percent difference between its various segments. Thus, when the responses to the first question cited above are analyzed according to income, 72 percent of the upper- and lower-income groups and 73 percent of the middle-income group hoped that Russia would defeat Germany. On the other hand, 2 percent more of the upper- than the lower-income group supported Germany (5 percent to 3 percent) while 2 percent more of the lower-income group was undecided (25 percent to 23 percent).

As could have been predicted from the distribution of opinions circulated through the religious media, the differences between Catholics and Protestants were greater. Twice as many Catholics as Protestants (6 percent to 3 percent) wanted Germany to win, and only two-thirds of Catholics, compared with three-fourths of Protestants, wanted Russia to win.[19] Still, these figures show that Catholics supported Russia over Germany by a margin of nearly eleven to one despite the open anticommunism of almost all of their religious leaders.

The decisive victory among the mass public for Russia was not achieved without an intense struggle, highlighted at the end of June when Herbert Hoover purchased time on nationwide radio to denounce "the whole argument of our joining the war to bring the four freedoms to mankind" as "a gargantuan joke."[20] Because Hitler was unpopular with Americans, isolationists and conservatives did not say that they wanted Germany to win. They certainly did not propose that the United States ally herself with Germany against Russia. But unlike the interventionists and liberals, the isolationists usually did not express the hope that Hitler would lose his latest campaign.

Actually, some of the more conservative organs were openly con-

Figure 1. Opinion of the Russo-German War, July 1941 (AIPO [Gallup] release, 13 July 1941)

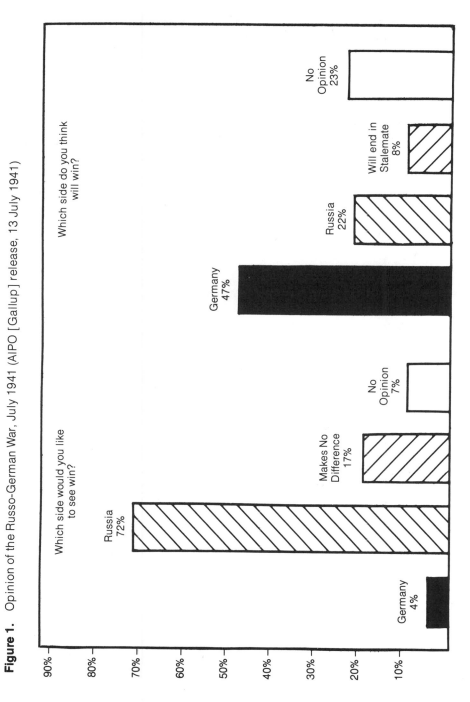

cerned about this possibility. "Suppose we aid Russia and Russia defeats Hitler," the *Wall Street Journal* inquired apprehensively, "who will then dominate Europe, and what will be the result of that domination? Will Stalin be a kindly master or will the entire continent be bathed in blood?"[21]

In the same editorial of 25 June, entitled "Tweedledum and Tweedledee," the *Wall Street Journal* hit upon a more common theme of the conservative response, one that we previously encountered in considering the late 1930s. "The American people know," it contended, "that the principal difference between Mr. Hitler and Mr. Stalin is the size of their respective mustaches. An alliance with either would be at the price of national self-respect."[22]

The hope of the *Wall Street Journal* and many other conservative organs was that these two alien ideologies would now destroy each other. "If, in the course of Hitler's mad lust for power," the *Cleveland Plain Dealer* hypothesized, "he should crush the Communist dictatorship and at the same time weaken himself so that he in turn could be destroyed by the combined efforts of Britain and America, the world would be better off in the end."[23] "It will be poetic and moral justice," the *Pittsburgh Press* chimed in, "if Schicklgruber and Djugashaili are now consumed in the conflagration of their own making."[24] Conservative columnist David Lawrence observed that the czarist regime had fallen during the last war, and he expressed the hope that "the same result may be in store for Stalinism."[25] And the *Philadelphia Bulletin* suggested on the same theme that Russians would be preferable to Germans as neighbors, "especially if time and circumstances should in the end emancipate them from Communist tyranny."[26]

Senator Harry S. Truman of Missouri, for one, was not sure that "time and circumstances" would be enough. "If we see that Germany is winning we ought to help Russia and if Russia is winning we ought to help Germany and that way let them kill as many as possible," Truman contended, "though I don't want to see Hitler victorious under any circumstances."[27] Because of Truman's subsequent prominence and because of the statement's forthrightness, this is probably the best known American reaction to the German invasion. Actually, it was unrepresentative and attracted only minor attention at the time.

Why this was true provides considerable insight into the opinion-circulating process in America at this time. In the first place, Truman, who was still essentially a congressional Democrat, spoke with the provincial's unique combination of isolationism and interventionism. To think that either of these self-respecting powers would have accepted aid under Truman's terms is to stretch beyond the breaking point the admittedly distended logic of international relations in wartime. Thus, Truman's statement was hardly of the caliber required by pundits and other politicians for additional circulation to the public. Secondly, the presidential Republicans who controlled most of the media primarily circulated their own views and those of the presidential Democrats. If Wendell Willkie, Thomas E. Dewey, or Robert F. Wagner had made this statement, it surely would have been circulated far more widely and intensively. Finally, Truman did not as yet have the stature of a national opinion maker on foreign policy. When one achieves such stature, almost anything one says on foreign policy is deemed newsworthy by at least a few leaders of the media; but until one does, it is extremely hard to have one's opinions circulated. Probably the only reason Truman received some attention on this issue was because his statement was pithy, frank, and somewhat outrageous.

The general position of the congressional Republicans and their supporters, as we have seen, was that any moral or material aid to Russia would make America the ally of international communism. However, the interventionists were able to prevail, as the polls attested, partially by using their domination of the media to define the argument in terms of Russia's acceptability as an enemy of fascism.[28] They also won, in part, because they had four major facts on their side. First, Russia was in mortal combat with fascism whether Americans liked it or not, and whether or not the isolationists would now have to abandon their pet theory that nazism and communism were the same thing. Second, Britain, America's major friend of the moment, would be given at least a short respite. Third, the Pope, while certainly not supporting Russia, refused to agree with von Ribbentrop and Hitler that the German thrust to the East was a "holy war." Fourth, at a time when Nazi domination of the entire world seemed possible, it was hard not to accept another enemy of Hitler.

Like competent high school debaters, the interventionists also used an important tactical principle to carry their argument: they structured their presentation in such a way as to concede in advance all material extraneous to the main point. The presidential Republicans and Democrats also advanced such similar positions that it was almost as if a strategy agreed upon in advance was being employed to rout the congressional Republicans and their Catholic allies.

In a sense, this is just what happened. There was Churchill's speech which had conceded all arguments against communism while insisting that Russia could be useful in the struggle against nazism. On the next day, 23 June, Undersecretary of State Sumner Welles issued a statement with President Roosevelt's approval that struck basically the same note. Welles said later that neither he nor the president had "seen the British text" before releasing their statement; but that would appear to be merely a devious semantic distinction, for it is most unlikely that neither of them had heard Churchill's address.[29]

Be that as it may, the State Department's release was very similar to Churchill's address in both structure and substance, if not in verbal virtuosity. It also began with a discussion of the "treacherous attack" on the Soviet Union and the manifest perfidy of the German leaders. Then, as an apparent sop to Catholic and conservative Protestant opinion, it stated that "freedom to worship God" is the "great and fundamental right of all peoples," and that this right had been "denied to their peoples by both the Nazi and Soviet Governments." "Neither kind of imposed overlordship," the statement continued, "can have or will have any support or any sway in the mode of life or system of government of the American people. But the immediate issue that presents itself to the people of the United States is whether the plan for universal conquest, for the cruel and brutal enslavement of all peoples, and for the ultimate destruction of the remaining free democracies, which Hitler is now desperately trying to carry out, is to be successfully halted and defeated."[30]

Welles's cautious statement promised no aid and did not even offer any real moral support to the embattled Russians. The best it could do on this score was to suggest, in conclusion, that "any defense against Hitlerism, any rallying of the forces opposing Hiterlism, from whatever source these forces may spring, will hasten the eventual downfall of the present German leaders, and will therefore redound to the benefit of our own defense and security."[31]

While borrowing their arguments, the leading presidential Republican and Democratic organs seldom referred to Churchill and Welles as their primary sources. The *Christian Science Monitor* conceded extraneous arguments and made its essential point in only one sentence. "Whatever the antipathy of capitalism for Marxism, whatever the dislike of free men for Stalin's despotism, whatever our recognition that Communism is a dangerous philosophy," the *Monitor* declared, "the immediate attack comes from Nazism."[32] "We are not going to pretend," the *New York Times* proclaimed, "that we have anything in common with the brutal despotism of Stalin."

Having assured its readers of America's moral superiority, the *Times* could point out that a "quick and complete German victory" would be "a catastrophe of the first importance for England and America." Germany, the *Times* feared, would then control the entire European and Asian land mass and "threaten the United States from both oceans."[33] "It is to defeat Hitler—not to help Russia—that American policy has long been directed," the *New York Herald Tribune* observed. "If the defeating of Hitler will incidentally help Russia, this also is beside the point."[34] Finally, the *St. Louis Post-Dispatch* stated, "We are choosing between evils, and the point about Nazism is that it is not only an evil, but that it is an unprecedentedly powerful and menacing evil."[35]

Whether nazism was in fact a more menacing ideological evil than Soviet Communism was a question whose answer tended to depend upon whether the observer's general orientation to political phenomena was conservative or liberal. But no one would have denied in June 1941 that Germany was the greater military threat. "Russian military power is the enigma of the age," the *St. Louis Post-Dispatch* editorialized with characteristic insight on 23 June.[36]

Most other opinion makers had definite ideas on this subject. "The efficiency of the Russian staff is not to be compared with that of the German, nor, except for a few divisions, can there be any comparison in the matter of equipment," George Fielding Eliot, the columnist and CBS military analyst, reported on nationwide radio on the evening after the attack. "The principal question which most military observers are asking themselves now is: How long can the Russians keep the bulk of the German Air Force busy in eastern Europe? Will it be long enough for the Royal Air Force to wreak such damage in the West as shall make it impossible for the Germans to stage another great offensive this year, this time against Britain?"[37]

The expert on Russia, Walter Duranty, whose columns were syndicated by the North American Newspaper Alliance, wrote that the "consensus of expert opinion is that odds in Germany's favor are five to one at least."[38] Even a month later Twohey could observe that the "press does not permit itself to hope Russia will hold out long but does hope that the upsetting of the Nazi timetable has postponed an attempted invasion of England for this year."[39]

In this climate of opinion aid to Russia was not a pressing issue. No one wanted American arms to fall into Hitler's hands. Moreover, full mobilization in the United States was still a year away, and the relatively few arms that were being produced beyond the pressing needs of American troops were committed to Britain under lend-lease. Many interventionists now urged that the opportunity afforded by Hitler's turn to the East be seized and that defense production be stepped up so that more weapons could be sent to Britain. Many isolationists, proceeding from different assumptions, thought that Britain and the United States should now relax and enjoy the spectacle of the dictators destroying each other. But in June and July neither side really injected the aid issue into the debate on the American stance toward the Russo-German war.

To complete this discussion of the opinion-making process during the two weeks after 22 June 1941, we should consider briefly the relative importance of the various branches of the media. Polls taken throughout the war showed that the mass public relied on radio more than on the press for most of its news of the world. It was easier, quicker, and more satisfying to listen to reports of unfolding events than to read about them in newspapers. In practice, most persons who listened to news programs on the radio read newspapers and periodicals as well, but their extremely significant first impressions usually were shaped by radio reports. Moreover, many people, aware of the press's persistent opposition to the president, believed that newspapers were biased and did not always reflect their readers' views. This image was fostered by radio, which sought to impress the public with its objectivity and fairness in using the nation's airwaves. And when events were tinged with drama, as they were when the Russo-German war erupted, the nature of radio gave it an obvious advantage.

In general, periodicals and other media such as books and movies were unable to present their more detailed analyses before most opinions had been basically formed.[40] These media could and did provide reinforcement, depth, and perhaps some alteration of opinions, largely among the attentive public and the opinion makers, weeks, months, and even years after Hitler's armies had crossed the Russian frontier.

By early July of 1941, as we have seen, Americans had concluded by the overwhelming margin of eighteen to one that they would like to see the Soviet Union defeat Nazi Germany. These results revealed a significant and convincing victory for the interpretation of events offered by Winston Churchill and his supporters in the United States among Democratic and presidential Republican opinion makers. Moreover, if Russia held out, and if supplies were available, most Americans were also prepared to condone aid to the nation which, only weeks before, they had equated with Nazi Germany almost as a matter of course.

But Russia was still not our ally in the sense that Britain and China were. Indeed ally, that term which is the symbol of implicit friendship, would never quite apply to Russia in the same sense; for, try as they might, even liberal Americans could not overcome their long-standing suspicion of Soviet institutions and ideals. And many Catholics and conservatives never really tried to alter attitudes established over a quarter of a century.

Religion in the modern era may not be the all-pervasive influence it once was, but the attitudes it fosters among believers are still probably the most deeply rooted. At least implicitly, that consideration hung heavily on President Roosevelt's mind in the late summer and early fall of 1941. Realizing that he was incapable of changing Catholic attitudes toward Russia by himself, Roosevelt wrote to Pope Pius XII on 3 September for help. It is important for an understanding of American attitudes to realize that Roosevelt apparently believed what he wrote; it is equally illustrative of the Catholic position that the Pope chose not to respond, an unusual choice indeed in the history of their wartime correspondence. Roosevelt's basic position on religion in Russia and his plea for help are set forth in the two major paragraphs of the letter.

In so far as I am informed, churches in Russia are open. I believe there is a real possibility that Russia may as a result of the present conflict recognize freedom of religion in Russia, although, of course, without recognition of any official intervention on the part of any church in education or political matters within Russia. I feel that if this can be accomplished it will put the possibility of the restoration of real religious liberty in Russia on a much better footing than religious freedom is in Germany today.

I believe that the survival of Russia is less dangerous to religion, to the church as such, and to humanity in general than would be the survival of the German form of dictatorship. Furthermore, it is my belief that the leaders of all churches in the United States should recognize these facts clearly and should not close their eyes to these basic questions and by their present attitude on this question directly assist Germany in her present objectives.[41]

Perhaps because of his dismay when he realized that a promise of assistance did not seem to be forthcoming, or perhaps because he believed that the level of Catholic opposition to Russia was intolerable at a time when Congress was about to include Russia under lend-lease, the president on 2 October authorized the release of a statement he had made at his most recent weekly press conference.[42] "As I think I suggested a week or two ago," Roosevelt began, "some of you might find it useful to read Article 124 of the Constitution of Russia," which dealt with freedom of religion. "Freedom of religion," the president continued, paraphrasing the language of article 124, was

freedom equally to use propaganda against religion, which is essentially what is the rule in this country; only, we don't put it quite the same way. For instance, you might go out tomorrow—to the corner of Pennsylvania Avenue, down below the Press Club—and stand on a soapbox and preach Christianity, and nobody would stop you; and then, if it got into your head, perhaps the next day preach against religion of all kinds, and nobody would stop you.[43]

If any American except the editor of the *Daily Worker* applauded Roosevelt's comments, no one has been able to discover it. His supporters thought that the statement was "unfortunate," and that America was going to aid Russia because of national self-interest, not because of similarities or differences in the religious practices of the two countries.

"President Roosevelt's interest in religious freedom, as emphasized on several occasions, merits deep appreciation," Luther A. Weigle, dean of Yale University Divinity School and president of the Federal Council of Churches, said on 5 October, "but it is to be hoped that he will not be misled into assuming that the freedom which is guaranteed under the Russian Constitution has any real resemblance to the religious freedom that we have known in America."[44]

Although American Catholics were divided at this time as to whether Communist Russia or Fascist Germany was the greater threat to civilization, they were united in vehement opposition to the president's remarks. As the official organ of the archdiocese of Chicago, *The New World*, put it, "In practice the regimes of Lenin and Stalin have leveled the most ruthless drive against Christianity since the days of Diocletian."[45]

Ironically, the furor over the president's remarks seemed to clear the air; and, as happened so often during his presidency, temporary embarrassment was followed by more lasting success.[46] The isolationist America First National Committee, growing ever more desperate, sent a poll to 34,616 priests asking whether they favored American participation in a "shooting war" outside of the Western Hemisphere and aid to Russia. According to a report on 5 October by ultraconservative Congressman Hamilton Fish of New York, "90 per cent of the priests" had answered no to both questions.[47] But the poll soon turned sour. Opponents of America First soon pointed out that fewer than 40 percent of the priests had bothered to return the questionnaire. More important, many Catholic leaders objected to this apparent attempt to use the opinions of clerics for partisan purposes.[48] Then, on 21 October, a petition supporting the president's aid policies, including aid to Russia, which had been signed by 1,000 prominent Protestant leaders, was delivered to the White House in a flurry of publicity by the editor of the *Protestant Digest*. Last and most important, the Pope agreed to draw up an interpretation of *Divini Redemptoris*, the encyclical which had instructed Catholics to devote themselves to utter opposition to communism. The crucial clarification, which was sent to the apostolic delegate in the nation's capital and quickly distributed nationally from there, was that there was a big difference between aiding the Russian nation and aiding communist ideology.[49] The president's letters and the pleas of his personal representative to the Vatican, Myron C. Taylor, had paid off.

The other broad religious groupings, Protestants and Jews, tended to avoid strictly religious grounds for attitudes toward Russia. Protestants, as usual, were divided. The most basic division on the question of the American stance toward the European war was placed in bold relief when Reinhold Niebuhr and other presidential Republicans and presidential

Democrats started a new religious journal, *Christianity and Crisis*, early in 1941 as an open challenge to the congressional Republican views of the *Christian Century*. It would not have been hard to predict correctly, on 22 June 1941, that *Christianity and Crisis* would support aid to Russia while *Christian Century* would oppose it. Jews, on the other hand, were generally the most fervent supporters in this country of aid to Russia after June of 1941. That they were for the most part New Yorkers, liberals, and anti-Nazis provides sufficient explanation for this fact.

Even though the German attack on Russia had blasted the neat dichotomy between "democracies" on the one side and "dictatorships" on the other, increasing numbers of Americans deserted isolationism and came to expect participation on the side of the Allies. The most notable defection from the congressional Republican camp was the powerful American Legion, which decided that the conservatism and rigidity of Charles A. Lindbergh and his congressional supporters no longer met the requirements of American self-interest in foreign policy. "Our present national objective," the legionnaires resolved in mid-September at their annual convention in Milwaukee, "is the defeat of Hitler and what he stands for, and all diverting controversies should be subordinate to the main objective." Probably the most important of these diverting controversies at the time, of course, was the question of aid to Russia. Implicitly if not explicitly, the legionnaires supported aid to Russia because the Russians were furthering America's "present national objective." They avoided ideological difficulties by insisting that their opposition to communism remained "unaltered," and that they still regarded "Communism, Fascism, and Nazism as equally false and dangerous." The legionnaires also resolved that the American Communist Party could not "be dignified by recognition on the part of the several states as a true political party and must be outlawed."[50]

In a real sense, the American Legion's interventionist stand cleared the way politically for the relatively uncontroversial extension of lend-lease to Russia by Congress in late October. Tired and on the defensive after two years of combat with presidential and congressional Democrats and the presidential Republican media on the issue of greater involvement in the European war, the isolationists in Congress could muster fewer votes on aid to Russia than they had been able to rally against aid to Britain at the first of the year. Their dilemma, they must have realized, was this: How could they possibly convince the majority of Americans of the justice of their position when almost all of the other opinion makers in America were either keeping silent or praising the heartening and unexpected tenacity of the Russian defense?

In addition, a daily barrage of news and comment about the Russo-German war appeared in American newspapers and could be heard over practically all of the more than one thousand radio stations in the country in the mornings, between soap operas in the afternoons, and in the evenings. Then as now, the average American spent several hours a day in the companionship of his electronic source of news and entertainment. And hardly an hour would pass between the summer of 1941 and June of 1944 when the progress of the Russian defense of the homeland was not mentioned on most radio stations. During the last week of June 1941, the Russo-German war and American-Russian relations occupied 72.3 percent of the front page of the average American daily newspaper.[51] That figure had dropped to 21.7 percent a month later, but even this smaller percentage represents several thousand words of news each week on the page most likely to be read.[52] Until Pearl Harbor, and then beginning again a month later for another two years, the Russo-German war was usually the leading item on radio news programs and on the front pages of American newspapers. With Russia being contrasted daily to the most powerful enemy of the United States, important changes in mass attitudes were almost certain to occur in theory and did occur in fact.

Probably the most important source of kind words about the Russians as people as well as soldiers was the network correspondent in Moscow. The primary CBS correspondents in Russia during 1941 were Erskine Caldwell and his wife Margaret Bourke-White. Caldwell, speaking as if from outer space because of poor radio connections, described in detail the major events on the front and behind the lines. On 3 July, for example, he reported on Stalin's speech to the Russian people, the first the Soviet leader had made "through live microphones" since 1939. The speech, which was translated to Russia's deaf and dumb in sign language, "impressed upon the people the seriousness of the hour. . . . As an observer, [Caldwell continued] I had the feeling that this announcement immediately brought about a new era in Soviet life." To one of the young Moscow girls who stood on the street to listen to the speech, "the winning of this war was now the sole objective of her life. . . . It is obvious, [Caldwell concluded] that the Soviet Union has mobilized its forces, both civilian and military, to wage an all-out war against Germany. If there is any such thing as so-called total war, this is to be it. The battle of the Russian steppes will make all previous wars seem like rehearsals."[53]

Miss Bourke-White told in rasping, sincere tones of the commitment of Russian women to the war effort and of the sacrifices which all were making. " 'I feel envy. I want to go to the front too,' " Miss Bourke-White quoted one young woman whose husband left for war duty.[54] Many women took over difficult factory jobs abandoned by their husbands. Sugar cost about a dollar a pound, and the ration of it was a maximum of two pounds per month. Old shoes would have to do, for new ones cost seventy rubles.[55]

Complementing the reports from Moscow were the comments on the Russian situation by leading newscasters in New York, Washington, and London. In the event that static had caused listeners to miss portions of Caldwell's reports, summaries of them or conclusions to be drawn from them were usually given by Elmer Davis and other leading commentators. "Mr. Caldwell's report," Davis added after the report discussed above, "bears out all the news that we have had from Moscow since the war started, that the emphàsis there is now entirely on nationalism, and not at all, outwardly at least, on communism."[56] Russian war communiqués were preferred to German ones, and battlefield reports on news programs were not unfavorable to Russia.

Most newscasters, having the cosmopolitan approach of many interventionists, thought that this was America's war as well as Britain's, China's, and Russia's. Edward R. Murrow had a gift for communicating the ideas of others so convincingly that they seemed to be his own. "His plea," Murrow said of Churchill's speech of 22 June, "was based on a combination of humanitarian principles and national self-interest. What he implied was that the Russians, after all, are human, but the Germans aren't. Russia's danger, he said, is our danger."[57] And Robert Trout, a CBS New York anchorman, liberally mixed interpretation with news in this introduction to a story on 6 July: "Within the past half-dozen hours Catholic bishops in Germany and, as you heard from Mr. [Albert]Warner, in this country have pointed out the untruth, the falsehood, in the Nazi propaganda campaign calling Hitler's war a 'holy war.'"[58]

Almost all major periodicals either joined in the pro-Russian chorus or maintained a discreet silence on the subject during the summer and fall of 1941. The liberal, or presidential Democratic, journals naturally were the most vociferously enthusiastic. "The future of the West and the chances of a viable international order," Max Lerner wrote in the *New Republic* in early July, "depend largely upon our finding common ground on which the American, British, Chinese, and Russian people can act."[59] "Time is on the side of the Russians," the interventionist editors of the same journal observed a month later, "and time is on our side too, if we will only use it instead of permitting it to be used against us."[60]

Later that month theologian Reinhold Niebuhr wrote that Americans might well "bring ourselves to thank God for the residual health of these Godless Russians."[61] "There is no doubt," Bruce Bliven wrote at the end of the summer, "that the spirit of the Russians in peace time was a great deal better than ours is at the present moment."[62] And at the moment of decision in Congress for aid to Russia, Freda Kirchway reminded liberals and those congressmen who read the *Nation*, "Russia is not going to win this war alone. It must have quick and decisive help from Britain and from the United States or it will go under; and if it is defeated, the position of the United States, not to mention Britain, will be desperate— as the President clearly told Congress."[63]

A week later a leading presidential Republican organ, *Life*, made the same point to its much larger audience. "Americans were confronted by the nightmare fact that, if Moscow falls and Stalin decides that bloody Russia deserves peace, the U.S.A. will find itself alone in the world, with only Britain as ally," *Life* noted in a story on the Russian battlefront with, it must have seemed to the readers, as many pictures as words. *Life* discreetly avoided the fact that the situation it now feared so markedly had existed only four months before.[64] "The Russian nation is harder to conquer than any other," *Time* said approvingly.[65] "Surely it is time we revised our views of Soviet policy," the well-known writer Kenneth Davis argued in September, "for if we continue to regard the Russians as 'enemies,' incredibly foreign to our ways of feeling and thinking, our chances for developing a permanently peaceful world at the close of this conflict will certainly be slim."[66] Virtually no national opinion maker would have taken public exception to Davis's contention.

Even in the conservative periodicals much of the comment was cautiously favorable to the Russians. *Business Week* praised Maxim Litvinoff, Stalin's new ambassador to the United States, as "one of the world's ablest diplomats."[67] Americans, conservatives assured their readers in a dramatic reversal of previous arguments, had little or nothing to fear from communism. Eugene Lyons and Freda Utley believed that Hitler's attack doomed Russian Communism just as the Kaiser's attack had brought about the downfall of the czarist regime. "One thing seems to me certain," Miss Utley wrote in *American Mercury*, "the Soviet state of the last quarter-century is finished. It will either be conquered, or split into several pieces, or reorganized on new non-communist lines."[68]

Reader's Digest, which distributed largely conservative thought to its millions of readers, published in condensed form an article by the economist Stuart Chase from *Forbes* which argued that "scientific progress has made the revolutionary theories of Marx obsolete." The main reason for this, Chase said, was that in the developed countries the proportion of the work force employed in the service trades and professions was rising while blue-collar jobs were disappearing.[69] And even those who could not quite follow Chase's reasoning could observe that American Communists were now the most fervent supporters of opposition to strikers and others who hindered production of war material.

Lest individual opinion makers, newspapers, radio networks, and periodicals do not quite enough to increase "understanding" of Russia, highly motivated promoters and scholars sprang into action in the summer and fall of 1941. The leading group promoting better relations between Russia and the United States was the American Council on Soviet Relations, which had been founded in 1938 but which virtually disappeared after the developments of late 1939. Not surprisingly, it was revived quickly after the Nazi attack.

Corliss Lamont, the son of New York banker Thomas W. Lamont and a staunch supporter of Russia through thick and thin, was the chairman of the group. In one of several pamphlets published by the council shortly after the German invasion, Lamont sought to put to rest the conservative argument that Russia and Germany were the same. The fact that even conservatives were willing to admit that their argument had been dealt a mortal blow by the new war did not lessen Lamont's zeal. He listed and then elaborated upon ten "contrasts" which, he believed, proved that Nazi Germany was the exact opposite of Soviet Russia.[70]

In November 1941, the first issue of the *Russian Review* appeared. "Of the need for a review that would endeavor to interpret Russia as it has been, as it may be in the future, there can be no doubt," editor William Henry Chamberlin wrote in the forward. He continued with an observation that, unfortunately, would remain largely true after American and Russian armies met in central Germany in April 1945.

> Russia is much less known to Americans than its size, its political importance, and its contributions to culture would warrant. Even the educated American rarely possesses the same grasp of the main facts of Russian history that he would have in regard to the history of the main countries of Western Europe. . . . While there is a substantial quantity of books about Russia since the Revolution, the quality of many of these works leaves much to be desired.[71]

Chamberlin could well have been referring specifically to the works discussed in the preceding chapter, which were violently anti-Russian, or to the pro-Russian volumes which appeared as he was writing late in 1941. "Whatever we Americans may have thought of the Soviet people," the procommunist journalist Anna Louise Strong contended in *The Soviets Expected It*, an example of the pro-Russian works, "they hold today our own front line for our democracy, our science, our equality, for all we have ever held dear. On them has fallen the military defense of civilization and human freedom against the dark forces that threaten to put back the clock of the world."[72]

In another representative work, *The Kremlin and the People*, Walter Duranty, a widely respected Kremlinologist, offered a revisionist account of recent Soviet internal and external affairs. Duranty defended Russian actions during the preceding few years at almost every turn. The purges were unfortunate, but they had, Duranty thought, eliminated fifth columnists in Russia. Munich was the "greatest humiliation which the Soviet Union had suffered since the Treaty of Brest-Mitovsk,' and it had paved the way for the Nazi-Soviet pact. In the perspective of German perfidy in 1941, the Finnish threat to the Soviet Union "was as obvious as if central Long Island, or Burlingame, California, were held by unfriendly little states which might at any moment agree with a great unfriendly power to unleash its war-dogs upon New York or San Francisco." Finally, Russians really were neither communists nor enslaved, contemptible creatures. Duranty cited wage differences and bonuses for overtime and hard work to buttress his argument that the Soviet economic system "might more accurately be described as State capitalism, rather than socialism." Russians might not worship at the altar of America's "rugged individualism"; but "in some ways, which perhaps are the ways of life, the basic ways of life, Russians are not less free than we are."[73]

It is very difficult to assess the impact of most books on the thinking of opinion makers, for outside of the academic community there is little citation of sources. Judging from Duranty's prestige as an expert on Russia and the way his ideas were assimilated into the thought of journalists and politicians, the indirect impact must have been profound. At the time, however, another book far eclipsed Duranty's in immediate impact. It was Joseph E. Davies's *Mission to Moscow*, the first great best seller on Russia since Lyons's *Assignment in Utopia*.

Like many a best seller, Davies's book was released at the most opportune moment. It was hardly in the bookstores before the Japanese bombing of Pearl Harbor brought America into the war. No longer were Americans virtuous observers of others' troubles. They were fighting for their lives, and like others in similar predicaments they needed reassurances. Most politicians and pundits spent much of their energy reassuring them that power and virtue were on the same side, and that America and her allies surely would win the war. Davies's self-assumed function at this time was to reassure them that Russia was all right.

This *Mission to Moscow* did. Unlike Duranty's somewhat scholarly approach, Davies told the "inside story" of his years as ambassador to Moscow in the late 1930s in the style of the sincere conversationalist. Davies was wealthy, aging, and known in the proper circles in American society; he was no radical. These facts made his message all the more palatable to those individuals, particularly in the eastern upper crust, who had a substantial say about whose opinions should be circulated widely and whose should not. The details of Davies's experience in Moscow and the reports he sent back to the State Department need not concern us here. The important thing is that many thousands of literate Americans found them to be valuable in solving the problem of friendship with Russia.

Davies set the tone in the book's preface: "Leaders of the Union of Soviet Socialist Republics I came to know. They are a group of able, strong men. I disagree with them in many respects; but I accord to them, that which I assume unto myself, namely, credit for honest convictions and integrity of purposes."[74] It seems unlikely that such remarks about the good faith of Russia's leaders would have made it to the printing presses of an established American publishing company six months before. After 22 June but before 7 December they were the words of a liberal; after Pearl Harbor they were words which almost any moderate could accept.

The radically altered positions of Russia in June and of the United States in December are crucial in explaining this change. Another reason was the tremendous feeling of national unity that developed after 7 December which emerges only when extreme views are moderated or laid aside. So far as is known, no one thought of Russia when President Roosevelt said in his war message to Congress and to the nation over radio that the "sources of international brutality, wherever they exist, must be absolutely and finally broken."[75] Germany, Italy, and Japan, Americans assumed, were the only sources of international evil. "In this country, on this Christmas," the *New Yorker* observed at the end of 1941, "there was probably more good will among men than there had been for many a long year. At war with a good-sized portion of the world, and settling down to the fourth week of it, we were, somewhat paradoxically, at peace with one another, and with ourselves."[76]

A prerequisite of genuine domestic peace in a democracy is basic agreement on foreign policy between the policy makers in the administrative branch on the one hand and the legislative branch and public on the other. This situation existed in the winter of 1942, and indeed generally until the beginning of 1945. No criticism of Russia or Britain now emanated from those who earlier had been quick to judge. As politicians or opinion makers, they knew that they could maintain their prominence only by permitting the sievelike memories of the public to forget the past. With America on the defensive everywhere, they could hardly suggest that the United States mount its offensive in the Pacific rather than in Europe. Similarly, the leftists scarcely could urge, as they would later in the year, that an offensive be launched in Europe immediately. And how could anyone—Left, Right, or Center—have the gall to criticize the British, who had first checked Hitler, or the Russians who, as the papers showed every day, were the only ones who were halting him now?

Even so, Americans early in 1942 still did not accept Russia as they accepted Britain and China. Hatred of communism, nurtured over many years, could not vanish in a few months. The old dichotomy persisted: China and Britain were "democracies," and Germany and Russia were "dictatorships." Germany might be evil and Russia good, but both were still dictatorships. If Chiang Kai-shek was as much a dictator as anybody, this fact had been carefully concealed from Americans. Chiang was our client in Asia who welcomed American economic and religious interests, and Madame Chiang was beautiful. If the Chinese had not yet perfected democracy, it was because they were backward and inexperienced. As for Britain, it was the home of English-speaking cousins and our deepest traditions; to dislike Britain too much was dangerously close to disliking oneself. But Russia was a remote country whose ideology Americans had been taught to consider a threat to all that was good. And even when the powerful and respected teachers shifted, it was hard to forget the axioms learned first.

Nevertheless, millions of Americans were changing their attitudes toward Russia in response to changed circumstances and the way their foreign-policy opinion makers presented these circumstances to them. In October 1941 and again in February 1942, *Fortune* commissioned Elmo Roper to conduct a survey on the question, "Regardless of how you feel toward Russia, which of these policies do you think we should pursue toward her now?" The respondent was given these four choices: (1)"Stop helping Russia in any way," (2)"Work along with Russia and give her some aid if we think it will help beat the Axis," (3)"Treat Russia as a full partner along with Britain in the fight against the Axis nations," and (4)"Don't know."

In October 1941, 14 percent wanted to stop helping Russia in any way; in February 1942, only 4 percent held this view. In October, 51 percent wanted to work along with Russia; in February, 43 percent gave this lukewarm response. In October, only 22 percent wanted Russia to be Britain's equal as a partner; in February, those making this choice had nearly doubled to 41 percent. Finally, in the wake of Pearl Harbor, those who declined to answer dropped from 13 to 11 percent.[77] These shifts in attitudes are illustrated in figure 2.

These changes, all favorable to Russia, are pronounced when considered in terms of percentages. They are even more significant in view of the fact that each percentage point represented about seven hundred fifty thousand adult Americans. Thus, nearly fifteen million more adult Ameri-

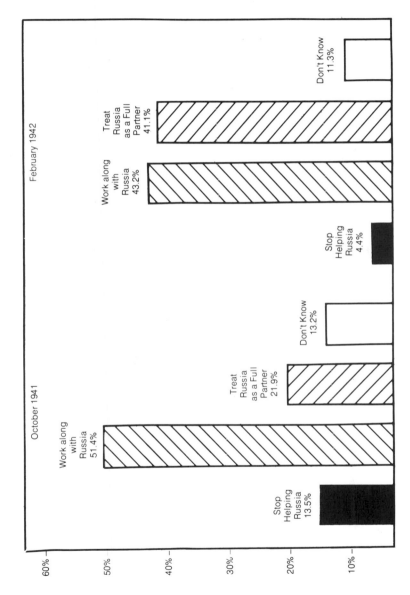

Figure 2. Opinion of Russia before and after American entry into the war (from "The Fortune Survey," *Fortune*, February 1942, p. 98)

cans favored Russia as an equal partner after Pearl Harbor and the Declaration of the United Nations on 1 January 1942 than at the time of the vote on lend-lease aid to Russia.[78] On the other hand, Russia was hardly an ally of the United States in the same sense as Britain even in February, for the "work along with Russia" response still received a plurality of all responses. President Roosevelt, a careful poll watcher, must have been well aware of the strength of this continuing distrust when the question of the immediate opening of a second front in western Europe came to a head in the summer of 1942.

FIFTEEN CENTS   JANUARY 1, 1940

TIME

THE WEEKLY NEWSMAGAZINE

Ernest Hamlin Baker

MAN OF THE YEAR
"Ivan the Terrible was right."
(Foreign News)

VOLUME XXXV   (REG. U. S. PAT. OFF.)   NUMBER 1

OCTOBER 6, 1941

Newsweek

10ᶜ

THE MAGAZINE OF NEWS SIGNIFICANCE

Red Cavalry Rides to Defend the Ukraine

(Reprinted by permission, Newsweek, Inc.)

One Year Against Hitler: Stalin Proved His Name Meant 'Steel'

(Sovfoto, reprinted by permission, Newsweek, Inc.)

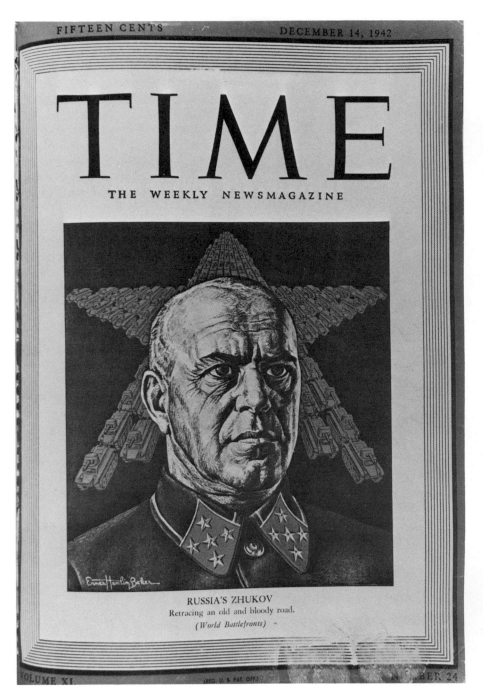

RUSSIA'S ZHUKOV
Retracing an old and bloody road.
(World Battlefronts)

FIFTEEN CENTS   DECEMBER 21, 1942

TIME

THE WEEKLY NEWSMAGAZINE

Boris Chaliapin

KATHARINE CORNELL, JUDITH ANDERSON, RUTH GORDON
Three bright stars in a Russian twilight.

(*Theater*)

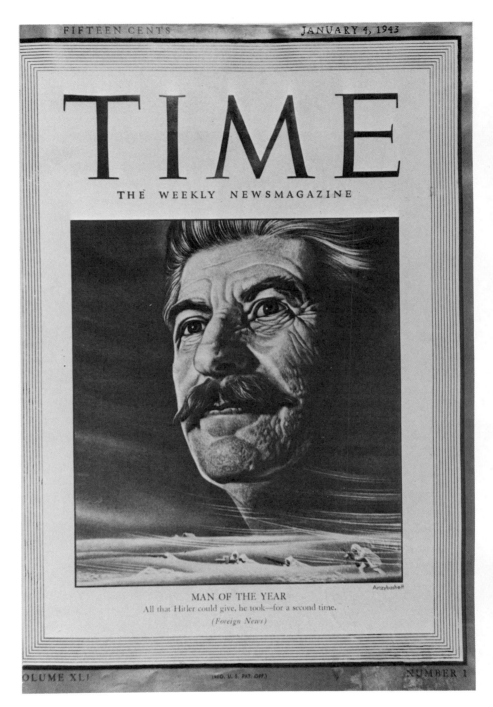

MAN OF THE YEAR
All that Hitler could give, he took—for a second time.
(Foreign News)

(Reprinted by permission from TIME, The Weekly Newsmagazine; Copyright Time Inc. 1943)

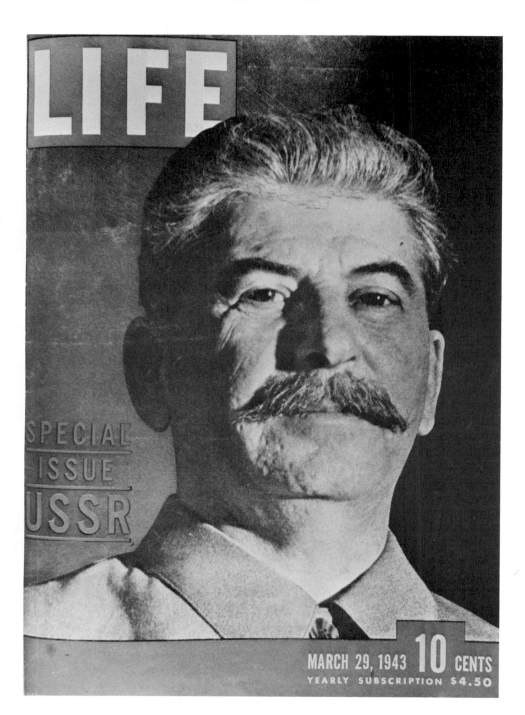

(Reprinted by permission, LIFE Photo by Margaret Bourke-White, Copyright © Time Inc. 1943)

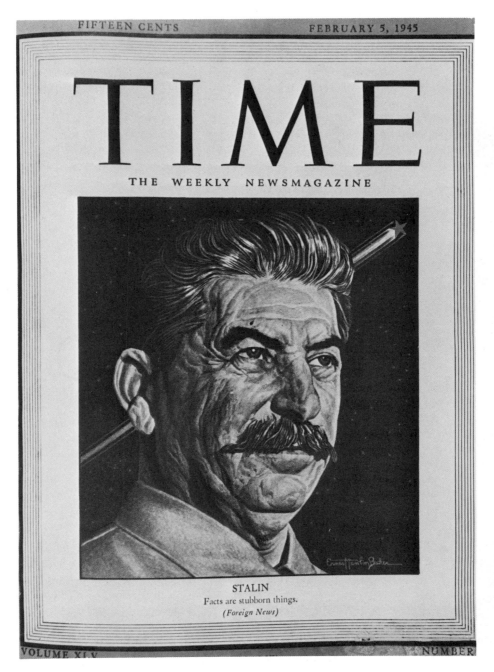

FIFTEEN CENTS   FEBRUARY 5, 1945

TIME

THE WEEKLY NEWSMAGAZINE

STALIN
Facts are stubborn things.
(Foreign News)

VOLUME XLV   NUMBER

(Reprinted by permission from TIME, The Weekly Newsmagazine; Copyright Time Inc. 1945)

Where Is the Second Front?

By the end of April 1942, the cold winter air had relinquished its tenacious grasp on the nation. Small peaches were visible in Georgia, where beautiful blooms had announced the advent of spring several weeks before. The cherries of Virginia had bloomed later, but they were already advancing past the peaches toward early maturity. And apple blossoms beautified the countryside from Maryland and southern Pennsylvania to Oregon and eastern Washington.

Orchardists from Augusta to Yakima could well worry about the supply of laborers to harvest this year's crop, for the Selective Service System had already called many of the able-bodied men to their fates in the war zones, while others had flocked to burgeoning defense installations in the nation's urban centers, attracted by the promise of a heretofore unknown level of affluence. But the farmers could take consolation in the fact that another winter of enforced idleness and accumulating debts had passed, and that wartime food prices offered hope that the hard-working and the fortunate would realize profits far beyond possibility during a dozen long years of depression.

Spring is the season of rebirth of not only such diverse phenomena as fruit trees and romance; it is also the season when war making traditionally begins or resumes on a massive scale. On the eastern front, the only major theater of operations in Europe at this time, the Russians had broken all polite rules of warfare by using their country's frigid winter to great advantage. In this season of rest and recuperation they recaptured hundreds of towns and seized thousands of German soldiers and tons of the Reich's prized equipment. But now spring promised a mighty thrust by the wounded but still immensely powerful German army, and American opinion was sharply divided as to whether the Russians could hold out for the seven months before winter would bring them its blessings again. After all, during the preceding year the Germans had nearly won everything: they had driven all the way from the Polish frontier to within sight of the Kremlin in the four short months before winter set in.

It was axiomatic to opinion makers in Britain and the United States that Russia should not become Hitler's greatest victim to date. Sympathy formed part of this concern, of course, but self-interest was at least an equal motivation, for without Russian assistance a successful assault on Germany from the west was virtually unthinkable. And if Hitler survived as the master of Europe, he would threaten indefinitely the security of the entire world. In practice, it was Britain's security which would be placed in the greatest immediate jeopardy by a Germany triumphant from Siberia to the English Channel. And it was in Britain, where the gratitude for Russian valor was greatest, that shrill demands for a second front first became most widespread.

Prime Minister Churchill sent Lord Beaverbrook, a prominent newspaper owner and statesman and the most powerful and persistent British voice for a second front, abroad in the spring of 1942. Beaverbrook's destination was the United States, one of the few remaining countries where Britishers, accustomed for two centuries to considering the world their province, were still welcome. Beaverbrook's official purpose in coming to America was to serve as British lend-lease coordinator.

If it was Churchill's hope that Beaverbrook would remain out of public view in America, as he had refused to do in Britain, the prime minister was to be disappointed, for Beaverbrook's mission to the United States was a minor sensation and a great success on matters beyond coordination of lend-lease. Beaverbrook's most important speech in America was to the Bureau of Advertising of the American Newspaper Publishers Association on 23 April 1942. The bureau was hardly one of the nation's leading organizations, but its proximity to a major channel of opinion circulation, coupled with Beaverbrook's prominence, assured the speech a wide distribution.

"I believe in the Russian system which holds to the faith that the best form of defense is attack," the visitor said with his usual candor. "And I believe that Britain should adopt it by setting up somewhere along the two thousand miles of coastline now held by the Germans, a second front in Western Europe." Beaverbrook continued with the reasoning behind his polite demand.

Now you may ask the reason for my advocacy of help to Russia. Is it due to confidence in a brave people or to the desire to help a hard-pressed comrade? Not at all.

It is the knowledge that Russia may settle the war for us in 1942. By holding the Germans in check, possibly even by defeating them, the Russians may be the means of bringing the whole Axis structure down.

This is a chance, an opportunity to bring the war to an end here and now. But if the Russians are defeated and driven out of the war, never will such a chance come to us again. Strike out to help Russia! Strike out violently! Strike even recklessly! But in any event such blows that really help will be our share and contribution to the Russian battle front.[1]

It is doubtful that Lord Beaverbrook's ideas had penetrated the consciousness of many of the delegates to the annual Southern Baptist Convention, which met in San Antonio, Texas, from 16 May through 20 May. If they had, they are not reflected in the minutes of the meetings. The only foreign issue discussed, except for missions, was the general orientation of this formerly isolationist church toward the war. "We are indeed living at a time when the hearts and minds of men are baffled and confused," the Home Mission Board reported to the convention. "We hesitate to hope lest our hopes be too sanguine or to fear lest our fears be not fearful enough."[2]

Having expressed doubt about the times, the Home Mission Board could proceed to affirm the necessity of the war for the individual, the church, and the nation: "The conflict today is not essentially a struggle for territory; that is included, but it is a clash of ideologies. We are fighting for the rights of the individual. If the Axis powers win, then totalitarianism will dominate the world. This ideology deifies the state and enslaves the individual. In such a world Christianity would have no place and the missionary who carries the Gospel of redeeming grace to lost men would find every door in the world closed."[3]

The two quotations, one from a liberal Briton and the other from a conservative American religious body, epitomize the wide range in American opinion in 1942 toward the global war which only recently had engulfed the United States. The Baptist leaders were still asking, in effect, if the war was truly just and if Russia was really our ally.[4] Part of their answer to the first question was that we were indeed at war for the survival of the individual and the church, and, to the second question, that the presence of Russia did not mitigate the war's democratic mission.

Like Beaverbrook, many cosmopolitan Americans had long since decided that the war was necessary, and their thinking naturally had advanced further. In 1942, many conservative, formerly isolationist Americans were still asking themselves whether Russia was indeed our ally in this war for democracy and against totalitarianism. The war aims of liberals and interventionists were not so dichotomous, and they had answered this question to their satisfaction in 1941. They could now turn to the problem of whether America was doing its part as Russia's most powerful partner in the war against Germany.

Not surprisingly, few conservatives spoke out either for or against a second front in 1942. In addition to wishing to avoid accusations that they were creating disunity among the Allies if they opposed a second front, they simply were largely unprepared for this question. Liberals in America and especially in Britain, in contrast, were so prepared for the question that they created serious difficulties for the civilian and military leaders of these two great Atlantic powers.

The argument for the second front, however, was slow to emerge. If someone at a sophisticated New Year's Eve party in uptown Manhattan had said to an acquaintance, "We must open a second front this coming year," the acquaintance probably would have shaken his head and suggested that his friend switch from whisky to ginger ale. If the acquaintance had been mildly interested in his friend's statement, he might have asked him what type of business transaction or stock manipulation he had in mind. And even if his friend had communicated effectively with him, he could well have dismissed any concern about inter-Allied conflict the next morning when the front page of the newspaper splashed news of the signing of the Declaration of the United Nations, which theoretically cemented the unity of the anti-Axis coalition.

Of course, Russia was not at war with Japan, but then how could she prosecute a war on two fronts, as the ultraconservative press insisted she should, when she might well lose everything on the one she had? And the implications, or even the details, of the British-American military conferences that were going forward in Washington over the Christmas holidays were not known to the friend as he read his newspaper or listened to the radio on 1 January 1942.

In a real sense, the millions of Americans who read the huge headlines and optimistic stories about the Declaration of the United Nations were being deceived, as they so often would be during the war when they read the glowing words of joint communiqués on the war and the peace to follow. But this is not surprising, for they had been deliberately deceived by diplomatic communiqués before. Moreover, they had become so accustomed to receiving in their newspapers and on the radio only what their government wanted them to hear that they naturally mistook appearances for a reality not revealed to them. For example, they, and probably most opinion makers as well, probably did not even consider the possibility that a tense struggle had developed among some of the signers over the wording of the declaration. They were not told, for example, that Roosevelt had assured Ambassador Litvinoff that the clause proclaiming "freedom of religion" as a central war aim really meant nothing.[5]

Almost surely most Americans were also unaware of two other

important facts about the "Grand Alliance" at the begining of 1942. First of all, the Declaration of the United Nations tended to disguise the fact that there was no institutionalized military alliance among the four major allied powers, that the only effective military alliance consisted solely of the United States and Britain, and that hence there was no joint war council of the United Nations to determine priorities in the struggle against the Axis. The contention here is not that such coordination would have been entirely desirable or feasible; it is simply that the American public tended to assume that there was much more effective military coordination among the allies than actually existed. And secondly, most Americans in early 1942 did not perceive the disparity between the relatively favorable military situation facing the United States and Britain on the one hand and the grim conditions facing Russia and China on the other. Whereas Russia and China were suffering from massive invasions which could not be repelled in the foreseeable future and which were causing large numbers of casualties, the United States and Britain were relatively secure and were suffering relatively few casualties. Strategically, the Russians and Chinese had to concentrate on blunting Axis attacks, whereas the western allies had several military options at any given time.

This striking contrast between Anglo–American flexibility and unity and Russian inflexibility and isolation was almost bound to contribute to friction sooner or later. In fact, with the Soviet Union facing possible extinction in 1942 and again in 1943 as the British and Americans dallied and debated alternative strategies instead of engaging large numbers of the German divisions, this friction was not long in coming.[6]

Signs of such frictions must have been evident to America's attentive public as early as the spring of 1942. Ambassadors, these people must have known, do not speak out on vital issues in the countries to which they are sent unless relations between their homelands and their hosts are strained. And even then they must speak with restraint and be quite popular in their host countries lest their efforts backfire.

There was no more popular and respected ambassador to the United States in 1942 than Maxim Litvinoff. Not only did he represent the primary foe of the Nazis, but he also had gained respect in some circles because he was Jewish, in others because he spoke pleasing English and had a British wife, and in all interventionist circles because of his reasoned pleas in the mid-1930s for collective security.[7] At a party which Litvinoff and his wife held in February 1942 for governmental and other notables, the Russian ambassador was literally the toast of American capitalistic society. Figuratively, he was frequently toasted by *Business Week*, *Time*, and other essentially conservative journals.

Litvinoff preceded Lord Beaverbrook in calling for a second front in

1942, but he may not have been quite as effective in his advocacy because of the obvious Russian self-interest involved and because his pleas came well ahead of public readiness to accept them. When Litvinoff, in an address to the Overseas Press Club in Washington on 26 February, called on Russia's allies to open a second front against Hitler that spring, for example, the *New York Herald Tribune* answered him indirectly in an editorial entitled "This Complex War." "All that American public opinion can ask of its leaders," the *Tribune* argued, "is that they act as fast as their equipment in men, planes, guns, and machines permits, that they think realistically not of withholding aid from this country or the other, but of smashing the common foe."[8]

What Litvinoff said in the speech actually differed little from the substance, if not the tone, of the *Tribune* editorial. "Don't get me wrong," Litvinoff said. "I don't for a moment mean to say that all the Allies should concentrate their attention on our front to the detriment of other fronts." But "identical quantities of armed forces and identical sorts of arms are not required on all fronts." After observing that the Russian theater of the war should "certainly be considered the most important"—a point of view which only ultraconservatives such as William Randolph Hearst were then denying—Litvinoff concluded with the strongest words of his mild, reasoned address: "Only by simultaneous offensive operations on two or more fronts separated by long distances could Hitler's armed forces be disposed of—and that is just why Hitler would dislike such operations."[9]

"It is sometimes objected," Litvinoff told an Economics Club dinner in New York on 16 March,

that practical ways to victory involve risk, and there is no denying the truth of this. Military operations between more or less equal forces generally do involve risk. Does not Hitler owe his considerable successes to highly risky ventures in Norway, Crete, and elsewhere? There may be much greater and more actual risk in waiting, in doing nothing, in letting slip one opportunity after another; and action involving risk has at any rate some chance of success, whereas inaction also involving risk is practically never crowned with success.[10]

Only two prominent Americans—Wendell Willkie and Joseph E. Davies—joined Beaverbrook and Litvinoff in the spring of 1942 in calling for a second front, and even they expended only a small part of their public energies in this effort. On 26 February, the same day that Litvinoff spoke to the Overseas Press Club in Washington, Willkie, in an address in Los Angeles, called for a major Allied offensive in the West. Both of these pleas made the front pages of many newspapers and the leading radio news programs and thus introduced at least the attentive public to the budding second-front issue. On a national radio program sponsored by the War Production Board at the end of April, Davies urged that "diverting fronts" be set up to remove some of the pressure from Russia.[11]

Davies's request may have been lost on his listeners because of his continuing emphasis on the need for trust and friendship toward Russia; yet Davies surely knew that trust in Russia obviously was required before a campaign to open a second front to help Russia regardless of risk could gain wide and intense popular support. The effort to increase public acceptance of "our Russian ally" (traced in some detail in chapter 3) thus forms a necessary backdrop to the heated campaign for a second front in the summer of 1942.

"The Russian people are fighting on our side and we should not forget that from the time of the American Revolution," Davies said in the same radio address, "the Russian people have never failed to be on our side in every war we have been in." Davies did not bother to elaborate how the "Russian people" had aided the United States in the Mexican or Spanish-American wars, but few of his listeners would have known enough about American history to notice this oversight. And in this time of friendliness toward Russia and to Davies, no one really took issue with the following assertion which formed the core of the former ambassador's entire campaign for friendship with Russia: "We must never lose sight of the fact that we are aiding Russia to help ourselves and helping the Russian Government to beat Hitler doesn't mean tolerance or approval of Russian Communism."[12]

Davies's primary efforts in the winter and spring of 1942, indeed those of many other presidential Republican and Democratic opinion makers in politics and the media as well, were directed not toward creating a clamor for a second front but toward improving public confidence in Russia. Davies alone must have written a dozen magazine articles and made fifty speeches around the country in addition to his radio appearances between December 1941 and June 1942.

"The man who represented this country through those amazing chapters of Russian and world history should make one of the most interesting speakers Atlanta has had at our old auditorium,"[13] Ralph McGill, a cosmopolitan young southern journalist wrote on 2 May in the *Atlanta Constitution* to boost Davies's imminent visit to that city. On 5 May the story of Davies's speech to the World Affairs Symposium sponsored by Atlanta's foremost department store made that newspaper's front page. As they drank their coffee at breakfast, Georgians could read the approving news story which reported Davies's comment that he was speaking in favor of Russia as a true believer in capitalism, a "member of the lodge."[14]

McGill's chatty column on the editorial page reinforced this view; it was entitled "A Member of the Lodge." "Joe Davies, capitalist, believes in Roosevelt and he believes that our new bedfellow, the Russian, is a good, worthwhile, dependable fellow much like our own pioneers," McGill wrote. "That is to say, he is willing to die for something." The column continued with a subtle comparison of Russian ideals with perhaps the most honored ideal of the South—the willingness to fight and die for one's beliefs. "Well,—times change," McGill concluded. "How about your mind?"[15]

Some of the mighty opinion makers who, unlike Davies, did not have to travel around the country to achieve broad circulation of their opinions, were presidential Republican Henry Luce and his unknown but powerful editors. They let eager subscribers and advertisers pay the Post Office Department for the circulation of *Time*, *Life*, and *Fortune* to personal mailboxes, hotel lobbies, and doctors' offices in every town and city in America. *Life* carried picture stories favorable to Russia with such concrete titles as "Russian Courage and Cold Rout Nazis"[16] and "Russian Parents Lament Dead Son at Scene of German Execution."[17] *Time* selected President Roosevelt as its man of the year for 1941 because of his foresight in supporting preparedness and aid to the Allies, and underlined the importance of unity by placing Stalin to Roosevelt's left and Churchill to his right on the cover of the 5 January 1942 issue. In the lead article Stalin was recognized as "the only leader who has yet to face a major German drive without a military disaster," and Roosevelt was hailed as the "leader of the democracies against Hitler."[18] Such recognition of Stalin as Roosevelt's partner in Allied leadership redounded to Russia's benefit among Americans. Of more specific assistance were the several Russian military leaders and strategists introduced to the public on the covers of *Time* during the year.

On 11 May, readers in New York, Oshkosh, and, indeed, everywhere in America opened their mailboxes and were greeted by the smiling face of Maxim Litvinoff. "Hitler has to destroy the Russian Army in 1942 or lose the war," *Time* observed in the succinct style which was its trademark. "And the U.S. has to keep Russia fighting or face a war that would be immeasurably longer and tougher." Litvinoff's importance thus indirectly established, *Time* could continue with a pithy assessment of the Russian ambassador: "To the U.S. public, traditionally suspicious of striped pants diplomats, he looks disarmingly undiplomatic. . . . If the U.S. is willing to be a tough guy it can play ball with tough Russia," *Time* concluded. "Against a common enemy they can operate together with profit and yet each for himself. That is what Litvinoff sensibly offers, a game as fair for one player as for another."[19]

If American publishers permitted any unfavorable comments about Russia to pass through their presses during 1942, the casual reader would have had difficulty finding them. Not only was Russia our partner, but nice words about her leaders and people sold, as Davies's *Mission to Moscow* demonstrated throughout the year. But because of the inevitable time lag between the conception of a book and its appearance on the market, there was virtually no comment on the possibility of a second front in this most durable of all media. Like most Americans whose thoughts on Russia were featured in print or on radio during the first half of 1942, authors were extolling friendship, or at least sensible cooperation, with the Russians.

The representative nonfiction work of 1942, if such may be said to exist, was *Prelude to Victory* by a young and obscure *New York Times* reporter, James Reston. *Prelude to Victory* appeared in June with the prestigious Knopf imprint and went through a second printing in August. By July it was well known among opinion makers and the attentive public, but it probably had its greatest impact on the thinking of the general public after it appeared in the drugstores and bus stations of the nation in a Pocket paperback edition in November. On its cover was the glaring injunction "Wake Up and Fight."

"It is necessary now that we admit the facts," Reston began; "many of the things we have laughed at, or taken for granted, or minimized, or despised in the last few years have risen up to plague us."[20] The British-born University of Illinois graduate of the class of 1932 then divided the work into eleven chapters, treating that number of ongoing "illusions" which be believed were hampering the war effort. These "illusions" were: (1) "that freedom comes easy"; (2) "that wars do not really settle anything"; (3) "that time and money will save us"; (4) "that this is entirely a war of guns, tanks, planes, and ships"; (5) "that we can win the war with our second team"; (6) "that the facts will speak for themselves"; (7) "that Britain and Russia are the enemy"; (8) "that it's always somebody else's fault"; (9) "that we are fighting to 'get back to normal' "; (10) "that everybody loves democracy"; and (11) "that you can do nothing about it."[21]

In his argument in chapter 2 that wars do settle things, Reston included a section entitled "The Fundamental Conflict between Totalitarian States and Our Ideals," driving this point home with quotations from the first two paragraphs of the Declaration of Independence and with the casual omission of the fact that America's largest ally had been considered totalitarian up until less than a year before. At another point in the same chapter he underscored the importance of the four freedoms by insisting that in order to avoid yet another world war, "every nation must possess the four freedoms."[22] "The point is simply this, and it means a whole lot to your children and mine," Reston said. "If, at the end of this war, some other dictator is able to deny freedom of religion, freedom from want, and freedom from fear to his people; if, in other words, it is possible for another dictator to keep the truth from men and poison their minds with lies and dreams of conquest, then it will be possible for that dictator to raise another warrior generation and challenge us on the field of battle."[23]

To be sure, Reston did not suggest that the United States keep fighting until Roosevelt's four freedoms were established everywhere. He also did not point out that Russia might not yet possess them and he did not even mention Russia at all. In fact, when Reston brought Russia into the discussion in chapter 7, he assured his readers that Russia was America's friend. The "main facts of this war . . . ," Reston asserted,

are that we are fighting against the Japanese and the Germans and the Italians, and that we are fighting alongside the Russians and the Chinese and the British. And since these are the main facts of the situation, what I want to know is: What is the point of carping at the British and Russians? What is the point of it? Where does it get us? It is not only plain bad manners and a free gift to the goons we are fighting against, but it is bad politics and bad strategy and it can help lose the war.[24]

"Suppose they are just as totalitarian as the Germans, which fortunately for us, they were," Reston continued in a reference to the Russians that in peacetime probably would have been seized upon by book reviewers as a contradiction of part of chapter 2. "Even suppose that they intend to spread Communism all over Europe after the war. What are we going to do about it now?"[25] Yet Reston was not sure how to put a stop to anti-British and anti-Russian talk. He inclined toward President Roosevelt's view that fifth columnists "put the rumors out" and that sixth columnists, or antiadministration groups, "spread the lies of the fifth columnists." But the latter could hardly be expected to desist when Reston mentioned Hearst, Patterson, and McCormick by name and labeled those to the right of them as the "Reptile Press."[26]

On 2 July, the French journalist Raoul de Roussy de Sales wrote in his diary that he had been reading three books, H. G. Wells's *You Can't Be Too Careful*, Herbert Hoover's and Hugh Gibson's *The Problems of Lasting Peace*, and Reston's *Prelude to Victory*. "There is no relationship between these three books," de Sales noted, "but their cumulative effect is irritating and disappointing. Three specimens of 'collective mediocrity.'" "It is discouraging," he wrote of Reston's book, "that after so many months and years it should still be necessary to make appeals of this sort."[27]

But Walter Millis, William Lyon Phelps, Malcolm Cowley, and other reviewers praised Reston for doing just this; and Clifton Fadiman hailed him as the "Thomas Paine of today."[28] Reston and these reviewers knew that, even in wartime America, true national unity remained a goal to be sought rather than a reality to be taken for granted.

Other books by journalists poured from the nation's presses with similar pro-Russian themes. Wallace Carroll carefully stated the facts and implications of the wartime alliance of communists and capitalists against fascists in *We're in This with Russia*.[29] In *Shooting the Russian War*, a book devoted largely to photographs, Margaret Bourke-White defended the purges because of their contributions to national unity. Less controversial but equally sympathetic statements permeated the book. "Stalin is fond of American cigarettes," Miss Bourke-White noted in a way that would tend to endear him to millions of smokers. "His visitors from our embassy know this and often bring him Camels, Chesterfields, and Lucky Strikes."[30] And John Scott published the record of his experiences in the 1930s in a Siberian industrial city. "Even if Moscow is lost," Scott argued, "the Red armies will be able to go on fighting for months, even years, basing themselves on the stronghold of the Urals supplemented by factories and skilled workers evacuated from the western parts of the Soviet Union."[31]

Two works in particular exuded optimism about Russia's armies. "Whatever the developments on the Russian front in the near future may be," Michel Berchin and Eliahu Ben-Horin wrote in *The Red Army*, "Russia will go on fighting."[32] Sergei N. Kournakoff, a captain in the Russian army, argued that "history" had "created all the prerequisites for a lasting friendship between our great peoples."[33] Kournakoff also insisted that a "second front must be opened on land, on the Continent of Europe, simultaneously with the unleashing of the forthcoming great battles on the Eastern Front." Such united and coordinated action, he thought, would permit victory over the Germans that very year.[34]

The aging Sidney and Beatrice Webb of England betrayed the effusive infatuation with Russia which characterized their last years when they wrote *The Truth about Soviet Russia*. They argued that "Stalin is not a dictator," and that, "tested by the Constitution of the Soviet Union as revised and enacted in 1936, the U.S.S.R. is the most inclusive and equalized democracy in the world."[35] Finally, Emil Ludwig's biography of Stalin in 1942 was as favorable as Eugene Lyons's work of 1940 had been unfavorable. To Ludwig, the "bolshevism of 1942" was the social order that most nearly equaled perfection at that time, and it was Stalin who had led the Russian people to this glorious state.[36]

Even those few literate Americans who were not aware of the thrust of at least some of these works would certainly have heard of *Mission to Moscow*, and they might also have read other works which concentrated on other themes but included explicit pro-Russian comments. One such book was a collection of Protestant religious lectures for 1942, whose contributors included the prominent lay and clerical religious leaders John Foster Dulles and William Paton. In criticizing the Streit plan for union of the English-speaking democracies, Dulles, whose viewpoint was much more open than in later years, argued that a "federation of the so-called democracies would, to others, appear as the banding together of the well-to-do to maintain the *status quo*."[37] Paton, a Britisher, said that his countrymen had found that Russians "live and fight, resist and sacrifice, as only people do who are possessed of moral integrity."[38]

In *A Time for Greatness*, Herbert Agar, a Catholic scholar and reformer, was itching to attack conservative opponents of Allied unity by name, but he refrained in deference to those who urged that the Left be "polite about them, for national unity, because since Pearl Harbor they are 'right about the war.' " "How can they be right about the war," Agar asked, "when they don't know what the war is about?"[39]

Finally, Quentin Reynolds, a popular journalist, positively praised Stalin for conducting the purges. "We forgot the meaning of the term," Reynolds contended. "The dictionary defines 'purge' as 'to make physically and spiritually clean.' That purge eliminated Russia's Fifth Column."[40] Of the Soviet leader, Reynolds wrote, "His appearance was a contradiction of everything we had ever been led to believe about Stalin. A British correspondent once wrote of Stalin, 'He looks like the kindly Italian gardener you have in twice a week.' You couldn't find a better description of the Soviet leader than that."[41]

To American ears, Stalin indeed was talking like a kindly Italian gardener in the spring of 1942. In his May Day "Order of the Day," Stalin described Mother Russia as "a force which is capable of saving the world from the Hitlerite plague." To the relief of the other Allied governments, he made no mention of the need for a second front. And then he said just what Americans wanted him to say: "We have no such aims as the occupation of foreign countries, the subjugation of other peoples." But to those Americans like Herbert Hoover and Secretary of State Cordell Hull, who insisted that other nations adhere in practice to the lofty moral principles which America actually honored primarily in theory, Stalin's reference to the intended incorporation of the Baltic states into Soviet territory must have been disturbing: "Our aim is clear and noble. We want to liberate our brothers, the Ukrainians, Moldavians, White Russians, Lithuanians, Latvians, Estonians, Karelians, from the shame and humiliation inflicted upon them by the German Fascist black-guards."[42]

Most American newspapers praised Stalin's speech. "Stalin was perhaps the most pointed when he disclaimed for Russia any desire to expand her territory or to impose her political domination on other peoples," the *Asheville Citizen* contended, highlighting like most other papers Stalin's apparent renunciation of territorial ambitions but forgetting that some of the peoples whom Stalin mentioned did not wish to be incorporated into the Soviet Union after the German defeat.[43] Walter Lippmann thought that "Stalin expressly meant to say to the Finns and to the Germans, as well as to the Hungarians and Rumanians, that the defeat of the German army and the downfall of the Nazi regime would not be followed by Russian military occupation of these 'foreign countries.' "[44]

But the *Cleveland Plain Dealer*, which had been militantly anti-Russian before 1941, was not so sanguine. "To most naive Americans," the *Plain Dealer* argued with complete confidence in American sophistication, "Finland, the Baltic States, Poland and Rumania are 'foreign countries' as far as Russia is concerned." But the *Plain Dealer* did admit that "toward military victory Russia is contributing more than any other nation. Her reward may come in an all-European understanding rather than in a settlement that seems to resemble outmoded imperialism."[45]

If Americans were beginning to feel much better about Russian Communists, they still could not stomach their American comrades. Surely American Communists knew this; they could confirm it by looking at any public opinion poll on the subject since scientific polling began about a decade before. They could also confirm it by reading any newspaper editorial on the subject except, of course, one from the *Daily Worker*. With this in mind, those American Communists who were sincerely interested in helping Russia would have done well to utter inanities about the need for unity to achieve victory or to remain silent. In fact, Earl Browder took a very conciliatory approach to American institutions after his release from prison.

Unfortunately, the *Daily Worker* and the leader in Browder's absence, William Z. Foster, leaped ahead in the spring of 1942 and demanded an immediate second front. Even before Litvinoff's address in Washington and Willkie's in Los Angeles had brought the issue before the mass public for the first time, Foster had published a pamphlet entitled "From Defense to Attack," which called for a western offensive. And scarcely a day passed later in the spring without the appearance in the *Daily Worker* of pleas for a second front. On 29 April, for example, the newspaper quoted at length from an article in a recent issue of the *Nation* by J. Alvarez Del Vayo, the exiled foreign minister of the Spanish Republic, on the desirability of an immediate second front.[46] "It only requires an end to the illusions and follies of 'waiting' to hurl immense armies against Hitler on the Western Front and bring him crashing to his doom," the *Daily Worker* editorialized on 2 May, the day after Stalin's order of the day.[47]

Franklin Roosevelt was, by all odds, the most effective American political leader of this century. But ever so often, during years in which he was not a candidate, this self-assured president would make a move the unpopularity of which almost every attentive person in the country could have assured him in advance.

Roosevelt's chief blunder of 1942 relative to positive attitudes toward Russia was his order releasing Earl Browder from the federal penitentiary in Atlanta just before Browder would have been released anyway. It is doubtful that the Russians were moved by this symbolic gesture at a time when they needed genuine help in the form of increased aid and a second front. It is certain that the move did not contribute to domestic unity, for the vast majority probably would have been pleased to leave Browder in prison for the rest of his life.

Right-wing columnist Westbrook Pegler, who had been scratching for material with which to attack the administration ever since American Communists had stopped sabotaging war industries in June 1941, rushed to the attack. Browder's release, Pegler proclaimed in his widely distributed column, "establishes the principle that under American justice today the politics of a criminal may be weighed in his favor."[48] An official of the American Legion asserted that the release was as great a shock to war morale as an announcement of the sinking of the nation's entire Pacific fleet would have been.[49] And Colonel R. R. McCormick, czar of the *Chicago Tribune*, was moved to write that paper's editorial on the subject himself. A major point in his tortuous prose was the admission—quite significant considering its source—that Communists no longer presented the danger to America that he had earlier thought they had: "Communists are cockeyed, of course; if they weren't they wouldn't be Communists. But they're no less dangerous for being cockeyed, just as the criminally insane are no less dangerous for being insane. But today we should draw not upon their dangerousness, but upon their cockeyedness."[50]

More moderate voices also took the opportunity provided by the president to vent latent hostility on communists and the Soviet Union. As the *Philadelphia Bulletin* put it, "What the Soviets would have done to any Browders who tried to destruct its preparations to meet expected attack from an enemy does not need telling."[51] "We don't like Earl Browder and what he represents," the *New York Post* told its readers. "We don't like his herd of home grown and imported commies. . . . We think both justice and national unity would have been better served by letting regular legal processes take their course."[52] The *Christian Science Monitor* was sure that the president had overstepped proper bounds: "Military aid, yes. Americans are willing that the Russians should have it in plenty as a powerful and proven ally against Axis military aggression. But as for political systems, Russia can have its communism and the United States will keep its constitutional republic."[53]

The *Philadelphia Inquirer*, which was slow to criticize the nation's leader during wartime, did not comment on the issue directly. Instead, it presented a story entitled "Browder is Member of Old U.S. Family," in which it informed Main Line Philadelphians that Browder's "family came to Virginia in 1650."[54] Only the *St. Louis Post-Dispatch* could muster enthusiasm for Roosevelt's action. "It would be a contradiction," the *Post-Dispatch* argued, "if President Roosevelt, on the one hand, should engage in every effort to aid Russia in its war against the Nazis and, on the other, fail to commute the unjust sentence of a Communist leader."[55] Although the *Post-Dispatch* stood alone alongside the *Daily Worker* in its assessment, it probably was right in arguing that the severity of Browder's sentence resulted more from the near hysteria of late 1939 than from judicial detachment. In any event, the fact was that Browder's release slowed for a time both the development of national unity and the growth of goodwill toward Russia.

Having described in some detail the early calls for a second front and the broad climate in America of increasing but still restrained friendliness toward Russia in the first half of 1942, we can now proceed to discuss the campaign for a second front which took place primarily between May and November of that year. The failure to establish a second front, which, intentionally or not, let Russians inflict and suffer at least 90 percent of the casualties in the European theater during World War II,[56] had profound impact on the diplomacy of the war and perhaps also an important though less direct impact on the shape of the peace.[57] It should prove worthwhile, therefore, after describing the debate on this issue, to assess some of the possible reasons for the campaign's failure.

Americans closer to the wellsprings of power than the foreigners and liberals we have discussed were also calling in the spring of 1942 for a second front to aid the valiant Russians as well as for other reasons. These advocates of an early second front were leaders of America's armies, who in 1942 were the nation's most respected civil servants. And rightly so, for they were civil servants in the noblest sense: they were totally dedicated, scrupulously honest, and completely apolitical in the performance of their jobs. Even those who were appointed by the president seldom spoke in public; that was not the civil servant's role. But these were extraordinary times; and the military leaders, like all civil servants, had some say in formulating the policy they would be asked to carry out.

Lieutenant General Dwight D. Eisenhower, then head of the Army's War Plans Division, did not speak out in public, but he frequently conveyed to his colleagues the conviction of what he wrote in his diary on 22 January: "We've got to go to Europe and fight—and we've got to quit wasting resources all over the world—and still worse—wasting time."[58] As he warned in a memorandum to General George C. Marshall on 25 March, "The loss of either England or Russia would probably give the Axis an immediate ability to nullify any of our future efforts."[59]

The cream of the American military echoed Eisenhower's sentiments publicly in the ensuing weeks. At the end of March, Admiral Ernest J. King,[60] chief of Naval Operations, and General Marshall,[61] the Army's chief of staff, stressed America's offensive plans without of course revealing their content. Toward the end of April, Secretary of War Henry L. Stimson[62] and President Roosevelt, the commander in chief,[63] said, respectively, that the United States was almost ready for offensive action and that it would take the offensive soon. In May, General Marshall told the graduating class at West Point that American forces would soon land in France,[64] and the prestigious *Army and Navy Register* called for the immediate opening of a second front.[65]

But none of these powerful military leaders had as great an impact on this issue as W. F. Kernan, a lieutenant colonel in the United States Army, who had been largely unknown as a soldier until the appearance, in February 1942, of his timely book, *Defense Will Not Win the War*. It went through six printings in February and March alone and was revived as a Pocket paperback in May.

In carefully reasoned chapters, Kernan depicted defensive strategy as the road to disaster. The participants in war are soon divided into winners and losers, Kernan argued, and the winners are those who seize opportunities, take chances, and mount offensives. "Shall the Nazis send armies to die in the snows of Russia and on the sands of Africa in order that freedom may perish from the earth," Kernan asked, "while we, the self-styled torch bearers of democracy, are content with an effort limited to the action of our navy and air force in the Pacific?"[66]

This sort of question must have been weighing heavily on the minds of President Roosevelt and General Marshall when they met with Soviet Foreign Minister Molotov in the White House in late May and early June. An able diplomat, Molotov possessed the ability to keep the discussion where he thought it belonged. And at this time, with Russia feeling the full fury of the German assault, even the president and the Army chief of staff had to admit that it belonged on the question of the second front. When Molotov finally pinned the president down on this question, Roosevelt turned to Marshall for a judgment of its feasibility in 1942. When the general replied affirmatively, as one would have expected he would after his West Point address two weeks before, Roosevelt assured Molotov that a second front in western Europe would be opened "this year."[67] "In the course of the conversations," the public communiqué of 11 June stated, "full understanding was reached with regard to the urgent tasks of creating a Second Front in Europe in 1942."[68]

Such scholars as Herbert Feis and Richard W. Steele, who have scrutinized the record of Molotov's meetings in Washington, make it clear that the foreign minister had every reason to believe that Roosevelt promised to open a second front in western Europe before the end of 1942, and that at Roosevelt's request Molotov surely conveyed this belief to Stalin.[69] But this does not mean that Roosevelt could be accused justly of perfidy when a second front in western Europe did not materialize that year. At the meetings with Molotov, Roosevelt did not specify the exact location of the proposed second front, though the entire context of the times and of the meetings suggested that the site would be in France, Belgium, or the Netherlands. Moreover, Marshall mentioned some of the difficulties involved in establishing a front in western Europe. The Russians also had to realize that changing circumstances could undermine even the firmest of intentions, and that, above all, Roosevelt could not dictate the timing of an invasion which probably would involve millions of Britons, and which in any case would have to be launched from the British Isles.

The response of opinion makers to news of the Roosevelt-Molotov meetings and the communiqué which marked their conclusion was as unanimously favorable as could ever be expected in this individualistic, pluralistic country. The opinion makers liked the fact that the meetings had taken place. They also liked the master lend-lease agreements and the apparent agreement on the second front.

"Three Greatest Nations Sign Alliances," *Life*'s bold headline read.[70] "The foundations of peace were laid last week," *Newsweek* announced. "Britain and Russia signed a twenty-year mutual-assistance agreement. The U.S. and Russia proclaimed a full understanding on the problems of safeguarding a durable peace."[71] "I am inclined to believe the President did well not to pitch the issue of a long-range alliance with Russia into the political debate," Freda Kirchway wrote in the *Nation*.[72] "The reference to a second front in Europe gained the most immediate attention here," CBS Washington correspondent Albert Warner told millions of listeners across the nation on the network's major evening news program. "The response in Congress was overwhelming," Warner continued.

Senator Hatch [New Mexico] said, "I want a second front opened just as quickly as possible." Senator Russell [Georgia] added, "A second front is going to have to come." Senator Smathers [Florida] added, "The quicker the better." But most people noted that the president's reference to the second front did not contain a definite statement. There is still the possibility that a tremendous aerial campaign will constitute the second front, or perhaps a series of strong commando raids. Perhaps, too, a second land front in '42 depends upon the circumstances that arise and the opportunities that open, while meantime we conduct a war of nerves which will keep the German troops in western Europe away from the Russian front. But whether it be in '42 or '43, it's certain that a British land offensive in western Europe is in the making.[73]

Other thoughtful opinion makers were also unsure of the precise meaning of the communiqué's statement on the second front. "Whatever this rather cryptic formula means," the New York Times editorialized, "there is no question that every prompting of self-interest supplements Mr. Molotov's plea to impel the British and American general staffs to stretch their resources beyond the limit to support the Soviet fighting forces as they face another great test of endurance."[74]

"The statement does not mean that agreement for opening a second front this year was reached, but it does not mean that such agreement was not reached," Edward R. Murrow commented from London. Murrow concluded, "If the precise meaning of that phrase is not clear to us, we may be sure that it is equally obscure—and more disturbing—to the Germans."[75]

President Roosevelt declined to clarify the "understanding." Instead, in a nationally broadcast message on the first United Nations Day, 14 June 1942, he launched into a series of grand platitudes. The president hailed the "great alliance dedicated to the defeat of our foes and to the establishment of a true peace based on the freedom of man. . . . The United Nations [he assured his listeners] have the power, and the men, and the will at last to assure man's heritage." Roosevelt concluded with some more lofty generalizations: "The belief in the four freedoms of common humanity, the belief in man created free in the image of God, is the crucial difference between ourselves and the enemies we face today. In it lies the absolute of our alliance, opposed to the oneness of the evil we hate. Here is our strength, the source and promise of victory."[76]

The British prime minister was usually much more forthright than the American president, and by the end of June the word had leaked to several leading American newspapers that Churchill doubted the feasibility of a second front in 1942. The occasion of these leaks was Churchill's visit to Washington soon after Molotov had boarded his plane for what he thought was a triumphant return to Moscow with the good news that the western powers would be opening a massive front in Europe that year.

Churchill thought otherwise and came to Washington essentially to convince Roosevelt that the two English-speaking powers should not attempt an invasion of western Europe in 1942.[77] The prime minister's mission turned out to be as effective as Molotov's mission seemed to have been. Obviously, Russia would have had much less cause for bitterness later if the western allies had agreed upon their common strategy before rather than after Molotov's visit.

A humorous note accompanied Churchill's departure from Washington by bomber on 25 June. A gala luncheon attended by British Ambassador Lord Halifax, Chinese Ambassador T. V. Soong, Prime Minister MacKenzie King of Canada, and other notables preceded Churchill's exodus. The "news" at the luncheon was Harry Hopkins's announcement that he planned to marry Mrs. Louise Macy, a wealthy socialite. But certain leftist groups in Washington were trying to make more substantial news. They placed picket lines in front of the District Building, the capital's equivalent of city hall, with placards demanding the immediate establishment of a second front to help the Russians. "A more unlikely place for the demonstration is unimaginable," a *Washington Star* reporter of the time has written, "since the politically-castrated commissioners could scarcely open a sewer for repair without a deep study of their skimpy budget."[78]

Even before Churchill left, Ambassador Litvinoff and Harry Hopkins told those who were attending a large Russian War Relief rally in New York that a second front was on the way. "There is now every ground to hope for it in the near future," Litvinoff said, reflecting the briefing that a joyous Molotov must have given him before leaving Washington. "A second front? Yes," Hopkins said, and it was five minutes before the enthusiastic crowd would permit him to complete the sentence, in which he promised, "and if necessary a third and fourth front, to pen the German army in a ring of our offensive steel." According to the *New York Times* reporter present, Hopkins's "closing message quoting the President as saying, 'We will attack at the right time and in the right place,' was as thunderously greeted as if he had added, 'and that is in Europe now.' "[79]

There was little doubt at the time that a second front was needed quickly to dampen Hitler's chances of becoming the unchallenged master of the great Eurasian landmass. "Hitler is winning in Russia," *Time* told its readers on 13 July in a typical comment. "If his armies continue to do as well as they did last week, and if the Red Army does no better, the Allies will then have lost their best chance to defeat Germany and win World War II."[80]

"Russia must be saved as one of the bulwarks of the Allied cause," the *Asheville Citizen* editorialized in agreement.[81] "The worse the position of the Red Army becomes, the greater the pressure upon Britain and America to open a second front in Europe this year," CBS newscaster Quincy Howe told his huge audience on 15 July. "Up to now the United Nations have tried to hold everything at any rate through this year and then attack somewhere next year. But this policy has already resulted in so many losses that we may be left holding almost nothing before 1942 is over. Hence the demand for the second front now." Howe concluded with some thoughts about the possible political and economic consequences of continued inaction.

The kind of war we fight will go a long way toward determining the kind of peace we get. If the United States makes its military power felt everywhere during the war, we are also likely to make our political and economic power felt everywhere after the war. If on the other hand we deliberately concentrate our military power on one or two fronts, we shall not carry so much weight during or after the war in other regions. The one front on which the United States has not made itself strongly felt yet is the European front.[82]

Time's influential readers were bombarded with sustained praise for all things Russian and sustained concern about the danger of continued delay. On 20 July Dimitri Shostakovich, the great contemporary Russian composer, appeared on *Time*'s cover. Already movies of Russia's resistance such as *Moscow Strikes Back* were appearing in the nation's movie houses, and *Time* gave them preferred treatment in presentation and kind commentary in review. On the following Sunday, Shostakovich's Seventh Symphony, a musical interpretation of wartime Russia, was presented on NBC. Seldom had a radio program been so well publicized in advance.

"The Germans in these July days of 1942," *Time*'s lead story in its "Battle of Russia" section began, "are fighting the battle that may decide the world's fate." The story continued in the same vein, referring to the direct calls of Russian leaders for an immediate second front and their circulation among the Russian troops of Roosevelt's promise to Molotov in June. *Time* implicitly supported this bold strategy of forcing American and British hands: "Now was no time for the diplomatic niceties and strategic reticences which blunted the first announcements after Molotov visited Eden and Roosevelt." Under a picture of Germans advancing in Russia was the pithy caption "The time to strike was now; the place, the back." "Perhaps the U.S. and Britain were not yet ready," *Time* editorialized openly, "but many a non-Russian who remembered Spain felt that the only unforgivable and irreparable failure would be the failure to try."[83]

Time's 27 July cover featured the dignified, intelligent face of

Marshal Simion Timoshenko, one of Russia's greatest military leaders of World War II. In an accompanying story, correspondent Walter Graebner reported that Russian soldiers "had one question uppermost in mind about England and America." " 'What,' they asked, 'is the feeling in your country about the second front?' " "They all said, in one way or another," Graebner reported, " 'If England and America hit Germany from the west she would collapse this year.' "[84]

After much obvious soul-searching, the powerful *New York Times* decided to join the chorus. Previously, the cautious *Times* had doubted the feasibility of a second front in western Europe in 1942, but in its widely circulated Sunday edition of 2 August the lead editorial was entitled "Second Front." "The two words most deeply engraved on the minds of the American and British people at this moment are *Second Front*," the editorial began. "These two words, together, are just now the most explosive words in the world. They can be the most dangerous words in the world. They can be the most hopeful. For our own safety we ought to be sure what they can mean."[85]

There were problems of transport, the Nazis surely had prepared for a second front, and American officials had cooled on the idea, the *Times* conceded in the body of the editorial. Having given the other side of the argument its due, this newspaper concluded with two of the most powerful paragraphs in its long history of reasoned advocacy.

Does this leave the ordinary citizen with nothing to do but wait and hope? Assuredly not. What the political and military high commands must wish to know is whether the public opinion of the United States and Britain is prepared for great risks and great sacrifices now in the expectation that these risks will be well taken and these sacrifices wisely made because they will shorten the war.

We are dealing in this matter with a great and irreplaceable treasure, the lives of a generation of young men. Agony of body and soul, the grief of long casualty lists, deprivations such as we have scarcely contemplated, are the facts we must certainly face if a bold stroke is now attempted. These facts are the facts of total war, which this country, at least, has not faced. Let us face them now. They are the Second Front.[86]

There were ample indications in the summer of 1942 that broad segments of the American public supported these demands for immediate military action in western Europe. "The decision rests, of course, with military leaders," George Gallup wrote in mid-July in the comment he regularly distributed with poll results to hundreds of American newspapers. "But when and if they make such a move it will be closely in line with the nation's armchair strategists, barber shop generals, and country-store tacticians whose military judgment on such matters as air power has, incidentally, proved better than that of many military experts."[87]

As usual, Gallup undergirded his witty comments with the poll data which many Americans apparently considered as solid and sound as reinforced concrete. On this question, 48 percent wanted to attempt an attack now, 34 percent thought we should wait until we were stronger, and 18 percent expressed no opinion. Gallup wrote that the chief argument in favor of the preferred response was that "every hour of delay works in Hitler's favor."[88]

Public-opinion polls apparently give a reasonably accurate estimate of the distribution of opinion in society on the specific questions asked, but they of course give no indication of the intensity with which those opinions are held. Here the student of attitudes must look for things which go beyond passive approval or disapproval, such as petitions, mass meetings, and letters to the editor. Descriptions of intensity of opinion can never be so precise as descriptions of the distribution of opinions within the confines of questions which must be answered yes, no, or no opinion. But intensity is something that must concern us if we are to go beyond the superficiality of most poll results.

Intense feelings about the issue of the second front existed briefly among large segments of the population for a few weeks at the end of July and in the beginning of August, but otherwise they were limited almost exclusively to elements on the Left. Leftist intellectuals—writers for the *Daily Worker*, *New York PM*, the *Nation*, the *New Republic*, and other journals of similar outlook, and professors in some universities—supported a second front enthusiastically from its inception as an issue in February and March until and even after its demise in November. A few liberal politicians such as Wendell Willkie and Fiorella La Guardia, mayor of New York, also spoke out on the issue.

Aside from intellectuals, whose numbers naturally were limited, the Left's primary power base on this issue, as well as on most others, was the Congress of Industrial Organizations, which still included many Communists and fellow travelers in key positions. The CIO did not speak for all of labor by any means: it had not yet joined with the older and more conservative American Federation of Labor, and John L. Lewis had resigned the CIO presidency and taken his United Mine Workers of America with him out of that union as he had promised he would do if Roosevelt was reelected in 1940. However, the CIO had several million members in the large industrial states of the Northeast and Midwest, and its leadership was convinced that reactionary forces in America and Britain were deliberately and maliciously delaying the beginning of the large front in western Europe which alone could ensure Russia's survival.

One of the CIO's tactics in the second-front issue was to have each member union which agreed with its stand issue a petition to this effect. Perhaps by accident but probably by design the issuance of these petitions was spread out over several months, with perhaps two or three being announced per week. If this was intentional, it showed that CIO officials had learned how to wring the maximum publicity from a generally hostile press. In any case, from June through September the statements of all types of unions, none of which could be considered to have any deep knowledge of foreign affairs or military strategy, were presented as news stories in the *New York Times* and other newspapers, albeit often on back pages near the obituaries or society column.

Another basic CIO tactic was to hold mass meetings on this issue as well as on others, all of which were well attended by the union faithful and some of which attracted considerably wider audiences as well. On 22 July, the New York Industrial Council, CIO, whose statements, resolutions, and petitions on the second-front issue received notice in the *Times* on several occasions, sponsored a Win the War Rally in Madison Square Park in New York City. The turnout was impressive: the throng filled Madison Avenue between Twenty-third and Twenty-fifth Streets and overflowed into the park and down Twenty-fourth Street in both directions.

Those who sent messages or spoke to the assembled multitude included most of the leaders of the American Left at this time. Wendell Willkie; Sidney Hillman, president of the Amalgamated Clothing Workers of America; and Representatives Emanuel Celler and Adam Clayton Powell, Jr., sent messages. The speakers included Senators James M. Mead of New York and Claude Pepper of Florida, both leading New Deal Democrats; Mayor La Guardia; New York Lieutenant Governor Charles Poletti; Joseph Curran, president of the National Maritime Union; Michael Quill, president of the Transport Workers Union; and actor Charlie Chaplin, whose voice came by telephone from Hollywood.

Not surprisingly, the brief time allotted to each speaker at the mass meeting did not result in any profound observations. In fact, what was said and the resolution that was passed are less important than the simple fact that this large mass meeting for a second front took place at all. For during World War II, almost all publicly oriented action among the mass of the population was directed toward nonpolitical projects such as war-bond and civil-defense campaigns and relief drives for Allied peoples ravaged by the war.

"We want to hit him with everything we've got so that he'll lose all this Fall," Senator Mead said, attempting a poetic touch as only politicians can. But Republican residents of uptown Manhattan and Westchester

County might have backed away from their support of a second front, as well as strengthened their antipathy toward Mead, when the Democratic senator added, "This is a people's war because we are determined to end it with a people's peace."[89] "You are declaring for all to hear," Willkie's statement read in part, "that there is no place in this nation for the temporizer, the appeaser, or the timid soul."[90] Again, some of those who read this statement in the *Times* probably were reminded that Willkie had been saying that there was no place in Ameria for the reactionary, the segregationist, or the secret isolationist.

The basic tenets of the liberal stand on the second front are epitomized in the meeting's message to President Roosevelt.

> We are united behind the nation's war effort.
> We are united in support of your policies.
> We are united in support of your agreement with the British and Soviet Governments upon the urgency of establishing a second front against Hitler in 1942.
> We stand ready, each according to his capacity, to make any sacrifice needed to carry your policy for a second front into immediate action.
> We denounce the forces of appeasement, the defeatists, the cowards and the traitors who slander our Allies and whisper against the prowess of our arms.
> We urge the immediate opening of the second front, now, before there is further risk of enemy gains. . . .
> We urge this for the security of America. We urge it for the hastened triumph of democracy and the freedom of mankind the world over.[91]

On the eve of the annual convention of the CIO's United Auto Workers in Chicago two weeks later, that union's president, R. J. Thomas, voiced the "disappointment" of labor at "the lack of imagination which has thus far been displayed by those in charge of our armed forces, and those who have been entrusted with supplying them." On the same day, the CIO sponsored a mass meeting in Grant Park in Chicago in support of a second front. Most of the speakers naturally championed the immediate opening of a second front and were cheered for their oratorical efforts. But Chicago's Mayor Edward J. Kelly, who greeted the delegates, took the position that the decision be left to the president, because "you and I don't know when it's time for a second front." In a speech before the New York State Federation of Labor on 18 August, George Meany, secretary-treasurer of the AF of L and a sharp critic of left-wing elements in the CIO who were spearheading the drive for a second front, also urged that "the question of when, where and how a second front will be established be decided by our commander in chief and our military experts."[92]

Some professors at New York University thought otherwise. A group of 104 of them, including two deans and twenty-one department chairmen, sent the following petition on the subject of the second front to President Roosevelt on 7 August. The petition read as follows: "We the undersigned members of the faculty of New York University, alarmed at the turn of events in Europe and the possibility of a serious and irreparable defeat on the Eastern Front, feel that the time has arrived for some decisive action on the part of the United Nations; therefore, we earnestly petition the President of the United States to give urgent consideration to the immediate opening of a second front."[93]

The characteristic conservative reaction to liberal demands for a second front was silence, about which it obviously is difficult to offer detailed comment. Conservatives—or, more properly, congressional Republicans, some congressional Democrats, and most attentive Catholics—had been quite willing in 1941 to let Russia and Germany slug it out on their own, and they generally did not alter this attitude greatly in 1942. Colonel McCormick, for one, argued vociferously that Russia was strong enough to take care of herself.[94] Unspoken but implicit in his argument was the feeling that he would not weep if his premises proved false.

Republican Senator Styles Bridges of New Hampshire, who had already cultivated anticommunism into the trademark for which he would become famous after the war, openly criticized Russia for not joining in the war against Japan. This was not in itself an unusual argument among congressional Republicans, but Bridges added the novel contention that a Russian second front against Japan should precede an Allied second front against Germany.[95] Such a move on any major scale obviously would have permitted Germany to defeat Russia. Like McCormick and some others, Bridges probably would have welcomed such an outcome.

Liberal, pro-Russian forces thus were basically canceled out by conservative journals like the *Chicago Tribune* and the Hearst chain,[96] by portions of the religious press, and by well-publicized politicians such as Senator Bridges and Congressman Fish. As the poll on the second-front question showed, the Left's views on this issue were probably more representative than the Right's, but the Right had greater access to such organs of opinion circulation as the mighty *Reader's Digest* and the other aforementioned newspaper chains and mass periodicals.

On the issue of the second front, as on most issues, the overwhelmingly powerful moderate media were able to carry the day. The *New York Times*, the premier moderate newspaper, naturally used its judgment in deciding which happenings were newsworthy as tested against its motto, "All the News That's Fit to Print." The Win the War Rally mentioned above, which almost certainly was the most important mass meeting in New York City in the summer of 1942, and which took place well before the *Times* openly supported an immediate second front, was relegated to page four. And this was not unrepresentative of the way in which the *Times* handled events or ideas which emanated from the Left or the Right.

Other moderate journals, of course, had not earned the reputation which the *Times* had for relative objectivity, while most journals on the Left did not claim to be scrupulously objective. The leading moderate periodicals, the Luce publications, were equally selective in emphasis.

Radio, a relatively new news medium, tended to follow the emphases of the established moderate newspapers and periodicals. Many radio newscasters and analysts had started their careers as writers for these organs, and some continued to do so on a part-time basis. Moreover, radio was especially receptive to governmental pleadings, for members of the Federal Communications Commission and others both within and without government were not then reconciled to the radio industry's thoroughgoing control of the airwaves.

During wartime, perhaps more than at other times, the moderate media were the established organs of opinion circulation in America. In return for the government's acceptance of continued modified private control of media content and continued unlimited profitability to the owners during the national emergency, the mass media performed many communications tasks for the government. The networks broadcast information programs from such agencies as the Office of War Information and the Office of Civilian Defense, recruitment programs for the armed services, and war-bond campaigns for the Treasury. In addition, they gave the president unlimited access to the nation's fifty million radio receivers, an access to the public which was limited only by the president's prudence in using it and by the people's ability to turn off their sets.

The beginning of the decline of an issue usually cannot be determined with full confidence, but for the second front it can be. It was not, as might have been expected, a specific presidential broadcast or statement that cooled the clamor; Roosevelt typically either declined comment or expresed full confidence in the military leadership's judgment on this issue. Such expressions of confidence were misleading, because the president as commander in chief naturally would make the final decisions on all crucial strategic issues. Besides, as we have seen, America's military leaders themselves favored the opening of a second front in western Europe that very year.

The decline of the second-front issue dates from an Office of War Information release of 7 August. "Our forces are being disposed," the release stated, "as and where the military commanders believe they get the maximum results according to the best professional judgment." It continued, obviously referring to the urgent appeals for the second front throughout the country, "Popular pressure for action on this front or that of many possible fronts can serve no useful purpose."[97]

Whether private appeals from the administration went out to politicians and leaders of the media would be an absorbing question for students of the internal workings of this wartime administration. My concern is the fact that media appeals for a second front declined precipitously the very next week.[98] Anne O'Hare McCormick, a leading *New York Times* columnist, now went against her previous position as well as that of the *Times* editorial of the week before when she entitled her 12 August column "The High Cost of Taking the Offensive."[99]

"Second-front talk has suddenly come to the fore again in today's news," Quincy Howe told his nationwide radio audience on 21 August. "One wonders perhaps that it did not come up sooner in view of the Dieppe raid."[100] In the rush of news headlines and thoughts of a late summer vacation, Howe might not have noticed that the second front was no longer a salient issue.

Only disastrous Russian reverses in the early fall of 1942 could have revived widespread demands for an immediate second front, and these did not occur. Instead, countless Americans watched and prayed as the Russians defended Stalingrad. This, it was sensed even then, was the crucial battle of the war, and millions of attentive Americans followed the shifting tides in the streets of the city and on the Volga plain as they would now follow a "crucial" televised football game. The hesitant American advances on small Pacific islands at this time were as nothing compared with the epic quality of this struggle. And the human-interest aspects of Stalingrad riveted the attention of millions of Americans who were unlikely to give a second thought to Stalin's speeches or the endless diplomatic dealings among the Allies.

"Americans may look about the quiet streets of their towns and attempt to picture them under the hail of destruction that has been visited upon Stalingrad," the *New York Herald Tribune* editorialized in words like those which appeared in all of the media and in speeches by politicians. "They may look at their neighbors and think of the men and women of Stalingrad contesting each bloody yard of each suburban street; they may be moved to awe; they must be moved to gratitude, for Stalin has been killing the men who would kill Americans; Stalingrad has been buying time for victory."[101]

There was one opinion maker in America outside of the administration—Willkie—who could turn some of the attention away from Stalingrad and the lackluster congressional campaign then in progress and redirect it toward the second front. The redoubtable Willkie did just that. President Roosevelt surely did not intend to send him around the world as his personal representative in order to revive the second-front issue, but that was the major immediate result of his trip. Willkie, the president learned to his sorrow, was always his own man. And in an age of slick politicians, Willkie's independence and candor contributed greatly to his popularity among cosmopolitan Americans, a popularity which peaked at the time of this trip and the publication of the best-selling book which resulted from it, *One World*.

"I am now convinced," Willkie told American journalists in Moscow just after his visit with Stalin near the end of September, "we can best help Russia by establishing a real second front in Europe with Great Britain at the earliest possible moment our military leaders will approve, and perhaps some of them need some public prodding. Next summer might be too late."[102]

Administration leaders back home were not amused by Willkie's widely circulated comment for three major reasons, Arthur Krock reported in his *New York Times* column. First, they thought that Willkie was viewed abroad as something of an official representative of the United States and hence should limit his remarks to the truisms of American policy. Second, "those responsible for the decision do not welcome anything that will stimulate civilian or political pressure." Third, administration leaders thought that Willkie's comments would intensify the British government's domestic difficulties on this issue, and they naturally opposed anything that would tend to undermine Churchill's leadership.[103]

Senator Burton K. Wheeler of Montana, an indomitable isolationist, told the Senate that he believed "the whole matter should be left up to the General Staff rather than to Mr. Willkie or columnists or other persons who are trying to tell the Army General Staff how to carry on the war."[104] And for once President Roosevelt was inclined to agree with his bitter adversary. "The trouble with typewriter strategists," Roosevelt said in a fireside chat on 12 October, "is that while they may be full of bright ideas, they are not in possession of much information about the facts or the problems of military operations. We, therefore, will continue to leave the plans for this war to the military leaders."[105]

Fortunately for the president, the issue had declined so markedly since early August that he was able to survive handily the flurry of comment created by Willkie's remarks and the first public appeals on this issue by another man Americans respected in the fall of 1942, Joseph Stalin. "As compared with the aid which the Soviet Union is giving the Allies by drawing upon itself the main forces of the German Fascist armies," Stalin wrote on 4 October to a surprised Henry Cassidy, the Moscow correspondent of the Associated Press, "the aid of the Allies to the Soviet Union has so far been little effective. In order to amplify and improve this aid, only one thing is required: that the Allies fulfill their obligations promptly and on time."[106]

Willkie took to the airwaves on 26 October to report on his trip and offer a wide-ranging critique of American foreign policy. "We must wipe out the distinction in our minds between 'first-class' and 'second-class' allies," Willkie said. "I reiterate: We and our Allies must establish a second fighting front in Europe." The earnest presidential Republican continued: "I say to you: there are no distinct points in the world any longer. The myriad millions of human beings of the Far East are as close to us as Los Angeles is to New York by the fastest railroad trains. I cannot escape the conviction that in the future what concerns them must concern us, almost as much as the problems of the people of California concern the people of New York. Our thinking and planning must be global."[107]

Opinion makers responded with overwhelming enthusiasm to Willkie's address. Republican politicians, wary of Willkie's prestige among the people and his refusal to adopt a partisan approach to the issues, generally remained silent, as did most Democratic politicians, who were accustomed to supporting the president fully on foreign policy issues. But editors and commentators were tired of the administration's vague, platitudinous approach to foreign policy, and they liked Willkie's forthright, reasoned advocacy of internationalism.

While praising the speech, however, most editors refrained from commenting on Willkie's continuing calls for a second front. The imprecise observation of the *Cleveland Plain Dealer* was typical: "It may have been a good thing all around that Wendell Willkie was not elected president. A man who can always hit the nail on the head is just as useful as the nail."[108]

So great was Willkie's prestige that both President Roosevelt and Secretary of State Hull held press conferences on the next day to respond. The president assured the reporters that he agreed with Willkie on practically everything, and Hull denied that the State Department was as reactionary as Willkie and other critics had charged. The president and the secretary were still speaking defensively, and they knew it. But Willkie's time at center stage was brief, for the president had the power to shape events, which Willkie lacked; and the president had not told his envoy to the world that American forces would soon be landing in North Africa to engage the enemy.

Just before that happened, Joseph Stalin delivered an address to the

Russian people on 6 November 1942 which was one of the finest speeches of this era of great speechmaking. Had Churchill made this address, it most probably would have been carried on American radio, and the ties between the two English-speaking powers would have been strengthened even further. But Stalin did not speak English, and an announcer translating over Stalin's voice would have undermined the speech's power. Consequently, most Americans had to settle for their radio and newspaper accounts from the wire service stories about the speech. The impact of the speech on most Americans, therefore, was probably fleeting as compared with a broadcast of Churchill's or one of Roosevelt's fireside chats. But the fact that the speech was quoted widely for the remainder of the war by writers and other opinion makers as a guide to Soviet policy is sufficient reason to consider its main points carefully.[109]

Stalin dealt first with the question of similarities between the current German invasion and Napoleon's invasion and the German invasion of World War I. Instead of the 140,000 troops equipped with single-firing rifles and horse-drawn cannon which Napoleon brought, the Soviet leader said, "we now have over 3,000,000 troops facing the front of the Red Army and armed with all the implements of modern warfare." Nor would comparison with the First World War "bear criticism." "First, in the First World War there was a second front in Europe which rendered the German position very difficult, whereas in this war there is no second front in Europe. Second, in this war twice as many troops are now facing our front as in the First World War."[110]

Stalin continued with a penetrating analysis of the effects of western inaction in the first ten months of 1942.

> Let us assume that a second front existed in Europe as it existed in the first World War and that a second front diverted—let us say—sixty German divisions and twenty divisions of Germany's allies. What would have been the position of German troops on our front then? It is not difficult to guess that their position would be deplorable.
>
> More than that, it would have been the end of German Fascist troops for, in that case, the Red Army would not be where it is now but somewhere near Pakov, Minsk, Zhitomir and Odessa.
>
> This means that already in the summer of this year the German Fascist army would have been on the verge of disaster and, if that has not occurred, it is because the Germans were saved by the absence of a second front in Europe.[111]

The remainder of the speech surely made American and British leaders feel much more comfortable. Reflecting the improved Russian military situation, Stalin's words were no longer like the hoarse calls for help from a sinking swimmer that had emanated from Russia in the summer, nor even like the pointed thrusts evident in the letter to Cassidy.

Instead, Stalin assured the Russian people that the Western allies would eventually open a second front because their self-interest dictated it. He then noted the existence of two great groupings of powers—the "Italo-German coalition" and the "Anglo-Soviet-American coalition"—which "are guided by two different and opposite courses of action." The existing wartime situation pointed to "progressive rapprochement between the U.S.S.R., Great Britain, and the United States of America" based on the following general principles: "Abolition of racial exclusiveness, equality of nations and integrity of their territories, liberation of enslaved nations and restoration of their sovereign rights, the right of every nation to arrange its affairs as it wishes, economic aid to nations that have suffered and assistance to them in attaining their material welfare, restoration of democratic liberties, the destruction of the Hitlerite regime."[112]

These noble ideals, which might well have been penned by Herbert Hoover or Cordell Hull, read like the Atlantic Charter. They did not include the objective that would have to be the most potent guide for a nation which was losing twenty million of its citizens due to the porosity of its borders: national security. In fact, although Americans of the time did not note it, the absence of a couple of paragraphs on this subject was the one glaring omission from this speech. Had Stalin only admitted that "the right of every nation to arrange its affairs as it wishes" might result in a future alliance between a revived Germany and an independent Poland, which might be fatal to Russia and therefore had to be prevented in the interest of Russia's survival, much of the confusion and opposition that developed as Russian policy unfolded might have been avoided. But of the Big Three, only Churchill was frank in public about probable future distributions of international power.

Meanwhile the overriding issue was, as Stalin put it, the "destruction of the Hitlerite regime." And, as the Sunday papers that were delivered to tens of millions of homes on 8 November 1942 attested, America was now ready to commit the blood of her sons to this end. "American Forces Land in French Africa; British Naval, Air Units Assisting Them; Effective Second Front, Roosevelt Says" was splashed across the top third of the *New York Times*. The Anglo-American attack, Roosevelt said, "provides effective second front assistance to our heroic allies in Russia."[113]

With these words and especially with the actions they described, the president snuffed out the already flickering debate over the second front. The Left was disappointed that a true second front had not been established in western Europe, and its spokesmen became more upset when the major western front was postponed again in 1943. But they could hardly trigger a public clamor for a massive front in France or Belgium, because Americans were by then dying in Italy. Elements on the Right might deplore the fact that the administration was not concentrating entirely on Japan, but Americans were killing Japanese in the Pacific, and Russia was still doing most of the fighting in Europe. And with Germans retreating everywhere, the urgency of creating a second front to save Russia was gone.

In view of the substantial popular demand in the United States, it might be asked in retrospect why there was no second front in western Europe until June of 1944. The answer lies primarily in the fact that the American form of government, like most other forms of government, works on the leadership principle. In America the people have a voice in choosing their leaders every four years; but between elections the leaders make the basic policies, and historically there has not been much that the public can do to change them. In 1942 the leader was Franklin Roosevelt. Roosevelt had been in office long enough and was far enough away from his next campaign so that he did not need to be too deeply concerned about any but the most powerful expressions of public discontent with his policies.

Roosevelt undoubtedly was a "strong" president. He pitted his opponents against each other, used his access to the media extensively and effectively to mobilize public support for his policies, and permitted the development of no significant independent power cells in the executive branch. His personal control usually dwarfed the combined influence of the legislative and judicial branches.

One would not have expected such a formidable and experienced wielder of power to permit the public to force his hand on a crucial strategic decision of the war, and Roosevelt of course did not. His enormous power was even greater in wartime than in peacetime, and he used it as we have seen to dampen the debate on the second front just as it was beginning to get out of hand. Only the executive branch had detailed estimates of British and American capabilities to launch a second front; the Office of War Information had—and often used—the power to withhold crucial information about the war from the press; if needed, the president could implicitly threaten more censorship if the media persisted in demanding an immediate second front. The military enjoyed great prestige; Roosevelt could say that this decision should be left up to the military without having anyone point out after his fireside chats that he was commander in chief of the American armed forces.

To be sure, the president had not cultivated all of his powers on his own. The successful application of the leadership principle depends on the implicit consent of the governed, and most Americans of this era surely would have acknowledged both the fact that they had chosen Roosevelt to be their leader and the corollary that they expected him to lead.[114]

The widespread public acceptance of the leadership principle explains why the July Gallup poll on the second front, which was discussed above, presents a superficial picture of American attitudes toward the issue. The poll showed that about 60 percent of those with opinions favored the immediate opening of a second front. Actually, the debate involved three basic positions: the leftist insistence that a second front be opened immediately, epitomized by Willkie's message to the New York rally; the rightist view that American forces should be concentrated in the Pacific because Japan was the main enemy, illustrated by McCormick's speeches and editorials; and the administration's view that the timing of military action should be left to it, summed up in Mayor Kelly's appeal to the members of the United Auto Workers to leave the second front up to the president, because he would make the proper decision when America was prepared militarily.

If Gallup had stated the question in these terms, probably 80 percent of the public would have backed the principle of presidential leadership in this crucial matter, and about 10 percent would have supported each of the other two positions. The fact is that most Americans have backed their presidents on foreign and military policy at least until their policies have seemed too expensive or dishonorable, or both.

Acceptance of the leadership principle as applied to the situation in 1942, then, would seem to be the major reason why Roosevelt was able to retain control of the situation. He was, to be sure, aided by other facts and developments. Most Americans were not extremely friendly to Russia in 1942. Some opinion makers such as Vice-President Wallace and Herbert Hoover precipitated considerable debate about the general principles of the peace even before, as Office of War Information Director Elmer Davis put it, America was "ankle-deep in the war." There was much discussion of important domestic issues such as taxation and rationing in wartime. And a congressional campaign soon occurred to direct some public attention away from the second-front issue. But these factors taken together were probably less important than Roosevelt's relationship to the people and a weak Congress in the formulation of foreign policy; and here of course the president held the better cards and could prevail so long as he played them with reasonable skill.

Yet the second front in western Europe was delayed until 1944, in the final analysis, not because Roosevelt wanted it that way, but primarily because Churchill insisted upon it. Despite America's greater power, the invasion would have to be launched from England under conditions of complete Anglo-American accord. And at least through the Casablanca Conference of January 1943, Roosevelt yielded to Churchill on every important strategic question of the European theater in order to achieve agreement.[115]

Thus to Winston Churchill belongs the principal credit, or blame, for keeping Anglo-American casualties at very low levels while Russia continued to be soaked in the blood of her sons. The 130,000 American deaths in the European theater during three years and five months of war did not even equal the average number of *civilian* casualties Russia suffered each *fortnight* before 1943. If postwar influence was to correspond even slightly to relative levels of sacrifice—and there is reason to believe Stalin thought that it should in eastern Europe and Roosevelt and Truman thought that it should in the Far East—the Russians surely were not overcompensated in peace for their sacrifices in war.

American Goodwill at High Tide

By the fall of 1942 Americans had grown accustomed to the war. The novelty and uncertainty of the previous winter had passed, and Americans had before them something which suited their individual temperaments: a specific job to be done. That job was the annihilation of the Axis armies and the restoration of world peace and prosperity. It was like building a skyscraper. No one knew exactly how long it would take, but all were confident that it could and would be done. There would be tragic risks for some and benefits for many, and when it was over the nation would find more pleasant risks and greater benefits. Most Americans did not permit global war to daunt their inveterate optimism.

This chapter and chapter 6 depart from the basically chronological framework of the previous chapters. In a sense this departure is warranted by the facts of American life between the fall of 1942 and the summer of 1944, for during those twenty months Americans were neither near the beginning, when the war was taking shape, nor near the end, when the postwar world was pressing upon them. Like builders with the site selected and foundations laid, Americans made their contributions to the war effort with such singlemindedness that history seemed to stand still. Because of this slackening in the pace of change, there is less need for the historian to concentrate on describing the changes taking place and the reasons for them. At the same time it becomes more appropriate to analyze enduring conditions and ideas.

The present chapter is divided into three sections. The first section focuses on the major events in Russian-American relations which captured the attention of opinion makers—and through them the general public—between the fall of 1942 and the end of 1943. It will be observed that a consistently friendly approach to Russia predominated despite the diversity of the situations which appeared during this time. The second part deals with circulators of opinion whose effectiveness peaked during 1943: films such as *Moscow Strikes Back* and organizations such as the National Council of American-Soviet Friendship. The last part is in many ways the most important portion of this study. Through examination of regional, economic, and other basic differences among the general population, I seek to establish the essential origins of differences in American attitudes toward Russia at this time.

Chapter 6 will complete the largely analytical center of the study. It will begin with a discussion of leading Americans' reactions to events, this time taking the story from the late fall of 1943 to the summer of 1944. Then it will describe the Polish imbroglio and projections of Russia's place in the postwar world, including the hope that Russia could contribute to prosperity for American business and full employment for American labor by providing a huge market for American goods. The most detailed and articulate thinking on the subject of Russia's place in the peace appeared in books, the medium which is so crucial to the circulation of opinions among opinion makers. This medium will provide the focus of the following chapter's analysis.

Considered together, these two central chapters should go far toward explaining what Americans thought about Russia and why they thought it during the war. Opinions obviously change in response to events such as the Nazi-Soviet Pact, the German assault on Russia, America's entry into the war, the calls for a second front, Stalingrad, Russia's break with the London Poles, the war's great conferences, the presidential election, and the end of the war in Europe. But opinions also change markedly, moderately, only a little, or not at all because of factors which cannot justly be linked to specific international events. They change perhaps most profoundly as a result of the individual's orientation to his environment. This concept embraces such diverse concerns as where one lives, which groups he belongs to or at least sympathizes with, and whether or not his thinking is likely to be influenced deeply by the dominant ideas of the day.[1]

America's paramount purpose in the war—the destruction of Axis military and political power—did not change between the fall of 1942 and the summer of 1944. Unaltered also was the people's boundless confidence that the goal would be accomplished fully. But if Americans were sure that they knew the drama's conclusion, they did not know exactly how it would develop. They did not realize in the fall of 1942 that they would have to think long and hard about the nature of the postwar world; and they did not know that Russia, then fighting for its very life, would play a primary role in it. In 1942 and during much of 1943, Americans could like Russians not only because of their success against the Germans, but also because they did not have to worry about them.

Criticizing Russia in the fall of 1942 was like criticizing one's son when he is struggling to recover from a crippling paralysis, and almost nobody except the ultraconservative Hearst-McCormick-Patterson newspaper axis was doing it. In fact, almost all opinion makers to the left of this group had nice words for Russia's courageous soldiers. Not surprisingly, portions of the Left dusted off and reinstated the discredited belief of the late thirties that Russia was earth's paradise. Even the Center felt forced to reevaluate its treasured contention that the Soviet government was inefficient and unpopular and to recognize the power of what the eminent British economist Harold Laski called "the majestic spectacle of Russian resistance in the face of a threat which seemed almost to have civilization by its throat."[2]

The changed situation in American attitudes toward Russia at this time was best summarized by the prominent Communist, William Z. Foster. "The anti-Soviet lies are falling one by one in the light of war realities," Foster exulted. "Thus," he went on,

the world is now learning that if it had adopted the collective security policy long advocated by the U.S.S.R. the war could have been averted; the so-called purge of a few years ago in the U.S.S.R. for which that country was wildly denounced, is now seen to be historically justified as the liquidation of the potential fifth column; justification of the Soviet Union's war against Finland is now obvious, with Finland lined up definitely in Hitler's camp; the infamous lie that under the Soviet-German non-aggression pact the U.S.S.R. and Nazi Germany were allies is being exploded; the democratic attitude of the Soviet Government toward religion is being graphically demonstrated by the fact that the Russian Orthodox Church is loyally supporting the Soviet Government in the war; the realization, too, is creeping into the minds of the American and British peoples that the wonderful fighting quality of the Soviet people originates in their unshatterable loyalty to their much-maligned Socialist system and Communist leaders.[3]

The significance of this statement is that it is a reasonably accurate analysis of the changes that were occurring in the attitudes of those Americans who were cosmopolitan enough to be keeping up with the thinking of the time. As we saw in chapter 4, most books on Russia in 1942 developed the themes that Foster summarized; and so did radio, newspapers, and political and religious leaders. On the day of the North African invasion, the circumspect *New York Times* exclaimed that "never in our history, certainly never during the past quarter of a century, has Russia stood so high in the respect and admiration of the free nations."[4]

During the summer of 1942, the second-front slogans and chants of the young and the workers in New York, Washington, and Chicago did not meet the standards of respectability of the wealthy inhabitants of Westchester County, Georgetown, and Evanston. In late 1941 and early 1942 they had opened their wallets and lent their names to the letterhead of Russian War Relief. As Russia's standing continued to rise, prominent Americans turned out to hear Russia praised in mighty metaphors.

Two such soul-searching affairs took place on 24 September 1942. In New York City about two hundred of America's most powerful businessmen met at a luncheon meeting of the Bankers' Club to hear praise for Communist Russia. Among the members present were Thomas W. Lamont, senior vice-president of J. P. Morgan and Company; Leon Freser, president of the First National Bank of the City of New York; and Thatcher M. Brown, a partner in the banking firm of Brown Brothers, Harriman and Company, who presided at the meeting. Like the members, the featured speaker, Robert A. Lovett, assistant secretary of war for air, had never been accused of leftist leanings. "No doubt the information that those [German] officers had on Russia came from those outrageous old geographies we studied in sixth grade," Lovett said, obviously implying that his listeners should revise their attitudes toward Russia. Lovett also declared, among other things, that he would rather have Russia on his side than to have to rely on the "complacent and illusory theory that we are bound to win because treasure and time are on our side."[5]

While magnates of the private sector were listening to Lovett over coffee and cigars in New York, governmental notables were gathering on the grounds of Joseph E. Davies's plush estate in northwestern Washington to hear Davies, Vice-President Henry A. Wallace, Secretary of Commerce Jesse Jones, and other speakers extol Russian heroism and trustworthiness. "The most decisive battle in all civilization is occurring at this moment— street by street, life by life—the fight goes on in Stalingrad," Davies declared. "God helping us, we'll be coming, fighting beside them for the freedom of the world." Overlooking the fact that Russia might yet fall, the ever-optimistic Wallace said, "We are over the hump." He said that a Chicago reporter had asked him, "What of Stalingrad?" and that he had replied, "Stalingrad is Chicago's first line of defense."[6]

The purpose of Davies's party was to publicize a mass meeting for American-Soviet friendship to be held in Madison Square Garden on 7 and 8 November. A better site for the meeting could not have been selected, for only in Russia was enthusiasm for the Soviet cause stronger than in New York City. Mayor LaGuardia proclaimed 8 November, the day of the meeting's climax, "Stalingrad Day." The Little Flower, as LaGuardia was fondly nicknamed, observed that "the great and heroic Russian people" were celebrating the twenty-fifth anniversary of their revolution and described the defense of Stalingrad as "the outstanding glorious event" of Russia's anniversary year. The mayor declared that his proclamation was a "tribute to our Russian ally, a sign of our fighting unity with them and a pledge of common action with them for total victory."[7]

The meetings were a great success. They began on Saturday, 7 November, with reasoned calls for friendship with Russia by two noted professors of philosophy. During the war it was not hard to find Catholic intellectuals who displayed at least some amity toward Russia, and Professor Francis E. McMahon of Notre Dame University was a good choice for this gathering. "I would consider myself disloyal at once to my religion and to my country if I did not raise my voice in behalf of Russia's struggle at this critical hour in world history," Dr. McMahon declared. "Because Russia has held, men of genuine religion have breathed more freely. Because Russia has held, the fighters for the dignity of man have gained new inspiration," the professor proclaimed. "We must help them now by the speedy opening of a second front," he concluded on the very day the North African campaign began. "Any unnecessary delay is a crime against culture and a crime against religion."[8]

Complementing the speaker from America's leading religious university was an eminent representative from its secular citadel of learning, Professor Ralph Barton Perry of Harvard. "The Soviets' greatness is of the future as well as of the past," Dr. Perry said, "and we will be fortunate indeed if we can associate our destiny with theirs." Already he detected an "underlying creed" common to both nations, composed in part of "respect for the dignity of man, . . . hatred of war, [and] . . . a sense of brotherhood uniting all mankind." Professor Perry argued that, for Russia, socialism was "a step forward in the direction of that Utopia which they call Communism, as our present capitalism is to us a halfway station toward the Utopia which we call democracy." The Harvard scholar concluded with an analysis of four stages in the development of American attitudes toward Russia since the Revolution and a call for a friendly fifth stage.

First we tried to destroy them, then tried to ignore them, and then treated them as poor relations. Some among us are now making an effort to treat them as a disagreeable necessity.

It is high time we passed on to a fifth and final stage in which we treat them as the great nation they are, now animated as we were in the 18th century by a sense of their destiny, and prepared to give their all for its realization.[9]

McMahon and Perry spoke at a luncheon meeting at the Hotel New Yorker to a relatively small audience. The next day twenty thousand persons jammed into Madison Square Garden for the major session of this Congress of American-Soviet Friendship. "We are gathered together," Corliss Lamont told the throng in the call to order, "to celebrate the deeply-rooted, firm-enduring friendship that joins the peoples of the United States of America and the peoples of the Union of Soviet Socialist Republics, to pay tribute to the magnificent battle the Soviet peoples are waging against the common enemy of mankind, and to further the objective of lasting cooperation and understanding between our two great countries."[10] The American national anthem then resounded throughout the coliseum.

The featured speakers at this gathering probably represented the most distinguished collection of Left-of-Center American leaders ever to appear on one platform. They included the keynote speaker, Vice-President Wallace; Davies; Mayor LaGuardia; New York Governor Herbert A. Lehman; Florida Senator Claude Pepper; United Auto Workers President R. J. Thomas; and the great black baritone, Paul Robeson; all of whose pro-Russian credentials were beyond question. To the Right of these, but still progressive, were Thomas W. Lamont; President William Green of the American Federation of Labor; and Lieutenant General Leslie C. McNair of the Army War College. Absent were leaders of the national Republican Party, including New York's governor-elect Thomas Dewey as well as spokesmen for conservative organizations.

"We salute the Red Army as it enacts its role of tremendous decisions," General McNair said. "We look forward to the day when the American Army can fight alongside the Red Army, bear our full share of the common burden, and go forward with it to Victory."[11] "To the people of Russia, to their gallant leader," Senator Pepper told the audience, "I bring the assurance of the American Congress and country—We shall keep our rendezvous with destiny. We shall be true to the race of man. We shall not, before God, betray our solemn duties."[12]

"There has never been a more glorious demonstration of the courage, fortitude and spiritual power afforded by either the bodies or souls of men than that which the great Soviet people, their Army and their leaders gave in their resistance to the Hun invasion,"[13] Davies declared in his thirty-minute speech, which was carried live over NBC. Davies concluded with a glowing introduction of the featured speaker of the day.

On May 8, 1942—a little less than six months after this country was attacked, a little less than a year after Russia was attacked—an American spoke to the world. The people of the world—the people upon whom the outcome of this war for freedom depends—heard, understood and cherished the words he spoke. For he had uttered their deepest thoughts. He spoke—as Lincoln at Gettysburg—for their aspirations and their will. On this twenty-fifth anniversary of the founding of the Soviet Union—a moment which this man himself names one of the milestones in human history—he is to speak to us, the man who said: "the century upon which we are entering—the century which will come out of this war—can and must be the Century of the Common Man." This is the Vice President of the United States of America, Henry A. Wallace.[14]

The tumultuous applause that greeted the vice-president's approach to the podium demonstrated the leftist leanings of the crowd, for Wallace was already the most controversial American. He was the brash, intense populist who seemed destined to be either loved or hated. "The new democracy, the democracy of the common man, includes not only the Bill of Rights, but also economic democracy, ethnic democracy, educational democracy, and democracy of the sexes," Wallace asserted. He continued.

Some in the United States believe that we have overemphasized what might be called political or bill-of-rights democracy. Carried to its extreme form, it leads to rugged individualism, exploitation, impractical emphasis on states' rights, and even to anarchy. Russia, perceiving some of the abuses of excessive political democracy, has placed strong emphasis on economic democracy. This, carried to an extreme, demands that all power be centered in one man and his bureaucratic helpers. Somewhere there is a practical balance between economic and political democracy. Russia and the United States both have been working toward this practical middle ground.[15]

Wallace's address surely did not disappoint the thousands who had gathered to demonstrate their friendship for Russia, but one of the earlier speakers may well have lingered longer in their memories. He was the imposing black man, Paul Robeson, an independent thinker and one of this century's outstanding singers.

In contrast to the rhetorical tributes offered by most of the speakers, Robeson spoke slowly, in short sentences. "I have been called an anti-fascist," Robeson said. "I am exactly that. Because I am an American and because I am a Negro."[16] Although he did not say so explicitly, Robeson conveyed the impression that fascists might exist outside of the enemy nations. But he obviously did not find any of them in Russia, and he ended his brief tribute with a song which he dedicated to an obscure Russian soldier from Kazakhstan, Baubek Bulkishev.

Wallace's contention that America and Russia were moving closer together, and Robeson's fervent hope that they would continue to do so, were shared by President Roosevelt. "I am delighted to see that excellent speech of yours at the American-Soviet Friendship meeting," Roosevelt wrote to Thomas W. Lamont on 12 November. "May I tell you a story which I have never yet committed to paper?" The remainder of Roosevelt's letter deserves to be quoted as a guide to his thinking, which he shared with Americans in many ways nearly every week.

In the Autumn of 1933, when I initiated with Stalin the question of renewing diplomatic relations, Litvinoff was sent over and we had a four or five day drag-down and knock-out fight in regard to a number of things, including the right to have American priests, ministers and rabbis look after the spiritual needs of Americans in Russia.

Finally, after further objections on Litvinoff's part, I threw up my hands and said to him "What is the use of all this any way? Your people and my people are as far apart as the poles."

Litvinoff's answer is worthy of an eventual place in history. He said, "I hope you will not feel that way, Mr. President, because I do not. In 1920 we were as far apart as you say. At that time you were one hundred per cent capitalistic and we were at the other extreme—zero. In those thirteen years we have risen in the scale to, let us say, a position of twenty. You Americans, especially since last March [Roosevelt's inauguration], have gone to a position of eighty. It is my real belief that in the next twenty years we will go to forty and you will come down to sixty. I do not believe the *rapprochement* will get closer than that. And while it is difficult for nations to confer with and understand each other with a difference between twenty and eighty, it is wholly possible for them to do so if the difference is only between forty and sixty."[17]

Several other examples of the barrage of praise for Russia after and outside of the National Congress of American-Soviet Friendship will elucidate the friendly attitudes being fostered at this time. "Never in the long centuries of modern history have men and women fought more gloriously than have the armies of the Soviet Union," Undersecretary of State Sumner Welles told an audience of businessmen in Boston on 8 October.[18] "However we may feel about Stalin and the tyrannies of Communism," the conservative *Saturday Evening Post* chimed in later that month, "we welcome Russia's millions of soldiers, knowing that their sacrifices have gained time for our better defense."[19] And Congressman Hamilton Fish, whose views made the *Post*'s sound liberal, felt compelled to tone down his anticommunism to improve his chances for reelection. On 12 September Fish had denounced, in his customary manner, "the mad rush to collectivism and Communism in America." But by 25 October, a week before the election, Fish was reduced to criticizing "the march to regimentation, collectivism, national socialism, and one-party and one-man government."[20]

In its November issue, *Reader's Digest*, which was read by tens of millions of Americans, featured a pro-Russian article by Maurice Hindus.[21] Admiral William Standley, the American ambassador to the Soviet Union, told the prestigious *New York Herald Tribune* Forum in mid-November that "it is just this united effort and self-sacrificing devotion of the people of Russia that has deeply touched my heart as much as it has won my everlasting respect and admiration."[22]

"Stalin has all the qualities of a great fighting leader," Averell

Harriman told a nationwide CBS radio audience late in the year. His glowing tribute to the Communist leader continued: "He has confidence in the Red Army and the Russian people, and they have implicit confidence in him. He knows that Hitler will be destroyed and that the Red Army will play a leading role in the glory of this achievement. But he looks upon the war against Hitler as a united effort with Britain and the United States."[23]

The culmination of the pro-Russian blitz in the fall of 1942 was the benign, almost saintly painting of Joseph Stalin with the snowy Russian winter as backdrop which appeared on the cover of *Time*'s New Year's issue. Stalin had been man of the year for 1939 as well, but what a different man he was now! In 1939 he had been Hitler's partner in evil, the shrewd, ruthless Bolshevik whose moves had thrown the world into war. Now he had almost supernatural wisdom and understanding. "Only Joseph Stalin fully knew how close Russia stood to defeat in 1942," *Time* said with genuine awe, "and only Joseph Stalin fully knew how he brought Russia through." Stalin's achievements were unequaled in the modern era, *Time* implied: "He collectivized the farms and built Russia into one of the four great industrial powers on earth." "The U.S., of all nations, should have been the first to understand Russia," the article stated in reference to the similarities between the two nations. "Ignorance of Russia and suspicion of Stalin were the two things that prevented it." "As Allies fighting the common enemy, the Russians have fought the best fight so far," *Time* concluded. "As post-war collaborators, they hold many of the keys to a successful peace."[24]

Meanwhile, followers of culture were feasting on the first American performance of Konstantin Simonov's war play, *The Russian People*, and the first major American production of Anton Chekhov's classic, *The Three Sisters*, both of which were staged in New York City. Chekhov's masterpiece drew most of the attention, both because of its intrinsic merit and because it featured what *Time* called "the most glittering cast the theater has seen, commercially, in this generation." Unlike most Broadway productions, which stand or fall with at most one big name, *The Three Sisters* featured the three great female stars of the American stage: Katharine Cornell, Judith Anderson, and Ruth Gordon. Male stars who had held title roles in the previous season on Broadway— Alexander Knox, Dennis King, and Edmund Gwenn—received only minor roles in this production. Remarkably, *Time* reported, the stars of this great hit of the 1943 season never tried to "upstage one another."[25]

The chorus of praise for Russia continued throughout the cold winter of 1943 as German troops retreated all along the eastern front in the wake of the decisive Russian victory at Stalingrad. A few voices like those of Westbrook Pegler and the *New York Daily News* began to object to possible Soviet postwar power, but these were drowned out in the din of praise from opinion makers who wholeheartedly appreciated Russia's contributions to victory. The Casablanca conference in January 1943, which found Roosevelt, Churchill, and their advisers debating the date for opening the second front in France, showed that the postwar world probably was still years away.

Yet Stalingrad forced some incipient consideration of Russia's future role even by those who were inclined to savor for a time the thought of certain victory. "The Soviet troops have not only proved themselves a great modern army, brilliantly led and excellently equipped," Anne O'Hare McCormick of the *New York Times* observed in a typical comment not yet tinged with fear of Russia, "they have made the Soviet Union a far weightier power in the world than Imperial Russia ever was. They have not only vindicated Stalin's policy and increased his prestige inside and outside of Russia; they give him a mighty instrument for carrying out his future aims."[26]

However, most opinion makers concentrated on praising Russia on seemingly every possible occasion, avoiding potentially unpleasant thoughts about the future. The *Christian Science Monitor*, for example, entitled its lead editorial of 12 February, "Gettysburg and Stalingrad." "At Stalingrad everything was lost but the battle, everything destroyed but the faith and faithfulness of men and women who did not ask to be masters, but would not be slaves," the *Monitor* proclaimed, adding, "One feels that Lincoln would have entered into their triumph wholeheartedly, knowing so well why it could be."[27]

The nation's largest and most cosmopolitan city continued to take the lead in paying tribute to the brave Russians. The birthdate of America's most famous soldier, George Washington, was chosen as the date for a gala dinner party honoring the twenty-fifth birthday of the Red Army, the earliest units of which fought against American troops sent to Russia by President Woodrow Wilson.

But bygones were bygones on 22 February 1943. Although many conservatives had supported Wilson's decision to send the troops, now they or their sons paid the large entrance fee at the Hotel Commodore in New York to dine for Russian War Relief and to hear Democratic Senator Elbert D. Thomas of Utah deliver the major address. "The tyrannies which Washington struck against were those which hindered the growth and development of individual man," Thomas asserted, summarizing several other typical after-dinner platitudes. "The tyrannies of old Russia kept the people submerged," he continued. "Freed by the people's army, Russia today knows what she is fighting for. . . . The world now sees the strength of men and women united in a fight for victory."[28]

     Two controversial statements by American leaders in early March 1943, and the tone of leading opinion makers' responses to them, illuminate diverse attitudes toward Russia as the war against Germany neared its midpoint. In a speech to a conference on "Christian Bases of World Order" at Ohio Wesleyan College in Delaware, Ohio, on 8 March, Vice-President Wallace warned that World War III "will be probable in case we double-cross Russia."[29] That same day, halfway around the world in Moscow, white-haired, aging Ambassador Standley publicly accused Russia's leaders of withholding information about American aid from the Russian people. "The American people in their sympathy are digging into their pockets, thinking that this help is going to the Russian people," Standley said. "The truth is that the Russian people don't know it."[30]

There was nothing predictable about either man's remarks, and in fact no one had predicted either. That the vice-president eventually would say something impolitic about American-Russian relations might have been expected, but not what he did say just when he said it. As for Ambassador Standley's criticism of the Russian government, no one would have predicted such a statement, for it not only went against established ambassadorial etiquette and the policy of the American government toward Russia, it also ran contrary to the admiral's previous remarks about the Soviet Union.

Wallace's remark was unfortunate not only because it was almost sure to grab the headlines the next day and be denounced on editorial pages the day after, but also because it would surely obscure the theme of his address. Wallace's theme, which deserved wide discussion, was this: "The future well-being of the world depends upon the extent to which Marxianism [*sic*], as it is being progressively modified in Russia, and democracy, as we are adapting it to twentieth-century conditions, can live together in peace."[31]

To be sure, a few journals generally favorable to Wallace urged that the speech be considered as a whole. "This remarkable address is not the utterance of a dreamer," the *Boston Globe* contended. "It is a clearheaded analysis of urgent realities known to every student of the political, social, economic, and spiritual trends of the times."[32] The *New York Post* and the *St. Louis Post-Dispatch* also supported the vice-president. But the responses of almost all other opinion makers probably help to explain why President Roosevelt sent Wallace on an extended goodwill tour of Latin America later that spring.

The generally friendly *Christian Science Monitor* said that Wallace's speech seemed "to promote untimely fears." "More positive and helpful emphasis," it added, "would be on more adequate appreciation of what Russia has done to win this war."[33] "Does he know of any desire or intent in this country to double-cross Russia?" the *Philadelphia Inquirer* asked indignantly. "Since when have we become a nation of double-crossers?"[34] "When has America ever double-crossed any nation?" the *Detroit Free Press* inquired angrily. The *Free Press* was also upset because Wallace, in its view, proclaimed "his terrible fear that pro-Fascist and anti-Russian interests in America may 'get control of our Government'—which implies that the Republican party, or any coalition of Republicans and old-line Democrats, are *ipso facto* Fascists and enemies of Russia."[35] "Certainly the mood of America today is to support Russia," the *Milwaukee Journal* averred. "But there is a shying away from disagreeable questions—how are we to insist on fair play for all nations if we acquiesce and encourage Russia in reconquest of peoples set free in the first World War?"[36]

If Wallace's remark evoked disgust from most of the nation's editors, who, though friendly toward Russia, saw no reason to consider America a double-crosser, they surely brought pleasure to the editor of the *Chicago Tribune*, who had been looking for an issue for some time. After waiting a day to prepare its attack, the *Tribune* contended on 11 March that "slap-happy Wallace had found some reason to say, if not believe, that the United States is about to doublecross Russia; and if it does, we'll prepare for world war number 3." The verbal barrage continued: "Henry's theme song is that the Russian people and the American people must work together for the salvation of the world. Just at present the Russian people and their foreign relations are Joseph Stalin and no other. If Mr. Wallace doesn't know Mr. Stalin's character and life work, someone should take him aside and talk to him—not, however, with the thought that it will do much good."[37]

The *Tribune* was equally pessimistic about the usefulness of Standley's remarks. "It is doubtful if anything we can do will enlighten the Russian people if their rulers are determined to keep them in the dark," Colonel McCormick's writers editorialized on 10 March, "but at least the American people can and should be told the truth."[38]

The antithesis of the *Tribune*, the *New York Times*, also doubted that words like those spoken by Wallace and Standley would have much effect. Russia, the *Times* thought, "will need to count on our collaboration in a new security system as much as we shall want to count on theirs. Words, however unwisely spoken, are not likely to affect these basic realities but if words could dampen the suspicion between the Soviet Union and the United States, Mr. Wallace's extraordinary suggestion that we might 'double cross' Russia would do more harm than the remarks of Ambassador Standley."[39]

Like the two great titans of the American press, most of the medium's lesser lights were unsure of the causes and effects of Standley's statement. The *Newark News* argued that Standley was in error: "Pravda, the leading Russian newspaper, more than a month ago told of United States aid in planes, tanks, and motor trucks."[40] "The 'calculated indiscretion' is a well-known diplomatic maneuver," the *Philadelphia Bulletin* contended.[41] Conservative columnist Paul Mallon agreed: "Standley is an adult personal representative of Mr. Roosevelt, and all such know enough not to criticize a diplomatic host without word from the boss."[42] "Admiral Standley did a good thing, we think, in calling Russian attention to the help they have been receiving," the *Wall Street Journal* wrote, "and Russia will be justified in replying that however great the help may be, it is not enough."[43]

All but the most conservative organs wanted to make sure that Standley's remarks did not lead to a rift in Allied relations. "Americans deeply appreciate the magnificent contribution of the Russians to the common cause, and we are sure the Russians appreciate our help," the *St. Louis Post-Dispatch* editorialized. "If they will say so, a possible cause of misunderstanding will be removed at once."[44] Standley's remarks were "harmful for the same reason that Stalin's statements, implying bad faith to his allies in second front promises, were unwise," the *Pittsburgh Press* thought. "When allies fall to sniping at each other, only the enemy profits."[45]

Ralph McGill—to cite a final example of press reaction to Standley's statement—made fun of the spat. He thought that Standley had "indulged in the ancient and honorable American custom of popping off. . . . As a great admirer of the ancient and honorable American custom of beefing," McGill concluded a bit more seriously, "I still wish our man had kept quiet. In the first place, he seems to be wrong about no publicity being given our aid. In the second place, the Russians are doing a fine job of killing Germans. And that suits me."[46]

Radio did not editorialize so openly, but it surely did the best job of disseminating the facts of the matter. Most Americans probably learned about Wallace's speech and Standley's statement not in their newspapers of 9 March, but on the radio the night before. CBS featured excellent reports from Bill Downs in Moscow, and NBC's Washington correspondent Carry Longmire explored the domestic implications of Standley's remarks. "His belief is that the American people and the Russian people should understand each other and their relative positions in this greatest of all wars," Downs reported, after giving a detailed account of Standley's remarks. "He considers this mutual sympathy between peoples as important to the future of the world as an Allied victory over the Axis."[47] "All the furor about the speech is not going to affect lend-lease at this end," Longmire assured NBC's listeners on 10 March.[48]

Longmire was right. Lend-lease was popular among both congressmen and their constituents, and appropriations to continue it passed virtually without opposition before the middle of the month. Moreover, at Roosevelt's bidding, Undersecretary of State Welles repudiated Standley's statement the day after it was made. Welles expressed confidence that Allied collaboration was "based upon complete trust and understanding between them all."[49]

At least publicly, most congressmen agreed with Welles. "While the statement of Ambassador Standley was an amazing one," Arthur H. Vandenberg of Michigan, the ranking Republican on the Senate Foreign Relations Committee, told his colleagues, "I still believe it was equally amazing for the distinguished Vice President of the United States yesterday to suggest that America is even capable of double-crossing Russia, of double-crossing anyone."[50] "As a matter of fact," Foreign Relations Committee Chairman Tom Connally of Texas said, "information of aid extended by the United States to the Russian armies has been given to the Russian people."[51] "I have not the slightest doubt that the statement was correct and true," dour Burton K. Wheeler of Montana said in obvious rebuttal to remarks like Connally's, "because Admiral Standley would not have made it otherwise."[52] But Wheeler seldom expressed the opinion of as many as 10 percent of his colleagues during the war, and the media no longer circulated his opinions widely.

Wheeler said a few days later that he was suspicious of "what Mr. Stalin wants, what he will demand and what he'll take."[53] Many other opinion makers, both within Congress and outside of it, were harboring similar thoughts, but they were not saying so publicly. Even Polish-American leaders were generally keeping their fears to themselves. "In considering the lend-lease bill this week, many of the Members deep in their hearts wanted to provide that no more lend-lease materials go to Russia until they sit down and tell us what her post-war intentions are," Alvin E. O'Konski of Wisconsin asserted in the House of Representatives on 10 March. But even this Polish-American and staunch supporter of the Polish government-in-exile in London did not advocate such a drastic step. "Should we face a showdown with Russia now or should we sit tight and help them finish annihilating Hitler and pray that we can get together when the fighting stops?" O'Konski asked. "I am inclined to do the latter."[54] Except for ultraconservatives and die-hard isolationists, almost all Americans probably agreed.

Left to right: Mrs. Eleanor Roosevelt; Mrs. Edward C. Carter, chairman of the New York Women's Division of Russian War Relief; and Mme. Maxim Litvinoff, wife of the Russian ambassador, 14 April 1942 (Reprinted by permission, United Press International Photo)

Crowd at Second-Front Rally, Madison Square Park, 22 July 1942 (Reprinted by permission, United Press International Photo)

Left to right: Foreign Commissar Molotov, Mr. Barnes, Joseph Stalin, M. Pavlov, Wendell Willkie, and Mr. Coates in Moscow, October 1942 (Reprinted by permission, United Press International Photo)

Left to right: Joseph Davies, Maxim Litvinoff, and Henry Wallace, Madison Square Garden, 8 November 1942 (Reprinted by permission, United Press International Photo)

Left to right: President Roosevelt, Secretary of State Cordell Hull, and Mrs. Hull, Washington, D.C., upon Hull's return from the Moscow Conference, 10 November 1943 (Reprinted by permission, Wide World Photos, Inc.)

Left to right: Eric A. Johnston, president of the U.S. Chamber of Commerce; and Thomas E. Dewey, Republican presidential nominee, Albany, N. Y., 21 July 1944 (Reprinted by permission, United Press International Photo)

President Roosevelt addresses Congress on the recent Yalta Conference, 1 March 1945 (Reprinted by permission, United Press International Photo)

American troops (left) reach out to grasp hands with Soviet soldiers after the historic junction at Torgau, Germany, 3 May 1945 (Reprinted by permission, United Press International Photo)

On balance, the Standley incident probably was a slight blow to Russian prestige. But Russia recovered what was lost when she promptly published full reports of American aid in *Pravda* and broadcast reports on Russian radio. In April and May, Russian prestige showed similar resiliency. In April, Russia felt compelled to sever relations with the London Poles when those anti-Soviet conservatives insisted that German reports of a Russian massacre of Polish officers at Katyn Forest before 22 June 1941 were accurate. The London Poles embraced Goebbels's assertions so gleefully that, regardless of the merits of the case, it appeared that they were siding with Germany against Russia. The Russians were so quick to break with the London Poles and to refuse to permit the International Red Cross to investigate the alleged massacre that it appeared that they had something to hide.

Most American opinion makers did not offer definite opinions about which side might be correct. They simply did not know the facts of the matter, which was fortunate for the Russians, who otherwise would have been embarrassed. Most opinion makers were content to deplore the break in relations as a blow to Allied unity. In fact, Twohey reported that the majority of newspapers blamed Hitler and Goebbels for the break![55] But the break in relations surely did not strengthen the Russian position in the United States, for Americans had long sided with the smaller, underdog nation in most disputes.

Stalin quickly undid whatever damage his acrimonious relations with the Polish government had cost him in American public support. In his May Day message of 1943 to the Russian people he took a conciliatory stance toward his western allies, assuring them of Russia's unity with them generally and of the need for unconditional surrender specifically and treading lightly on the touchy question of the second front.

Together with an amicable article in *Pravda*, Stalin's speech marked, in the words of CBS military analyst George Fielding Eliot, "the coming into being of a far better relationship between Russia and her western allies than has previously been apparent."[56] The *Washington Star*, which tended to have fairly typical reactions on most questions, was also pleased: "Those who have been circulating the rumor—probably of Axis origin—that Russia is toying with the idea of a separate peace will find nothing to comfort them in the May Day message of Joseph Stalin."[57]

Russia's image in the United States was further enhanced by the dissolution of the Soviet state's international revolutionary agency, Comintern, on 23 May 1943. Even though it had been quiescent for several years, Comintern had remained a hindrance to Allied unity, and American opinion makers were happy to see it go. "The bogeyman that Nazi propaganda has been holding up to frighten the world is no more," exulted the *Buffalo News*.[58] "The Russians are fighting today, not for world revolution, but to save the Russian nation," the *Chicago Daily News* argued, repeating a common theme of the day.[59] And the *Detroit Free Press* added, "Russia has gone 'national' and as such can be accepted in the family of nations."[60] The *Minneapolis Star-Journal*'s analysis of the implications of the move, unthinkable except in a climate of opinion at once friendly to Russia and optimistic for the future, was typical of the responses of hundreds of American opinion makers.

> Russian dissolution of the Communist International brings Russia still further toward an area of wholehearted cooperation with the other United Nations. There is still a long way to go. But without minimizing the formidable barriers which still exist, or glossing over frictions, it must be conceded that walls of suspicion erected by Russia and her present allies against each other in the past generation are breaking down as rapidly as we have any practical right to hope. It becomes more and more possible that common ground can be found, if we persist, which involves no surrender of basic principles and tenets by the democracies.[61]

One cause of the favorable and optimistic response in the press may have been a heady discussion of the dissolution on the day it was announced by the young CBS correspondent Larry Leseuer and *New York Herald Tribune* reporter Walter Kerr. In their five-minute discussion, which took place in CBS's New York studios, Kerr and Leseuer spared no words in praising Stalin's latest move. So strong was their support of Russia that they must have known that they were contributing as much to Soviet-American friendship as to an understanding of Comintern's demise. "Well, Larry," Kerr said at one point, "I'm sure that right now men and women are talking about this near Pushkin Square, in Gorki Street, in Moscow's famed subway, out in the Park of Culture and Rest, and probably at the ballet between the acts. I think you will agree with me that they are glad to hear about the dissolution of the Communist International. The people in Moscow are tired of that sort of thing. They are fighting a hard war, they're interested only in winning that war and rebuilding their homes, and after the defeat of the Axis, to live their lives in peace."[62]

"Well, today Hitler is still trying to claim that dissolution of the Comintern means nothing, and that he's still the protector of Europe, saving it from Bolshevism," Leseuer said at another point. Kerr replied, "We know differently: that Moscow's abandonment of world revolution will have a great effect in strengthening the United Nations during this great battle for their existence. It looks to me like just another nail driven into the Axis coffin."[63]

Whether Leseuer and Kerr really believed all their sanguine words, or whether they had decided in advance that any unfavorable comments might hinder Soviet-American understanding, is something that probably cannot be known. But programs like this one surely had a profound effect on public attitudes for, as I have noted, Americans relied more on radio than on the press for news. On the one hand, they probably relied more on the printed media for opinion, and this would have been especially true of the better educated. On the other hand, many Americans who were not among the better-educated minority were surely aware of the two most significant products of the printed media in 1943: Wendell Willkie's *One World* and *Life*'s special issue on Russia.

Willkie's *One World* was the *Mission to Moscow* of 1943. It blasted the remaining isolationist bulwarks as Davies's work the previous year had dealt a severe blow to anti-Russian sentiment. Willkie's book eclipsed Davies's, as Willkie himself eclipsed everyone else of importance in America but the president. It sold more copies than *Mission to Moscow* in bookstores where records of sales were kept. Exactly how many more unabridged copies were sold in a magazine format in the nation's drugstores and bus and train stations is unknown, but the number must have run well into the millions. And then there were spin-off articles in *Reader's Digest*, *Look*, the *Saturday Evening Post*, and other periodicals.

Willkie called for the leadership of a humble America in an interdependent world in which the "peoples of each nation" could be "free from foreign domination, free for economic, social and spiritual growth." The peoples of Asia and other developing nations, Willkie said, "want us to join them in creating a new society of independent nations, free alike of the economic injustices of the West and the political malpractices of the East."[64]

In the euphoria of 1943, the realization of Willkie's ideals for a peaceful world seemed certain; yet they remain ideals three decades later. Willkie thought that self-interest and goodwill would combine inexorably to unify the world. His early death in 1944 probably saved this man who considered himself a pragmatist much grief.[65] Willkie also was certain that an America confident of its capacities yet tolerant of the different paths of other nations could live in peace with Russia. He expressed the liberal's confidence in future cooperation succinctly:

Many among the democracies fear and mistrust Soviet Russia. They dread the inroads of an economic order that would be destructive to their own. Such fear is weakness. Russia is neither going to eat us nor seduce us. That is—and this is something for us to think about—that is, unless our democratic institutions and our free economy become so frail through abuse and failure in practice as to make us soft and vulnerable. The best answer to communism is a living, vibrant, fearless democracy—economic, social, and political. All we need to do is to stand up and perform according to our professed ideals. Then those ideals will be safe.

No, we do not need to fear Russia. We need to learn to work with her against our common enemy, Hitler. We need to learn to work with her in the world after the war. For Russia is a dynamic country, a vital new society, a force that cannot be bypassed in any future world.[66]

Such was the argument and appeal of the last two paragraphs of chapter 4 of *One World*, "Our Ally, Russia." Most of the chapter described the author's two weeks in Russia in the early fall of 1942. He had been surprised that the Soviet government had given him every chance to find out what he wanted to learn.[67] He had not realized, but Americans would be glad to learn that Russia "is ruled and composed almost entirely of people whose parents had no property, no education, and only a folk heritage."[68] The upward social mobility of millions of Russians, Willkie believed, went far to explain their devotion to Stalin's government. He was surprised by the efficiency of the collective farm he visited and of the huge Soviet aviation plant which produced the Stormovik, Russia's great fighter plane of World War II.[69] And Willkie was pleasantly surprised by Stalin. "He has, I would say, a hard, tenacious, driving mind," Willkie reported. "When we talked of the causes of the war and the economic and political conditions that would face the world after the war, his comprehension was broad, his detailed information exact, the cold reality of his thinking apparent." Americans were sure to like Stalin's democratic character: "On the personal side Stalin is a simple man, with no affectations or poses. He does not seek to impress by any artificial mannerisms."[70]

What had happened to the paragon of evil who had purged his ablest subordinates and joined with another wicked dictator to plunge Europe into war? Anyone who still found questions like that surfacing from the subconscious at odd hours of the night probably was somewhat shocked by the smiling photograph of Joseph Stalin that greeted him from the cover of *Life* magazine on 29 March 1943. Had not Henry Luce been as staunch in his enmity toward Russia as in his amity toward China? What had happened to the Christian convictions of this son of missionaries and the "Americanism" of this self-made American capitalist? Luce did not say. But there was this bulging issue praising Communist Russia as one would hesitate to praise his native land lest he be accused of chauvinism.

The many warm pictures of the Russian people and their American friends cannot be reproduced here, but representative sentences can. "Of all the great countries of the world, the U.S.S.R. is the least known to Americans," *Life* observed in an article on lend-lease. "These two countries seem likely to emerge as the two greatest powers of the post-war era," that article concluded. "Without their full and honest co-operation, there can be no stable, peaceful world."[71] An editorial followed, stating that the purpose of the special issue was to create "popular sympathy and understanding" for Russia. "We respect the mighty Russian people and we admire them," the editorial went on. "It is safe to say that no nation on earth has ever done so much so fast."[72] An article entitled "The Peoples of the U.S.S.R." was next, followed by "The Father of Modern Russia." "Perhaps the greatest man of modern times was Vladimir Ilyich Ulyanov [Lenin]," *Life* judged.[73] The next article was entitled "Red Leaders, They Are Tough, Loyal Capable Administrators."[74]

Following a section entitled "Russian Painting" came Joseph E. Davies's article, "The Soviets and the Postwar: A Former Ambassador to Moscow Answers Some Perplexing Problems." This culminating article consisted of Davies's replies to twenty-one questions about Russia submitted by the editors of *Life*. The editors' first question probably was the most important: "Can we assume that the rulers of Russia are men of goodwill toward other nations and that they desire a peacefully stable world?" "Yes," Davies replied. "Their public statements of policy and their deeds in the past decade both establish that. . . . Abyssinia, Spain, China, the attitude of the Soviets in agreeing to stand by Czechoslovakia with France against attack by Germany—all attest to their sincerity as 'Men of Good Will.' It is, also, to their practical best interest to have peace with, and in, the world."[75]

The corollary to the first question was the second: "Will Russia pursue a lone-wolf policy after the war or will she seek to cooperate with the other Great Powers in creating a stable world?" "That will depend," Davies replied,

upon what kind of world they will then face, or upon what kind of a world they think they are facing. If they believe in, and trust the proposals of Great Britain, China, and ourselves, and the United Nations, they will, in my opinion, go as far as any of these in a high-minded and altruistic effort to cooperate in creating a stable and decent world.

If, on the other hand, they believe they are not getting a square deal on a reciprocal and high-minded basis, they will not hesitate to go it alone. They will not be 'taken for a ride.' Nor will they be used to pull anyone's chestnuts out of the fire. They will do exactly what we would do, if in their shoes.[76]

Probably the greatest military victory of this century occurred at Stalingrad in the fall of 1942; the fastest-selling book ever published in America up to that time, *One World*, appeared in the early spring of 1943; and so did the most remarkable and perhaps the most influential issue of a magazine ever published by the Luce empire. All of these happenings and others had a marked effect on public opinion toward Russia. Suffice it to say for now that opinion on the basic question, Can Russia be trusted to cooperate with us after the war? was evenly divided in the spring of 1942.

By the spring of 1943, and from then until the end of the war in Europe, the yeses outnumbered the noes by nearly two to one. As illustrated in figure 3, the great change of several million Americans from doubt to assurance occurred during this year of great victories by Russian soldiers and lavish praise by American opinion makers.

In the last half of 1943, as in the first half, Russia showed great resiliency in American opinion. Russian bitterness over Anglo-American failure to establish the second front in 1943 surfaced when Stalin permanently recalled Ambassadors Maisky from London and Litvinoff from Washington in mid-August. These acts of displeasure, combined with continued inflammations of the Polish sore, caused concern among Americans about the depth of Allied unity. And since Americans almost automatically adopted an American perspective on events, any signs of Allied disunity hurt Russia's image primarily.

Most Americans were not told and thus could not know how bad Anglo-American relations with Russia were in the summer of 1943, but their leaders knew. Washington's oppressive heat during August left tempers short in the wake of Stalin's actions and his continued refusal to meet with Roosevelt and Churchill. Moreover, Secretary of State Hull seemed to believe that his authority at the State Department was undermined by the very presence of Roosevelt's brilliant friend Sumner Welles, and, in late August, Hull dismissed him. This abrupt move led columnist Drew Pearson, who was sometimes wrong, but who knew more about Washington's inner workings than administration leaders liked, to charge that Hull was "anti-Soviet" and that he and other reactionaries had forced the pro-Russian Welles to resign. "I do not ordinarily take notice of attacks made on either the State Department or myself," the aging Tennessean replied promptly and indignantly at a press conference on 30 August. "When these attacks, however, concern our relations with an Allied Government, I must take notice of them. . . . I desire to brand these statements as monstrous and diabolical falsehoods."[77] President Roosevelt put Pearson's name and his own on the front pages of American newspapers by taking time from his duties on 31 August to call the columnist a "chronic liar."[78]

Columnist Arthur Krock of the *New York Times*, like Pearson a Washington insider, argued that Hull and Roosevelt attacked Pearson in order to prove their friendship for the Russians.[79] Whether or not this appraisal was correct, the fact was that the Russians were bearing the brunt of the German fury for the third straight year; and with lend-lease shipments continuing to fall behind schedule, there could be little doubt that something needed to be done to demonstrate American friendship.

Outside of government much continued to be done to convince the

Figure 3. Trend in opinion of Russian postwar cooperation, 1942–1943 (adapted from a table in Warren B. Walsh, "American Attitudes toward Russia," p. 186)

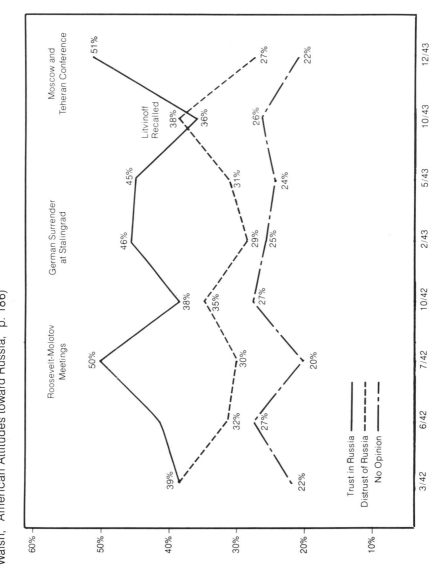

remaining doubters of Russia's esssential goodness. No one did more in the late summer of 1943 than Captain Eddie Rickenbacker, a daring pilot and World War I hero. Like Charles Lindbergh before he became too deeply involved in political issues, Rickenbacker was an authentic American hero. To qualify as one, a man must have a remarkable military record or have shown skill in mastering technology or both. George Washington, Robert E. Lee, and Dwight Eisenhower had the first distinction; Eli Whitney, Henry Ford, and Charles Lindbergh had the second. Eddie Rickenbacker was one of the very few Americans to have both, and he reminded his countrymen of these qualities when his plane was missing for a time on a daring flight in the Pacific theater early in World War II. Finally, Rickenbacker, like Ford and Lindbergh, had sterling anticommunist and antilabor credentials.

So when this middle-aged, All-American boy returned from a 55,000-mile airplane tour of the world's battlefronts, Americans listened to his radio report as they had listened to Willkie's when he had returned the previous fall. "Bolshevism in Russia is not as we have been led to believe by communist enthusiasts in this country," Rickenbacker reported, shrewdly mixing praise for Russia and censure for American Communists in a single phrase. "They have been constantly turning to the right, as evidenced in many ways, during the past twelve months."[80] The best proof of this contention, Rickenbacker thought, was to be found in practices in the Russian Army. "Nowhere in the world have I seen so much respect for progressive rank in the Army as I witnessed in Russia from the bottom to the top which is in the direction of Capitalism and Democracy,"[81] Rickenbacker asserted, apparently unaware of the gross irony in the last phrase.

Ever since Roosevelt had failed to carry through on his second-front commitment of 1942, he had been seeking a face-to-face meeting with Stalin. Not without reason did Roosevelt consider himself a charmer, and he wanted to ground American relations with Russia on the bedrock of personal trust. By the fall of 1943, broad segments of the American media were also calling for such a meeting to iron out some of the difficulties that had developed in Russo-American relations. Stalin also was interested in such a meeting to halt the deterioration in Allied relations, and it was agreed tacitly that a summit conference would occur at Teheran in December if a meeting of foreign ministers scheduled to take place in Moscow in October was successful. The stage was set to recoup among the American public the prestige both of American foreign policy and of the USSR.

The Moscow Conference had its intended effects.[82] Not only did it cement Allied unity for the prosecution of the war, but it also improved substantially the State Department's and Russia's standing with Americans. The aging Hull, who made the arduous journey to Moscow as the head of the American delegation and received in America most of the credit for the conference's success, was the hero of the hour, and he was praised and feted upon his return as never before. Hadley Cantril of Princeton University, one of the most sophisticated students of public opinion during the war, reported to Roosevelt that trust of Russia had jumped 16 percent in the wake of the Moscow Conference. To the basic question on Russia throughout the war, "Do you think Russia can be trusted to cooperate with us when the war is over?" 36 percent answered yes and 38 percent answered no in October just before the Moscow meetings. On 2 November, the day after the public results of the Moscow Conference boomed out of radio speakers and were splashed across the front pages of newspapers, 54 percent answered yes and only 26 percent answered no to the same question.[83]

The optimism and euphoria touched off by the Moscow Conference marked the high tide of American friendship toward Russia during World War II. One reason for this, surely, was the fact that most American opinion makers no longer portrayed Russia as a revolutionary power. Indeed, as we have seen, Rickenbacker and other opinion makers considered Russia less revolutionary than the United States in such matters as military discipline. The resurgence of the conservative Russian Orthodox Church, the dissolution of Comintern, the presence of wage differentials, and the absence of labor unrest were other signs that Russia was becoming more conservative. But the period of overwhelming friendliness toward Russia was short-lived. Roosevelt at Teheran was unable to maintain the two-to-one margin of friendliness toward Russia. On 6 December, just after the publication of the communiqué from the Teheran Conference, 51 percent answered yes to this study's standard question and 27 percent answered no.[84] Before proceeding to the other concerns of this chapter we should discuss briefly the reasons for this decline of 3 percent in trust of Russia.

At this point it must be emphasized that no one ever knows exactly why public opinion changes. In fact, when the change is only 3 percent, one cannot be sure that there was any change at all, for the same persons are not polled twice, and there is a margin for error of about 3 percent when samples change. Assuming that opinion did change for the worse, which is at least 90 percent probable in this case, there was no precise way then to determine why, and there is of course no way now to be more precise statistically. And one can never be sure which of several forces operating deep in the individual's consciousness was the most compelling in causing a specific change of opinion.

This having been said, it is possible to point out some differences in the situations in early November and early December which might have contributed to the slight downward trend. Probably the most basic reason was that there was exuberant praise and almost no criticism of the Moscow Declaration in the mass media. Some of the Hearst papers praised Hull's efforts, and Colonel McCormick's *Chicago Tribune* was reduced to faint grumblings about the possibility of Russia making a separate peace.[85] Twohey reported that 58 percent of the press responded enthusiastically to the conference's results while only 5 percent took "an attitude in any way inimical and even here the expression inclines more to a mixed or noncommittal position than to positive disapproval."[86]

The *Asheville Citizen* explicitly, and many other organs implicitly, hailed the Moscow accords as "perhaps the best news of the war."[87] "Our relations with Russia were long bedeviled by irresponsible Communists in this country who injured every cause they took up, including the cause of international peace," the *New York Times* contended. "The Moscow Conference has established new relations on a different footing."[88]

Some of the journals became almost lyrical in their comments. "Figuratively speaking, the conferees succeeded in building a bridge over a wide and turbulent river," the *Wall Street Journal* wrote. "Nobody knows yet whether the bridge will be strong enough to bear up under all the loads of conflict and national aspirations that must attend the passage, statecraft being a less exact science than engineering. But the bridge stands, and the four powers must use it, seeking always to stop short of overloading." The *Wall Street Journal* concluded buoyantly: "It may well prove to be the turning point in man's age-old struggle up from savagery."[89]

Raymond Clapper, whose importance as a columnist may have exceeded even Walter Lippmann's until his death in an accident in the South Pacific in 1944, also offered an extended metaphor to suggest the possible importance of the Moscow Declaration. "The declaration of Moscow is a start from which a new age can come," Clapper wrote on 2 November.

A door is opened, and we see outside not the distant clouds of a third world war, as so many had feared, but we see instead lying off to the horizon the green, peaceful fields of hope. Until now victory had been something that would serve only as a pause before more inescapable war. We had felt imprisoned in a room where there could be no peace, only more war. Now we can see out through the door that has opened at Moscow the bright highway over which we can go forward together into better days. At last we have the promise that our men far away are not dying in vain.[90]

Commentator Raymond Gram Swing was more concise. "It has been a foregone conclusion for some time that the Allies will win the war," Swing told his audience of several million over NBC's Blue Network. "The Moscow Conference holds out to the world the promise that they will also win the peace."[91]

More vindictive opinion makers were pleased to have the opportunity to strike out at alleged reactionaries. "The conference report gives the lie to McCormick-Patterson-Hearst propaganda about the danger of a separate peace between Russia and Germany," Max Lerner wrote in *New York PM*. "There must be consternation today in Disunity Row all over the country."[92] Howard Brubaker of the *New Yorker* lacked charity: "The news that the conference in Moscow was making progress depressed Senator Wheeler. He had been hoping all along that the boys would end up shaking fists instead of hands."[93]

The *New Yorker* of that day was not above engaging in a bit of snobbery and racism to make a point. However, a story which appeared in the 13 November issue seems so illustrative of how millions of ordinary Americans may have reacted to the news of the Moscow successes that it bears repeating.

> We wish to report that the most cogent comment we have heard on the Moscow pact was made in front of Macy's Broadway entrance at 4:43 P. M. on the day the afternoon papers broke the news. It was delivered to a colored woman by a medium-sized colored man wearing yellow shoes, who looked up from the *Journal-American* he was reading and addressed his companion firmly in the following words: "Now we and the Bear has *got* somewhere."[94]

"Now we and the Bear has *got* somewhere." That is what the lofty opinion makers who had a greater gift for better grammar but no finer gift for direct expression thought also. In fact, that is what practically everyone thought, as the rise in trust of Russia in the polls and other indications of public opinion suggest. But no American outside of the government really knew how closely appearances coincided with realities in this case, for the communiqué from the Moscow Conference only underscored the positive and blotted out the negative results of the meeting. Most of the opinion makers and all of the public could believe only that the vague statement was an accurate reflection of existing relations among the Big Three. In the fall of 1943, America's will to believe reached a peak.

The American response to the Teheran Conference could hardly have been as enthusiastic as the reaction to the Moscow Conference, and in fact it was not. The Moscow meeting had brought needed reassurance that the Allies were going to see the war through together and cooperate in the coming peace. The Joint Declaration from Teheran was disappoint-

ingly brief and vague, considering the fact that the entire future of Europe
was still in doubt. Americans were of course pleased that the Big Three
left Teheran "friends in fact, in spirit, and in purpose."[95] But what, many
asked, were the facts and purposes agreed upon?

Conservative opponents of the president, surprised by the Moscow
Declarations and realizing that Hull was a less suitable target than
Roosevelt, had remained silent in November. They found their voices
after Teheran. "Mr. Roosevelt's and Mr. Churchill's junkets are becoming
tiresome," the *Chicago Tribune* observed. "It ceases to be impressive when
journeys to the far corners of the earth and meetings surrounded by the
panoply elected by dictators and inappropriate to the leaders of self-
governing people result only in the announcement of trivial arrangements
in earth-shaking terms. The trick theatricalism is becoming comic and the
country is sick and tired of it."[96] George Rothwell Brown, a widely
syndicated, ultraconservative columnist, also was not amused: "Why,
hang it, not even Napoleon Bonaparte buckled down to a Czar of Russia
as Churchill and Roosevelt have knuckled down to Stalin, in meeting
him, as it were on his home grounds, only sixty miles from Russian soil
and in a country virtually dominated by Russia." "The incident isn't
flattering to American pride," Brown concluded. "Still, there it is."[97]

Most editors were not displeased with the site of the meeting, but
they were angered by the fact that details of the meeting were withheld
for a week after it was completed. Even that would have been bearable if
the three nations' information agencies had agreed on a time for release
of the meeting's communiqué. As it happened, Radio Moscow released
the news first, and some American newspapers thought that this was
both a blow to American pride and further evidence of the Roosevelt
administration's inefficiency.

In a word, the long-awaited summit conference turned out to be an
anticlimax. The Moscow Conference was supposed to lead up to the
summit at Teheran, and it did chronologically. But it did not substantively,
for almost nothing new could be found in the communiqué from Teheran.
With so few outstanding questions about the nature of the peace answered
at Moscow and Teheran, many observers concluded, there had to be
serious differences among the Allies. But as we shall see in the next
chapter, much of the discussion in America about Russia's place in the
postwar world proceeded as if major differences simply did not exist.

Perhaps fundamental differences did not exist after all, at
least not if one's frame of reference is a crude version of idealistic
philosophy. Many Americans did not want to think they existed, and

these people probably blocked serious dilemmas entirely out of their conscious minds. All of the media aided in performing this common mental function, including the most striking, visually, of the media at this time, the cinema.

The golden age of American movies would soon pass, as Hollywood declined and television kept more and more people at home on Saturday nights. But the cinema was still thriving during World War II. Newsreels, OWI and military shorts, and documentaries made it a medium of information as well as perhaps the premier medium of organized mass entertainment. Those of generally liberal persuasion had more control over this industry than any other, and they used it to spread the good word about Russia during the war.

Since World War II there have probably been fewer than five major American movies which have portrayed modern Russia favorably; during the war there were about twenty-five which did this. On the theme of the valiant Russian struggle for survival, there were, among others, *Moscow Strikes Back*, *The Siege of Leningrad*, *The City That Stopped Hitler–Heroic Stalingrad*, *We Will Come Back*, *Day After Day*, and *The Battle of Russia* from the War Department's Why We Fight series. The Russian people and their leaders, past and present, were depicted in *Peter the Great*, *Alexander Nevsky*, *North Star*, *Song of Russia*, and the controversial, effusively pro-Russian rendition of Davies's relatively noncontroversial book, *Mission to Moscow*.[98]

Several friends and casual acquaintances have told me that *The Battle of Russia*, which was one of the Army's orientation films, is the only thing they really remember about the circulation of opinion on Russia during World War II. Beginning in 1943, this extremely favorable portrait of a courageous ally was shown to each of the several million Americans who entered the services. With equal courage and willingness to sacrifice, the film implied strongly, Hitler would soon be doomed. It was a patchwork movie, bringing together highlights from several previous movies about Russian resistance. *The Battle of Russia*, which was released for commercial showing in the fall of 1943, was in many respects the culmination of the official and private campaigns in this country for friendship toward Russia.

Moscow Strikes Back was released a full year earlier. It was a sophisticated propaganda film, so sophisticated, in fact, that even such a cosmopolitan person as TVA director David Lilienthal seems to have been taken in. "Never have I felt that a picture was more authentic," Lilienthal wrote in his diary after seeing it on 8 January 1943. Ironically, Lilienthal thought that some who had seen the film with him were the ones who had been taken in. He had seen it at a large cocktail party which the

Russian Purchasing Commission gave in honor of the lend-lease adminis-
trator, Edward R. Stettinius, Jr., at Washington's Shoreham Hotel. In
attendance was an assortment of governmental and business leaders
involved in getting war material to the Russians. Lilienthal noted that
"every time Stalin was pictured there would be vigorous applause.
Imagine watching the former chairman of the United States Steel Cor-
poration, who sat two seats from me, pounding his hands, together with
the Russians and all the rest of us, for good old Joe—and this in the sacred
precincts of the Shoreham. . . . Page Martin Dies!"[99]

Actually, Stalin made only two appearances in the film, so the
viewers at the Shoreham must have been cheering as well every time
Russian soldiers raced across a snow-covered field and liberated one of
their villages. The movie begins with racy Russian band music accompanying fast-stepping Russian soldiers as they march through Red Square
in August 1939. Soon the deep, powerful voice of Edward G. Robinson
begins to describe the Russian people and the beloved capital they fought
to save in November and December of 1941.

Sardonic comments about the Nazis spice the film. Robinson refers
to one pretty Russian girl as the "kind of northern blond Hitler would
like to be." "A great fighting man speaks to his men" is the narrator's
description of Marshal Timoshenko. Determined Russian soldiers are
presented, followed by "the women of the Red Army." These in turn are
contrasted with Hitler's legions—"brutalized young men drunk with
success. . . . Their pure blood circulates poorly on Russian soil," Robinson
says of shivering captured Germans. After the fury of battle the cameras
take us to the destroyed home of Tchaikovsky. "The Nazis came to give
the word barbarian a streamlined meaning," Robinson editorializes.
"In the midst of a forest they used his furniture for firewood." There
are more battles, and pictures of dead children who, frozen, look like
disfigured dolls. "On all of us rests the mission of world liberation,"
Robinson concludes. If other viewers were moved by this picture as was
Lilienthal, they could hardly have failed to agree.[100]

By the beginning of 1944 the wave of Russian war films had already
begun to recede. Voluntary pro-Russian organizations also peaked long
before the war was finally won. The role of the scholarly organization,
the American Russian Institute, can be described quickly. In fact, it
described itself accurately as "an American organization for factual
information on the Soviet Union." The institute, whose headquarters
were on West Forty-fifth Street in New York City, did not seek to
influence opinion on Russia. It sought simply to inform those scholars,
writers, and others who wanted to visit its excellent library and the

relatively small number of persons who subscribed to its informative bulletin, "Russia at War."

It was hard to get accurate, objective information about Russia in this country during the war. The wave of appointments to American universities in Russian studies came only after the Soviet Union was widely viewed as a military threat to the United States, and that was not during World War II. Much information gathered by the institute was passed on to the public in books, speeches, and articles. But its role in circulating opinion remained basically indirect, and its influence is therefore very difficult to assess.

The purpose of the National Council of American-Soviet Friendship (NCASF) was to "promote better understanding and strengthen friendly relations between the United States and the Soviet Union as essential to the winning of the war, and the establishment of world-wide democracy and enduring peace."[101] That, basically, was also the goal in the fall of 1942 of the National Congress on American-Soviet Friendship, from which the National Council developed.

The ambitious aim of the National Council, under the leadership of Corliss Lamont, was to gain grass-roots support for the thoughts of the speakers at the National Congress and to develop an ongoing organization with branches around the country which could publicize issues in Russian-American relations and even pressure congressmen to support continued cooperation.[102] To this end the central office in New York published a regular newsletter, sold pamphlets on Russia in bulk, and provided speakers for other organizations. It also sponsored additional congresses in the fall of 1943 and in subsequent years.

At its peak in the summer of 1943, the National Council was a vibrant organization. It had active chapters in twenty-eight cities from Springfield, Massachusetts, to Los Angeles, and from Miami to Minneapolis. It had musicians', artists', scientists', and architects' committees to proselytize among these groups. It was furnishing its chapters with photographic exhibits on such subjects as "Scenes and People of the Caucasus," "Collective Farming," and "Original Water Colors and Drawings by Soviet Children." Aware of the importance of the childhood years in forming attitudes, the council was selling books like *Sasha and the Samovar* for ages three to six, *Igor's Summer* for ages eight to ten, and *Young Heroes of the War* for ages ten to fourteen.

Most impressive, perhaps, was the fact that its speakers had been heard by such traditionally conservative groups as American Legion Posts in Parkchester, New York; Lakewood, New Jersey; and elsewhere; by the Masonic Lodge of Newark; and by the Veterans of Foreign Wars of New York City. Obviously, interest in Russia was not the exclusive province of the Left during World War II.

By the fall of 1943, the National Council was showing signs of incipient decline. The attendance at the Congress of American-Soviet Friendship, which it sponsored in November, did not match the impressive number which had gathered a year before. The keynote speaker, Secretary of Interior Harold L. Ickes, did not have the stature of Henry Wallace in 1942. The director of Palmer Memorial Institute, Dr. Charlotte Hawkins Brown, could not fill Paul Robeson's shoes. Nor was the young, soft-spoken Soviet ambassador, Andrei Gromyko, the equal of the departed Litvinoff. And by the next fall, Stalingrad would be a distant memory and Roosevelt's reelection a more important goal than outward amity toward Russia.

By 1944, in short, Russia the ally was pretty much taken for granted, as Britain had been after Hitler turned the world's attention eastward in the summer of 1941. If American concern was aroused at all, it was by the plight of other nations; and Russia now seemed able to take care of herself as her armies drove the Germans back toward their homeland.

When Russia's fate had been the concern of all but the most conservative groups in Britain and America, Russian War Relief was an extremely popular organization in the United States. Even those who doubted the wisdom of sending lend-lease assistance to Russia did not oppose voluntary contributions of clothing, household goods, medical supplies, and foodstuffs to Russia.

In fact, helping the unfortunate abroad was something of a national obsession at this time. Giving to the disadvantaged abroad did not interfere with the harsh economics of scarcity and the cultivated realities of status in the United States; and that perhaps is one reason why wealthy New Yorkers rushed to place their names on the letterhead of Russian War Relief and contributed generously to feed and clothe avowed Communists in Russia, while many Americans in Harlem and elsewhere went to bed hungry every night. A further irony is that the same middle-class matrons who knitted sweaters for Finns to use against Russians in 1939 sent clothes for Russians to wear in their struggle against Finns and Germans in 1942.

Whereas the National Council had a maximum of twenty-eight local committees (that figure being reached in the summer of 1943), Russian War Relief already had exactly twice that number a year earlier, at least two-thirds of which were in the cosmopolitan Northeast.[103] Unlike the National Council, Russian War Relief steered clear of political questions. The slogan of the Greater New York Campaign in the spring of 1942, for example, was straightforward: "Aid to Russia Helps Us."[104] Under the able leadership of Edward Carter, Russian War Relief was able to send $46 million in aid to Russia in 1943 and 1944 alone.

๛ Whatever the exact motivations of the donors, it is fairly certain that all contributions tended to strengthen and solidify friendly attitudes toward Russia. That this process occurred—that attitudes toward Russia changed markedly during the first two years of American participation in World War II—cannot be doubted. Opinion on the crucial question of trust in Russia, as we have seen, changed from one doubter for every truster to two trusters for every doubter between March 1942 and November 1943. Assuming that the polls were reasonably accurate— and the question was asked frequently of enough different people to give one confidence that they were—the change toward friendliness to Russia involved a net gain of about fifteen million adult Americans. This was enough to shift those expressing trust in Russia's willingness to cooperate after the war from a decided minority to a clear majority of all respondents. Because the American people had no independent sources of opinion about Russia other than the few Russians who came to the United States at this time and intermingled with a minute percentage of the population, most of the credit for the shift must go to the overwhelming majority of American opinion makers from the president and Henry Luce's periodicals down who supported greater friendship with Russia.

Gains in favorable attitudes toward Russia were made among people of all economic and social positions and of all political and religious persuasions. The suave Wall Street banker who speculated in soybean futures and the unsophisticated southern sharecropper who grew soybeans were both likely to be more favorably disposed toward Russia in 1943 than they were in 1942, and their opinions of 1940 would have been discarded long ago—assuming, of course, that they had earlier been sufficiently exposed to the circulation of opinion in America. The physics professor at Yale and the Catholic priest in Milwaukee were no longer so hostile to Russia, if they were still hostile at all.

But differences in attitude remained among both individuals and the larger groups in society to which either they formally belonged or toward which they were oriented. On an individual basis, the historian can study only persons who left writings or recordings or who were widely written about or discussed on the radio. Such rare persons cannot serve as satisfactory guides to general public attitudes. Those who can may be described according to the various social groupings to which they may be said to have belonged. This mass of Americans would remain anonymous were it not for census takers, pollsters, journalists, and other observers of American life. This great body of individuals—the American people—will occupy us for the remainder of this chapter.

It may be said with considerable confidence that economic distinctions were not the major reason for differences in attitudes toward Russia during World War II. Economic differences there were, of course, but they simply do not seem to have been fundamental. The people themselves did not think they were fundamental, for 98 percent described themselves in 1944 as belonging economically to the middle class, and 88 percent thought that they belonged socially to this great American class. Only 1 percent thought that they belonged economically to the upper class.[105] For convenience and possible analytical utility, pollsters tended to divide the population into upper-, middle-, and lower-income groups of approximately equal sizes. Such distinctions, however useful analytically, obviously did not correspond to the public's essentially egalitarian self-image.

Perhaps in deference to the American aversion to thinking about economic differences, relatively few polls were analyzed on the basis of this criterion. The two main ones that were—one by the Gallup organization of Princeton and the other by the National Opinion Research Center of Denver—did record statistically significant differences. On the basic question of whether or not Russia was trustworthy to cooperate with the United States when the war was over, asked by Gallup in April 1943, 53 percent of the upper-income group, 45 percent of the middle-income group, and 41 percent of the lower-income group answered yes; 31, 38, and 31 percent said no; and 16, 17, and 26 percent had no opinion.[106]

In November 1943, NORC asked the public, "Do you think Russia ought to have as much to say as the United States about the peace that is made with Germany?" Of those with opinions, 81 percent answered yes and 19 percent said no. By occupation—again considering only those with opinions—87 percent of "professional, business, and white collar" respondents, 77 percent of "farmers," and 68 percent of "factory and construction" workers answered yes. By economic level 86 percent of upper-, 83 percent of middle-, and 75 percent of lower-income respondents with opinions answered affirmatively.[107]

The polls show that, as usual, Americans at all income levels disagreed with others at the same income level. Thus, while 53 percent of the upper-income group in the 1943 Gallup poll thought that Russia could be trusted to cooperate, 31 percent did not. The middle-income group was most evenly divided, 45 percent having said yes and 38 percent no. And just as the middle-income group is usually the most evenly divided, the lower-income group usually has the largest percentage of undecided respondents. Here it had 26 percent, 9 percent more than the middle-income group and 10 percent more than the upper-income group. But failure to express an opinion surely resulted more from lack of interest and lack of information than from low income.

The differences at the same income levels are most striking when the poll results are fleshed out with examples. At upper-income levels were both President Roosevelt and his supporters such as Averell Harriman and, on the other hand, the many wealthy people who voted against Roosevelt every time he ran for office. At middle-income levels in small towns and large cities were liberal professors who tended to think like the editors of the *New Republic* and conservative merchants who tended to think like the editors of the *Reader's Digest*. At lower-income levels, CIO workers who followed their union's leadership contrasted sharply with Appalachian farmers who may not even have heard of Russia, and who, like most people with little knowledge, tended to distrust the unknown.

There surely were some persons in all classes whose economic position determined their attitudes toward Russia more than any other factor, but these must have constituted a very small minority of the population. As indicated, the highest percentages of favorable attitudes toward Russia occurred among upper-income respondents, whose personal economic interest would be most threatened by communism. These positive attitudes almost certainly stemmed much more from education and from awareness of Russia's new role in international affairs than from economic status.

Three factors which are fixed at birth—age, sex, and ethnic background—also do not appear to have had major effects on general public attitudes toward Russia. At any rate, the pollsters of the time did not think so, for they almost never analyzed their data on the basis of any of these factors. That alone is not sufficient reason to discount them, of course, but one can judge from other sources and from general immersion in crosscurrents of the period that these factors were not crucial keys to differences in attitudes toward foreign policy generally and toward Russia specifically.

Age was not crucial because the generation gap as we know it did not exist at this time. Indeed, there was no such term in general usage. Contemporary youth were relatively enthusiastic about the administration, the war, and ongoing American values.[108] If anything, the generation gap as we know it was reversed. Older people were more likely to oppose the federal government because many distrusted the deficit spending, centralization of power, and other changes that Roosevelt had wrought since 1933. The young tended to view the New Deal favorably as a necessary response to changing conditions and as a blow to the power of the wealthy. Older people who remembered the "good old days" before 1929 did not know what to think of the New Deal, but many surely thought that change was coming much too fast.

At a time when women's liberation in most cases still meant marriage to a forceful, kind, and relatively affluent man, there were not likely to be major differences between the sexes on most issues of domestic and foreign policy. According to political scientist Alfred O. Hero, women generally "were less inclined to vote, less informed about most aspects of foreign policy, less likely to read international coverage and analysis in magazines and newspapers, and less apt to pay attention to programs on radio" than men.[109]

The major reason for this apathy surely was not less intelligence but rather the social custom which dictated that women, especially those at the lower- and middle-income levels, should defer to men on political questions. William Lydgate, a leading student of public opinion in the 1940s, reported that on one interviewing trip around the country he asked a Maine woman her opinion on an issue that had been hotly debated in the press for several weeks. Her reply would shock today's feminist: "I don't know what I think about that. I haven't talked to my husband yet."[110]

Many women surely had considerable influence on their husbands' thinking, and what they read about Russia on their own is therefore quite significant. The *Ladies' Home Journal* was mostly favorable to Russia throughout the war. In 1943, for example, the *Journal* featured friendly articles by Ella Winter, Dorothy Thompson, and Walter Lippmann. Miss Thompson and Lippmann stressed Russia's crucial role in the peace just as they did in their syndicated columns, and Miss Winter had nothing but praise for Russian institutions. "For those who don't like commercials in Radio," she said, "Russia would be a paradise." She added, "There are private doctors, but everybody can attend the best hospitals and clinics free."[111] Those and similar comments must have appealed to American women, who generally disliked the commercials which interrupted their favorite soap operas and feared that staggering hospital bills might wreck fragile family budgets.

Finally, differences in attitudes toward foreign policy resulting from varied ethnic and racial backgrounds probably were not crucial for most people, though they may well have been more important than differences resulting from gender and date of birth. Both because they generally did not have very much formal education, and because their attention tended to be riveted to pressing domestic injustices, most blacks apparently took very little interest in foreign affairs. Even their leading newspapers—the

Chicago Defender, the *Amsterdam News*, *The Pittsburgh Courier*, and the *Baltimore Afro-American*—devoted little space to foreign affairs, and of course even less to relations with Russia. Only readers of the *Crisis*, the journal of the National Association for the Advancement of Colored People, would have been exposed to frequent references to Russia. "There are many undemocratic features of Soviet administration which I would like to see eliminated," George Padmore wrote in a typical comment in that journal, "but nevertheless, I think the Soviet Union can teach the so-called Anglo-Saxon democracies much in the sphere of interracial relations."[112] The noted black leader Ernest Johnson wrote in *Christianity and Crisis* in March 1942 along much the same lines: "And let those who remain unimpressed with the necessity of revolutionizing their own racial attitudes reflect on the fact that Russia, whose associate in a mortal combat we have now become and whose future influence our conservatives greatly fear, has won no small measure of her power by dealing effectively with race prejudice. Certainly blinding of our eyes is not only a crime; it is a historical blunder."[113]

The most important ethnic group with respect to attitudes toward Russia were the Polish Americans, six to eight million strong, who could swing elections in the large industrialized states of the Northeast and Midwest. As will be demonstrated in chapter 6, however, Polish-American opinion was neither intensely nor unanimously opposed to Russia. Many recognized the unequaled contribution that Russia was making to the common war effort which would free Poland from Nazi domination, and others doubted that the conservative Polish government-in-exile really represented the Polish people. Moreover, the friendliness toward Russia of Russian-American Jews and Jews who had left Poland tended to counterbalance antagonistic Polish-American opinion.

The attitudes toward Russia among other leading ethnic groups were probably more profoundly influenced by religious than by ethnic considerations. The religion of many German Americans and virtually all Polish, Irish, and Italian Americans was Roman Catholicism. It must not be assumed, of course, that religion was the most important influence on the thinking of most of these forty million Americans, but it surely was a major influence for many of them.

The validity of this proposition is underscored by the most thorough analysis of poll data on the basis of religion, which was made by NORC toward the end of the war on the question of trust in Russia's willingness to cooperate. In the middle-income group it was only 3 percent more, but in both the upper- and lower-income groups fully 14 percent more Catholics than Protestants believed that Russia could not be trusted. The exact percentages were these: in the upper-income group, 59 percent of the Protestants and 50 percent of the Catholics expressed trust, and 30 and 44 percent respectively did not; in the middle-income group, the respective percentages were 48 and 48 and 31 and 34; for the lower-income group, these percentages were 44 and 32 and 34 and 48.[114] The 32 percent expressing trust in Russia against the 48 percent who expressed distrust among lower-class Catholics was almost the exact reverse of the attitudes toward Russia of other Americans, including middle- and upper-class Catholics.

Probably the most brilliant American observer of contemporary affairs during World War II was the eminent theologian Reinhold Niebuhr, who edited *Christianity and Crisis* and contributed frequent articles to other periodicals. "The relations between the Communist and the democratic world after the war will be somewhat analogous to the relations between Catholicism and Protestantism after the Thirty Years' War . . . ," Niebuhr wrote in the *Nation* in January 1943. "In a sense, the liberal-democratic world is a secularized version of Protestantism, while communism is a secularized version of Catholicism, which may be one reason why the Church hates the Kremlin with an almost pathological hatred."[115]

Characteristically, Roman Catholic leaders did not comment publicly on Niebuhr's observations, but they did continue to warn of the dangers of communism throughout the war. "Religious freedom in Russia, so long as the Communists continue to rule, is impossible," Fordham professor N. S. Timasheff warned in his widely quoted book on religion in Russia published in 1942.[116] And Father Ralph Gorman wrote in the April 1942 issue of *Sign*, the "National Catholic Magazine," that a "victorious Russia, astride two continents, supplied with unlimited resources, flushed with victory, and headed by a regime solidified by success, would constitute a menace difficult to exaggerate." Father Gorman continued, "We can recognize the dangers inherent in the Communist ideology and the threat to democratic and Christian ideals that might result from a Red victory, and limit our aid in such a way that we shall not be helping to forge the chains of a Communist-dominated Europe."[117]

By 1943 even the Catholic leadership had lost some of its fear of Russia, if not of communism. "It may well be that the rise of the totalitarian states has passed the crest and that its vicious philosophy has been discredited," Ignatius Kelly wrote in July in the *Ecclesiastical Review*.[118] "I say that we Catholics would be mad if we did not recognize this thing for what it is, an upsurge of the human spirit, drawing its strength from buried and perhaps long forgotten Christian holiness," J. L. Benvenisti wrote in *Commonweal* of the heroic Russian resistance.[119] And the same magazine editorialized early in 1944 that "we must study

Soviet institutions to see how they are able to inspire the sense of purpose that we lack."[120] But an editorial the previous summer conveyed the warning that periodicals and priests obviously were emphasizing to Catholic parishoners: "A policy of continuing nationalism in Russia by no means signifies the end of all our fears and worries about Russia or about her social revolution."[121] And *United States News* pointed out, at the height of American-Soviet friendship in the summer of 1943, that President Roosevelt's "effort to heal the breach between Russia's Government and the Catholic Church appears not to be succeeding." "There had been hope," the news magazine concluded, "but this was something even America's most persuasive politician was unable to bring off."[122]

The president did not have to bother to convince American Jews of the desirability of American-Soviet friendship. Jews had a dozen reasons to approve of all forms of collaboration. At home they tended to sympathize with the more radical forms of organized labor and to regard themselves as being the victims of considerable overt anti-Semitism. Abroad, they appreciated both the apparent absence of anti-Semitism in the Soviet Union and Russia's tremendous sacrifices against the world's premier anti-Semites. American Jews were always among the most generous contributors to Russian War Relief and the most persistent supporters of an early second front.

Domestic as well as international grounds for their support of Russia pervaded nearly every wartime issue of leading Jewish periodicals. Russia's reluctant entry into the war in June 1941 brought an immediate response from the *American Hebrew*. "Now that the American Clivendon Set is free to link 'international Jewry' with 'international Bolshevism,' " that important periodical prophesied, "we can confidently anticipate the appropriate changes in their propaganda."[123] By 1943 that same weekly was also praising the treatment of Jews in Russia. "They enjoy not only all the political and cultural rights with the rest of the population, but what is more unique, also economic and social equality such as the Jews do not enjoy in some democratic countries," William Zuckerman pointed out in April 1943. "Anti-Semitism has been literally wiped out. A country which throughout the nineteenth century was the bulwark of Jew-hatred and gave birth to the Jewish pogrom, now does not know the meaning of anti-Semitism. The new generation of Russia looks upon it as one of the legends of a dark past."[124]

To refer to the remaining religious groups in America at this time as Protestants is to risk the implication of a unity which simply did not exist. Theologically, Protestants ranged from the millions who believed that every word in the Bible was divinely dictated to the thousands who doubted that God existed and believed that the Bible was written by fallible mortals. Protestants included brilliant social critics and mystics who probably did not know there was a war going on. Protestants in America were those who were neither Catholics nor Jews.

Relative to foreign policy, there were three major groups of Protestants. On one side were the fundamentalists, who took religion seriously, but who tended not to have much sustained interest in foreign policy. When they did, their approach was largely conservative and nationalistic. In the middle was the great mass, for whom religion was at least partially a cultural requisite and foreign policy basically a separate matter. On the other side were the children of the social gospel, who took their liberal approach to religion seriously and thought that it should be applied to solve man's problems on earth.

The first two groups need not detain us long. The fundamentalists usually kept their religion pure in part by avoiding political questions. Occasionally they would offer a sweeping comment, such as the statement of the Social Service Commission to the Southern Baptist Convention in 1942 that Christianity "is greater than man's isms, more powerful than arms and planes and submarines."[125] But that was more an affirmation of faith than an analysis of existing conditions, for Nazism had thrust the world into war, and the nation's goal at that time was to produce enough weapons to be able to destroy it. The second group, which included the great majority of Protestants, viewed religion largely as a matter of personal salvation, and often as a relatively secondary concern at that. There is no evidence that religion had much effect on their attitudes toward American foreign policy.

The leaders of the vigorous social gospel minority typically participated in such interdenominational organizations as the Federal Council of Churches and subscribed to such nondenominational periodicals as *Christian Century* and *Christianity and Crisis*. They included the cosmopolitan cream of American society: Reinhold Niebuhr, John Foster Dulles, Rhoda McCulloch, John C. Bennett, Harold Robbins, Henry Sloane Coffin, and many others.[126] In contrast to the fundamentalists, the liberals were overwhelmingly favorable to Russia. They were not Communists or even fellow travelers, but during the war they were certainly more charitable toward Russia than they were toward America's shortcomings.

The social gospel group developed a fairly coherent ideology of Christian internationalism, a major tenet of which was insistence that America and Britain should bend over backward to ensure Russian and Chinese participation in a humane, progressive world order. To Eduard Heimann, the Soviet Union was both "part of the scourge sent to the democracies as a consequence of their sins" and "also part of the

Christian democratic world."[127] John Foster Dulles criticized the Streit plan for federation with Britain because "a federation of so-called democracies would, to others, appear as the banding together of the well-to-do to maintain the status quo."[128] "Without a religious sense of humility and responsibility the Anglo-Saxon world will fail to come to terms with the two great non-Christian nations, Russia and China," Niebuhr warned in October 1943. "It will fail to understand to what degree what is good in the new Russian order represents values of equal justice which we should have, but did not, achieve; and to what extent the evils of tyranny in Russia are simply a false answer to our own unsolved problem of social justice."[129]

Niebuhr, who differed theologically from the social gospel group but shared their social concerns, was disturbed about the thrust of the group's thinking. In April 1943 he wrote that "the more 'idealistic' forces of America, whether secular or religious, are inclined to plan for a world community in such abstract terms as not to engage the actual historical realities at all." Niebuhr warned that the idealists' chaste blueprints "are so completely irrelevant to the real problems which the world faces and so far from the actual possibilities of a tolerable system of mutual security, that the realists can afford to disregard them. Thus our policy moves toward a cynical expression of American power, while our avowed war aims are pure as gold."[130]

Except that he had served on the commission which helped to formulate the document, Niebuhr could have been referring to John Foster Dulles's widely circulated "Six 'Pillars of Peace,' " which called in very general terms for such things as "continuing collaboration of the United Nations, . . . an organization to adapt the treaty structure of the world to changing underlying conditions, . . . the goal of autonomy for subject peoples, . . . procedures for controlling military establishments everywhere, [and] the right of individuals everywhere to religious and intellectual liberty."[131] Exactly how harried State Department officials, much less officials of the Soviet Foreign Ministry, were to build a temple of peace upon pillars such as these was not spelled out, and Niebuhr doubted that they would or even could perform this feat.

Niebuhr must have been shaken when 144 leaders of America's religious establishment came out in October 1943 with a "Joint Catholic, Jewish and Protestant Declaration on World Peace." The signers of the declaration included the Reverend Henry Sloane Coffin, president of Union Theological Seminary; Dr. Stephen S. Wise, chairman of the War Emergency Zionist Committee; and the Most Reverend Saul Alphonsus Stritch, archbishop of Chicago. The declaration urged the implementation of the following seven-point program:

1. The moral law must govern world order.
2. The rights of the individual must be assured.
3. The rights of oppressed, weak or colonial peoples must be protected.
4. The rights of minorities must be secured.
5. International institutions to maintain peace with justice must be organized.
6. International economic cooperation must be developed.
7. A just social order within each state must be achieved.[132]

Such abstract prescriptions for heaven on earth did not speak to Americans longing, quite literally, for nothing more than a peace they could live with. By insisting upon an ideal peace settlement, these religious leaders helped neither the administration nor the general public to plan and prepare for the peace to come.

🙞🙜 Much more noticeably than was the case before the 1930s or after the 1940s, politicized Americans tended to be divided into forces of order and forces of movement at this time. Sometimes the differences between them were not drawn sharply; sometimes they were. But most American opinion and decision makers had to make decisions which cast them on one side or the other, and even voters who took little interest in politics between elections had to choose between the generally conservative Republicans and the generally liberal Democrats. Only the most apathetic could think that many American politicians were successfully straddling the political fence on basic issues.

The forces of movement in America in 1943 were composed of presidential Democrats and some presidential Republicans and congressional Democrats. The members of this mighty grouping were at least reasonably sympathetic to organized labor, progress for blacks, deficit financing when required, and solidarity with Britain and Russia in the war and the peace to follow. President Roosevelt and Vice-President Wallace were the leading presidential Democrats, Wendell Willkie and Thomas Dewey were the leading presidential Republicans, and Senators Connally and Barkley were the leading congressional Democrats in 1943.

The views of these leaders were the majority views we have encountered earlier in this chapter and in previous chapters; they do not require further elucidation at this point. Obviously, the very fact that the adminstration, powerful congressmen, and leading Republicans all were favorably disposed toward Russia goes far to explain Russia's popularity in America in 1943.

The forces of order—congressional Republicans, some congressional Democrats, and some presidential Republicans—tended to oppose the administration in almost every aspect of domestic and foreign policy. In domestic policy, resentful western Republicans, southern Democrats, and conservative northern Republicans had few qualms about joining to block innovative administration programs after 1936. On foreign policy, most southern Democrats and some northern Republicans had broken with western Republicans on the issue of preparedness and aid to Britain, but now all three groups were tending toward a strongly nationalistic approach. Senators Burton K. Wheeler of Montana, Gerald Nye of South Dakota, and Albert "Happy" Chandler of Kentucky did much to develop the nationalistic position, which was described by its opponents as the "New Isolationism." The forces of order were as unwilling to shed their longstanding suspicion of the Soviet Union as they were loath to drop their opposition to the New Deal, and it is quite likely that the one was related to the other.

On balance, Henry Luce probably belonged with the forces of order in America; but as an intelligent and cosmopolitan New Yorker, with personal knowledge of foreign lands, Luce maintained in his publications a delicate balance between the two positions that surely contributed to their immense popularity. Just as he was lauding Russia in *Life*, Luce was offering a reasoned critique in *Fortune* of American foreign policy in general and official policy toward Russia in particular. Good relations with Russia, *Fortune* argued, would result neither from the unlimited, unreasoned praise of Russia by the Left nor from self-righteous prognostications of future perfidy from the Right. "The nationalist reaction in the U.S. has not yet turned into isolationism," *Fortune* editorialized in its April 1943 issue, "but it threatens to do so unless the confusion about the rules is cleared up." And just what was the "nationalist reaction" then in evidence? "The nationalist reaction in the U.S. is at bottom a desire to come down from the clouds," the editors of *Fortune* thought. "It is a desire to argue over real issues, not just words."[133]

Two months later these general complaints were applied to American-Russian relations. The three major paragraphs of this excellent editorial merit our consideration. They also merited (but did not really receive) the consideration of both the forces of movement, who were letting praise be a substitute for realistic efforts to establish a durable relationship with Russia, and the forces of order, who did not think that any nation should be permitted to limit American power in the world. *Fortune*'s central argument was this:

> Mutual interests of the two nations heavily outweigh conflicting ones—which exist nevertheless and will worry any U.S. Secretary of State this side of Earl Browder. Yet to mention such conflicts is taboo. Why? Because the American people supposedly have to be sold on cooperation with Soviet Russia, and nothing must interfere with that delicate educational purpose.

The people already have been sold on this idea—not by Elmer Davis but by Hitler. The delicate task of leadership of course is not the hopeless attempt to make an intelligent people overlook possible points of friction, but to satisfy them that their government is as hardheaded as they and the Russians are. . . . If Hitler, Franco, and the U.S. communists could not prevent the American people from desiring, by an overwhelming majority, close cooperation with Soviet Russia, nothing can—except a U.S. foreign policy that offends the self-respect of this nation and makes the self-respecting Russians doubt the value of an alliance with nincompoops.[134]

An important poll taken three months later showed that, whether or not self-respecting Russians wanted an alliance with "nincompoops," most self-respecting Republicans did not want a permanent military alliance with Russia after the war. Early in September 1943, the Gallup organization asked its customary sample of 3,000 this question: "After the war, should the United States and Russia make a permanent military alliance, that is, agree to come to each other's defense immediately if the other is attacked at any future time?" Overall responses were yes, 39 percent; no, 37 percent; and no opinion, 24 percent. Forty-five percent of the Democrats answered yes and 31 percent no, but 36 percent of the Republicans responded yes and 43 percent no. When Great Britain replaced Russia in the same question, 67 percent of the Democrats and 57 percent of the Republicans answered yes.[135]

This poll showed that those who supported the party representing the forces of movement in America favored a military alliance with Russia after the war by almost the same margin as those who supported the party representing the forces of order opposed it. That is not to suggest, of course, that all Democrats favored movement and all Republicans supported order, but it is likely that conservative Democrats and liberal Republicans largely canceled out each other's responses at this time, so that poll results analyzed by political affiliation provide a reasonably accurate reflection of the division of opinion within the public between the forces of order and the forces of movement.

The division of opinion within each of the groups (as well as between them) is powerful evidence that Russia remained a controversial topic during the war. In the previous poll, as we have seen, 31 percent of the Democrats opposed a military alliance with Russia after the war. In a poll on the question of trust taken just after the Moscow Conference, 21 percent of the Democrats did not believe that Russia could be trusted to cooperate after the war. But 50 percent thought that Russia could be trusted, and 29 percent did not know.

Again, the contrast with Republicans was marked. More than one-third of the Republicans—34 percent to be exact—thought that Russia could not be trusted, 43 percent thought that she could, and 23 percent were undecided.[136] Despite this relatively high negative vote of 34 percent, never during the entire war did a smaller percentage of Republicans believe that Russia could not be trusted.

The questions of postwar trust and a possible military alliance revealed sharp regional as well as political differences in opinions about Russia. The west central states had the most confidence in Russia's willingness to cooperate, followed in order by the Northeast, the Far West, the South, and the east central states. The percentage of yes answers in April 1943 was 48 in the states west of Illinois and east of the Rockies, 45 in the states from Maryland northward, 45 in the states west of the continental divide, 39 in the states which had fought for independence in the Civil War, and 41 percent in the states through which flow the eastern tributaries of the Mississippi River.

The only reason that the South had a slightly smaller percentage of confidence in Russia than the eastern Midwest was because the South had 6 percent more undecided respondents (28 percent to 22 percent). The Northeast also had 22 percent undecided on this difficult question, while the west central and western states each had 18 percent undecided.[137]

On the question of a military alliance with Russia after the war, the South, which had trailed all other sections in positive responses on the question of trust, easily led them. The favorable percentage in the South was 47, in the Far West 40, in the Northeast 39, and 37 in each part of the Midwest.[138] Obviously, prewar attitudes had lingered to some extent: the South had been the most interventionist region and the Midwest the most isolationist before Pearl Harbor.

Regional differences there obviously were, but what caused them and what did they mean? Did they result essentially from cultural differences fostered by the search for regional identities over many decades or did they reflect basically fortuitous differences in the traits of their inhabitants? These are big questions which, implicitly or explicitly, have occupied the attention of many scholars for many years. The answer here will be neither exhaustive nor definitive, but the thrust of this chapter's argument suggests that the importance of regional differences as causal factors in modern America has often been greatly overemphasized.

"One of the greatest delusions of our time is that America is torn by deep sectional differences over foreign policy," William A. Lydgate wrote in 1944.[139] If it was a delusion in 1944—and the polls show that it was far from a total one—it had not been a delusion three years earlier when some midwestern congressmen were scarcely on speaking terms with their interventionist colleagues from the South and the Northeast. Moreover, Lydgate based his argument largely on public opinion on a question that was all but dead by 1944, namely, "Do you agree with those people who think that the United States should take an active part in world affairs after the war, or with those who think we should stay out of world affairs?"

On this question, in a Gallup poll of May 1944, 72 percent of midwesterners and 73 percent of all Americans thought that the United States should take an active part. As might have been expected on a dead issue, the regional differences were not statistically significant. The more important question at this time was whether America should adopt an essentially unilateral approach or an essentially multilateral one to international problems. And the new isolationists, unilateralists, imperialists, or whatever one chose to call them, were strongest in the Midwest and South.

The Northeast was the most cosmopolitan section of the country during these years of global war; it was also the most complex. The region's complexity and diversity applied to even the names of its two major parts. The northernmost part, New England, was, as John Gunther observed later, "neither new nor very much like England."[140] Of the two great Middle Atlantic states, New York and Pennsylvania, the one reached the Atlantic only at New York City and the other did not reach it at all.

The Northeast probably had as many truly cosmopolitan persons as all other regions combined. It also probably had as many of what the sociologist Herbert Gans has called "urban villagers"[141] as all other regions. It had immigrants from Europe whose families had arrived in America in every decade since 1620. It was receiving an influx of black Americans from the South during this war as it had during the last; it also had black residents whose ancestors had lived there as free men long before the Civil War. New York and other great cities were as vibrant and fluid as cities anywhere in the world; Kent, Connecticut, and other small towns were as tranquil and unchanging as the small towns of Europe and the Far East. The essential unity of the Northeast was its utter diversity.

Compared with citizens of other regions, northeasterners were probably the most friendly toward Russia. As we have seen, midwesterners who lived west of the Mississippi shaded them in the polls on this issue, but the intensity of support for Russia found in the Northeast did not exist in any other region. Jews, Communists, organized labor, pro-Russian organizations, and newspapers were all strongest in the Northeast; and it was these groups which made the greatest effort to force Roosevelt's hand on the issue of the second front. Many conservative but cosmopolitan northeastern Republicans also supported Russia during the war.

On the other hand, the Irish in Boston and Brooklyn offered considerable opposition to both Britain and Russia; and some German, Italian, and Polish Americans did likewise for ethnic or religious reasons. The powerful presence of Catholicism in the Northeast is probably sufficient reason for the higher level of support for Russia in the polls in the western Midwest.

❧ It must have occurred to the reader that none of these standard "independent variables"—economic standing, ethnic origin, religious heritage, political preference, and regional background—even begin to provide an adequate explanation of differences in attitudes toward Russia during World War II. Each offers insights into reasons for some of the differences, but it obviously will not do to conclude this chapter with a few glib remarks about how some variables probably were more salient for some persons and others were more salient for others. Not only would such remarks be facile; they would also be false. For there appears to have been a profound but subtle force at work in American society at this time which makes the great standard "independent variables" seem superficial.

This force is essentially the same as that which Robert K. Merton described in contrasting the "local" and "cosmopolitan" leaders of a northeastern community during the Second World War. Concerning differences in attitudes toward Russia, it would be useful to extend this concept to all adults in America at that time. If this is not done, the most fundamental division in American society and in American attitudes toward Russia will be ignored.

The most fundamental differences in American society at this time seem to have stemmed from differences between cosmopolitan and provincial Americans. And what did *cosmopolitan American* and *provincial American* mean in practice? The basic differences between them lay in their approaches to the exciting, turbulent world of the twentieth century. Provincials were fundamentally narrow-minded, a term used here analytically, not pejoratively. Their worlds were restricted primarily to their families, jobs, pleasures, and the events and personalities in their localities which impinged upon their lives. When one shrewd journalist said that most people were more interested in a fire in Brooklyn than a war in Europe, he was referring primarily to provincial Americans.

Cosmopolitans thought of themselves as residents of the state, nation, and world as much as of the locality. They wanted to know what was happening and what people were thinking in Washington, New York, London, and Moscow as much or more than they were interested in business transactions and minor scandals in small towns like Hightstown, New Jersey; in modest cities like Macon, Georgia; and in large metropolitan areas like Chicago.

Cosmopolitans in Hightstown wanted to know how communism

and national socialism worked as well as whether these systems threatened their community. Provincials in nearby New York City were more concerned about the price of bread than about whether the victorious allies would be able to agree upon an effective international organization. Cosmopolitans in Hightstown read the *New Yorker* and *Time*; provincials in New York City read the *New York Daily News* and sometimes bought the *Reader's Digest* at the newsstand.

It should be possible to develop criteria for cosmopolitans and provincials and to determine from existing data how many of each lived in different places at different times according to any of several possible definitions. Such work should prove to be eminently worthwhile, but it obviously is far beyond the scope of this study.

At present, the prime indicator of probable provincial or cosmopolitan status would seem to be educational achievement. It seems reasonable to assume that at least 80 percent of adult Americans in 1943 with grade-school educations or less were provincial, and that at least 80 percent of those with college educations were cosmopolitan. As of the 1940 census, about 60 percent of Americans twenty-five years of age and older had never gone beyond the eighth grade. The other 40 percent had attended high school, and about 17 percent of these had benefited from at least one year of some form of college training.[142]

The approximately 6 percent of adult Americans who had been to college were overwhelmingly cosmopolitan according to the standards of the time. Without them such cosmopolitan journals as the *New York Times*, the *Christian Science Monitor*, *Time*, *Fortune*, and the *Nation* probably would have folded for lack of readers. The decision makers, opinion makers, and attentive public were drawn almost exclusively from their ranks. They were the leaders of the American commercial, governmental, religious, and educational establishments, and they generally favored continued cooperation with Russia after the war.

The 60 percent who had never gone to high school were at the bottom of most social and economic indices. To earn a living, they usually had to either do the menial work of modern industrial society or practice subsistence farming. They were not abreast of the popular and intellectual currents of their time; thus, for example, many of them probably did not know that it was now fashionable to be friendly toward Russia. If they knew it, they kept it much better concealed from the pollsters than did the better-educated groups.

The vague fear of Russia which had been nurtured by the nation's opinion makers for a generation lingered among the very poorly educated and also among many of those who really did not have much better educations. These included the approximately one-fourth of adults who had been beyond grade school but who had not been graduated from high school; and it also included many of those who had finished high school but who lacked the intelligence, ambition, or money to continue on to college. Quite possibly, there was very little difference between the outlooks of those who went no further than grammar school and those who went no further than high school. As Alfred O. Hero has pointed out, the "sharpest differences on most aspects of world affairs have been between those who went to college and those who did not."[143]

Just as there existed a spectrum of provincials from the illiterate, isolated small farmer to the urban industrial worker who had gone to high school, read *Life* occasionally, and heard about Russia infrequently at union meetings; so were there differences in cosmopolitans from, say, Walter Lippmann to the small-town doctor who had to fight to maintain an essentially cosmopolitan approach. Hero has demonstrated that throughout America in the late 1940s there were significant differences in the international orientations of college graduates

according to college attended, course of study, and level of performance. People whose parents also went to college or were of the more sophisticated social strata have been more likely to fit the criteria of interest, thoughtfulness, and responsibility in world affairs than those from less-educated or privileged homes. Those who majored in the humanities and social sciences have been more apt to be realistic internationalists than others who majored in technology, premedicine, commerce, and other subjects unassociated with world affairs. Those who received technical, graduate, or professional education have tended more in this direction if they had broad undergraduate educations rather than technical ones. Those who majored in the purer sciences have on the whole been more interested, informed, and thoughtful about foreign policy than those who focused on the applied sciences. Those who made high grades have been on the average more sophisticated about world affairs than those whose grades were average or, particularly, poor.[144]

Whatever the exact differences in attitudes toward Russia among college graduates, the differences between them and other Americans were surely more striking on the whole. When Americans were asked just after the Moscow Conference, "Do you think Russia ought to have as much to say as the United States about the peace that is made with Germany?" 89 percent of the college-educated respondents said yes, as did only 81 percent of the high-school-educated respondents and 76 percent of grade-school-educated respondents.[145]

College-educated respondents were also much more willing to give freedom to Russia's domestic spokesmen. "In peace time, do you think members of the Communist Party in this country should be allowed to speak on the radio?" NORC inquired in February 1944. Nearly twice as many college-educated as grade-school-educated respondents—67 percent to 38 percent—answered yes. As usual, high-school-educated respondents were in the middle, with 50 percent. Moreover, five times as many grade-school-educated as college-educated respondents, 20 percent to 4 percent, declined to offer an opinion.[146] On the basic question of trust in Russia's willingness to cooperate, 62 percent of the college-educated group, 60 percent of the high-school-educated group, and only 51 percent of the grade-school-educated respondents answered yes in March 1945.[147]

A more specific variable than education for probing the cosmopolitan-provincial continuum is information. Information about foreign affairs and the ability to use it in making judgments about policy alternatives is perhaps the basic difference between cosmopolitans and provincials in the field of foreign policy.

Elmo Roper analyzed the results of several polls during the war according to three categories: "well informed," "poorly informed," and "uninformed." Roper presumably placed respondents into these categories according to the questions of fact which preceded questions of opinion in his polls. In any case, the results parallel those tabulated by Gallup and NORC on the basis of differences in formal education.[148]

"Do you expect that Russia will want about the same kind of peace that we do or that she will make demands that we can't agree to?" Roper's interviewers asked approximately five thousand Americans in June 1943. The results showed that 33 percent of the well informed, 30 percent of the poorly informed, and 27 percent of the uninformed thought Russia would want about the same kind of peace as the United States.[149]

"Do you think we should or should not try to work with Russia as an equal partner in fighting the war?" Roper also asked at the same time. Of the well informed, 89 percent said yes, compared with 84 percent of the poorly informed and only 71 percent of the uninformed.[150]

Finally, Roper asked, "Do you expect that Russia will stay in the war until Hitler is completely defeated, or that she is likely to make a separate peace with him as soon as she finds it to her advantage?" The results were the most striking of all: 67 percent of the well informed, 58 percent of the poorly informed, and only 46 percent of the uniformed expressed confidence that Russia would stick with the Allies to see the war through.[151]

The well informed probably were more confident of continued Russian cooperation, because they were more aware of Stalin's public position on the war, believed that Russia had little real choice in the matter, and were more conscious of the pro-Russian position which was then being taken by most of the nation's opinion makers.[152] Different factors naturally went into the thinking of different cosmopolitans; in fact, there surely were more factors than the three which I have mentioned.

But the exact reasons for the positive response in specific cases matters little. The point is simply that the cosmopolitans—in this case the well informed—had the approach to changing circumstances which was likely to make their responses much more reasoned than those of the provincials.

Dozens of additional polls could be cited in support of the crucial role of information in shaping attitudes toward Russia during World War II; none, to my knowledge, support the contrary argument. To cite one final example, when the Gallup organization asked in mid-November 1943 whether Russia could be trusted to cooperate after the war, the overall result was 47 percent yes, 27 percent no, and 26 percent no opinion. But of the 70 percent of the sample who had heard or read about the Moscow Conference two weeks before, 57 percent answered yes, 27 percent said no, and only 16 percent had no opinion. In contrast, among the 30 percent of the adult sample who, remarkably, had neither heard nor read about the Moscow Conference, the result was 26 percent yes, 27 percent no, and 47 percent no opinion.[153]

The great wave of American goodwill toward Russia peaked in 1943 among cosmopolitan Americans, many of whom were reading such hopeful works as Wendell Willkie's *One World* and listening to such optimistic speeches as Secretary of State Hull's report on the Moscow Conference. The negative attitudes toward Russia at this time were concentrated among provincials, many of whom would have been hard pressed to tell an interviewer whether Willkie had ever visited Russia and what his general views on Russia were. Cosmopolitans and provincials were the two basic American social types during World War II. They also epitomized the two basic approaches to Russia at this time. One of these was based on knowledge, however imperfect it might now seem. The other was grounded on ignorance and continuing fear.

Russia in the Postwar World

When wars drag on, the questions people ask become more pointed as the early euphoria fades. With such questions in World War II came increased American skepticism about the righteousness of Russia's aims. The overwhelming evidence between the spring of 1943 and the beginning of 1944 that the Russians and their Western allies were going to win gradually became somewhat unsettling. What will the Russians do after Hitler is beaten? Americans asked apprehensively. Will they go home, or will they try to communize Europe? Nobody knew, and that fact probably contributed as much to the prevailing uneasiness as anything Russia did or did not do at the time.

Absence of knowledge did not seem to hinder discussion. Before the Anglo-American invasion of Europe and the presidential campaign captured the nation's attention in the summer of 1944, Russia's place in the postwar world was the premier subject of public debate. This occurred not only because opinion makers sensed that Russia's position would be crucial to the maintenance of peace, but also because there seemed to be little else to discuss. Domestic issues had been of secondary importance for several years, and the American theaters of war in Italy and the Pacific were going well enough but not spectacularly.

In this relative vacuum, American opinion makers could discuss the implications of events involving Russia. They could express concern about the festering Polish sore which threatened at times to undermine the Allied partnership. They could consider Russia's potential contributions to America's postwar prosperity. And they could talk and write generally about Russia's internal evolution and her role in the family of nations after the war. As usual, they discussed all of these subjects at once. Here, in the interest of clarity, the four basic topics will be considered in turn.

146

❧☜☞❧ Before the summer of 1943, almost all discussion of Russia's postwar role had been disparaging, euphemistic, or simply platitudinous. The regnant idea on this subject in 1942 was that the United States and Britain would determine the shape of the peace. As Protestant leader Henry Pitt Van Dusen put it, "Any realistic envisionment of the peace must recognize that, granted decisive Allied victory, predominant power at the cessation of hostilities will rest with the British Empire and the United States."[1]

This observation, so common in learned works on the peace as well as in hastily written newspaper editorials and radio commentaries, was not intended as a threat to Russia or anybody else; it was simply an apparent statement of fact. Russia, after all, would do well to survive as a nation; and Germany, Italy, France, and Japan were sure to be much weaker than before. By the simple process of elimination, Britain and America would be the only industrialized powers left.

After Stalingrad, American opinion makers were compelled to admit that Russia would have some say in the shape of the postwar world, but they were not forced to consider the implications of this admission. The very fact that Russia was to be a great power somehow made her benevolent, just as the other great powers, Britain and America, were assumed to be benevolent toward other nations. As we have seen, American opinion makers in March 1943 were generally displeased when Ambassador Standley criticized our Russian ally, and they were universally unhappy when Vice-President Wallace suggested that the United States might double-cross Russia if conservatives came to power. The goodwill toward Russia of the winter of 1943 had culminated in *Life*'s special issue on Russia at the end of March.

Three major events in the late spring and summer of 1943 awakened many Americans from their dreams and focused their attention on the possibility that Russia might be difficult to deal with after the war. The first was Russia's rupture of diplomatic relations with the Polish government-in-exile, which has been mentioned, as has the third, the recall of Ambassadors Maisky and Litvinoff from London and Washington. The second event, Russia's formation of a "Free Germany" committee in July, concerned American leaders and led to speculation in the media that Russia might be seeking a separate peace with Germany. In view of the apparent deterioration of Soviet-American relations, it was somehow fitting that one of the most virulent wartime attacks on Russia and on American liberals should fill the first fourteen pages of the July 1943 issue of *Reader's Digest*, which was regularly circulated to twice as many Americans as any other periodical. It was an article by one of the foremost Russophobes of the 1930s, Max Eastman, and it was entitled "We Must Face the Facts About Russia."

Eastman began by praising the "heroic fight of the Russian armies and people against Adolf Hitler's military machine," which was hardly praise any longer, because it was such a cliché.[2] "It is natural, since she fights so brilliantly beside us," Eastman went on, "to be a little undiscriminating in our praise of the Soviet Union."[3] Most opinion makers would have agreed so far, but Eastman was barely on page 2. Considering the pro-Russian climate of opinion, the remainder of the article was courageous even for the staunchly conservative *Reader's Digest*.

Eastman criticized Russia, of course, but he aimed his main attack at the "mushheads and muddleheads" in the United States who "are doing us in."[4] Like Joseph McCarthy's targets later, some of these were professors, but most were liberal bureaucrats. " 'Don't say a word against Stalin or he won't accept our tanks' seems to be the attitude of some of those who are now giving away the national treasure so avidly," Eastman remarked, adding, "This is an attitude of spirit which I find diplomatically foolhardy, morally disgraceful and *dangerous to the survival of democratic institutions* within this country."[5] Four pages later, the author returned to this ominous theme: "If ever strong, hard-minded patriots of democracy were needed in our public life, it is now."[6] "Our sole weapon against their [Russia's] darkness," Eastman concluded, "is our light."[7]

Few opinion makers outside of the ultraconservative press adopted Eastman's approach, but his article stimulated thought about Russia and her postwar intentions. Only a small part of this resulted directly from Eastman's article, but the article did come at a time when Americans wanted a more down-to-earth discussion of the postwar world. The article helped to precipitate this phase of the debate.

"Suddenly the subject of American foreign policy broke into flame," *Fortune* noted in its issue which reached the newsstands in October. "It became subject No. 1 in public discussion."[8] This "flame" was not a hopeful one, Reinhold Niebuhr thought. The theologian sensed a "general pessimism" caused by the "increasing evidence that an accord with Russia, broad enough to guarantee a stable world, is a desperately difficult achievement, and may be beyond the resources of present statesmanship."[9]

However, the Moscow and Teheran conferences seemed to belie all pessimistic premonitions. Had not the foreign ministers of the Big Three reached agreement at Moscow and the leaders of the world powers met amicably in the capital of Iran? In his fireside chat of Christmas Eve 1943, which was devoted largely to discussing the recent Teheran meetings, President Roosevelt continued the tradition of buoyant optimism which he had never really relinquished since he first took office more than a decade before.

"On the basis of what we did discuss, I can say even today that I do not think any insoluble differences will arise among Russia, Great Britain, and the United States," the nation's premier opinion maker reported. The president conveyed the false impression that there were no major outstanding differences between Russia and the Western powers, but stated correctly, "I got along fine with Marshal Stalin." Indeed, his praise of Stalin was lavish: "He is a man who combines a tremendous, relentless determination with a stalwart good humor. I believe he is truly representative of the heart and soul of Russia, and I believe that we are going to get along very well with him and the Russian people—very well indeed."[10]

The euphoria of the holiday season—which had continued from the Moscow Conference through Thanksgiving and from the Cairo and Teheran conferences through Christmas—did not last. "Four weeks after Teheran," *Time* noted in its New Year's issue, "the first exuberance was soberly shaking down."[11] Roosevelt's expressions of confidence, many opinion makers now pointed out, were phrased more in terms of future than of present accord.

American concern was soon heightened by anti-Western campaigns in *Pravda* and *Izvestia*, the official Soviet newspapers, in the winter of 1944. *Pravda* opened with an attack against Wendell Willkie, probably Russia's most effective American friend during the war. The ostensible provocation was Willkie's article in the *New York Times Magazine* of 2 January 1944 entitled "Don't Stir Distrust of Russia." In it Willkie pleaded with his fellow Republicans not to attempt to make political capital with ethnic Americans out of Russia's possible postwar relations with her east European neighbors. "Of course," Willkie added parenthetically, "one of the most pressing questions in everybody's mind is what Russia intends to do about the political integrity of small states around her borders—Finland, Poland, the Baltic and Balkan states."[12]

To this statement, David Zaslavsky of *Pravda* responded immediately in a highly irritated tone. "The question of the near Baltic republics is an internal affair of the Union of Soviet Socialist Republics. . . ," Zaslavsky insisted. "With respect to Finland and Poland," the Russian wrote sarcastically, "it must be said that the Soviet Union will be able to get an agreement with them itself and does not need the help of Mr. Willkie."[13]

On 1 February, *Izvestia* charged that the Vatican's foreign policy had "earned the hatred and contempt of the Italian masses for supporting fascism."[14] Predictably, Monsignor Fulton Sheen of Catholic University charged immediately that Russia was plotting a separate peace with Germany, and Bishop Edwin O'Hara of Kansas City said that *Izvestia*'s contention was "totally false."[15] Walter Lippmann, epitomizing the view of the moderate establishment, thought that *Izvestia*'s publication of the anti-Papal article was a "highly improper action."[16]

Pravda continued its attacks throughout the spring, adding likely targets such as William Randolph Hearst and Red-baiting columnist Karl Von Wiegand and unlikely ones such as the *New York Times* military analysts Hanson W. Baldwin, thus multiplying its offenses against the American way.[17] Not until D-Day in June were Americans again praised, and the praise was just as lavish as the censure had been harsh.

On 1 February 1944 the Soviet government announced formal diplomatic and military autonomy for each of the sixteen Soviet "republics." Most American opinion makers did not know how to assess Russia's latest move, so they drew conclusions on the basis of their general attitudes toward Russia. "This means," Hearst's *San Francisco Examiner* editorialized on page 1 with typical self-assurance, "Russia will have sixteen votes in any future League of Nations and at the peace table when Germany is defeated. The United States will have only one vote."[18]

But the *Minneapolis Star-Journal* and most other newspapers were not inclined to criticize the Soviet Union for anything at this time other than Zaslavsky's attacks, and certainly not for its ambiguous move. "It is a step away from authoritarianism and totalitarianism, and toward 'democracy' and representative government," the *Star-Journal* assured its readers.[19] "A few years ago it would have been regarded with intense suspicion," the *Kansas City Star* observed astutely. "The change in attitude is a measure of how far Russia has risen in world esteem largely through its magnificent feats of arms and its diplomacy."[20]

The Russians, obviously, were already planning for the postwar world, but American foreign policy had not kept pace. As the warm breezes of spring returned to the nation, the end of the war did not seem to be far away. Russians were moving into eastern Europe, and the Western Allies were obviously preparing to land in France. In America, opinion makers and the attentive public were wondering more persistently than ever whether the United States had a concrete, workable foreign policy for the remainder of this difficult war and the beginning of what promised to be a difficult peace.

"What is America's foreign policy, anyway?" thousands of opinion makers asked. Responding to the clamor in his usual unimaginative way, Secretary of State Hull, on 21 March, issued a seventeen-point rehash of his previous statements and speeches. President Roosevelt did no better. "The United Nations are fighting to make a world in which tyranny and aggression cannot exist," Roosevelt told the reporters who had anxiously gathered in the White House four days later to hear details of America's foreign policy; "a world based upon freedom, equality and justice; a world in which all persons, regardless of race, creed or color may live in peace, honor and dignity."[21]

After disappointing the reporters, the president insulted them, as he had done so often during the war. He accused them of wandering around asking bellhops if the United States had a foreign policy, and he assured them that they could stop looking, because he was giving it to them. He resumed reading his statement, which ended with an urgent "call upon the free peoples of Europe and Asia temporarily to open their frontiers to all victims of oppression." Did this mean, a reporter asked, that America would open its doors to these predominantly Jewish refugees? Roosevelt replied that the United States had no policy on this matter as yet. American foreign policy, *Time* said in a pithy statement that summarized what many were saying, was "long on ideals, short on plans."[22]

Unfortunately, the plans that many opinion makers outside of government were advocating in 1944 were also long on ideals. Former Undersecretary of State Sumner Welles, for example, said in a widely circulated speech in New York City on 18 May that the United States should seek to implement its ideas on international organization immediately rather than waiting until the end of the war. Welles argued that such nations as Brazil, Mexico, Norway, and the Netherlands should have a say in plans for the reconstruction of France, Italy, and eastern Europe.[23]

There was an indisputable tendency among even the most sophisticated advocates of international organization such as Welles to consider it a panacea for solving the world's outstanding problems. In the 18 May speech, for example, Welles did not bother to suggest how the addition of most of the remainder of the world's nations would facilitate working out complicated settlements which would be satisfactory to Russia, the Western powers, and the nations involved, much less to Brazil and Norway. Moreover, Welles and other knowledgeable internationalists who had been in the administration should have known that neither Roosevelt, Churchill, nor Stalin was expecting a strong international organization to develop after the war. And whatever strength it had would have to result more from direct consultation among the Big Three than from permitting Mexico, Norway, and other small nations to determine what the Big Three and the parties involved should do in any given situation.

꒰∗☜✿☞∗꒱ The debate that developed on Poland makes this point clear. If anybody in the entire world had a solution to the Polish problem that promised to satisfy both the Polish government-in-exile and the Russian government, he kept it a secret throughout the war. The differences between the Soviets and the conservative, anti-Russian London Poles seemed so irreconcilable that they should have shaken the faith of those optimists who believed that all disagreements could be worked out.

However, most American opinion makers blithely hoped and expected that the Soviet government and the London Poles would achieve a means of coexistence before the end of the war. This attitude, based on the belief that the two governments would have to compromise their differences, persisted even after Russia broke diplomatic contact with the Polish leaders in London on 26 April 1943. Strangely, it persisted even after Russia set up a rival, leftist Polish government in Lublin on 21 July 1944.

What did the break with the London Poles mean? What did Stalin want? After the war such questions tended to go unanswered; during the war most of them were at least partially answered. Just after the break, two major questions were posed to the Soviet leader by the Moscow correspondents of the *London Times* and the *New York Times*. "Does the Government of the U.S.S.R. desire to see a strong and independent Poland after the defeat of Hitlerite Germany?" the reporters inquired. "Unquestionably, it does," Stalin replied. "On what fundamentals is it your opinion that relations between Poland and the U.S.S.R. should be based after the war?" the reporters asked. "Upon the fundamentals of solid good neighborly relations and mutual respect," Stalin responded, "or should the Polish people so desire, upon the fundamentals of an alliance providing for mutual assistance against the Germans as the chief enemies of the Soviet Union and Poland."[24]

Both the questions and the answers were extremely general, and Stalin gave no indication that he would be willing to accept any sort of anti-Russian regime in Warsaw; but American writers seized upon the exchange as they had seized upon Stalin's speech of 6 November 1942. The theme of the discussion of postwar Russo-Polish relations in two dozen books published during 1943 and 1944 was that Stalin's "strong and independent Poland" would be a Poland which Americans—and perhaps even the London Poles—could accept.

But what else could Stalin have said that might not have endangered Allied wartime unity? Moreover, the answer to the second question implied strongly that his concept of postwar Poland was that of a nation which could not threaten Russian security either singly or in combination with Germany or other powers. And the break with the London Poles indicated clearly that this virulently anti-Russian group was not what Stalin had in mind.

To comprehend Stalin's position, Americans did not have to follow the loud demands of the London Poles that all the lands Poland had taken from Russia at the time of the Russian Revolution be returned to them. They could simply think about the vicious anti-Russian campaign which some Poles in America were conducting even as Russia was bearing the brunt of Hitler's attack. "Soviet Russia is morally and deeply responsible to the people of the entire world for the spread of this war," *Nowy Swiat*, a New York paper reaching sixty thousand Polish-Americans asserted just after Pearl Harbor. "One must not tell the Poles, French, Turks, Letts, Lithuanians, Hungarians, Serbs, 'Fight!' " the same journal asserted on 21 March 1942, "because when Hitler is conquered with your help, you will be given over to the 'benevolent' care of Stalin."[25] The author of these words, which were very similar to what Hitler and Goebbels were telling conquered Europeans, was Ignacy Matuszewski, director of the Pulaski Foundation in Washington. The essentially pro-German organization which systematically spread his and similar views among Polish-Americans was the National Committee of Americans of Polish Descent.

Such sentiments were opposed by many prominent Polish-Americans, notably among professionals and labor leaders. "We appeal to Americans of Polish descent to detach themselves from the poisonous propaganda of the National Committee of Americans of Polish Descent and its supporters, because their activities are beneficial only to the enemies of the United States and Poland," a declaration of 1 July 1943 signed by Oskar Lange of the University of Chicago and other leading Polish-Americans stated. "We call upon them to give complete support to the efforts of President Roosevelt and the American Government, because they are striving to win the war and to secure the peace."[26]

Another large group of Polish-Americans meeting in Detroit declared on 7 November 1943 that the "present Polish Government is a prisoner of reaction."[27] Exactly a month later the president of Milwaukee's American Polish Trade Union Council sent a statement to President Roosevelt and Secretary of State Hull praising their achievements at the recent conferences with Russia and Britain,[28] and there was also a mass meeting attended by fifteen hundred Polish-Americans in New York City later that month to demonstrate friendship for Russia.[29]

Most opinion makers were as uncertain as Polish-Americans were divided on the question of support for the London Poles. The opinion makers hoped that Stalin would settle his differences with the London Poles, but they were unsure of how they would react if he did not. This did not apply to most Roman Catholic opinion makers, who tended to criticize the Russians for anything they did or might do relative to their predominantly Catholic neighbor, but most others sought to disguise the unpleasant fact that they had no real solution to the dispute.

Faced with these dilemmas, some generally cosmopolitan organs like the *Washington Post* resorted to dubious assertions based on unrevealed sources. "The Polish government-in-exile is, in the opinion of those best qualified to know, as representative of the Polish people as any government-in-exile can be," the *Post* editorialized on 24 November 1943.[30] The

editorialist who wrote these words presumably was the one "best qualified to know" in this case.

Others like the Columbia sociologist Robert Morrison MacIver
engaged in sweeping geopolitical reasoning aimed at solving the entire
problem in one redrawing of the map. "Estonia and Latvia should be
restored to Russia which badly needs an outlet on the Baltic," MacIver
wrote in 1943 in *Towards an Abiding Peace*. "Lithuania should become a
province of Poland, with which it was in former days conjoined. This
territory, including the Memel area, would give Poland in turn an appropriate access to the sea and serve as compensation for the loss of the war-
breeding Polish Corridor."[31]

Still others like the *New York Herald Tribune*, not to mention the
ultraconservative press, could offer little more to the problem's solution
than vague threats. "If Russian publicists imagine that whatever Russia
chooses to do in the Baltic states and Poland will meet with the enthusiastic applause of a 'majority' of Americans," the *Herald Tribune* warned on
6 January 1944, "then they are laboring under a delusion quite as dangerous as that which seems to afflict the Poles."[32]

Finally, a few opinion makers like the journalist Irving Brant stressed
the seeming intractability of the problem. Brant noted that the dispute
involved the "triple complication of a boundary dispute between two
countries militarily allied with each other, politically hostile to each other,
and disputing over the nationality of the peoples involved."[33]

In fact, the dispute involved even more: it involved communists
versus economic feudalists, atheists versus Catholics, Russian versus
Polish ethnicity, and a pregnable border which throughout modern history each side had been willing to cross to conquer territory and people
on the other side. It is not surprising that the only "answer" liberal
Americans could seriously offer was "international organization," which
was supposed to solve this as well as all other outstanding questions.

The persistence of the Polish problem probably did more than
anything else to dampen the enthusiasm which had greeted the Moscow
and Teheran communiqués. Before the ink was dry on these documents,
the London Poles were loudly insisting that Poland must regain its
prewar borders. Most American newspapers supported Russia's insistence on something like the Curzon Line as the postwar boundary,[34] but
they did not like Russia's refusal late in January 1944 to agree to American
mediation of the Russo-Polish dispute.

"The reaction to all this—the whole Russo-Polish affair—is now
mounting to the point where we can no longer pass it over as one of those
differences of opinion bound to arise, causing temporary friction but sure
to be settled to the satisfaction of everyone if we'll all just be patient,"

commentator Chet Huntley told West Coast listeners on CBS on 15 February 1944. "We can no longer ignore it, no longer turn our backs on it. By arguing that it doesn't concern us, we're taking a long step backward toward the days of isolationism."[35]

By swinging all the way from ill-considered isolationism to the belief that America's vital interests were everywhere, Americans like Huntley were drifting from the attitudes which had made World War II possible to the attitudes which would help to bring not accommodation but the Cold War. Only a few perceptive thinkers like Walter Lippmann and Carl Becker sensed the development of this dangerous swing from one extreme in America's approach to the world to the opposite extreme. Most Americans simply did not have any serious forebodings about international politics in the postwar world. They not only had no idea what a cold war was, but they also did not expect serious tensions to develop with Russia or any of our other allies. To those who did fear such a tragic development, it was the Polish imbroglio that was primarily responsible for their fears.

👁️‍🗨️ If one were Polish-American or particularly worried about possible Russian power in Europe, he might have been concerned about the Russo–Polish dispute during World War II. But if he were a cosmopolitan businessman or labor leader interested in maintaining prosperity after war orders had subsided, he probably thought more about doing business with Russia after the war than about whether Poles and Russians could get along. After the experience of depression in the preceding dozen years of peace, businessmen had to think seriously about how depression was to be averted after the war. For if millions of Americans lost their jobs again, the entire structure of American capitalism might well collapse.

The man whose ideas on this subject had the greatest impact early in the war was one of the nations's most successful businessmen during the depression as well as a leading opinion maker, Henry Luce. Early in 1941 and again a year later Luce wrote articles in his most widely circulated journal, *Life*, about the coming "American Century." The first article, "The American Century," is better known; but the second, "America's War and America's Peace," gave a more penetrating presentation of Luce's views.

In both articles, this exemplary presidential Republican took a much broader view than would have been dictated by purely pecuniary considerations, and in fact he did not discuss the financial implications of his ideas in any detail. But his world order provided the setting for more specific thinking about America's international capitalism after the war, and it therefore merits close consideration.

"It is a war against the cleavage of mankind into Right and Left which, tearing Europe asunder, made Hitler's victories possible," Luce began in his 1942 article. Having started auspiciously with one of the better summations of American war aims, Luce plunged into the heart of his argument. Those who accepted his premises must have found his logic impeccable as he proceeded.

> Because America alone among the nations of the earth was founded on ideas which transcend class and caste and racial and occupational differences, America alone can provide the pattern for the future. Because America stands for a system wherein many groups, however diverse, are united under a system of laws and faiths that enables them to live peacefully together, American experience is the key to the future. . . . Only when Americans see the whole war as America's war, and the whole peace as essentially America's peace, only then will they give what it will take—in resourcefulness, in initiative, in risk and courage—to win the war and the peace. . . . America must be the elder brother of the nations in the brotherhood of man.[36]

The most prominent person to take issue with Luce's premises was Henry Wallace. The vice-president's most famous utterance was his statement on 8 May 1942 that the ten decades to come would be not the "American century" but rather "the century of the common man." Wallace was much more convinced than Luce that America had not lived up to her ideals, and that until she did she did not deserve to be the standard for the world. Wallace also feared that the "elder brother" might exploit the "younger brothers" in the family of nations. The vice-president's ideal was a combination of America's political and individual democracy with Russia's economic and ethnic democracy.[37]

To put it mildly, Luce and other American businessmen were less than enthusiastic about Russia's form of socialism. But throughout the war they were enthusiastic about the business they were doing with Russia through lend-lease and about the even greater business they hoped to do with her after the war was over. Surely this was a major reason why leading business men, who were overwhelmingly conservative cosmopolitans, were so friendly toward Russia during the war.

In 1941 almost all American businessmen still feared Russia. In an important speech in Detroit on 23 September, J.O. Downey, a personal assistant to the chairman of the board of General Motors, asserted that there would be hope for the postwar world "if Russia can be purged of Communism."[38] But Russia's successes against the Nazis, combined with evidence that she was growing more conservative and the general climate of goodwill toward her, purged most cosmopolitan businessmen of their worst fears about her.

By the fall of 1942 industrialist Thomas A. Morgan could argue, as did many others, that "the United States has a great deal to gain by proper trade relations with Russia and that Russia, on the other hand, has a great deal to gain by having an opportunity to carry on business with us in a normal manner."[39] Senator Josiah W. Bailey of North Carolina, who had never been one of Russia's best friends in the United States, entered Morgan's speech into the *Congressional Record*. The fact that Bailey and many others were contemplating trade with Russia after the war may well have been one reason why they did not criticize Russia publicly during the war.

By the fall of 1943, Luce's dream of an open world dominated by American capital was apparently becoming a reality. The Axis were clearly on the road to defeat, and all other major powers except the United States seemed to have been weakened substantially by the ordeal of total war. Russia in particular would need much foreign aid to effect speedy recovery and satisfy the demands of her citizens for consumer goods. "Russia's respect for American industrial technique and business methods is extremely high," Raymond Moley reported in his column in *Newsweek* on 18 October 1943. He went on:

> Her needs, after the war, will be enormous. The building of her industry will require American goods, built here by American labor, and the past record indicates that payments for these goods will be scrupulously maintained. The objection that by such trade we shall be creating a great competitor living under an alien system can be dismissed. Russia will build her own economic system in any event, and hesitation on our part because of political differences will merely hand over this trade to other countries.[40]

Actually, nobody was objecting openly to the prospect of lucrative large-scale trade with Russia after the war. The 1943 Congress of American Soviet Friendship featured a session at which leading businessmen verbally celebrated Russian-American friendship. "The traditional friendship between the American and Russian peoples, marred for a while by misunderstanding, has reasserted itself in a dramatic manner during these years of heroic self-sacrificing struggle against a common enemy," the general manager of the Esseness Trading Company observed in a typical comment which led to another: "Welded in the crucible of war, the continued cooperation between our country and the Soviet Union will be a potent force in reconstructing the world on a foundation of peace, prosperity and international good will."[41]

Averell Harriman thought that America's desire to help Russia after the war reflected its humanitarianism. But it was humanitarianism tempered by self-interest, and Harriman did not hesitate to juxtapose the two seemingly contradictory impulses in consecutive sentences: "The American people have the greatest sympathy for the Russian people, who have suffered so much, and it is in their hearts to attempt to be of the greatest assistance. We will have plants to produce machinery and equipment needed by the Soviet Union and in so doing we will help our own people to convert from war to peace."[42] "Russia is not a competitor of America," another leading administration official, Donald Nelson, contended in *Collier's* early in 1944, "but she can develop into an excellent source of business for America."[43]

Economist Harland Allen was even more convinced that America's prosperity—yes, even the "future of the private-enterprise system"—rested with Russia. Allen argued that America's "pent-up domestic demand" would "not suffice indefinitely." Latin America, Europe, and the Far East would be too poor to pay for huge quantities of American goods. That left Russia, "the great hope for sustained post-war volume and employment." Allen hailed Russia as *"the largest single market ever known,"*[44] which to many Americans was the ultimate compliment one could bestow upon a foreign country.

Two of the nation's premier business periodicals played heavily on this same theme. At the end of 1943, *Business Week*'s lead editorial was entitled "Stalin's Challenge to American Business." In addition to stressing the possibilities of massive penetration of the Russian market, the editors of *Business Week* also urged that the United States put east Europeans to work lest Russia use them herself. "Russia has a huge, ready-made rehabilitation project on which it will be natural to employ thousands of these workers if their own governments cannot find jobs for them," the editors warned and added, "First glimpses of Russia's dramatic postwar plans provide a measure of the imagination and the boldness which the Anglo-American nations must show if they are to meet this economic challenge."[45]

Nation's Business featured several articles on Russia's economy by Junius B. Wood during 1944 and capped its year with an article on Russia by Eric Johnston, the buoyant president of the United States Chamber of Commerce, who had just returned from a well-publicized trip to Russia on behalf of American business. "Many people cannot understand that the Soviet Union is not a turmoil of talk, inefficiency and incomplete plans," Wood wrote in March.[46] The corollary to this, Wood's basic point, was best stated in the July issue: "The Red army, only one part of the Soviet system, symbolizes the changes which have come in Russia. The war will end and armies will cease to hold world attention, but the foresighted manufacturers, the exporters and the businessmen of other countries must be prepared to meet the Soviet Union of the future."[47] Johnston wrote that during his three-hour meeting with Stalin, the marshal told him that Russia "looks forward to a continuing flow of supplies for postwar replacement, reconstruction and expansion." The Russian people "venerate the United States," Johnston thought, "not because of its system of government about which they know so little—but because it is the greatest industrial nation in the world."[48]

The activist president of the Chamber of Commerce naturally preferred America's "democracy" to Russia's "communism," but he was careful not to criticize the economic system with which America might trade so profitably. "They call that system State Socialism," Johnston wrote, adding, "How it is defined is no concern of ours, but how it works concerns us vitally, because, in the postwar world, Russia is going to turn to the United States for the multitude of things she will need not only to rebuild her war-torn economy but to give her people the higher standard of living she has been promising them for 20 years."[49]

Although no one stressed the point, Russia was to benefit from American capital by becoming essentially an economic appendage of the United States. Russia was to provide raw materials like manganese, chromite, platinum, lumber, and fur to American industry and receive in return expensive manufactured goods like machine tools, mining and agricultural machinery, and electrical and transportation equipment.[50] The businessmen and economists who dreamed of huge profits and full employment for Americans grounded on billions of dollars in trade with and investment in Russia apparently did not consider the possibility that Soviet leaders might prefer slower growth based on economic independence instead of more rapid development based on dependence on American capitalists.

Meanwhile, a significant group of intellectuals had begun to wrestle with some of the fundamental problems of current and future Soviet-American relations. Fortunately, there is no need here to present a general definition of intellectual and intellectuals, for our concern is limited to the relationship between public opinion and foreign policy. Stated simply, most intellectuals in the field of foreign affairs who get their views circulated widely are those who write books.

Almost all of the books we shall be discussing never made those indices of broad public circulation, the best-seller lists. But that was not too important because many of them were surely read by opinion makers such as Raymond Clapper, Raymond Gram Swing, Henry Wallace, and Arthur Vandenberg. And what these and other influential men were reading and thinking between 1942 and 1945 had an indisputable effect upon both the opinion–circulating and the decision-making processes in America during the war.

It is apparent in retrospect that three basic approaches dominated intellectual discussion of Russia's role in the postwar world. Many writers joined fellow liberals and internationalists such as Henry Wallace in singleminded praise of everything Russian. Others, more conservative and nationalistic in outlook, liked neither Russia's social system nor her rapidly growing power in world affairs and said so subtly, as the spirit of the time required. Still other intellectuals discussed probable postwar realities without excessive sympathy for either the liberals' ideal of an increasingly socialistic world patterned on Russian precedents or the conservatives' ideal of a world ordered by American capital. Those liberals and conservatives whose social ideals lent basic structure to their arguments may be called idealists; those in the third group may be called realists. The labels are not intended to suggest unanimity of outlook within each group but simply to suggest a basic similarity in approach to the question of Russia's place in the postwar world.

During World War II, the liberal idealists probably wrote as many books on contemporary affairs and future problems as the conservative idealists and the realists combined. Dozens of works each year after 1941 extolled continued cooperation among the Allies as the only path to lasting peace, proclaimed that a powerful international organization alone could ensure such cooperation, and warned that conservatives and isolationists in America and Britain might seek to block the path to peace as they allegedly had done after World War I.

Robert A. Divine has ably demonstrated that liberals spent a remarkable amount of time and energy drawing up blueprints for international organization and presenting them to the American people.[51] Proportionately, they spent very little effort on the subject of Russia's postwar intentions, which to them seemed to offer no serious threat to the realization of their aims. Was not Russia a progressive nation which stood for peace? And had it not proved during the past decade that it would collaborate with the Western democracies through international organization and by other means to prevent aggression?

Scores of liberal writers were careful during World War II not to say anything against Russia. They often avoided the entire subject of Russo-Polish relations, Russia's annexation of the Baltic states, and potentially disturbing questions about the postwar world. "No territorial problem has been posed by the Soviet Union," Henry C. Cassidy, the Associated Press correspondent in Moscow, wrote in 1943.[52] Like so many of the idealists, both liberal and conservative, Cassidy offered a sweeping, internally inconsistent generalization to make his point about postwar Russia: "I should say victorious post-war Soviet Russia would be socialistic, but not internationally revolutionary; atheistic, but not violently anti-religious; autocratic, but not anti–democratic."[53]

Apart from soothing generalizations about the apparent emergence of a less revolutionary social order within Russia, liberal idealists expounded upon the tenet which they considered tantamount to proof of Russia's continued good behavior after the war. This tenet was that Russia required peace for internal reconstruction. "Mainly Russia wants her own land back and protection against invasion," journalist Walter Graebner wrote in *Round Trip to Russia*. "Then she wants to get back on her feet, reconstruct her country, and catch up in every way with all the other countries in the world."[54] "After the victory of the United Nations," journalist Bernard Newman argued, "Russia, whether victorious in her own right or prostrate, must be preoccupied again with internal reconstruction. This task, in the future as in the past, will continue to have a sobering effect."[55] Hiram Motherwell, a prominent writer and lecturer, judged that Russia would be strong militarily after the war, but he also believed that "Russia will have little urge to meddle in the internal politics of postwar Europe." Compared with the urgent and staggering task of reconstruction, Motherwell thought, "the gratification of adding a few thousand square inches of map to a territory already comprising a sixth of the land surface of the globe is trivial."[56] And Basil Mathews, a British-born writer living in Vancouver, ridiculed the fear of conservatives that Russia might try to communize Europe by force. "The idea that within ten or even twenty years Russia would have the power, even if she had the will, to go out on the adventure of Bolshevizing Europe," Mathews wrote, "is surely 'such stuff as dreams are made of'; indeed, it is 'the baseless fabric' not of a vision but of a nightmare."[57]

Finally, many liberal idealists expressed much more concern about possible domestic sources of American and British foreign policy than they did about Russia's intentions. Historian Denna F. Fleming, for example, was deeply concerned about the "prime danger that American conservatives and British Tories will team together, or take alternate roles in playing power politics against Russia through the length and breadth of Europe."[58] As justification for his fear, Fleming said that the administration had "already solemnly promised Franco that we will not use even a suspicion of force to upset the cruel tyranny which the three great democracies helped him to set up over the Spanish people."[59] Fleming pleaded for support to keep the conservatives from wrecking the peace: "Russia did her level best to co-operate with the British and French for five years to prevent this war from breaking out, but they would not co-operate. If the Soviets are willing to try again, the result must be different."[60]

Conservative idealists started from starkly different premises and reached starkly different conclusions from those of the liberal intellectuals. The conservatives thought that the New Deal had been a step in the wrong direction; the liberals believed the reverse. The liberals thought that some fairly basic aspects of the Soviet experiment deserved to be emulated; a few years earlier the conservatives had hoped that these same social and economic developments would be destroyed. The liberals looked forward to increased public power and a further leveling of status and income in America and the world; the conservatives hoped for a resurgent international capitalism centered in Wall Street. And on the question of Russia's role in the postwar world, the liberals implied strongly that America should seek accommodation with Russia; the conservatives contended that Russia should be expected to seek accommodation with the United States. The conservatives began to develop this approach shortly after America joined the war.

Henry Luce's second American century article and Herbert Hoover's and Hugh Gibson's *The Problems of Lasting Peace*, both of which were published in the first half of 1942, marked the advent of the conservative idealistic position.[61] Neither of these works singled out Russia for special attention, but both postulated the necessity for Anglo-American moral, political, and economic leadership throughout the world after the war. In 1942, with Russia's very survival as a nation in doubt, there was little reason to expect that the Russians would soon be able to challenge Anglo-American hegemony.

Intellectuals on the Right also showed relatively little concern about Russian power in 1943. This was the height of the era of good feelings toward Russia, the year in which one offered only guarded criticisms of possible Soviet intentions. Yet the desire for Russian accommodation to the West existed even then. "We may hope that, perhaps by means and processes we cannot now foresee," William Henry Chamberlin wrote in his book of that year, "there will emerge, out of the present ordeal of humanity, in which the Russian people have played a heroic part, a Free Russia, an integral and inseparable part of the Free World."[62]

In the sobered atmosphere of 1944, no conservative idealist reiterated Chamberlin's exuberant hope. By then these intellectuals, with the exception of Joseph M. Jones, would have been satisfied if Russia accepted American economic and political leadership after the war. Jones, whose book, *A Modern Foreign Policy for the United States*, was derived from a series of well-publicized articles in *Fortune* in 1943, argued that American foreign policy should be "based upon, protect, and extend the principle of freedom in the world."[63] He elaborated in regard to Russia and China:

> Intervention in the Soviet Union and China to assure the conditions of freedom is inconceivable. At this point we must frankly compromise principle with expediency. But such a compromise in part of the world in the interests of peace, and in the interests of freedom elsewhere, would seem to be an advance

upon our policy in the past of merely giving lip service to principle and compromising it in all parts of the world. Moreover, in making this compromise, we should make fully and continuously known to the Soviet Union and China that the principle of freedom is at our masthead, and that a successful job of order-keeping in the world, in which they have as great a stake as we, is possible only if it is based upon the protection and extension of freedom.[64]

Such sentiments obviously boded ill for an uncontested maintenance of Soviet influence in the occupied countries of eastern Europe after the war. But Jones was talking about more than eastern Europe; he was talking about Russia as well, and he thought that "we should work with the Soviet Union on the assumption that the conditions of freedom will develop there."[65]

What form would the conservative idealistic argument take when carried to its logical conclusion? In *An American Peace*, published in 1944, *New York Times* managing editor Neil MacNeil provided an answer. "Russia's postwar policies gravely concern the rest of the world," MacNeil wrote. "Without her continuing collaboration with the other United Nations a just peace is impossible, and even if an expedient one were arranged it could have little hope of survival. . . . Russia's great need is security," MacNeil observed, and he left no doubt that he thought she should have it only if she accepted the leadership of the capitalistic powers.[66]

If she is willing to accept her security as part of world security, she can have it. If she insists on making her own security at the cost of the rights and interests of other peoples, she will face a hostile world instead. We shall have a good chance of realizing the ideal of a world of free and prosperous peoples in our time, provided Russia co-operates in making that world. But if she decides to go her own way she will force the other powers into coalitions to counter-balance her influence, which must inevitably lead to tension and war.[67]

MacNeil argued that advantages would accrue to Russia as a result of her voluntary acceptance of Western leadership, to which she probably would have to yield whether she liked it or not. Full collaboration with the West, MacNeil pointed out, would give Russia "a security from attack that hitherto she has not known." No longer would there exist any "basis for the Russian dread of encirclement by the capitalistic nations and fear of destruction by them would vanish abruptly."[68] "Both the United States and the world need a peace based on American principles— a Pax Americana," MacNeil concluded. "We should insist on an American peace. We should accept nothing less."[69]

The realists rejected the premises and conclusions of both the liberal and conservative idealists. To the liberals they said that capitalism and nationalism would continue to be powerful forces in the postwar world. To the conservatives they suggested that Russia would continue to be communist and that it would exert substantially more influence outside of its borders than it had before the war. The key to a workable peace, the realists predicted, would be respect by each of the two emerging "superpowers"—Russia and the United States—for the fundamental national interests of the other. What is remarkable, given the vagaries of history and the scope of the conflict that developed between the United States and Russia after the war, is that all of the leading realists foresaw not only the probable preconditions of amicable relations between the two nations, but also the manner in which the wartime allies could well become bitter enemies.

Although there were some realists among journalists and other groups throughout the nation, the foremost ones had been trained as scholars. David Dallin and Joachim Joesten were recognized experts on Russia; Carl Becker taught history at Cornell University, and William T. R. Fox taught political science at Yale; and Walter Lippmann was a distinguished publicist and scholar before becoming a syndicated columnist.

Even the casual reader of Dallin's work of 1943, *Russia and Postwar Europe*, would have grasped its theme, for it was restated cogently throughout the book. "The Soviet Government sees the guarantee of its security in the widening of its influence over the multinational territory along its western borders," Dallin said at one point.[70] "The Soviet Government has not the least faith in the durability of postwar alliances, in assurances of friendship, or in pacts of collective security," he argued even more compellingly at another point, guiding the reader through Russia's experience with such diplomatic devices during the 1930s. "For this reason it seeks, and will seek even more as time goes on, to ensure its interests by means of widening its sphere of influence in Europe, in the territory which separates Russia from Germany and Italy."[71] Polish-American readers in particular could take no comfort from Dallin's concise analysis. As he summarized that portion of his argument which dealt with Poland: "A Soviet security sphere would include Poland as its most essential component part."[72]

If anyone accurately foresaw the preconditions of cold war, it was Dallin. As shown in the preceding paragraphs, he judged that Russia would insist upon the establishment of a security sphere in eastern Europe. His discussion of the possible consequences of this Russian step was fascinating and prophetic:

> It is hardly probable that Russia's chief allies would comply with her desires for a considerable expansion in any form whatever. But it is another paradox that the consequences of Soviet expansion would in both cases be almost the same, i.e., whether it is achieved with or without the consent of the powers. In both cases the world press would be full of alarming reports from every corner of the

security sphere, the diplomacy of the small countries would be working without let-up, air forces would be concentrated in the Anglo-American sphere of Europe.

This would be the "encirclement" which Soviet Russia has always feared more than anything else. This time the encirclement might involve an Anglo-German Alliance, the most dangerous combination Russia could face. This process of encirclement is certain to take place after Soviet Russia crosses the Vistula, enters the Balkans, and moves up to the Mediterranean. Neither arguments nor appeals nor pacifism will be able to check the development of this conflict.[73]

"Any attempt to get at the roots of the present peace problem must start with the realization that Europe, in particular Central Europe, today is to all intents and purposes a vacuum," Joesten wrote in his work *What Russia Wants* in 1944. "There is no established political, economic, or social order and no legitimate authority anywhere outside of the neutral enclaves of Sweden and Switzerland."[74] One implication of this fact, he thought, was that this vacuum would not remain. Another was that Russia, "the predominant power on the European continent," would be the only country that really could be expected to fill it.[75]

Joesten also argued that Russia was as entitled to fill the vacuum as Britain was to have friendly governments in western Europe and the United States was to oversee the Carribbean.

Every country is deeply concerned with the political outlook and mentality of its neighbors; every great power sees to it that its smaller neighbors do not become tools of its potential enemies. Would the United States look on while a Nazi dictatorship established itself in Canada or Mexico? Would it tolerate a revolutionary hotbed in Cuba or the Bahamas? In the same way we cannot expect a triumphant Soviet Russia to tolerate in her dooryard reactionary monarchies, semi-Fascist republics, or clerico-feudal autocracies. It is self-evident that she will seek to surround herself with a belt of bordering states that are, if not like-minded, at least sympathetic and cooperative. And is she not entitled, after the harrowing experiences of the past, to seek security in friendly surroundings?[76]

In 1944 Carl L. Becker was near the end of one of the most distinguished careers in modern historical scholarship. He had made noteworthy contributions to American history, European history, and historiography; and his stylistic talents were probably unsurpassed in modern nonfiction prose. Becker clearly was disturbed about the course of the debate over the postwar world. He heard liberals insisting that a powerful universal organization was the only hope for peace and conservatives contending that American hegemony was the only path to postwar stability, and he disliked both arguments. His book *How New Will the Better World Be?* was addressed to both sides.

"After the war is over," Becker informed the internationalists, "nationalism, whatever its defects, will remain for any foreseeable future what it has been for a long time past—the strongest political force in the modern world; and this force will be exerted in the form of many sovereign independent states."[77] "Let us not be hypnotized and befuddled by words," Becker told the nationalists who had been denying that American hegemony could possibly be imperialistic. "Let us say that Great Britain, Russia, China, and the United States are great imperial states, since that is what in fact they are. Let us admit, if it eases anyone's conscience, that they are 'imperialistic' states."[78] "The present moment," Becker added caustically, "is indeed a singularly inopportune time for the people of the United States, who cannot even repeal a poll tax designed to deprive Negroes of their rights as citizens, to cherish tender scruples about the purity of British imperialism."[79]

Chapter 4 was entitled "Can We Abolish Power Politics and End Imperialism?" Becker's answer for the foreseeable future was a convincing no. If not, what would constitute the basis of a European settlement all sides could live with? Britain's and America's basic requirements in Europe, Becker thought, "will be naval ascendancy in the Atlantic, a strong France, the restoration of Belgium, Holland, and the conquered Scandinavian countries, the destruction of Nazi power and the establishment in Germany and Italy of governments that are democratic in some sense of the term, or at all events that bear no resemblance to the Fascist or Nazi systems." Becker could find "no reason to suppose" that such a settlement would "run counter to the national interest of Russia," for "Russia is not directly interested in the Atlantic Community or the settlement of western Europe."[80]

And what about Russia's basic requirements? In a passage that merited careful attention then as now, Becker made it clear that an intelligent, noncommunist American of 1944 could comprehend the reasons for Russia's demands and could argue intelligently that they must be accepted if true peace among the great powers were to follow the war.

The primary interest of Russia in the European settlement arises from the fact that her western frontier, from the Baltic to the Black Sea, brings her into intimate relations with Poland, Czechoslovakia, Hungary, the Balkan states, and Germany. In the region of border states east of Germany, Russia has a major interest which the countries of the Atlantic Community do not share. Stalin has already made this clear by stating that Russia will retain certain parts of Poland and certain other strategic territories taken by Russia in 1939. He has also stated that he will oppose the creation of any federation of the border and Balkan states under Polish leadership. Something like eighty per cent of the people of these border and Balkan countries are peasant farmers. They are on the whole bitterly hostile to the Fascist or semi-Fascist governments supported by the upper classes and too often maintained only by Quisling adventurers with German or Italian backing. They are strongly in favor of governments by and for the farmers—

governments which, although not Communist, would not be hostile to Soviet Russia. Stalin will certainly be in favor of such governments, and will certainly be opposed to any attempt, on the part of Great Britain and the United States, to set up governments or federations of goverments, on the Russian frontier that are designed, or seem to him to be designed, to serve as a European barrier against Russian influence or the spread of Russian political ideas. It would be unwise, and futile besides, for Great Britain and the United States to make any such attempt, or otherwise to antagonize Russia in the settlement of eastern Europe, where Russia has the major interest, has made the major sacrifices, and will in any case have the major power.[81]

It is no slight to William T. R. Fox's book, *The Super-Powers*, to give it much less attention, because the views it expounded were very similar to Becker's. Fox warned the internationalists that they would never achieve the goal of world order "by ignoring the differences between the elephants and the squirrels of international politics."[82] The author also had a direct warning for those who dreamed of universal American hegemony. "Britain and America," Fox insisted, "can do no more by direct action to prevent the Soviet Union from being its own judge as to what constitutes a friendly, anti-fascist regime in Eastern Europe than Britain or the Soviet Union could prevent the United States from making a fresh landing of marines in Nicaragua."[83]

The last word in this chapter belongs to Walter Lippmann, whose books, articles, and syndicated columns circulated his ideas much more broadly than Becker's and Fox's books were able to circulate theirs. And because Lippmann's ideas were similar to theirs, the opinion maker or ordinary citizen who wanted to be reasonably well prepared for the postwar world needed only to have followed his columns or to have absorbed the major points of his book, *U.S. War Aims*, published in 1944.

"More than upon anything else," Lippmann wrote, "the outcome depends upon the relations between the Soviet Union and the United States." That thought had become a truism by this time, but how satisfactory relations between the two nations were to be maintained most definitely had not been explained to the public. Lippmann proposed a regional system of security based on the preeminence of a great power in each part of the world. "Russia and America can have peace if they use their alliances to stabilize the foreign policy of their allies," Lippmann prophesied. "They will have war if either of them reaches out for allies within the orbit of the other, and if either of them seeks to incorporate Germany or Japan within its own strategical system."[84] Lippmann proceeded to illustrate what his regional system would mean in practice.

Under the regional principle which I am advocating, it would be held an overt act of aggression for any state to reach out beyond its own strategical orbit for alliance with a state in another orbit. . . . No one questions our alliances with Canada and Mexico. But if Mexico made an alliance with the Soviet Union, everyone would know at once that the peace was troubled. If we made an alliance with Iran or with Romania, all the world would have every right to think the worst of our intentions.[85]

The crucial concern of the United States in the postwar world, Lippmann contended, was "maintaining and perfecting the Atlantic Community." And just as the United States and Britain had clear rights in the Atlantic community, so Russia had the right, under the new distribution of power that was emerging from the war, to maintain and perfect its new community in eastern Europe. Accordingly, Lippmann urged that the United States "recognize as valid and proper the strategic system of the Russian Orbit, as including within it the states east of Germany and west of the Soviet Union."[86]

Walter Lippmann was an upper-class American whose home news-paper was the *New York Herald Tribune*, the most representative organ of America's cosmopolitan upper class. Lippmann was no admirer of communism as an economic system or of Joseph Stalin as a political leader. But Lippmann's views on the peace were very similar to Stalin's; more significantly, they also coincided basically with Winston Churchill's. But what were Franklin Roosevelt's? Lippmann and other Americans could only hope that they would find out during the country's first wartime presidential election in exactly eighty years.

Ominous Drift:
The Election of 1944, Yalta, and Beyond

Presidential politics never depart entirely from the consciousness of Americans. No sooner are the ballots tabulated in an election than
Americans of all levels of political sophistication begin to think and talk
about the next presidential contest. The issues and candidates in the
midterm congressional and gubernatorial campaigns briefly divert attention from presidential politics, but the results of these campaigns heighten
interest in the next presidential contest to a new level by indicating
which party, which issues, and which candidates are in favor.

Unfortunately, as Robert A. Divine has noted in a recent study of
the three presidential elections in the 1940s, American fascination with
presidential politics has not resulted in anything approaching an adequate
elucidation of foreign-policy issues. "Ideally," Divine observes, "a presidential campaign should be a great educational experience, in which
would-be leaders make clear the issues confronting the nation and offer
positive programs to the voters." In practice, candidates often seek "not
to enlighten the voter, but instead to appeal to the emotions by over-
simplifying and frequently distorting complex world problems."[1] In
the election of 1944 the question of future relations with Russia was
oversimplified and distorted largely by Democratic generalities and
denials that the issue existed and by Republican innuendoes about international power politics and the power of domestic Communists.

เ๛๛ Republican gains in the 1942 midterm elections gave that
ever-optimistic party hope of finally unseating President Roosevelt
in 1944. Newly elected GOP congressmen came to Washington early
in 1943 prepared to embarrass the administration at every turn. "Rarely, if

169

ever has any national campaign developed so bitterly so long in advance of an election," *Washington Star* columnist Gould Lincoln pointed out on 1 May 1943. "The Republicans already are seeking to raise the 'dictator' issue, on the theory that a fourth term would so entrench the President that he would be able to do anything he wished, whether the war was on or had ended. The Democrats counter with the cry that President Roosevelt is the only man who can handle the war."[2]

The Democrats had their candidate for 1944. Franklin Roosevelt may or may not have been indispensable to the country, but he was assuredly indispensable to the Democratic party. There was no other Democrat at this time with anything like the stature or vote-getting potential of the four leading Republican candidates in 1943. These included Wendell Willkie on the Left, Governor Thomas E. Dewey of New York in the Center, and General Douglas MacArthur and Governor John W. Bricker of Ohio on the Right. Public-opinion polls consistently showed the president leading each of these potential candidates, but no other Democrat was ahead of any of them. Of the three Republicans, the voters favored Dewey. To Gallup's question of September 1943, "Which ONE of these men would you prefer as the Republican candidate for President next year?" 35 percent picked Dewey, 29 percent chose Willkie, and 15 percent favored MacArthur.[3]

After Willkie, MacArthur, and Bricker had become "unavailable" for the top spot on the ticket during the months preceding the convention, Dewey won the nomination without a fight when the Republican delegates assembled in Chicago in June. The generally conservative mood of the convention was underscored not only by the enthusiastic nomination of Bricker as Dewey's running mate, but also by the fact that the man who had done more than any other to revive the Republican Party, Wendell Willkie, had not even been invited to attend. Moreover, the keynote address by Governor Earl Warren of California showed that he—and undoubtedly much of his party—was not immune to thoughts of American hegemony in the postwar world. Warren called "for effective co-operation with all the peaceloving nations of the world" to keep the peace. By 1944 such appeals were clichés. In the very next sentence, Warren began to suggest that the "arch" joining the four great Allied powers would have to be constructed primarily of American materials or it would not be constructed at all. "But beyond that is the task of establishing order, maintaining peace and extending prosperity," this moderate Republican told the delegates. "We stand ready to welcome every nation that is prepared in honesty and good will to join us in the accomplishment of that purpose."[4]

Except for taking the step (unprecedented in this century) of dumping an incumbent vice-president against his will, the Democratic convention, which met in Chicago in July, was routine. Roosevelt was renominated, and the glories of the Democracy were duly reiterated for the benefit of the wire service correspondents and the national radio audience. Dewey's main point in his acceptance speech had been that the tired old men of the administration needed to be replaced by vigorous young ones. With appropriate modesty, Roosevelt in his acceptance speech broadcast from San Diego implied his own indispensability. "I shall not campaign, in the usual sense, for the office," Roosevelt said in this speech on 20 July. "In these days of tragic sorrow, I do not consider it fitting. And besides, in these days of global warfare, I shall not be able to find the time."[5]

The administration's great triumph early in this quadrennial contest was achieving an agreement with the Republicans that issues of foreign policy should be almost entirely excluded from partisan debate. For a few days in mid-August it appeared that this was not to be. Dewey said on 16 August that he was concerned about the "cynical trip to power politics" which seemed to be occurring behind closed doors at the Dumbarton Oaks Conference.[6] The next day he deplored signs of a "unilateral approach to the problems of Poland and eastern Europe."[7] "As Americans, we believe in the equality and the rights of small nations and minorities," he said in a statement released through his Albany office. "They must not be lost," the governor went on, "in a cynical peace by which any four powers dominate the earth by force."[8]

Secretary of State Hull, moving with uncommon dispatch, told reporters the next day that Dewey's fears were "utterly and completely unfounded."[9] The secretary invited Dewey or a representative to meet him to discuss American foreign policy in detail. That same week John Foster Dulles, Dewey's chief foreign-policy adviser, met with Hull for three days in Washington. At the conclusion of their meetings, the two men issued a statement removing the basic questions of international organization and inter-Allied relations from the campaign. Herbert Brownell, another of Dewey's advisers, was asked later if he had "any recollection of either Governor Dewey or Mr. Dulles as being discontented with the general direction of wartime policies." "No, I don't," Brownell replied.[10] This basic agreement on fundamentals probably goes far to explain the general absence of foreign policy as an issue in the 1944 campaign.

Another reason, of course, was that Roosevelt's foreign policies at the time were highly popular. America's unity with her allies clearly was contributing to an early and decisive victory over the Axis powers, and the prospects appeared bright for the continued unity after the war which could assure peace and prosperity in the future. Even if he had been so inclined, Dewey would have needed to be hesitant to attack the president's foreign policies lest he be accused of threatening wartime unity and hence, as American politicians say, of jeopardizing the lives of American boys.

In fact, Dewey had to call upon all his political talents to attack the administration at all, for in the domestic sphere he had to face the facts of unprecedented prosperity and full employment. Thus the Republicans were forced to rely on innuendoes about the president's age and health, about creeping domestic communism, and about the growing power of bureaucracies in American life. They could only hope that the president would commit an egregious blunder, or that the apparent conservative trend in American politics would pull them through.

Lacking widespread grievances about the nation's domestic affairs or its foreign policies upon which to base an effective campaign, the Republican candidates and the forces of order which rallied to their cause gravitated to innuendoes about the communist threat to America which, they suggested openly, could only be quashed by a Republican victory. Their favorite target was Sidney Hillman, the outspoken director of the CIO's Political Action Committee, which was formed in the spring of 1944 to ensure Roosevelt's reelection by rallying the working classes of America to the Democratic cause and by seeing to it that these generally apathetic groups actually voted on election day. To conservatives, Hillman seemed to stand for everything that was wrong with America: he was the head of a powerful union centered in New York City, he was a Jew of recent Russian extraction, and he had radical ideas concerning the distribution of power in American society.

In his acceptance speech on 9 September, delivered to a friendly audience in French Lick, Indiana, John W. Bricker of Ohio, the Republican vice-presidential candidate, attacked Hillman by name. "I am sure that the great majority of working people, union members and union leaders alike, resent the intrusion of Sidney Hillman into their private business of casting a free and unintimidated vote," Bricker asserted. "They know as you and I know that any impairment of that right by a radical and communistic labor element will in the end defeat the honorable and legitimate aims of organized labor in this country." He also promised that a Republican victory would enable the people to "give full scope to individual incentive and American ingenuity and turn our back finally and completely on alien philosophies of government."[11]

Powerful periodicals added Russia explicitly to the conservatives' arsenal. "The greatest potential menace to permanent peace is Soviet Russia," Catholic World editorialized in its October issue. "Fascism is not and never was as dangerous as Communism."[12] Farm Journal and Farmer's Wife, the nation's leading agricultural periodical, openly campaigned against the Left throughout 1944. Its position linking the American Left with alien evil was epitomized in an editorial in its last issue before the election.

The coalition of the machine bosses with the spokesmen of radicalism and Communism is ominous for freedom, and a challenge to all American ideals both of liberty and decency. There are no morals to Communism. It is the avowed enemy of human freedom and of human rights in property. Its record of purges and murder, of sabotage and deceit, is written in recent history. It has even "dissolved" its American branch to hide under the cloaks of others. . . . Farmers of America! You are laboring 365 days this year to help protect American ideals from foreign aggression. Will you give one day, on November 7, to preserve these ideals at home?[13]

Dewey himself carefully avoided attacking Russia, which remained an honored ally. But in the last month of the campaign he joined the chorus of those who were attempting to discredit Roosevelt by linking him with the detested domestic Communists. Responding to a radio speech of 5 October in which the president denied any interest in support from Communists, Dewey charged in a broadcast speech two days later that "My opponent softly denies that he welcomes 'the support of any person or group committed to communism or fascism.' " The challenger proceeded to link Roosevelt with "Earl Browder, now such a patriot, who was convicted as a draft dodger in the last war, convicted again as a perjurer and pardoned in time to organize the campaign for the fourth term."[14] In a speech in Boston just before the election, Dewey summarized his charges: "In this campaign, the New Dealers attempt to smother discussion of their Communist alliance. They smear any discussions of this major question of our day. They insinuate that Americans must like communism or offend our fighting ally, Russia. Not even the gullible believe that. . . . In Russia, a Communist is a man who supports his government. In America, a Communist is a man who supports the fourth term so our form of government may more easily be changed."[15]

Roosevelt followed Dewey to Boston and in one of his most brilliant political speeches made it clear that he considered Dewey a muddleheaded man who lacked faith in America. Sarcasm rather than bluntness was his bludgeon, and he used it with enormous effectiveness. He pointed out that Dewey had accused the New Deal of going communist and of becoming a monarchy in two different Bay State cities on the very same day. "Now, really—which is it—Communism or monarchy?" Roosevelt inquired mockingly.[16]

The president assured his listeners that he wanted neither. "And, if this were a banquet hall instead of a ball park," he said, tailoring his speech to the situation, "I would propose a toast that we will continue to live under the Constitution for another hundred and fifty-five years. . . . When any poltician or any political candidate stands up and says, solemnly, that there is danger that the Government of the United States—your Government—could be sold out to the Communists," Roosevelt continued, "then I say that the candidate reveals—and I'll be polite—a shocking lack of trust in America."[17]

Not surprisingly, Roosevelt carried Massachusetts as well as the other large northeastern states that seemed to be going for Dewey only two months before. No other Democrat since the Civil War, except Lyndon B. Johnson in 1964, would be elected president without the solid support of the South. But in 1944, as in his three previous campaigns, Roosevelt would have won if all the southern states had gone for Dewey, for Roosevelt polled 432 electoral votes to Dewey's 99. The consummate campaigner had done it again.

What effects had the campaign had on American attitudes toward Russia? Not very many, to judge from the rough gauge provided by public-opinion polls. To the basic question, "Do you think Russia can be trusted to cooperate with us after the war?" 47 percent of Gallup's respondents answered yes in both July and December 1944, and the percentage of noes actually dropped from 36 to 35.[18]

But, alas, polls do not tell the entire story. The campaign had brought Americans six months closer to the end of the war with the basic questions of the postwar world still as unanswered as they had been when MacArthur and Willkie had been forced to drop out of the campaign. What would be done with Germany and Japan? How would the great powers continue to cooperate after the guns had grown cold? Would it be through the machinery of international organization, through informal consultation, or terror of terrors, not at all? What would be the fate of eastern Europe?[19] Dewey could not provide the answers, and Roosevelt did not attempt to do so.

Roosevelt the politician was in winning form, but Roosevelt the statesman was providing no solutions to the thorny problems of the postwar world. In the absence of presidential leadership, many of the answers that were being circulated during the summer and fall of 1944 were not very promising for peace. "Common sense indicates that we shall require air power superior to that of any potential enemy or group of enemies," famed air-power advocate Alexander de Seversky said about the first of August.[20] Seversky was but one of many advocating peace through American military supremacy at this time. *Life* magazine, which had featured Joseph Davies's views of Russia in March 1943, was featuring in September 1944 those of William C. Bullitt. Bullitt thought that the American aim for the remainder of the war should be to counter aggressively Russian moves in eastern Europe, and he said so without mincing words in the 4 September issue of *Life*.[21]

On 23 August 1944 the Salt Lake *Deseret News*, official newspaper of the Mormon Church, printed a leading article entitled "Just How Friendly to the U.S. Are the Soviets?" Its major implication was that Russians were selfish people to whom generosity should not be extended. Ten days later, this newspaper denounced a Mormon radio commentator who had supported a Russian War Relief drive and intimated that he was a Communist sympathizer. In the future, good Mormons were not to listen to his broadcasts.[22]

The *Deseret News* was not the only important opinion maker attacking Russia savagely during the campaign of 1944. Also on the offensive were other newspapers such as the *New York Daily News*, the *Chicago Tribune*, and the *San Francisco Examiner*; national commentators and columnists such as Upton Close and Frank Kent; senators such as Robert R. Reynolds of North Carolina and Burton K. Wheeler of Montana; and private citizens with a ready access to the media such as William C. Bullitt and Max Eastman. In wartime, these and other voices of confrontation were muted by the overarching need to maintain unity for victory. Whether they would come to the fore in the inevitable strains of adjustment to the different conditions of peace was an increasingly disturbing question as peace grew ever more imminent.

President Roosevelt was in a jovial mood when he returned to Washington after the election; but he, along with many other Americans, was disturbed by persistent rumors that Churchill and Stalin not only had plans for Europe but were proceeding at that very moment to implement them. Soon these rumors would be confirmed strikingly: Churchill would send British troops into Greece to fight leftist elements there, and Stalin would finally recognize the pro-Communist Lublin regime as the legitimate government of Poland. Was the United States going to permit Churchill and Stalin to divide Europe into spheres of influence?

The president would not comment, and the State Department could not, for Hull was stepping down after a dozen years in office and Roosevelt had not chosen his successor. Nearly all other national opinion makers tried to fill the huge vacuum. In mid-November 1944, friends of Russia held another mass meeting in Madison Square Garden, featuring Acting Secretary of State Edward R. Stettinius, Jr., and Soviet Ambassador Andrei Gromyko.

"The friendship between our two countries is a cherished heritage of our peoples," Stettinius said, forgetting the generation of mutual hate before 1941 and the fact that less than a majority of the American people thought even then that Russia could be trusted to cooperate after the war. "Of course, differences occur within and among nations," Stettinius granted. "But there is abroad in the world today a greater conviction than ever before that whatever differences may arise among nations, they can and must be solved, peacefully in a spirit of common understanding and goodwill, and for the greater good of all." Gromyko argued that the "necessity of coordinated action by the Allies is dictated by their fundamental national interest." Other than expounding on that point, Gromyko echoed Stettinius's fine generalities.[23]

Other friends of Russia were more specific. Alvarez Del Vayo warned in the *Nation* that "we shall soon hear all kinds of complaints, even from people not fundamentally antagonistic to the Soviet Union, that the Russians are trying to become the dominant political factor on the continent." Del Vayo thought that such complaints were useless if the United States had nothing better to offer than "the theory of free enterprise, big business as usual . . . and Prince Humbert, Archduke Otto, and Franco."[24]

Life also thought that what was happening in Europe was not Russia's fault. "Whether or not they were planned or controlled by Moscow, the uprisings in all countries seemed spontaneous," *Life* assured its millions of readers in early December.[25] "It is a common experience that whatever is essential usually comes about," the *New York Times* editorialized optimistically. "The continued cooperation between the United States and Russia is so essential to future world peace that no remaining differences can be permitted to interfere with it."[26]

CBS commentator Joseph C. Harsch warned that differences among the Big Three must not "lead to a fixed idea that any one of the big allied powers had superior claims to virtue." Harsch had noticed that Britain had received heavy American criticism for her recent actions in Greece, and that Russia was getting a similar amount of American moralizing for her moves in Bulgaria and Rumania. "In outside eyes we dominate two continents without opposition," Harsch pointed out. "Therefore we have greater security than either Britain or Russia should feel. They both envy us our greater security, which adds to the sting of any criticism."[27]

More conservative spokesmen were not paying much attention to the way "outside eyes" were seeing things. Karl Von Wiegand and Benjamin de Casseres of the Hearst newspapers were attacking Russia in column after column during the fall of 1944 and the winter of 1945, as were other writers for the ultraconservative press. The *Saturday Evening Post* was warning Russia that she must allay Allied fears "with a broad and generous policy toward her neighbors and more assurances that she has no plans for a new hegemony over the European 'heartland.' "[28]

Meanwhile William Green, president of the AF of L, was openly battling the CIO on the question of attending an international gathering of trade unions in London which would include Russia's. The CIO planned to send representatives, the AF of L did not, and both were calling each other names. In an editorial in the AF of L's *American Federationist* in December, entitled "The Free and Not Free," Green said that the Russians "do not have free trade unions" and that the American and Russian workers' "fundamental philosophies and objectives are diametrically opposed."[29]

Another powerful institution, the Roman Catholic church, was also speaking out against Russia in late 1944. Since 1942, American Catholic leaders had been fairly restrained in their discussions, but the attack was renewed in the fall of 1944 as it became clear that the position of the Church in eastern Europe would be diminished after the war if Stalin had his way.

Leading Catholic bishops issued a six-page statement in mid-November which implicitly criticized the results of the Dumbarton Oaks meetings and urged the administration to take strong steps to put the principles of the Atlantic Charter into effect in eastern Europe. The bishops then said, without noticing the gaping contradiction, that power politics must end and be replaced with a "universal institution" in which "every nation stands on its rights and not on its power."[30]

In this ethnocentric view, which was coming to be held by many who were not Catholics as well, the United States and other "just" bodies like the Catholic church could use the required power to achieve their ends, but other nations or bodies could not. Considering the prevalence of such views—though assuredly not because of them—Gerald P. Nye, the stalwart isolationist turned champion of American hegemony, could plausibly argue in his farewell address to the Senate on 19 December that within the next ten or twenty years America would be "called to war with Russia."[31]

In striking contrast to Nye's speech was an article by Reinhold Niebuhr entitled "Russia and the Peace," published in *Christianity and Crisis* just after the election. It was a revealing commentary on the American mass media that Nye's fatalistic assertions received much wider circulation than Niebuhr's carefully reasoned thoughts. It was ironic and significant that Nye, who had been rejected by the voters of small and isolated North Dakota, and whose isolationist, anti-British and anti-Russian views had not been in favor for years, was able to make his views known to most cosmopolitan Americans; and that Niebuhr, who was widely acknowledged to be one of the most brilliant men in America, was able to communicate his views only to the readers of the journal he edited and to those who saw scattered references to the article in other liberal publications.

"The intransigence of Russia on questions affecting her Western frontier and sphere of influence have aroused the not unnatural fears that Russia will seek to dominate the whole of Europe," Niebuhr noted, "and it must be conceded that there is always the possibility that we may pay too high a price for Russian cooperation by delivering Europe into her hands."[32]

That was the only concession Niebuhr made to the increasingly prevalent fear of Russia. "On the other hand," he went on, "it is important to recognize that what seems from one perspective as the impulse to dominate, is from another perspective a desire to guarantee one's own security. What seems like a threat is usually meant by the agent as a defensive measure." The result, unless special care were taken, was the "old vicious circle of mutual fear in international relations." Americans would have to understand that the Russians "are not going to put their full trust in any system of mutual security. They are going to insist upon some measure of special security. It will be well to remember that we will do the same in terms of our naval strategy for instance."[33]

In addition to the general use by great powers of special security, four unique facts dictated Russia's insistence on it, Niebuhr thought.

What are the Russians afraid of? They remember that there were vast numbers of people in the Western world who would have gladly bought immunity from the Nazi peril, if they could have turned its fury toward the East. That was Munich.

Secondly, the Russians know that there are even now many people in the West, particularly in the religious world, who think that Russia is a more deadly enemy of civilization than Hitler was. They have heard Father Fulton Sheen's broadcasts.

The Russians are, thirdly, not at all certain that the constitutional and other difficulties which America faces in determining our relation to the community of nations, may not result in America's withdrawal from world responsibility. . . .

Finally, the Russians know that the rich democracies have a divided soul. They are democracies and they would like to establish democracy in Europe; but they are also rich democracies and are afraid of all the revolutionary ferment on the continent. Their inclination, as proved in both Italy and France, is to come to terms with the conservative elements in the hope of avoiding the radicalism which fizzes in the wine of democracy as soon as the stopper is removed.[34]

While Niebuhr and many others were talking and writing about the peace, the president was playing for time, as was his wont. There was nothing he could do to stop Senators Wheeler and Nye from ranting about British and especially Russian intentions, but he was able on 23 December to persuade several internationalist senators who were visiting the White House to avoid opening a debate in the Senate which could embarrass the United States government and its allies.[35]

Exactly a week later Roosevelt was pleading with Stalin by cable to postpone "formal recognition of the Lublin Committee as a government of Poland."[36] Stalin let Roosevelt know by his actions that the time for postponement had passed: he recognized the Lublin government on the very next day.

Unless the president was thoroughly inured to disappointment, the news of Stalin's move must have ruined his celebration of New Year's Eve. If he still tended to be reflective, it is hard to imagine that he got much sleep that night. The year 1945—the year of decision in Europe and perhaps in Asia as well—had begun. Germany surely would be subdued in six months, perhaps even in three. Would the Allied powers fall apart as soon as the shooting stopped? Already there were strong pressures in the media and in Congress for the American government to seek to block the achievement of British and Russian aims.

Equally important, were the American people prepared for the realities of the actual peace that would follow the fighting? Perhaps Roosevelt thought that they were; but even if they were not, he, the "indispensable" leader, expected to be at the helm of the ship of state to guide it through troubled waters. Had not he provided twelve years of effective leadership in foreign affairs, and could he not be expected to provide four more?

In his written message to Congress on the state of the union on 6 January 1945, Roosevelt came closer to explaining his perceptions of the postwar world and of America's role in it than he had in the previous three years of war or than he would in the three remaining months of his life. Coupled with his usual upbeat optimism that all problems could and would be solved and his tendency to lapse into generalities about unity and peace were warnings about the complexity of international relations and the danger of "any nation assuming that it has a monopoly of wisdom or of virtue." The problems in such liberated areas as Greece and Poland, Roosevelt said, "are not as easy or as simple to deal with as some spokesmen, whose sincerity I do not question, would have us believe. . . . It is only too easy for all of us to rationalize what we want to believe and to consider those leaders we like responsible and those we dislike irresponsible."[37]

The president noted that, when the Atlantic Charter was signed in August 1941, "certain isolationists protested vigorously against our right to proclaim the principles—and against the very principles themselves.

Today many of the same people are protesting against the possibility of violation of the same principles." He pointed out that "the statement of principles in the Atlantic Charter does not provide rules of easy application to each and every one of the war-torn world's tangled situations. But it is a good and useful thing—it is an essential thing—to have principles toward which we can aim." Disputes growing out of the war could not be resolved "overnight," Roosevelt concluded, but "only through institutions capable of life and growth."[38]

Obviously aware of the president's desire to avoid a divisive congressional debate on foreign policy until after the Yalta meetings, Senator Tom Connally of Texas, head of the Foreign Relations Committee, pleaded with his colleagues to postpone debate on America's foreign policy and that of her allies. The loyal senator, apparently hoping that a folksy metaphor would remind restless senators of the importance of maintaining Allied unity until the war was won, asked those in attendance at the Democratic caucus on 5 January "not to run off across the field after a rabbit while the fox is going down the road."[39] Shortly thereafter he told the president that he was finding it difficult to control the pressure for a "country-by-country debate on the floor" and admitted that he himself was concerned about Russia's Polish policy.[40]

The ranking Republican member of the Foreign Relations Committee, Arthur H. Vandenberg of Michigan, was also concerned about Russia's actions in Poland and other unilateral actions by America's allies. His concerns led to what is probably the most famous American speech of World War II. And in contrast with Roosevelt's moderate-to-liberal State of the Union message four days earlier, Vandenberg's speech on the Senate floor on 10 January was an excellent articulation of moderate-to-conservative attitudes toward the coming peace.

Like many other famous speeches, Vandenberg's has been cited much more often than it has been read. It has usually been hailed as a renunciation of isolationism by a leading prewar Republican isolationist. But this was not its primary purpose for two reasons. First, Vandenberg was no die-hard isolationist before America's entry into the war; he had supported Roosevelt on lend-lease and some other measures for American cooperation with Britain and Russia before 7 December 1941. Second, Vandenberg simply was not an isolationist after Pearl Harbor. He supported all possible measures to aid the Allies; participated in the important Mackinac Conference of Republican leaders in Michigan in 1943, which specifically supported international collaboration after the war; and openly supported Dewey's internationalism during the 1944 campaign.

Thus, Vandenberg's frequent references to international cooperation after the war surely did not surprise his colleagues or constitute the main argument of his address, for they had become staples of the rhetoric of responsible Republicans. Instead, such references in this speech served primarily to emphasize Vandenberg's ideological distance from die-hard isolationists of World War II such as Gerald P. Nye and Burton K. Wheeler and secondarily to buttress the senator's thesis.

Vandenberg's main point was that American foreign policy had to be changed from unquestioning and unlimited alliance with Britain and Russia to an approach based on vigorous implementation of the Atlantic Charter and other statements of American ideals. At innumerable points, Vandenberg elaborated on this theme. "It seems to me . . . that the first thing we must say, beyond misunderstanding," the Senator declared, "is that we have not altered our original commitments; that we have not lowered our sights; that we have not diluted our dedications; that we are not fighting to pull ancient chestnuts out of alien fires; that the smell of victory is not an anesthetic which puts our earlier zeals to sleep." "We are standing by our guns with epic heroism," Vandenberg said at another point. "I know of no reason why we should not stand by our ideals." The senator concluded with a stirring appeal for "honest candor in respect to our ideals, our dedications and our commitments, as the greatest contribution which government can now make to the only kind of realistic peace which will most swiftly bring our victorious sons back home, and which will best validate our aspirations, our sacrifices and our dreams."[41]

In view of the fact that equally idealistic statements could be found in nearly every paragraph of the speech, it is not surprising that Vandenberg sharply criticized the foreign policies of each of the three great Allied powers. He attacked "a great American illusion . . . that we, in the United States, dare not publicly discuss these subjects lest we contribute to international dissension and thus encourage the very thing we all need to cure." "I do not know why we must be the only silent partner in this grand alliance," Vandenberg continued. "There seems to be no fear of disunity, no hesitation in Moscow, when Moscow wants to assert unilateral war and peace aims which collide with ours. There seems to be no fear of disunity, no hesitation in London, when Mr. Churchill proceeds upon his unilateral way to make decisions often repugnant to our ideas and our ideals."[42]

The senator singled out for criticism "Russia's unilateral plan" which appeared "to contemplate the engulfment, directly or indirectly, of a surrounding circle of buffer States, contrary to our conception of what we thought we were fighting for in respect to the rights of small nations and a just peace." Vandenberg called on Russia to accept "collective security" to assure that it never again would be attacked by Germany, the fear of which, Vandenberg thought, was causing Russia's unilateral actions in eastern Europe. As an immediate step toward implementation of collective security, Vandenberg urged that the Allies conclude a treaty forthwith guaranteeing the permanent disarmament of the Axis nations.[43]

Vandenberg reserved his severest criticisms for American foreign policy, which he thought was ultimately responsible for the other Allies' ability to violate American ideals. The American government had been sitting back watching Britain and Russia pursue their unilateral ends. For a while its leaders had mouthed the principles of the Atlantic Charter; but only recently the president had given it an "almost jocular, and even cynical" dismissal. And how should this tacit acquiescence in the ignoble aims of our Allies be halted? Generally, "the greatest contribution we can make to the realities of unity at this moment when enlightened civilization is our common stake" is "honest candor on the high plane of great ideals" by American officials. Specifically, "the first thing we must do is to reassert, in high places, our American faith in these particular elemental objectives of the Atlantic Charter," which, in Vandenberg's view, were the basic statements of American war aims. If the Atlantic Charter were not to guide America's approach to the peace, the senator implied strongly, administration officials should not have referred to it so reverently and so frequently throughout the war.[44]

What makes understanding of the thrust of Vandenberg's address so crucial is that it was only a more coherent and eloquent summation of the views that were being circulated at this time by most conservative opinion makers in the press, in periodicals, and on the radio. On the question of the values that had to prevail in the peace settlement, conservatives were, in their own way, as profoundly idealistic as the world federalists. The great ideal of those placing their faith in international organization was that international harmony could be assured through procedures and institutions patterned on those of America's federal government. The great ideal of the conservatives was their belief that a workable peace could be based only on the loftiest of American ideals: open covenants, territorial integrity, self-determination of nations whose leaders were to be chosen in free elections, and collective security based on American principles.

Except for some skepticism about international organization, Vandenberg could have borrowed most of the remainder of the general principles in his speech from any of several speeches by Woodrow Wilson in 1919. And the Republican senator whose party had blocked America's entry into the League of Nations on Wilson's terms now claimed to hold to most of Wilson's principles with nearly the same tenacity which that great Democrat had exhibited. Wilson surely would have been resting uneasily in his grave if he could have known that William Randolph Hearst, R. R. McCormick, and other conservatives both to the Right and to the Left of Vandenberg were insisting that Russia adhere to Wilson's basic ideals or remain out of the United Nations with the same ferocity with which similar elements had opposed America's entry into the League of Nations because Wilson was too "idealistic."

Time, an enormously influential moderate-to-conservative organ, featured Joseph Stalin on the cover of the 5 February issue. In contrast to the saintly depiction of two years before, the Soviet leader was now portrayed as an enigmatic, powerful "historic force" moving inexorably westward from the Russian steppes. As the key to whether a peace acceptable to Americans would be achieved, Stalin was "the most important person in the world last week . . ."; for "with military success in sight the Big Three were split apart as never before." Both Russia and the Western Allies had ample grounds for mistrust, *Time* acknowledged. "But his allies, too, were driven by a historic force, for they knew that if they failed to persuade Joseph Stalin to a united peace, even their united military victory would be a defeat."[45]

Most educated Americans to the Left of Vandenberg and *Time* had dreamed throughout the war of peace insured by an organization like the League of Nations, which Wilson had been primarily responsible for creating. Now many liberals thought that some of Wilson's international ideals had proved inadequate. "After the last war," the *New Republic* argued on 8 January, "men of good will relied upon plebiscites and self-determination as the hopeful formula for the future, but today the world is disillusioned about the mechanisms."[46]

In "What Do We Want in Europe," an article by the liberal foreign-policy expert, Vera Micheles Dean, which appeared the next week, the *New Republic* again turned the tables on the conservatives. At the end of World War I, conservatives had urged liberals to face up to a reality which differed from cherished liberal ideals. Now Miss Dean was doing the chiding.

Our tendency to admonish Britain, and less frequently Russia, in lofty moral tones is due to the belief that the United States alone is guided by idealistic considerations, as contrasted with the sordid motives of other nations. . . . This aspiration toward ideal settlements of international problems is responsible for current enragement over the prospect that the Atlantic Charter may not be applied in Poland and Greece. But our tendency to demand perfect solutions of international problems constitutes a real threat to postwar stability. . . .

What troubles our conscience is that Britain and Russia are resorting to what we call, in derogatory tones, "power politics." But, as an English newspaper put it, do we want "powerless politics"? Any individual or nation who is seeking to achieve political ends is always using some form of power—the power of arms or

economic favors, or ideas. We can question the ends Britain or Russia are seeking
to achieve. That is quite another matter. But we would find it much easier to deal
with other nations if we stopped taking a holier-than-thou attitude.[47]

Both conservatives and liberals—both Vandenberg and Dean—spoke
glowingly of establishing collective security after the war, but they did
not mean the same thing by this fine phrase. Conservatives tended to
warn Russia and Britain that collective security would result from collaboration on American terms or it would not exist at all. Naturally the
phrase *American terms* was not used. The phrase *on the basis of American
ideals* was used instead, but a foreigner probably would have had some
difficulty in distinguishing between the two in practice. Liberals, in
contrast, tended to think that collective security would be grounded on
international organization or it would not exist after the war. Because
Russia (with American consent) had insisted on the veto at Dumbarton
Oaks, and because most Americans were unprepared to relinquish much
national sovereignty, liberals were no more aware of the realities of the
times in their insistence upon the panacea of world organization than
were the conservatives in their insistence upon an American peace.
For either group to impugn the common sense of the other—and this
happened much more frequently than either group examined its own
assumptions in the light of existing facts—simply kept the real issues
from emerging and prevented a realistic approach to the peace from
being adopted by either side.

As the *New Yorker* never tired of pointing out, there obviously
was much unsound thinking among both conservatives and liberals in
January 1945. The president of the United States surely thought so too,
for his basic view of the peace was that the Big Three should use their
power to guarantee world stability. This basic approach was shared by
the two other men who actually wielded great power in world affairs at
this time—Churchill and Stalin.

Before departing on the long trip to Yalta, where he was to meet
Stalin and Churchill on 4 February for a full-dress discussion leading to
agreement on impending postwar problems, the president might well
have sought to demolish several unrealistic tenets of American thought.
But Roosevelt no longer had the courage (or the energy) that he had
shown when he told the Left in the early 1930s that capitalism was not
dead and the Right that capitalism would not work without the balance
wheel of a powerful federal government. The president probably assumed
that he did not need to do more than he had done in scattered passages of
the State of the Union address to attack the regnant ideas on foreign

policy because he would be present to see that a peace based on power and pragmatism was implemented. The events of tomorrow, he must have judged from experience, tended to make people forget today's predictions.

As useful to the cause of peace as forthright speeches would have been an absolutely honest communiqué from Yalta. At Teheran, the powers were in the middle of a war which was far from being won, and it was perhaps necessary to report a degree of unanimity that did not exist. But the historic Yalta Conference took place near the end of the war; the misconceptions which emanated from it, the three astute leaders should have reasoned, surely would return to haunt them.

But politicians are often like bartenders: they would rather make people happy, if only for a short time, than tell them the truth. If the Big Three had been truthful, they would have reported that most of the differences that had developed over the past three years had not disappeared as if by magic; that Britain and America would do much to determine the destiny of western Europe and most of the rest of the world, and that Russia would be determining the destiny of eastern Europe and a small part of non–Russian Asia; and that while this or any other possible solution would not satisfy everybody, they believed—as did Walter Lippmann in the United States and the *London Times* in Europe, among others—that this was the best they could do at this time to provide for enduring peace.

Instead of saying something to this effect, the Big Three professed to be united on every question. They were united on establishing a United Nations organization and on the future of Germany, eastern Europe, and Asia. "The Premier of the Union of Soviet Socialist Republics, the Prime Minister of the United Kingdom and the President of the United States of America have consulted with each other in the common interests of the peoples of their countries and those of liberated Europe," the "Declaration on Liberated Europe" began. "They jointly declare their mutual agreement to concert during the temporary period of instability in liberated Europe the policies of their three governments in assisting the peoples liberated from the domination of Nazi Germany and the peoples of the former Axis satellite States of Europe to solve by democratic means their pressing political and economic problems."[48]

The leaders could well have devoted the next five thousand words of the communiqué to explaining what this paragraph's generalizations meant in practice. Instead, the remaining six paragraphs of this section introduced at least a dozen more gaping generalizations. Then the communiqué proceeded to its famous and ultimately unfortunate generalizations about postwar Poland, of which more will be written later in this chapter.

Perhaps because of its cultivated ambiguity and emphasis on unanimity, the communiqué had its intended immediate effect: it was approved by 75 percent of Twohey's sample of the American press, while only 11 percent disapproved.[49] A wirephoto of Churchill, Roosevelt, and Stalin smiling and looking pleased with themselves was featured on the front pages of hundreds of American newspapers on 13 February. Those who could recall the similar picture from Teheran might have noticed that Roosevelt now looked much older and more tired; he was a striking contrast to his two partners, who had changed little and looked rested and robust. The headlines gave the impression that permanent peace had been made, and everyone wanted to believe, after a half-dozen years of international turmoil, that the headlines were right.

Almost all liberal and moderate newspapers took the communiqué at face value and praised it accordingly. The *Boston Globe*, resorting to the frequently used metaphor of forward motion, said that the Yalta meetings "carry the hopes of men and the problems of war and peace valiantly forward."[50] The *Daily Worker* used an ancient maritime metaphor: "The agreement of Crimea proclaims to the world that the storm-tossed ship, the United Nations, is definitely going to reach port."[51]

Other exulting editorialists employed metaphors which suggested that dissension had disappeared and unity had been assured. "We have agreed to agree," the *Asheville Citizen* declared. "Our unity has found its bedrock in a mutual association of power and principle which nothing can shake."[52] "To read the statement by the leaders of the three powers is to feel that the air has been cleared," the *Providence Journal* wrote, hardly contributing to the demise of diplomatic obfuscation.[53] "All the winds at Yalta blew strongly toward cooperation," the *Philadelphia Bulletin* editorialized and added: "It was a most promising development, full of good omen for the difficult period following the war."[54]

"All in all, the Crimea conference was amazingly promising," the *Milwaukee Journal* exclaimed. "Its accomplishments stand out like a light, offering hope in a world torn by years of war."[55] The *Detroit News* assured its readers that the meetings "actually swept the board clear of every pending issue that threatened, or had seemed to threaten, cordial relations between the Big Three."[56] Even the *Chicago Tribune* was inclined to be generous. "No American in his right mind can fail to hope," it pointed out, "that the decisions and agreements reached at Yalta will produce a stable and peaceful Europe."[57]

Only a few newspapers were uncertain that the three statesmen and their staffs had performed miraculous feats. "There is some skepticism about the practical operation of the agreement for joint action in liberated countries," the *Christian Science Monitor* reported.[58] "The customary generalities in which the communiqué from the Big Three conference is phrased contain sufficient specific information to let the world know that little progress was made toward settling Europe's political difficulties," the *Cleveland Plain Dealer* noted gloomily.[59] Nor did the *Casper Tribune-Herald* think the communiqué said very much. "The real test of the postwar program will come, of course, when the details are evolved and revealed."[60] These doubtful souls generally agreed that the Polish problem would be the acid test of the meeting's accomplishments. "One is tempted to say, at the risk of some exaggeration, that if the three powers can find a way out of the Polish confusion, they can find a way out of anything," the *Baltimore Sun* stated with characteristic caution.[61]

Arthur Sears Henning of the *Chicago Tribune* and conservative columnist David Lawrence were not so circumspect. "The conference is widely viewed as a victory for the Russian dictator Stalin who has substantially gained all his objectives and has forced President Roosevelt to back down from the position he took on the Atlantic Charter and the rape of Poland less than two months ago," Henning asserted.[62] "American idealism has been defeated as conspicuously at the Crimea conference as it was at Paris 26 years ago," Lawrence wrote, reflecting the idealism of avowed realists like Vandenberg. Lawrence's major grievance was that "a Polish puppet state under Russian domination has been set up and now its title and authority are confirmed."[63]

Those who were pessimistic about the results at Yalta were divided on the Polish problem. Most, like Lawrence, thought that Poland, in a common metaphor of the day, had been "sold down the river." "This fine-sounding solution is the death-knell for that Poland which fought through four years of German occupation," the *Cleveland Plain Dealer* contended, forgetting for a moment that the London Poles had little power in Poland during the war.[64] "The tragedy of Poland leaves all the people of the world with the greatest and gravest misgivings," the *New York Journal-American* proclaimed, ignoring for the moment the existence of the Russians and the Lublin Poles.[65]

The *Casper Tribune-Herald* disagreed vociferously with such sentiments. Its argument of 12 March underscored the fact that cosmopolitans lived in America's most remote regions as well as in New York, Chicago, and San Francisco: "Those who challenge the so-called decision of the Yalta conference regarding Poland should also explain how it could have been avoided if Russia is to be a party to the world peace program. As a matter of fact the decision was made by Moscow long ago. And if any objections were to be raised, that was the time to protest."[66]

Conservatives' attitudes toward Russia were still colored by a vague fear of both that nation's social system and of the intentions of the forces of movement in America. The *Wall Street Journal* revealed this thinking on its editorial page on 15 February just after the Yalta communiqué was released: "The Russian government is founded on the theory that the ruler is possessed of a superior wisdom, the same theory that is so assiduously propagated in certain quarters in this country."[67] Obviously that sophisticated organ of the business community was still unhappy because the inhabitants of those "quarters" had not been turned out of office in the recent elections.

On the next day, columnist Felix Morley offered some of the most incisive criticisms of the Yalta declarations that were to be found before criticizing Yalta became fashionable after the war. The declarations, Morley argued in the *Wall Street Journal*, were a "pitifully threadbare attempt to combine an affirmation of high principles with specific provisions that make a complete mockery of those principles." Morley obviously would have appreciated more candor from the parley's participants. He also thought that the American and British effort to become involved in eastern European affairs in competition with Russia hampered the prospects for enduring peace. "To divide with Russia responsibility for the policing of Central Europe," Morley wrote, "can only lead to increasingly unsatisfactory relations between the United States and Russia."[68]

So far as can be determined, most radio commentators joined most other opinion makers in hailing the Yalta accords. "No great instrument of compromise satisfies all men," Joesph C. Harsch said on CBS; and, to buttress his favorable response, he added that "the violent and more telling propaganda comes from our enemies." To deny the possibility that the Polish problem had been solved, Harsch thought, "would be to pass a judgment of insincerity on the men who met at Yalta."[69] "The constructive spirit of give-and-take has come into evidence . . . ," Raymond Gram Swing said on NBC, "the specter of unilateralism has vanished."[70]

All opinions circulated by the networks, of course, were not so favorable. NBC's Washington correspondent, Richard C. Harkness, mentioned criticism of the communiqué by Senators Burton K. Wheeler of Montana, Edwin Johnson of Colorado, Hendrik Shipstead of Minnesota, and Alexander Wiley of Wisconsin.[71] He did not point out that these four gentlemen probably would have opposed any possible result of the conference except a statement by Stalin that Russia wanted no influence outside her borders after the war. NBC commentators Lowell Thomas and H. V. Kaltenborn, who tended to oppose Russia but who did not say so very frequently after 1941, essentially declined to comment on the accords.[72]

Politicians such as Senators Connally and Wheeler were more than willing to present their mutually contradictory views on the air, which they did on CBS on 20 February and 27 February, respectively. As might have been expected of one of the administration's staunchest supporters in the Senate, Connally praised every aspect of the accords. "Recognition was not to be given to either the London or the Lublin governments," Connally commented on the Polish settlement. "A new government incorporating representatives of the various parties and groups to be established under the supervision of the three great powers is provided."[73]

The senator from Montana denied that such compromises had taken place. "When we realize that at Yalta the decisions that were reached were the result of abject appeasement of Stalin," Wheeler asserted, "we can picture the firm nature of the struggle that is already going on between Russia and Britain in every country in Europe, toward which we will never be permitted to remain neutral." Like Vandenberg, Wheeler obviously had abandoned his earlier isolationism, though not to the extent of supporting international organization as much as did the Republican from Michigan. If anything, Wheeler was more insistent on the necessity of Allied acceptance of America's ideals than Vandenberg had been the month before: "We must demand the principles of the Atlantic Charter be incorporated into any future plans for world organization. We must insist upon the amendment of the present Dumbarton Oaks proposals to bring about the changes that are imperative if the world is not to be run on the basis of brute force in the hands of the few. If we do not want our boys to have fought and died in vain, we must act now in the name of humanity."[74]

The other great medium of opinion circulation, periodicals, made up in insight for what they lacked in immediacy. *Time*'s first thought, in an article entitled "Moment in History," was that all remaining "doubts about the Big Three's ability to cooperate, in peace as well as war, seemed now to have been swept away."[75] By the next week the great "moment in history" was turning out to be just that, for *Time* was having "Second Thoughts." "Yalta could be taken as an incomplete check on a race for spheres of influence," *Time* asserted.[76] "Yalta is a chance for a solution, rather than a solution itself," *Life* said soberly that same week. "Since the wording of the agreement does not necessarily rule out 'spheres of influence' (nor modify Russia's one-sided agreements in Rumania and Bulgaria), Poland will be the crucial test of how well the Big Three can combine their policies in practice."[77]

Journals as opposite in outlook as *Business Week* and the *New Republic* informed their readers that Russian influence would predominate in postwar Poland if the Yalta accords were carried out. *Business Week* stressed the fact that "Poland is going to become a Russian satellite, dependent on Moscow both in building its economy within the new borders that will be assigned to it and in maintaining its security in the face of a bitter and vengeful Germany."[78] The *New Republic* obviously wanted to make sure that liberals realized that Russia had achieved its major goals at the conference in the Crimea: "On the whole, the results at Yalta represent a substantial victory for Stalin. He gets his way, without serious modification, in regard to Poland and in regard to reparations. If anything is to be done regarding the Balkans that he does not like, the recorded results do not show it."[79]

President Roosevelt did not agree publicly with this view. In his address to Congress in person and to the people over radio upon his return from Russia, he implied that at Yalta everybody had won everything, everywhere. "The Conference in the Crimea was a turning point— I hope in our history and therefore in the history of the world," the president said in the words of a vigorous optimist but in the tones of a tired man. "There will soon be presented to the Sentate of the United States and to the American people a great decision that will determine the fate of the United States—and of the world—for generations to come," the president added, changing in one sentence from historian to prophet.[80]

The chief executive then adopted a third familiar role, that of dissembler. The results at Yalta, he said, "ought to spell the end of the system of unilateral action, the exclusive alliances, the spheres of influence, the balances of power, and all the other expedients that have been tried for centuries—and have always failed. We propose to substitute for all these a universal organization in which all peace-loving Nations will finally have chance to join."[81]

Despite these and similar comments there was no evidence that Roosevelt had abandoned his conception of the "Four Policemen" ruling the world by force when necessary.[82] For the president of the United States to continue to conceal his plans for the postwar world from the American people, who had elected him to lead them and their democratic government, was completely unwarranted and ultimately damning to world peace. During World War II, Joseph Stalin and Winston Churchill were much more candid with their peoples about their governments' foreign policies than was Franklin Roosevelt. Stalin and Churchill each made several major addresses to their peoples about their nations' goals in the war. President Roosevelt did not make any such pronouncements. This fact explains much of the confusion about and disillusionment with foreign policy which occurred in America during the last six months of the war and afterward.

A few implications of the president's lack of leadership on foreign policy must be mentioned at this point. Most opinion makers of the time acknowledged that peace would bring conflicts among the Allies which the exigencies of war had prevented from surfacing earlier. If true peace were to emerge, the president, as the preeminent opinion maker in the nation, obviously would have to prepare the people for these problems and their solution within the framework of continued Allied cooperation. This the president and other administration leaders like Secretary of State Hull simply did not do. In fact, they compounded the confusion by insisting that no real problems existed and by implying strongly that none would surface after the war. Given such a dearth of leadership, what were Americans to think when difficult problems began to emerge with ever-increasing frequency and intensity in March 1945?

The absence of executive leadership at this time naturally becomes more striking in retrospect, but it concerned many thoughtful contemporaries of the president as well. Such prominent persons as Vandenberg, Dulles, Lippmann, and Niebuhr expressed concern about it throughout the war, as did *Time* in numerous biting criticisms of the administration's foreign policy after 1943. Dewey was near the mark when he said early in 1944 that the Republicans at the Mackinac Conference were the first political party to spell out a fairly comprehensive plan for American participation in maintaining the peace, and he apparently was sincere as well as seeking to score a political point when he expressed his utter disappointment in October 1944 about the content of the president's speech to the Foreign Policy Association.[83] Hull's attempts to inform the public were even more disappointing, and Secretary of State Stettinius did little better in his first few months in office.

Outside the ranks of opinion makers and the attentive public, however, there was much less concern about the absence of executive leadership in foreign affairs. Most Americans remained relatively uninterested in foreign policy and uninformed about it. They had traditionally left such matters up to the nation's political leaders, who, it could be assumed, knew much more about them than did the average person. Even during a war for America's survival, Hadley Cantril reported late in 1944, the "intensity of public interest in domestic affairs is almost twice as great as the intensity of public interest in foreign affairs."[84] The greatest concern among the mass public from 1943 on was not whether the Big Three could remain united in the peace, but whether there would be jobs when Johnny came back and war orders ceased.

Considering the fact that they might well have to vote in 1946 and afterward for or against politicians who were campaigning primarily on some aspect of foreign policy, most Americans knew far too little about the outside world. This fact was underscored by at least a dozen polls conducted during the war to find out what the general public knew about American foreign policy and about other countries.

One of these was conducted just before the end of the war on the question of knowledge about Russia: "Are the people in Russia, as far as you know, allowed to have private property, such as a house, car, or any money they save up for personal use?" That question had been answered in at least twenty books and forty articles in major periodicals during the preceding three years. Yet only 30 percent of the sample answered correctly when they said yes. The answer to the second major question had been even more widely circulated. "Do you think," the pollsters from the Office of Public Opinion Research asked, "all people in Russia are paid about the same amount of money for their work or are there wide differences in the amounts people are paid?" The correct answer, wide differences, was given by only 36 percent. To both questions nearly half of the respondents answered don't know. The final question was this: "Do you think most of the war materials the Russian army has used, such as tanks, planes, and guns, have been made in Russia, or do you think most of them have been obtained from this country or England through Lend-Lease?" It was obviously very important that this question be answered correctly, for Americans could hardly understand Russia's general status as a great power and her specific role in the European peace settlement if they did not comprehend the scope of her contribution in the European theater of war. Yet only 22 percent gave the correct answer, made in Russia, while 58 percent said obtained through lend-lease. The fact was that Russia had made more than 90 percent of her war material herself.[85]

Efforts to educate the public often would not even have been controversial. For example, the public was polled in January 1945 on the question of relative power in the new world organization. American domination was favored by 26 percent, 43 percent wanted an equal voice by all countries, and Big Three domination was supported by 19 percent.[86]

Here was a sterling opportunity for the president to convey to the country his idea of leadership by the great powers in the peace without stating it too bluntly. He could have taken a few minutes in a fireside chat to explain that American domination was an impossibility if the organization was to be accepted by Britain and Russia; and that an equal voice by all countries ranging in population from China to Iceland and in size from Russia to Morocco might be nice in theory, but that it simply would not work because power in the international organization would have to reflect the distribution of power on earth.

Another idea that the president and his associates needed to convey if there was to be peace was the fact that Russia planned to dominate eastern Europe after the war whether Americans liked it or not, and that there was really nothing short of war that they could do about it. This was an unpleasant thought, of course, and any intimation of it would have created a brief storm of protest. But in early March 1945 the next congressional elections were still twenty months away, and the president surely could have told the great mass of people what the *New Republic*, *Business Week*, and other opinion makers were already saying.

As good a time as any for Roosevelt to have explained the realities of international politics as he saw them would have been soon after his return from Yalta, perhaps in his report to Congress. Again, the president could have used the results of a recent Gallup poll to clinch his point. "Russia's Army is driving the Germans out of a number of the smaller countries in eastern Europe," the Gallup interviewers reminded the respondents, and then asked, "Do you think that Russia should decide what to do with these countries by herself, or should all the United Nations have something to say about it?" Only 11 percent thought Russia should decide by herself, whereas 83 percent said that all the United Nations should have a voice.[87]

The president could have reported these results and then said that they were misleading because the question established too great a dichotomy. He could have told Congress that Russia would have the preeminent voice in eastern Europe just as the United States and Britain would predominate in western Europe and everywhere else. The Western Allies could not really stop Russia from doing what she wanted in the lands occupied by her troops any more than Russia could stop Britain and America from doing as they thought best in the countries they occupied, but both sides could exert moral suasion in the spirit of goodwill that had to prevail after the war. But Roosevelt was silent on this crucial issue throughout his tenure in office.

In the spring of 1945 Americans wanted very much to agree with the rosy predictions of their president that the peace would bring an age of international goodwill. They were pleased that the Axis powers were nearing devastating defeat, and they did not want to spoil the optimism of the time by entertaining forebodings about the future of international relations. Moreover, there was too much to do at home after the war to let people worry very much about what might happen abroad.

The euphoria of the moment, fed by the apparently satisfactory results of the recent Yalta conference, was reflected in popular attitudes toward Russia. George Gallup reported on 10 March that more Americans than ever trusted Russia to cooperate with the United States after the war. In March 1942, only 39 percent trusted Russia to cooperate; by November 1943 the percentage had risen to 47, where it remained with slight variations through December 1944. Now the figure was an impressive 55 percent, which represented an increase of about six million adult Americans in the four months since December.[88]

If education is accepted as a rough measure of cosmopolitanism, the cosmopolitans were still the most favorable toward Russia, as they had been throughout the war. Nearly two-thirds of the respondents who had attended college (62 percent), expressed trust in Russia's willingness to cooperate after the war. Adults who had been to high school but not to college followed closely with 60 percent favorably disposed, while only 51 percent of those who had no more than a grade-school education gave affirmative responses.[89]

These differences were made somewhat less striking by the fact that almost all of the differences resulted from the progressive increases in the percentage of undecided respondents in the high-school-educated and grade-school-educated groups as compared with the college-educated group. Thirty percent of the college-educated group answered no, 8 percent expressed no opinion; 29 percent of the high-school-educated group answered no, 11 percent expressed no opinion; and 31 percent of the grade-school-educated group said no, 18 percent expressed no opinion. Because of the lower percentage of both yes and no responses among the high-school-educated group, that group actually would have expressed virtually the same amount of confidence in Russia as the college-educated group if the undecided responses had been excluded from consideration.

If one's vote in the 1944 election can be accepted as a rough measure of whether one belonged to the forces of order or to the forces of movement in America—and there is every reason to believe that it can, except in the case of southerners—then the division along these lines was even more striking in this case than was the division by educational background. Sixty-two percent of those who voted for Roosevelt believed that Russia could be trusted to cooperate, 25 percent did not, and 13 percent were undecided. Of those who voted for Dewey, 51 percent answered yes, 38 percent said no, and 11 percent were undecided.[90]

At the end of February 1945 very few American opinion makers were predicting the collapse of the Grand Alliance; by the beginning of April many were. What had happened in these five weeks to cause such a violent turn in opinion? It is hard to say with precision. But it is not hard to agree with James MacGregor Burns's observation that "in just one month . . . everything seemed to come unhinged." To observe that "Poland was the engine of conflict, just as it had been in 1939 and before" does not explain it fully, and Burns wisely does not suggest that it does.[91]

Poland was indeed the primary "engine of conflict," as anyone who has read the periodicals and newspapers and has listened to the commentators of the time would know. During March, criticism of Russia's uncompromising position in Poland was fairly restrained, but by April almost all newspapers were criticizing Russia for dominating the Poles. Only a few journals such as the *St. Louis Post-Dispatch* and a few columnists like Walter Lippmann still argued that Russian actions in that unfortunate land were comprehensible. Respected senators were speaking out on the Senate floor and writing urgent inquiries to Secretary of State Stettinius by the end of March. The president was mumbling to his doctor in Warm Springs, Georgia, about the Polish problem during the last days of his life,[92] and President Truman was lecturing Soviet Foreign Minister Molotov about it in the White House shortly thereafter.

In addition to the situation in Poland, many other developments were undermining positive American attitudes toward Russia during the less than three months between the Yalta Conference and V-E Day: concern about the situation in Rumania after the downfall of the Radescu government on 28 February; complaints about the paucity of non–Russian news sources in eastern Europe; criticism of the secret Yalta agreement on Soviet voting in the proposed General Assembly, admitted by the White House on 29 March; disappointment with the Russian announcement, subsequently reversed, that Foreign Minister Molotov would not attend the United Nations Conference in San Francisco; and a tendency to view that conference, which opened on 25 April, as a struggle for power by the United States and Britain on one side and Russia on the other.

All of these issues were featured in newspapers, periodicals, newscasts, and speeches during these weeks. To be sure, much discussion of Russia continued to be positive. The *Atlanta Constitution*, for example, editorialized on 11 April that "there is every reason to expect Russia to be one of, if not the most powerful, factor in the cause of world peace."[93] On 24 April the *St. Louis Post-Dispatch* admonished "the handful of distrustful Americans to banish their enmity toward our Russian Ally."[94] In regard to the situation in Poland, Walter Lippmann wrote on 28 April that "it is quite clear that the trouble has not been a matter of the Anglo-Americans adhering to the Yalta Agreement and the Soviets reneging on it."[95] In describing the meeting of the American and Russian armies in central Germany the day before, CBS correspondent Richard C. Hottelet stressed the unpretentious comradery of the occasion: "Just some men meeting, shaking hands, getting together on the banks, saying they were glad to see each other."[96] And on 2 May correspondent Paul Appleby gave a generally optimistic analysis of the first week of the San Francisco Conference: "The fact is that in this important week the nations have worked sufficiently well with Russia, and Russia with them."[97]

Nevertheless, the preponderance of news and commentary on Russia carried in the media between Roosevelt's report on Yalta in early March and the end of the war in Europe in early May was negative. In a nationwide radio address on 10 March, Socialist Norman Thomas warned that Russia "can extend its dominion from Tokyo to Dakar. . . . From the hypocrisy of Yalta can spring no peace," Thomas said bitterly.[98] "The great powers are learning to their sorrow that the Titan of the Steppes still considers the capitalist world his mortal enemy," Catholic leader Edmund A. Walsh told the Export Managers Club in New York three weeks later.[99] And in a speech in Philadelphia on 17 April, Herbert Hoover condemned Russia by quoting "an old Quaker friend who said, 'If thee does not repent in a measure and change thy ways considerably, thee will be damned to a certain extent.' "[100]

Magazines and newspapers joined in the attack. "Why are the Russian people deprived of the real news about America?" the editors of the *Saturday Evening Post* asked in the 24 March issue.[101] "Had the sacrifice of Poland been reported by our President as a grim but unavoidable act of military necessity, we might have swallowed our pride but salvaged some remnants of our consciences," Eugene Lyons wrote in the April issue of *American Mercury*. "When it is passed off on a gullible public as a just settlement—more, as a magnificent Rooseveltian triumph—we are face to face with a moral outrage that will haunt our history whatever the ultimate consequences. . . . The crime of Yalta, the virtual surrender of Eastern Europe to totalitarianism, can be explained only on grounds of urgent expediency."[102]

In a 3 April editorial entitled "Two Sides to Unity," the *Christian Science Monitor* warned Soviet leaders that "concessions won from American statesmen are far from being won from the United States."[103] And the Washington correspondent of *Farm Journal and Farmer's Wife* wrote on 10 April that "shocked observers here conclude that the Yalta decisions were not decisions at all, and that our foreign policy as a whole is as vague and erratic as ever."[104]

The attack on Russia in the Hearst newspapers also intensified in the spring of 1945. On 5 April, for example, a virulent editorial was reprinted from a New York Catholic weekly: "For Czechoslovakia, substitute

Poland, Lithuania, Latvia, and Estonia; for Munich, susbstitute Yalta; for Chamberlain substitute Churchill; for Hitler substitute Stalin. . . . We have won the war; LET US NOT LOSE THE PEACE."[105] And Drew Pearson wrote an "Open Letter to Stalin" in his enormously popular column on 7 April.

> Perhaps your embassy has reported that in the last two years, much of the old anti-Soviet suspicion has vanished and that the great bulk of the American people are anxious to cooperate with Russia for future peace as they have for winning the war. In the past two weeks, however, this friendly feeling has received a jolt. . . . It has received a jolt because of the general impression that the Yalta promises are not being kept and that the rights of little nations are being trampled on. To put it bluntly the American people are beginning to wonder whether Russia is really sincere about keeping the peace after the war, unless that peace is one which she dominates.[106]

It is not surprising that the sharp criticisms of Russia were reflected in poll results. Comparable polls by Cantril and Gallup made in late February and mid-May showed that trust in Russia's willingness to cooperate after the war dropped from 54 to 45 percent in the Cantril polls and from 55 to 45 percent in the Gallup polls.[107] Equally important, whereas in January 1945 a plurality of those who were "dissatisfied with the way in which Russia, England, and the United States are cooperating at the present time" considered England most responsible for inter-Allied difficulties, by May a majority of those who were dissatisfied saw Russia as the chief culprit. And the proportion who were dissatisfied jumped from 15 percent in April to 33 percent in May.[108] Finally, it is not surprising that, as the war in Europe came to an end in early May, such diverse opinion makers as David Lawrence, Cecil Brown, the *Philadelphia Inquirer*, and the *New York Times* were calling for a new Big Three conference to achieve "specific" agreements on "democratic" governments in eastern Europe and to discard the Yalta Conference's "high-sounding generalities."[109]

The dominant attitude of America's opinion makers around V-E Day was exemplified in an editorial in the *Trenton Times* on 25 April. The *Times*, which had been consistently friendly to Russia until March 1945, now blamed the world's problems in general and those of the newly convened San Francisco Conference in particular on the "intransigence of Russia, which is apparently determined to establish in Warsaw a government subservient to Moscow and to fix the status of Poland as a vassal of the Soviet Union. The U.S. and Britain cannot concur in such a repudiation of the agreement at Yalta."[110]

In this brief portion of the editorial the *Times* took two positions common to many American opinion makers in the spring of 1945 which contributed greatly to the coming of the Cold War. The first was the assumption that the Yalta agreement on Poland was unambiguous, and that it could be understood by reading the brief statement on the subject. The key sentence in the text under the heading "Poland," and the only one of real consequence, was this: "The provisional government which is now functioning should therefore be reorganized on a broader democratic basis with the inclusion of democratic leaders from Poland itself and from Poles abroad."[111] At first glance that seemed clear enough, but what did it mean in practice? It meant virtually nothing that Stalin did not want it to mean, for it left the following fundamental questions unanswered: How many of the "democratic leaders" within Poland and in the London government must be included? What types of positions should this undetermined number of leaders have? Must they really have any significant power in the new Polish government at all? And when did the ambiguous requirements of this agreement have to be implemented? Was it before the first of March 1945, or by 1995?

Similar ambiguities pervade the communiqué's discussion of "free and unfettered elections" in Poland. In the first place, these elections were not to occur until after the new Polish government was established. Second, it is unclear whether the elections were to take place before or after the Big Three nations were to "establish diplomatic relations with the new Polish Provisional Government of National Unity." Third and most important, in no part of the communiqué were the Soviet Union or the other two powers required to compel the Poles or any other liberated peoples to hold elections. It is one thing to agree, as the Big Three did, to "jointly assist" the liberated peoples or even to try to form a Polish government "pledged" to hold elections; it would have been quite different for the Big Three to require each other to force the liberated peoples to hold elections, and this they did not do.[112]

Given the incompleteness and ambiguity of the Yalta agreement on Poland, the position of the Red Army in Poland, and the fact that the agreement surely did not mean that the real power of the Lublin group was to be assumed by the "democratic leaders" who were to be taken in, Stalin could hardly be criticized for not living up to the letter of the statement on Poland. And given Russia's intention to retain veto power over postwar Polish politics—an intention underscored on two dozen occasions during the war—it was only slightly more just to accuse Stalin of bad faith in carrying out these agreements.

The second position that the *Trenton Times* adopted in this editorial, one which many other opinion makers also were adopting at the same time, was the suggestion that Britain and the United States should team up against Russia, a course of action President Roosevelt had warned against in a conversation with his son Elliott in December 1943.[113] If Russia interfered in western Europe, Britain and the United States could and probably would have combined to expel her from their sphere of influence. But Russia had sacrificed twenty million people, and she was sure to insist that she decide what security measures were necessary in the region between Russia and Germany. The unposed question was this: how were Britain and America supposed to stop this unless they wanted to bury their dead in western Europe and sacrifice heavily all over again in a war with Russia?

In a world of ruthless power politics which had already culminated in two world wars in a generation, why should Russia agree to trade her own efforts to provide security for promises which could end up as badly as those that were made between Germany and Russia at Rapallo in the early 1920s and in Berlin on 22 August 1939? There had been many holy wars in man's bloody history, and the next one, which could come as early as 1950, might pit a holy alliance of capitalistic nations—the United States, Britain, Germany, France, Japan, and others—against communistic Russia. If the reader is skeptical that this was even possible, he should read what was being written about Russia even during the war in many of America's tabloid newspapers and Catholic publications; he should hear what was being said publicly by Senators Nye, Reynolds, Taft, and Wheeler; and he should remember that in international politics prophets have rarely considered all the possibilities.

Chapter 8

Conclusion
From Partnership to Cold War

Having dealt in some detail with changes in attitudes toward Russia and in the political culture which nurtured them, it should prove useful to focus once again on the four issues raised in chapter 1: the shape of attitudes toward Russia during World War II; the process by which these attitudes were formed; the role of national leadership in influencing wartime attitudes toward foreign policy; and the process by which, to most Americans' surprise, a Cold War with Russia occurred so quickly after the Allied triumph.

Changes in public thinking about Russia were frequent and far-reaching. Before the Nazi-Soviet pact, Americans probably disliked Germany even more than they disliked Russia. After the signing of that treaty—and especially after Russia's attack on Finland—Russia became Germany's equal in infamy. Even before the German attack on Russia, the Soviet position had improved relatively, for Russia had been reasonably quiescent in international affairs for more than a year while Germany was devouring Scandinavia, the Low Countries, and France, and threatening the existence of Great Britain. Russia's position in American opinion improved much more rapidly after Hitler attempted to make Russia his next victim.

Only after Americans themselves had become embroiled in the conflict did true friendship for Russia begin to take root and grow. The struggle was for America's survival as a free nation; France and the small European countries which had gone under proved that. And in 1942, as Americans were losing ground in a foreign war for the first time in their proud history, Russia's continued resistance held out the best hope for ultimate victory. Unhindered by a second front in western Europe, the Germans advanced in Russia during the summer over the dead bodies of millions of courageous Russian soldiers and civilians. By late fall, after the epic struggle on the streets and in the houses of Stalingrad, it was the

Russians who were advancing over the frozen bodies of dead Germans. Stated simply, the average American appreciated from the bottom of his heart the tenacity and ultimate success of the Russian resistance.

This sincere appreciation of Russia's sacrifices in 1942 led to many acts of goodwill toward Russia during 1943. Russia was the toast of the nation. The enduring legacy of friendliness toward Britain and China kept their standing with Americans higher in absolute percentages than Russia's, but toward no other land was the intensity of positive feelings so pronounced. The euphoria touched off by the communiqués, news photos, and headlines from the Moscow and Teheran conferences in the fall climaxed the year in which Russia stood higher in American esteem than at any other time in this century.

The year 1944 brought less favorable attitudes toward Russia. The Russians themselves contributed to their decline in favor, which was reflected in the polls and in the writings and speeches of American opinion makers. Communist spokesmen in *Pravda* and *Izvestia* lashed out against respected American leaders and institutions, most of which had held highly favorable opinions toward Russia. They refused either to get along with the London Poles or to announce their full support for the Lublin Poles. And they began their drive into eastern Europe which, although welcomed as a necessary step toward Hitler's demise, was feared because many Americans did not want eastern Europe to be dominated by Russia after the war. This reason for declining American confidence clearly was not due to Russian malfeasance; nor was it Russia's fault that the presidential election contributed directly to disunity in America and indirectly to growing distrust of Soviet intentions.

The apprehension of Americans about Russia's place in the postwar world and their own role in it increased during late 1944 and early 1945. Britain and Russia obviously were working toward specific objectives, but the Roosevelt administration did not seem to have any specific objectives for the peace which now appeared to be only months away. The conferences at Moscow and Teheran had served fine public relations functions for the administration, and the Yalta Conference did also. But the Yalta accords had unfortunate consequences. They gave the appearance that the three great powers would share the responsibility for forming governments in liberated lands all over Europe, whereas in reality nothing of essence was changed. As perceptive opinion makers observed at the time, the Yalta meetings basically did not alter the power relationships in either eastern or western Europe. In fact, there is no evidence that Roosevelt and Churchill were willing to see them changed in the West, or that Stalin was willing to see them altered in the East.

From March 1945 onward, American goodwill toward Russia declined sharply. This happened, generally, because almost all Americans simply were unprepared for the realities of the rapidly approaching postwar world. Manifestations of this unfortunate situation have been described in preceding chapters; they will receive more intensive treatment later in this one. The decline in good will after March 1945 occurred specifically because Americans decided that Russia was not living up to the Yalta accords. American bitterness and disillusionment in the wake of Yalta—a bitterness reciprocated by Kremlin leaders—stimulated the tangible beginnings of the Cold War.

In short, dominant American attitudes toward Russia changed from prewar fear to midwar friendship and back toward postwar fear and distrust. These changes confirm an important but fairly obvious point in public-opinion theory as we considered it generally in chapter 1, namely, that opinions do indeed change markedly over time.[1] Perhaps more significant is this study's specific finding that a period of perhaps ten to twenty months was required to transform generally negative attitudes into generally positive ones (roughly, from the summer of 1941 to the fall of 1942), and that, looking ahead, it took a similar period to transform the generally positive attitudes into generally negative ones (roughly, from the winter of 1945 to the spring of 1946).

How were these shifting but generally friendly wartime attitudes toward Russia formed? This study suggests that most people's attitudes changed less as a result of specific events than according to the way opinion makers interpreted events and personalities for the public.[2] Why was it so much worse for the Russians to attack Finland in December 1939 than it was for them to occupy the Baltic states in July 1940? The Letts, Lithuanians, and Estonians probably did not think that it was. But American opinion makers treated the attack on Finland as dastardly aggression worthy of daily headlines, which thereafter exacerbated attitudes toward Russia. In contrast, the media gave the seizure of the Baltic states relatively little notice. No real change in public attitudes toward Russia occurred at that time.

Or consider the American response to the German attack on Russia. Why should Americans necessarily have adopted a solidly pro-Russian position, leading to the extension of lend-lease to Communist Russia even before the United States entered the war? Many Roman Catholics and conservatives like Herbert Hoover and Colonel R. R. McCormick thought that their countrymen should not adopt pro-Russian attitudes. They argued that Germany's social and political ideas were less threatening to America than Russia's, that Germany tolerated religion whereas Russia did not, and that the overthrow of Stalin's despotic regime should be welcomed. Moreover, they thought that Hitler's thrust to the East was just what the Western democracies should have been hoping for all along.

These and related arguments had considerable plausibility, yet they were almost totally rejected by most opinion makers and subsequently by the bulk of the public as well. It is extremely doubtful that they would have been rejected by the public if most leading opinion makers had found them compelling.

Another hypothesis about the process of opinion change concerns the mass and attentive publics, which on matters of foreign policy correspond quite closely to the provincials and cosmopolitans described in chapters 1 and 5. Students of public opinion usually contend that the attentive public is quite stable in its opinions and attitudes toward foreign policy, whereas the mass public is quite changeable.[3] The findings of this study seem to suggest the reverse. Here it was the cosmopolitans who changed their opinions and attitudes toward Russia most noticeably from December 1939 to December 1943. Provincials, who did not keep as abreast of changing ideas, were much more likely to retain most of their prewar opinions and attitudes throughout the war.

For cosmopolitans and even more for provincials, these attitudes included a visceral hatred of communism, a hatred Republicans tried to exploit in the 1944 campaign. During the 1930s most Americans knew little of Russia, and they tended to consider her backward, strange, and unimportant.[4] Whereas during the thirties most Americans were strongly anticommunist and vaguely anti-Russian, during the war most Americans were anticommunist but pro-Russian, thus creating the likelihood on a large scale of what psychologist Leon Festinger has called cognitive dissonance.[5] As we have seen, and as this theory would tend to predict, some Americans reduced dissonance in their thought processes during the war by (1)insisting that Russia was evolving away from communism; (2)avoiding information contrary to their new view of Russia; and (3) repressing information which tended to "play the Axis game" of undermining Allied unity. By early 1945 Russia was increasingly recognized as the dominant power on the European landmass. Given the instability of attitude explained partly by cognitive dissonance and the absence of pro-Russian governmental leadership, it proved relatively easy within a year of V-E Day to restore the godless, dictatorial, and world-revolutionary images of Russia and to add land-grabbing, domineering, and saber-rattling ones.

Another conclusion about the formation of attitudes toward Russia during the war involves the role of well-publicized Allied conferences in raising the level of favorable opinions regarding probable postwar cooperation between Russia and the United States. In fact, as demonstrated in figure 4, 50 percent or more of Americans polled on the question of trust in Russia's continued cooperation after the war answered yes *only* after the Roosevelt-Molotov meeting in June 1942, after the Moscow and Teheran conferences in late 1943, and after the Yalta and Potsdam conferences in 1945.

It is ironic in view of the conference's goal of increasing unity among nations and significant in view of the success of previous conferences in raising the level of favorable attitudes that the April through June 1945 San Francisco conference to form the United Nations did not increase confidence in continued Soviet-American cooperation, and that the September 1945 London Foreign Ministers' Conference contributed to a decline in confidence, a decline which was to increase sharply after the beginning of 1946.[6] Moreover, the apparent success and high-sounding generalities emerging from each wartime conference left a legacy of disappointment as the glow wore off and basic differences remained. Whether on the second front, on Poland, or on other issues, the cost of the appearance of unanimity and a jump in the opinion polls was great— greater, perhaps, than the cost of increased candor.

If, as is argued here and in much of the literature on public opinion, the president and other leading opinion makers can largely shape dominant attitudes toward foreign policy, the recent emphasis on domestic constraints on American policy toward Russia in the mid-1940s needs to be reconsidered.[7] It would have required courage and leadership, but there is strong reason to believe that Presidents Roosevelt and Truman and their secretaries of state could have told the American people throughout 1945 of America's and Russia's new power and of the new realities of the international order. Given the tradition of deference to the president in foreign policy, the desire for continued friendship among the Allies, and the renewed faith in American institutions growing out of the war effort, it is quite likely that most Americans would have accepted their leaders' assessment of the postwar world order. In fact, that is precisely what the majority of the people had done when their governmental and other leading opinion makers favored pro-Russian attitudes during the war, and it is also what the people did when these leaders adopted a "get-tough-with-Russia" stance in 1946 and 1947.

Viewed as a whole, the preceding analysis of the opinion-making process demonstrates the enormous power of national leadership in the United States to influence wartime attitudes toward Russia. One segment of that leadership, the media, occupies a crucial and unique place in the communication of ideas in modern society. We have seen in this study that general American views on Russia during the war never differed markedly from those which predominated in the media at any given

Figure 4. Percentage expressing confidence in Russian postwar cooperation, 1942–1945 (adapted from a table in Warren B. Walsh," American Attitudes twoard Russia," p. 186)

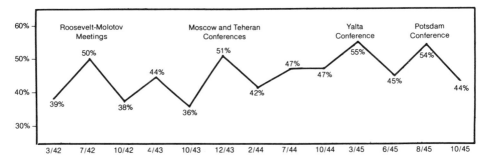

time. Coincidence is not cause, of course, but it would be difficult to deny on the basis of this striking evidence that the media play an extremely important role in shaping opinions on foreign affairs.

Even more important, however, is the president's potential power as an opinion maker on foreign affairs. The president stands far above any one of his countrymen in this regard. One reason for this is his personal prerogatives in this area. Because he is the nation's decision maker in foreign much more than in domestic affairs, the public looks to him for leadership in this area more than in any other. His views on international problems are sought persistently, and when he gives them they are almost always widely circulated in the media. Only the president has immediate access to the electronic media to explain his views on foreign policy to the people, and no one has really contended that he should not possess this unique privilege. But with all of his immense power and privilege in foreign affairs goes the responsibility to keep the people informed of his ideas about the world and America's role in it.

Most modern American presidents and their assistants have done just that. Two years after explaining to Americans why he believed they must go to war, Woodrow Wilson sought by every possible means to explain to them why he thought the country must join the League of Nations. Herbert Hoover and Secretary of State Henry L. Stimson explained the situation in the Far East during the Manchurian crisis as they saw it and indicated their response to it. And Harry S. Truman and General George C. Marshall told the people their views on the European situation after the war and how they wanted the nation to react to it.

As we saw in preceding chapters, many American opinion makers of the time viewed with alarm the administration's lack of leadership in formulating foreign policies and in explaining them to the American people. More recently, scholars such as Robert Beitzell, James MacGregor

Burns, John Lewis Gaddis, and Lloyd C. Gardner have criticized Roosevelt sharply for his failure to explain to the public the changing realities of Soviet-American relations.[8] George F. Kennan's observations in an interview with me in March 1970 highlight this crucial failure in the context of entire the war.

I think it never pays not to tell the people the truth. And I think what we should have told them is: "Look here, we and the western Europeans are weak. We cannot defeat Hitler with our own forces. We are going to have to take the help of the Russians in defeating him; and let nobody think there won't be a price for that. It's going to be a bitter price. We're going to have to pay it someday. There will have to be compromises made, and postwar Europe will not be all to our liking."

But the trouble is that our people are convinced that you don't get people to fight if you tell them this sort of thing. Personally, I don't think that's true, because I think military units fight much more on the basis of unit pride and morale than they do on the basis of political indoctrination. I think a proper leadership would have told us all the way through: "This is all right. We will stand up loyally as allies of the Russians. We will meet all our commitments to them and will do the best we can to help them defeat the Germans. But we should not forget that these people have an entirely different ideological orientation than we have and that their aims, as evidenced by the first two decades of their power in Russia, don't resemble our own. We can't expect that we're going to want the same things."

This was the great deceit that was practiced on the American public: to try to make them believe that really, at bottom, the Russians and we were after the same things. This was not right.[9]

In fairness, there can be no doubt that Roosevelt did much during his years in office to improve relations between the United States and Russia. He recognized the Soviet Union soon after taking office, and he defended his decision so ably that it never really became a political issue in the United States. He opened some channels of trade and communication between America and Russia with similar boldness and success. He helped to maintain an effective partnership with Russia throughout the war despite much residual anticommunism in America and despite much resentment in Russia about the Western powers' tardiness in opening the second front and in sending lend-lease aid on schedule. In this as in many other areas, it is difficult to fault the president's diplomacy.

But Roosevelt never really faced the culminating task of his leadership: preparing the American people to live in a peaceful world given structure and order by the continued cooperation of the three great powers which were about to win the largest war in human history. Moreover, there can be little doubt that he knew that most Americans were not prepared for the probable realities of postwar international relations.

The American people were unprepared not because provincial Americans continued to ignore the entire spectrum of international politics and to look to the administration for leadership, but because most cosmopolitan Americans had not accepted Russia, power politics, or both. Most conservative and Roman Catholic leaders were not averse to power politics as practiced by the United States or Britain, but they would not accept the fact that Russia was then and in the future would continue to be a great power exerting decisive influence in some countries outside her borders, notably Catholic Poland. Most liberals were willing to grant Russia virtually the same prerogatives the United States exercised in international affairs, but they made it clear that they were going to be unhappy if any nation played power politics after the war.

The president was the only American who had the power and prestige to alter these rigidifying attitudes significantly. He might not have succeeded entirely, but if he did not acquaint the people with his judgments about the implications of increased Russian and American power in a world of sovereign states, he could well expect the people to sour on the shape of the peace and turn against Communist Russia soon after the war ended. And the only time to prepare the people for the postwar world obviously was during the war.

Most other opinion makers, and indeed the people themselves, shared responsibility for the failure of most Americans to understand the probable realities of the postwar international order. In fact, a crucial point in considering the origins of the Cold War is not to determine degrees of responsibility for this failure but simply to state that the overwhelming majority of Americans were unprepared for the postwar world. Their unpreparedness for the peace was a primary reason for the coming of the Cold War.[10]

The basic question confronting Americans in the spring of 1945 was whether a preponderant percentage of international influence in the postwar world would suffice, or whether the United States should resist any spread of Russia's economic and political ideas, even if that spread essentially was confined to eastern Europe, and even if contention might well lead to acrimonious conflicts between the United States and Russia. That was the question Carl Becker had posed so clearly in 1944, and it was the question which he, Walter Lippmann, Reinhold Niebuhr, and a few others had answered by advocating the first alternative.

Careful students of the thought and behavior of Franklin Roosevelt, such as Robert A. Divine and James MacGregor Burns, have concluded that this was the president's own basic position. To be sure, he wanted Russia to exercise her power in eastern Europe judiciously and with some regard for international amenities. Thus, for example, he wanted her to include some Poles from outside the Lublin committee in the new Polish government, but he knew that the ambiguous Yalta accords appeared to permit the preeminence of the Lublin Poles under Russia's guidance, a fact of which he reminded Churchill two weeks before his death. Unlike many of her supporters on the Left, Roosevelt had little faith in a new world organization, and he definitely wanted it to be an organization of sovereign states rather than a true world government. And unlike many of his opponents on the Right, Roosevelt realized that another superpower existed, and that visions of American hegemony all over the globe were just dreams. He also realized that, despite the existence of a strong Russia with preeminent influence in eastern Europe, the United States would be the most powerful nation in human history.

In retrospect, the president's basic ideas about the postwar world seem sound. They grew out of careful thinking about international relations dating back to the campaign for the League of Nations and from experience in diplomacy during a dozen tumultuous years of uneasy peace and global war. They corresponded essentially with the ideas on the subject of many of the most penetrating thinkers in America—men like Walter Lippmann, Carl Becker, Henry L. Stimson,[11] David Dallin, and Reinhold Niebuhr.

Unfortunately, Roosevelt never shared his overarching conception of the postwar world with his new vice-president, Harry S. Truman, much less with the American people as a whole. Unlike the experienced cosmopolitan president, the provincial vice-president's entire career had been devoted to domestic politics and administration. In Missouri, Truman had advanced in county government with the support of the Pendergast machine; in Washington, he had come to prominence by watching over waste, inefficiency, and profiteering in defense contracts. There is little evidence that he knew much about the realities of international politics or the awesome problems that he might have to face in foreign policy. Yet the tired president met with Truman only twice in 1945.

As I have emphasized in the preceding chapter, the American people desperately needed instruction in international affairs. Even sophisticated liberals like the editors of the *New Republic* judged the Yalta accords primarily by their possible contribution to the development of international organization. On the Right were many advocates of American hegemony whose views of the postwar world were just as unrealistic. Most of these opinion makers would have denied vehemently that they were insisting on American hegemony, but they could hardly have denied that they were demanding that specific American ideals like free enterprise, free elections, and religious freedom prevail everywhere on earth. Liberals like the editors of the *New Republic* and conservatives like Herbert Hoover had very strong convictions about the new world in which either a world organization patterned after America's federal government or American power and ideals would reign supreme. In the spring of 1945 the dreams of both of these relatively cosmopolitan groups seemed to be crashing into concrete roadblocks, and neither the liberals nor conservatives liked it at all.

Meanwhile most Americans did not know what to think. They were provincials who looked to the president for leadership in foreign policy. Roosevelt, for his part, had told them time and again in his soothing radio voice that all was well, that the Allies were getting along fine, and that the new world after the war would emerge without such evils as power politics and spheres of influence. In the weeks before and after the president died they occasionally read in the newspapers and heard on the radio that Russia was playing power politics and jeopardizing the peace. Living as they did in an age of virulent nationalism and having been told little about the facts of American and Russian power outside their borders, they naturally began to believe that Russia was threatening the peace, and in sharply increasing numbers they began to tell the pollsters that Russia could no longer be trusted.

The American people and their government in the spring of 1945 had two basic choices. They could accept Russian predominance in the lands between Russia and Germany and have the strong likelihood of accommodation among the great powers, or they could contest virtually every move Russia made outside of her borders and have Cold War. If the new president in the White House, the peddler in Dubuque, and most people in between had been better informed about the realities of international politics and the limits as well as the strengths of American power, the nation probably would have chosen a course in which disagreement between the new superpowers might have been put in perspective, one in which at least some of the domestic and international consequences of bitter hostility might have been averted. The tragedy of the situation was that hardly anyone even knew what the alternatives were.

Notes

1. In a 1964 poll, for example, Lloyd A. Free and Hadley Cantril asked, "Which do you think will turn out be be the greater threat to the United States—Soviet Russia or Communist China?" The response was 54 percent China and 19 percent Russia. In an October 1966 Gallup poll, 56 percent answered, "Communist China should not be admitted as a member of the United Nations," but in answering another question 55 percent favored admission "if it would improve U.S. and Communist China relations" (Lloyd A. Free and Hadley Cantril, *The Political Beliefs of Americans*, pp. 88–89).

2. In regard to policy, it can be argued generally that the hardening of the American position toward Russia's policies in eastern Europe, symbolized by President Truman's blunt conversation with Soviet Foreign Minister Molotov on 23 April 1945, reflected in part the end of the necessity of the Russian military contribution to victory over the Axis. On this point see, for example, John Lewis Gaddis, *The United States and the Origins of the Cold War, 1941–1947*, p. 212 and passim. A specific incident just after V-E Day was the "sudden, drastic, even rude stoppage" of lend-lease shipments to Russia on 12 May 1945 (George C. Herring, Jr., *Aid to Russia 1941–1946*, p. 206). Contemporary studies of media and public attitudes reported significant "stiffening" of opinion toward Russia in May 1945. See, for example, U.S. Department of State, "Fortnightly Survey of Public Opinion on International Affairs," no. 27, 23 May 1945. Herbert Feis aptly titled his work on the May to June 1945 period *Between War and Peace*.

3. For some indication of the vitality of the effort among American private citizens to plan for a new world order, see Robert A. Divine, *Second Chance*, pp. 52–58 and passim.

4. John R. Deane, *The Strange Alliance*. The following is an obviously incomplete but suggestive sampling of books on wartime Soviet-American relations published in the United States: Gar Alperovitz, *Atomic Diplomacy*; Robert Beitzell, *The Uneasy Alliance*; Diane Shaver Clemens, *Yalta*; Raymond H. Dawson, *The Decision to Aid Russia, 1941*; Herbert Feis, *Churchill, Roosevelt, Stalin*; Gaddis, *United States and the Origins of the Cold War*; Lloyd C. Gardner, *Architects of Illusion*; Herring, *Aid to Russia, 1941–1946*; Martin F. Herz, *Beginnings of the Cold War*; Gabriel Kolko, *The Politics of War*; William H. McNeill, *America, Britain, and Russia*; William L. Neumann, *After Victory*; Thomas G. Paterson, *Soviet-American Confrontation*; Lisle Rose, *After Yalta*; and Richard W. Steele, *The First Offensive, 1942*.

5. Two articles on this subject, published shortly after the war, are Warren B. Walsh, "American Attitudes toward Russia," and Paul Willen, "Who 'Collaborated' with Russia?" A recent article which gives some attention to attitudes toward Russia during the war is Les K. Adler and Thomas G. Paterson, "Red Fascism." Another recent article is Melvin Small, "How We Learned to Love the Russians," pp. 455–78. In addition to these articles, most studies of American-Soviet relations during World War II make at least some reference to American attitudes toward Russia. For a perceptive recent analysis of some aspects of American attitudes, see Gaddis, *United States and the Origins of the Cold War*, pp. 32–62.

6. Meno Lovenstein, *American Opinion of Soviet Russia*; Peter G. Filene, *Americans and the Soviet Experiment, 1917–1933*. Three works dealing primarily with attitudes of Ameri-

can intellectuals are Christopher Lasch, *The American Liberals and the Russian Revolution*; Frank A. Warren III, *Liberals and Communism*; and William Welch, *American Images of Soviet Foreign Policy*. A documentary collection is Peter G. Filene, *American Views of Soviet Russia*, *1917–1965*.

7. James F. Best, *Public Opinion*, p. 6. Social psychologist Wilbur Schramm has formulated the following definition of *attitudes*: "By attitudes we mean inferred states of readiness to react in an evaluative way in support of or against a given stimulus situation" (*The Process and Effects of Mass Communication*, p. 209). Schlitz and Cook define an attitude as "a disposition to evaluate, or to respond to, an object or class of objects in a given way, this disposition being inferred from consistence of response to the object or members of the object class" (quoted in Herbert McClosky, "Personality and Attitude Correlates of Foreign Policy Orientation," in James N. Rosenau, *Domestic Sources of Foreign Policy*, pp. 55–56).

8. Bernard Berelson and Gary A. Steiner, *Human Behavior*, p. 102.

9. For a detailed discussion of belief systems, see Milton Rokeach, *The Open and Closed Mind*, pp. 233–310.

10. On this issue see, for example, Filene, *Americans and the Soviet Experiment*, pp. 2–3.

11. I am convinced that however useful oral history may be in reconstructing participation in events, it is much less useful in reconstructing attitudes. Perhaps this is especially the case when (1) the attitudes involve issues of foreign policy, (2) there was such a shift in attitudes toward Russia shortly after the war, and (3) the attitudes were held about thirty years ago.

12. M. Brewster Smith, Jerome S. Bruner, and Robert S. White, *Opinions and Personality*, pp. 48–287. In 1947 these authors conducted a thorough study of ten men of diverse social background and political outlook, concentrating on their attitudes toward Russia.

13. George Gallup, the leading pollster of the 1940s, argued in a pamphlet written in 1939 that "the New England town meeting idea has, in a sense, been restored by the development of opinion polling." As the qualification in his comment implies, Gallup must have known that residents of a typical New England village surely knew more about the structure of their neighbors' ideas than Americans knew of each other's from poll results (George Gallup, *Public Opinion in a Democracy*, p. 2).

14. James N. Rosenau, *Public Opinion and Foreign Policy*, pp. 19–20. Rosenau, in turn, was indebted to Gabriel A. Almond's important study, *The American People and Foreign Policy*.

15. Rosenau, *Public Opinion*, p. 20.

16. For Soviet-American relations during the war, the decision-making process, diplomacy, and (less systematically) the opinion-submitting process have been treated in detail in the works listed in note 2 above, as well as in other works on the war such as James MacGregor Burns's *Roosevelt: The Soldier of Freedom*.

17. Rosenau, *Public Opinion*, p. 28.

18. Rosenau, *Public Opinion*, p. 28. An important sidelight is that "opinion leaders" whom Lazarsfeld, Berelson, and Gaudet credited with influencing opinions at the local level in their famous study of the 1940 election in Elmira, New York, are opinion holders because they simply do not have access to the society's impersonal channels of communication. For elaboration on "opinion leaders," see Paul Lazarsfeld, Bernard Berelson, and Hazel Gaudet, *The People's Choice*, pp. 49–52.

19. Rosenau, *Public Opinion*, pp. 27, 35–37, and 41.

20. Ibid., p. 59. Most of these examples were taken from a table on this page.

21. Ibid., p. 56.

22. In the research for this study there naturally was much greater concentration on newspapers, periodicals, books, radio broadcasts, public-opinion polls, and similar sources and less on private papers and governmental documents than there would have been, for example, in a study of the decision-making process.

23. Bernard C. Cohen, "The Relationship Between Public Opinion and Foreign Policy Makers," in Melvin Small, *Public Opinion and Historians*, pp. 70–71. Many other students of the presidency could be cited to substantiate Cohen's argument. One of the most recent and

perceptive is Emmet John Hughes: "The modern network of mass media has given the Presidency an almost revolutionary opportunity to create, to control, to distort, or to suppress the news" (*The Living Presidency*, p. 218). For recent discusssions of the importance of the mass media in America life in the 1930s and 1940s, see Erik Barnouw, *The Golden Web*, pp. 74–90 and 190–215; Richard H. Pells, *Radical Visions and American Dreams*, pp. 263–68; and Geoffrey Perrett, *Days of Sadness, Years of Triumph*, pp. 20 and 481.

24. Martin Kriesberg, "Dark Areas of Ignorance," in Lester Markel, *Public Opinion and Foreign Policy*, pp. 45–56. Kriesberg estimated that only 25 percent of the adult population showed "knowledge of foreign problems" (ibid., p. 51). Polls conducted in the spring of 1964 showed that about one-fourth of those interviewed did not know that China had a communist government; about one-fourth also had not heard that fighting was taking place in Vietnam (Free and Cantril, *The Political Beliefs of Americans*, p. 59).

25. Robert K. Merton, *Social Theory and Social Structure*, p. 451.

26. Ibid., pp. 451 and 454.

27. Ibid., p. 262.

28. Ibid., pp. 461–62.

29. Scott Greer, "Urbanization, Parochialism, and Foreign Policy," in Rosenau, *Domestic Sources*, p. 255. See especially Greer's article (pp. 253–62) and Herbert Gans, *The Urban Villagers*.

30. Alfred O. Hero, Jr., *The Southerner and World Affairs*, especially chapter 1.

31. Arno J. Mayer, *Political Origins of the New Diplomacy* and *The Politics and Diplomacy of Peacemaking*.

32. In his excellent recent study of American social thought during the depression, Richard H. Pells points out that unquestioned enthusiasm for Russia among the American Left was being challenged increasingly by the late 1930s. But many intellectuals remained highly sympathetic to Russian ideals, if not to practices such as the purges. (*Radical Visions and American Dreams*, pp. 304–10).

Notes to Chapter 2

1. Raoul de Roussy de Sales, *The Making of Yesterday*, p. 90.

2. Alice Payne Hackett, *Fifty Years of Best Sellers*, pp. 79–80.

3. AIPO Poll no. 138, November 1938, Roper Center. (AIPO stands for American Institute of Public Opinion, the Gallup organization.)

4. AIPO Poll no. 90, 5 July 1937, Roper Center.

5. AIPO Poll no. 147, February 1939, Roper Center. The question was, "Which do you think is the greater danger to America—the Communists living in this country or the Nazis living in this country?"

6. Eugene Lyons, *Assignment in Utopia*, p. 622.

7. Ibid., pp. 639–40.

8. Ibid., p. 606.

9. Consider, for example, Raymond Buell's assertion in *Reader's Digest* that "the whole of Central Europe today fears that sooner or later Germany and Russia will reach an understanding" ("Poland: Key to Europe," p. 101).

10. Quoted in Meno Lovenstein, *American Opinion of Soviet Russia*, pp. 152–53.

11. Westbrook Pegler, "What Strange Bedfellows!" p. 10.

12. Ibid., p. 11.

13. Ibid., p. 54.

14. Both quotations are from Irving Howe and Lewis Coser, *The American Communist Party*, p. 387.

15. Obviously, to call the *Nation* a leading liberal journal is to make a judgment, albeit an uncontroversial one. James N. Rosenau argues in *Public Opinion and Foreign Policy* that all questions of relative influence among opinion makers should be eliminated so that the flow of opinion can be described with thoroughgoing objectivity. I do not see how this can be done. I think judgments about relative influence, whether conscious or unconscious, are bound to enter into any conceivable study of the opinion-making process.

16. "To All Active Supporters of Democracy and Peace," *Nation*, 26 August 1939, p. 228.

17. National Municipal League, *People Must Think*, p. 62.

18. Editorial, *Federal Council Bulletin* 12 (June 1939): 4.

19. It now seems that the sharp dichotomy between democracy and totalitarianism in vogue at this time and later was a gross simplification of the facts. The growth of governmental power over the lives of individuals was proceeding rapidly in all industrialized countries, including of course the United States.

20. Clarence K. Streit, *Union Now*, p. 111.

21. Ibid., p. 114.

22. Quoted in Howe and Coser, *American Communist Party*, p. 387.

23. *Daily Worker*, 23 August 1939, p. 2.

24. To most American opinion makers, capitalism and democracy tended to mean the same thing, and socialism and dictatorship meant the opposite. Whether they were aware of the possibility of democratic socialism and simply did not pass this idea on to the public, or whether they were unaware of this possibility, is not clear.

25. *New York Times*, 22 August 1939, p. 18.

26. Ibid., 24 August 1939, p. 18.

27. *New York Daily News*, 23 August 1939, p. 31.

28. *New York Herald Tribune*, 24 August 1939, p. 18. For a brief but perceptive analysis of the effect of the Nazi-Soviet pact on the linking of Russia and Germany in American thought, see Les K. Adler and Thomas G. Paterson, "Red Fascism," pp. 1049–51.

29. Ibid., 25 August 1939, p. 14.

30. *New York Mirror*, 23 August 1939, p. 23.

31. *New York World-Telegram*, 23 August 1939, p. 16.

32. Ibid.

33. *New York Journal-American*, 23 August 1939, p. 1.

34. *Christian Science Monitor*, 22 August 1939, p. 18.

35. *Trenton Times*, 25 August 1939, p. 10. In order not to give disproportionate emphasis to large metropolitan areas, I have examined daily throughout the war the leading newspapers of three smaller cities: Trenton, New Jersey; Asheville, North Carolina; and Casper, Wyoming. These cities and their suburbs averaged about eighty thousand in population. Almost all of the other newspapers which I examined served metropolitan areas having more than ten times as many people.

36. *Philadelphia Inquirer*, 25 August 1939, p. 19.

37. *Baltimore Sun*, 23 August 1939, p. 8.

38. *Washington Post*, 23 August 1939, p. 6.

39. *Washington Star*, 22 August 1939, p. 6.

40. *Washington Times-Herald*, 23 August 1939, p. 8.

41. *Asheville Citizen*, 22 August 1939, p. 8.

42. *Atlanta Constitution*, 23 August, 1939, p. 8.

43. *New Orleans Times-Picayune*, 23 August 1939, p. 10.

44. *Houston Post*, 23 August 1939, p. 6.

45. *Cincinnati Enquirer*, 23 August 1939, p. 4.

46. *St. Louis Post-Dispatch*, 22 August 1939, p. C2.

47. *Cleveland Plain Dealer*, 23 August 1939, p. 18.

48. *Detroit News*, 23 August 1939, p. 18.

49. *Milwaukee Journal*, 22 August 1939, p. 8.

50. *Chicago Tribune*, 23 August 1939, p. 10.

51. *Chicago Daily News*, 23 August 1939, p. 12.

52. *Denver Post*, 22 August 1939, p. 8.

53. *Casper Tribune-Herald*, 23 August 1939, p. l.

54. *Los Angeles Times*, 23 August 1939, p. 8

55. *Seattle Times*, 23 August 1939, p. 6

56. See, for example, the findings reported by Harold Lasswell and Paul Lazarsfeld in Lazarsfeld and Patricia Kendall, *Radio Listening in America*, p. 54.

57. On this point (and others about radio at this time) see Erik Barnouw, *The Golden Web*, esp. pp. 74–83.

58. Benjamin Stolberg, "Communist Wreckers in American Labor," p. 6.

59. W.G. Krivitsky, "When Stalin Counterfeited Dollars," p. 8.

60. "Harvest Notes," *Saturday Evening Post*, 14 October 1939, p. 26.

61. Demaree Bess, "Stalin Over Europe," p. 50.

62. "Playing the Red," *Saturday Evening Post*, 8 November 1939, p. 26.

63. Mark Sullivan, "Uproot the Seeds of Totalitarianism," p. 6.

64. William Henry Chamberlin, "Letter to Editor," pp. 380–81.

65. Herbert Solow, "Stalin's Great American Hoax," p. 394.

66. "Subject to Change," *Saturday Review of Literature*, 9 September 1939, p. 8.

67. Louis Fischer, "Russia Goes West," p. 310.

68. Paul V. Harper, *The Russia I Believe In*, p. 267.

69. At the end of August, for example, the *Daily Worker* pled for American aid for Poland; ten days later, with the USSR attacking Poland from the East, it was pleased by the downfall of Poland's government.

70. *New York Times*, 1 December 1939, p. 22.

71. *New York Post*, 1 December 1939, p. 14.

72. *University of Washington Daily*, 5 December 1939, p. 4.

73. "The Attack on Finland," *Christian Century*, 13 December 1939, pp. 153–54.

74. *Chicago Tribune*, 1 December 1939, p. 6.

75. *Trenton Times*, 3 December 1939, p. B3.

76. *Pittsburgh Press*, 1 December 1939, p. 34.

77. *Detroit Free Press*, 2 December 1939, p. 6.

78. *New York Times*, 2 December 1939, p. 1.

79. *San Francisco Examiner*, 1 December 1939, p. 4.

80. *New York Times*, 1 December 1939, p. 11.

81. Quoted in Ellsworth Barnard, *Wendell Willkie*, p. 154.

82. The scholar would naturally be interested in the exact composition of the newspapers used, but that is information which Twohey did not provide. From my own work in the newspapers of the period, I am convinced that Twohey used, as he claimed, a balanced sample of newspapers of the various regions and political outlooks.

83. "Twohey Analysis of Newspaper Opinion," 2 December 1939, p. 5.

84. Ibid., 9 December 1939, p. 2.

85. Ibid., 16 December 1939, p. 2.

86. AIPO Poll no. 179, December 1939, Roper Center. The question was "In the present crisis, are your sympathies with Finland or Russia?" The results cited in the text underscore the importance of the media in circulating opinions. The media was also at least 99 percent pro-Finnish. Imagine how the results would have differed if the media had pictured the war as "defensive" and "necessary," or even had considered it "unnewsworthy" and ignored it.

87. *New York Times*, 7 February 1940, p. 4. After the war, the United States would *give* arms to virtually anybody who expressed animosity toward communism and would intervene with its own troops in such places as Korea, Lebanon, Vietnam, and the Dominican Republic, none of which was as well liked as "poor little Finland" in 1939 and 1940. The American stance toward the Russo-Finnish War was a sterling example of what isolationism meant in practice.

88. AIPO Survey, 5 January 1940, Gallup organization files. The question was, "Which of the following do you consider more important for the Dies Committee to investigate—Communist activities in this country or Nazi activities in this country?"

89. "Man of the Year," *Time*, 1 January 1940, p. 15.

90. Samuel I. Rosenman, *The Public Papers and Addresses of Franklin D. Roosevelt*, 9: 54.

91. Governor Herbert Lehman of New York, for example, said on 30 September that "nothing that could happen in the United States could give Hitler, Mussolini, Stalin and the Government of Japan more satisfaction than the defeat of the man who typifies to the whole world the kind of free, humane government which dictators despise—Franklin D.

Roosevelt" (quoted in Robert A. Divine, *Foreign Policy and U.S. Presidential Elections*, p. 60).

92. Secretary of State Cordell Hull even told Herbert Hoover in February 1941 of developments in the East, to which Hoover replied that the United States should patiently "wait for the Great Dictators to destroy each other." Hoover's remark is quoted in Eugene Lyons, *Herbert Hoover*, p. 365.

93. *New York Times*, 2 February 1941, p. 23.

94. *New York Herald Tribune*, 14 March 1941, p. 16.

95. *New York Times*, 21 April 1941, p. 18.

96. Alfred E. Smith address, 28 May 1941, Tape 3577, Phonoarchive of radio recordings, University of Washington (hereinafter cited as Phonoarchive).

97. There is need for a careful study of the sociology of publishing. In view of the swiftness of the change from early 1941 to late 1941 in authors and views featured by leading publishers, however, it is clear that publishers respond to intellectual and political currents more than they might prefer to admit in choosing the subjects and approaches to be emphasized.

98. Hewlett Johnson, *The Soviet Power*, p. 343.

99. Eugene Lyons, *Stalin*, pp. 13, 287.

100. Max Eastman, *Stalin's Russia and the Crisis in Socialism*, p. 6.

101. Freda Utley, *The Dream We Lost*, p. 297.

102. T. A. Taracouzio, *War and Peace in Soviet Diplomacy*, p. 295.

Notes to Chapter 3

1. *New York PM*, 23 June 1941, pp. 6–7.

2. Ibid.

3. Ibid.

4. Ibid.

5. Ibid.

6. Ibid., p. 24.

7. *New York Post*, 23 June 1941, p. 10.

8. *Baltimore Sun*, 23 June 1941, p. 12

9. *Casper Tribune-Herald*, 23 June 1941, p. 6.

10. *New York PM*, 23 June 1941, p. 5.

11. "Twohey Analysis of Newspaper Opinion," 28 June 1941, p. 4. Sixty-three percent of the newspapers, including all interventionist organs, took this view.

12. As Ralph Ingersoll put it, "It went through one's mind that it could happen this way. But so did a dozen other alternatives" (*New York PM*, 22 June 1941, p. 1).

13. *New York Times*, 25 June 1941, p. 1.

14. This dichotomy provided an organizing principle for Raymond H. Dawson's *The Decision to Aid Russia, 1941*, an important study of the entire opinion-policy relationship on the question of aid to Russia.

15. See James MacGregor Burns, *Roosevelt: Soldier of Freedom*, pp. 36–40. In presenting these four groups, I probably have placed emphasis where Burns would not have, but basically these ideas are his.

16. AIPO Release, 13 July 1941, Gallup organization files.

17. Ibid.

18. This does not mean, of course, that the opinions circulated by the media necessarily originate in the media. In fact, most opinions on almost all issues originate elsewhere. If all opinions did originate in the media, the scholar's task would be simplified immensely: the views of media opinion makers would be the sole object of study in this area!

19. AIPO Release, 13 July 1941, Gallup organization files. Income and religious differences were the only variables analyzed in this poll.

20. Quoted in Eugene Lyons, *Herbert Hoover*, p. 366. The "four freedoms"—freedom of speech, of worship, from want, and from fear—were proclaimed as broad aims by President Roosevelt in his state of the union address on 6 January 1941. Conservative critics feared that the four freedoms might involve an attempt to extend the New Deal to the entire world.

21. *Wall Street Journal*, 25 June 1941, p. 4. This fear was also expressed, among others, by the *New York Journal-American*, the *Trenton Times*, the *Milwaukee Journal*, the *Chicago Tribune*, and the *Minneapolis Star-Journal*.

22. *Wall Street Journal*, 25 June 1941, p. 4.

23. *Cleveland Plain Dealer*, 24 June 1941, p. 8.

24. *Pittsburgh Press*, 23 June 1941, p. 4.

25. *Washington Star*, 24 June 1941, p. 9.

26. *Philadelphia Bulletin*, 23 June 1941, p. 7.

27. *New York Times*, 24 June 1941, p. 1.

28. National debates often are confusing because they do not center on the same definitions of given arguments. All sides naturally tend to define an issue so that their positions can be presented logically and forcefully. The "winner" is usually not the side which attempts to defeat the other arguments, but the one which can present its own the most potently both in terms of the persuasiveness of the argument and in terms of the opinion-circulating capacity that it can command.

29. Quoted in Raymond H. Dawson, *The Decision to Aid Russia*, p. 119.

30. Ibid., pp. 118–19.

31. Ibid., p. 119.

32. *Christian Science Monitor*, 24 June 1941, p. 22.

33. *New York Times*, 26 June 1941, p. 18.

34. *New York Herald Tribune*, 23 June 1941, p. 18.

35. *St. Louis Post-Dispatch*, 24 June 1941, p. 8.

36. Ibid., 23 June 1941, p. C2.

37. CBS Tape 1826, "The World Today," 22 June 1941, Phonoarchive.

38. *Detroit News*, 23 June 1941, p. 1.

39. "Twohey Analysis of Newspaper Opinion," 26 July 1941, p. 7.

40. This is not to deny, however, that prestigious journals such as *Time* and *Reader's Digest* had powerful effects on their readers' overall orientation to events, as well as specific perspectives as soon as *Newsweek* or the *Nation*, for example, arrived in the reader's mailbox several days after the event.

41. Myron C. Taylor, *Wartime Correspondence between President Roosevelt and Pope Pius XII*, pp. 61–62.

42. During the war the president still could determine which of his comments at press conferences were "for the record" and which were "off the record."

43. *Department of State Bulletin* 5 (4 October 1941): 246.

44. *Federal Council Bulletin* 23 (November 1941): 6.

45. Quoted in Dawson, *Decision to Aid Russia*, pp. 259–60.

46. It was as if the public were reassured by reminders of Roosevelt's humanity! More to the point, Twohey argues at several points in his ongoing analysis of the Roosevelt administration and the press that Roosevelt often provoked controversy and then turned it to his own ends. Probably the most famous case of this was the third-term issue, brought up by Roosevelt late in 1939 in a provocative manner. The media and other politicians discussed and debated it throughly at the time, so that by the summer of 1940 it was largely a dead issue.

47. *New York Times*, 6 October 1941, p. 8.

48. Dawson, *Decision to Aid Russia*, p. 265.

49. Ibid., pp. 265–68.

50. *American Legion Magazine*, November 1941, p. 27.

51. "Twohey Analysis of Newspaper Opinion," 28 June 1941, p. 7.

52. Ibid., 26 July 1941, p. 7.

53. CBS Tape 1838, "The World Today," 3 July 1941, Phonoarchive.

54. CBS Tape 1845, "The World Today," 10 July 1941, Phonoarchive.

55. CBS Tape 1852, "The World Today," 17 July 1941, Phonoarchive.

56. Ibid.

57. CBS Tape 1826, "World News Tonight," 22 June 1941, Phonoarchive.

58. CBS Tape 1841, "World News Tonight," 6 July 1941, Phonoarchive.

59. Max Lerner, "Russia and the War of Ideas," p. 18.

60. "When Winter Comes to Russia," *New Republic*, 11 August 1941, p. 3.

61. Reinhold Niebuhr, "The Russians and Our Interdependence," p. 1.

62. Bruce Bliven, "Russia's Morale—and Ours," p. 274.

63. Freda Kirchwey, "Congress and Russia," p. 361.

64. "Muscovites Take up Their Guns as Nazi Horde Approaches Russian Capital," *Life*, 27 October 1941, p. 27.

65. "Morale," *Time*, 29 September 1941, p. 18.

66. Kenneth Davis, "Have We Been Wrong About Stalin?" p. 7.

67. "Litvinoff—He Capitalizes a Failure," *Business Week*, 15 November 1941, p. 28.

68. Freda Utley, "The Limits of Russian Resistance," p. 300.

69. Stuart Chase, "The Twilight of Communism in the U.S.A.," p. 34.

70. Lamont's contrasts were: "The ideal of international peace and cooperation [versus a nation] permanently geared to war and conquest; a free brotherhood of peoples versus ruthless persecution of minorities; a socialized economy operated for use versus a monopolist economy run for profits; socialist planning for abundance versus totalitarian planning for war; the expansion of trade unions versus the destruction of trade unions; the emancipation of women versus the degradation of women; an unprecedented advance of culture versus the debasement of culture; science in the service of the people versus science perverted to the uses of war and racism; evolution toward fullest democracy versus democracy considered 'a putrid corpse'; and a nation in which civilization moves steadily ahead versus a nation which moves civilization steadily backward" (Corliss Lamont, *Soviet Russia versus Nazi Germany*, p. 1).

71. William Henry Chamberlin, "Forward," *Russian Review* 1 (November 1941): 1.

72. Anna Louise Strong, *The Soviets Expected It*, p. vii.

73. Walter Duranty, *The Kremlin and the People*, pp. 138, 173, 184, and 161.

74. Joseph E. Davies, *Mission to Moscow*, p. xviii.

75. CBS Tape 838, Franklin Roosevelt address, 9 December 1941, Phonoarchive.

76. "Talk of the Town," *New Yorker*, 3 January 1942, p. 9.

77. "The Fortune Survey," *Fortune*, February 1942, p. 98.

78. The Declaration of the United Nations and its relation to American attitudes toward Russia will be considered in the next chapter.

Notes to Chapter 4

1. Lord Beaverbrook, "Opportunity to Win War in 1942," p. 459.

2. "Home Mission Board Report," *Annual of the Southern Baptist Convention*, p. 252.

3. Ibid.

4. It is ironic that these basic questions arose as they did. In 1941 Americans were asking whether Russia was acceptable as "our" ally, even though the United States was not formally at war and Russia was. In 1942 the question of whether we were really Russia's ally arose even though both nations were belligerents against Germany.

5. On this point see James MacGregor Burns, *Roosevelt: Soldier of Freedom*, pp. 183–84.

6. The most detailed study of American decision making and diplomacy in regard to the second front is Richard W. Steele, *The First Offensive, 1942*. Soviet thinking on this issue is discussed in Alexander Werth, *Russia at War, 1941–1945*, pp. 377–80 and 484–86.

7. It was an axiom of thought after 1941 that if the Western democracies and Russia had banded together in the late 1930s to stop Hitler, the current bloodshed would have been averted. Litvinoff was hailed in retrospect as a prophet in a wilderness of appeasing Tories and smug Americans.

8. *New York Herald Tribune*, 28 February 1942, p. 10.

9. Maxim Litvinoff, "More Fronts to Win the War Now,"p. 325.

10. Maxim Litvinoff, "Russia's Contributions," p. 358.

11. *Daily Worker*, 28 April 1942, p. 2. For additional information on Davies, see *Current Biography*, 1942 ed., s.v. "Joseph E. Davies"; and John Lewis Gaddis, *United States and the Origins of the Cold War*, pp. 34–37.

12. *Daily Worker*, 28 April 1942, p. 2.

13. *Atlanta Constitution*, 2 May 1942, p. 4.

14. *Atlanta Constitution*, 5 May 1942, p. 1.

15. Ibid., p. 6.

16. "Russian Courage and Cold Rout Nazis," *Life*, 12 January 1942, pp. 19–25.

17. "Russian Parents Lament Dead Son at Scene of German Execution," ibid., 4 May 1942, p. 29.

18. "Man of the Year," *Time*, 5 January 1942, pp. 13–14.

19. "Tough Baby from Moscow," *Time*, 11 May 1942, p. 17.

20. James B. Reston, *Prelude to Victory*, p. 3 (references are to the more widely circulated Pocket edition).

21. Ibid., contents.

22. Ibid., p. 32.

23. Ibid., p. 33.

24. Ibid., p. 121.

25. Ibid., p. 122. Reston's contention that it was fortunate that Russia was totalitarian was common at this time. If the Soviets had not operated with totalitarian efficiency, it was believed, the Germans would have conquered Russia in 1941.

26. Ibid., p. 144.

27. Raoul de Roussy de Sales, *The Making of Yesterday*, p. 257.

28. Reston, *Prelude to Victory*, front cover.

29. Wallace Carroll, *We're in This with Russia*. Carroll assured his countrymen that "for a generation or more after this war—if Americans go forward courageously—the Soviets will not be able to exert a direct revolutionary influence on America by the example of their achievements" (p. 239).

30. Margaret Bourke-White, *Shooting the Russian War*, p. 215.

31. John Scott, *Behind the Urals*, p. 263.

32. Michel Berchin and Eliahu Ben-Horin, *The Red Army*, p. 258.

33. Sergei N. Kournakoff, *Russia's Fighting Forces*, p. vii.

34. Ibid., p. 257.

35. Sidney and Beatrice Webb, *The Truth about Soviet Russia*, pp. 16, 19.

36. Emil Ludwig, *Stalin*, p. 193.

37. John Foster Dulles, "Toward World Order," in Francis J. McConnell et al., *A Basis for the Peace to Come*, p. 47.

38. William Paton, "The Ecumenical Church and World Order," in ibid., p. 77.

39. Herbert Agar, *A Time for Greatness*, p. 289.

40. Quentin Reynolds, *Only the Stars Are Neutral*, p. 93.

41. Ibid., p. 94.

42. *Washington Star*, 1 May 1942, p. 1.

43. *Asheville Citizen*, 2 May 1942, p. 4.

44. Ibid., 6 May 1942, p. 4.

45. *Cleveland Plain Dealer*, 2 May 1942, p. 8.

46. *Daily Worker*, 29 April 1942, p. 2. Del Vayo correctly prophesied, "The clamor for a second front is not going to diminish; on the contrary, it will become overwhelming as soon as the stupendous struggle on the Russian front regains its former intensity."

47. Ibid., 2 May 1942, p. 1.

48. *Atlanta Constitution*, 19 May 1942, p. 6.

49. *New York Herald Tribune*, 18 May 1942, p. 16.

50. *Chicago Tribune*, 17 May 1942, p. 12.

51. *Philadelphia Bulletin*, 16 May 1942, p. 10.

52. *New York Post*, 19 May 1942, p. 19.

53. *Christian Science Monitor*, 18 May 1942, p. 20.

54. *Philadelphia Inquirer*, 17 May 1942, p. B9.

55. *St. Louis Post-Dispatch*, 17 May 1942, p. C2.

56. America and Britain combined suffered fewer than 500,000 military and civilian deaths, while Russia was suffering about ten million soldiers and another ten million

civilians killed in the war against Germany. Thus Russia received about 95 percent of the Allied casualties in the European war. On the basis of sacrifices, it would be extremely difficult to argue that Russia demanded too large a sphere of influence after the war. In fact, if there is an argument to be made on this point, it would be that Britain and America received too much, for their soldiers overran much of western Europe after Germany had been largely defeated.

57. James MacGregor Burns believes that the postponement of the second front from 1942 until 1944 was the greatest single cause of the Cold War. As Burns puts it at one point in his recent work on World War II, "The resulting cynicism was the breeding ground of postwar disillusion and disunity. The second-front delay far more than any other factor aroused Soviet anger and cynicism" (*Roosevelt: Soldier of Freedom*, p. 374).

58. Quoted in Kenneth S. Davis, *Experience of War*, p. 187.

59. Alfred D. Chandler, Jr., *The Papers of Dwight David Eisenhower*, 1:205.

60. *New York Times*, 27 March 1942, p. 7.

61. Ibid., 31 March 1942, p. 3.

62. Ibid., 18 April 1942, p. 1.

63. Ibid., 29 April 1942, p. 1. Roosevelt was well aware throughout the war of his role of commander in chief, and Stimson was a forceful and sagacious secretary of war. Both they and the leaders of the military services believed firmly in the principle of civilian control.

64. *New York Times*, 30 May 1942, p. 1.

65. Ibid., 31 May 1942, p. 3.

66. W. F. Kernan, *Defense Will Not Win the War*, p. 51.

67. Quoted in Burns, *Roosevelt: Soldier of Freedom*, p. 233.

68. Ibid., p. 234.

69. On these points see Herbert Feis, *Churchill, Roosevelt, Stalin*, pp. 65–69; and Steele, *The First Offensive, 1942*, pp. 136–41. Steele argues that "Molotov was probably deceived by the President's declaration" (p. 138). The Roosevelt-Molotov meetings are also discussed in Robert Beitzell, *The Uneasy Alliance*, pp. 40–41; in Burns, *Roosevelt: Soldier of Freedom*, pp. 233–35; and in Gaddis, *United States and the Origins of the Cold War*, pp. 68–69.

70. "Three Greatest Nations Sign Alliances," *Life*, 22 June 1942, p. 15.

71. "Russia's Hopes Turn Westward in Deals with the Democracies," *Newsweek*, 22 June 1942, p. 17. The Washington accords were similar to those which Molotov had negotiated in London two weeks before. The major difference was that no formal alliance was concluded between Russia and the United States.

72. Freda Kirchway, "Russia and the Future," p. 701.

73. CBS Tape 2216, "The World Today," 11 June 1942, Phonoarchive.

74. *New York Times*, 12 June 1942, p. 20.

75. CBS Tape 2216, "The World Today," 11 June 1942, Phonoarchive.

76. CBS Tape 852, "FDR's Special Message to Celebrate Flag Day" (United Nations Day), 14 June 1942, Phonoarchive.

77. For the context of Churchill's visit, see, for example, Burns, *Roosevelt: Soldier of Freedom*, pp. 235–36.

78. Scott Hart, *Washington at War*, p. 109.

79. *New York Times*, 23 June 1942, p. 1. On the same day, 22 June 1942, General Douglas MacArthur said that the "world situation at the present time indicated that the hopes of civilization rest on the worthy banners of the courageous Red Army" (quoted in William Z. Foster, *The USA and the USSR*, p. 9).

80. "Hitler Is Winning," *Time*, 13 July 1942, p. 20.

81. *Asheville Citizen*, 12 July 1942, p. B2.

82. CBS Tape 2249, "The World Today," 15 July 1942, Phonoarchive.

83. "Time Will Not Wait," *Time*, 20 July 1942, p. 20.

84. "Dispatch from the Volga," ibid., 27 July 1942, p. 20.

85. *New York Times*, 2 August 1942.

86. Ibid.

87. Ibid., 17 July 1942, p. 2.

88. Ibid.
89. Ibid., 23 July 1942, p. 4.
90. Ibid.
91. Ibid.
92. The Chicago rally is described in the *New York Times*, 3 August 1942, p. 14; Meany's remarks are in ibid., 19 August 1942, p. 11.
93. Ibid., 8 August 1942, p. 2.
94. As McCormick put it on 28 November 1942, during Russia's defense of Stalingrad, "With this long tradition of a warlike nation, only deceitful propaganda could have made people think that Russia was not equipped to make war with the Axis. The Russians are savage; they endure tyranny; they know nothing about popular institutions or justice, but as soldiers they are tops" (in Robert McCormick, *Addresses and Editorials, 1941–1944*, p. 31).
95. *New York Journal-American*, 26 March 1942, p. 1.
96. Hearst's *New York Journal-American* was attacking lend-lease, which was popular, and, implicitly, a second front, which was not really an issue as early as March 1942. "Let us stop subsidizing all the greedy and ungrateful nations of the universe that hold out a mendicant hand for Lend-Lease alms," the *Journal-American* editorialized on 19 March. And on 26 March it said, "We know that Russia will continue to protect itself and, while making friendly treaties with Japan, to repel successfully German invasion."
97. *New York Times*, 8 August 1942, pp. 1, 6. The final decision to proceed solely with the African operation (TORCH) had occurred at a White House meeting on 30 July (Steele, *The First Offensive, 1942*, pp. 177–78).
98. The Office of War Information statement was released on Friday, 7 August, and hence could not affect expressions of opinion for the week ending 8 August. For the decline in newspaper demands for a second front, compare the "Twohey Analysis of Newspaper Opinion" for 8 August and 15 August 1942.
99. *New York Times*, 12 August 1942, p. 18.
100. CBS Tape 2293, "The World Today," 21 August 1942, Phonoarchive. An elite force of British and American troops had just staged a commando raid on Dieppe, a French seaport. The Allies suffered heavy losses, leading some opinion makers to conclude that a second front in western Europe that year would be premature. Others, however, judged that a major second front might be imminent.
101. *New York Herald Tribune*, 13 September 1942, p. B12.
102. Quoted in Foster R. Dulles, *The Road to Teheran*, p. 249.
103. *New York Times*, 29 September 1942, p. 22.
104. U.S., Congress, Senate, *Congressional Record*, 77th Cong., 2nd sess., 1942, 88, pt. 6:7707.
105. CBS Tape 864, Roosevelt "Fireside Chat," 12 October 1942, Phonoarchive.
106. Quoted in Dulles, *Road to Teheran*, p. 249.
107. *New York PM*, 27 October 1942, p. 3.
108. *Cleveland Plain Dealer*, 28 October 1942, p. 7. Twohey found that only 3 percent of his sample criticized Willkie's speech. Another 18 percent criticized Willkie for his harsh words for Britain but praised the rest of the speech ("Twohey Analysis of Newspaper Opinion," 31 October 1942, p. 5).
109. Those relatively few Americans who read the better journals of information and opinion probably knew much more about the speech than the average citizen. For example, in its November 16 issue, *Newsweek* featured a two page analysis of the speech entitled "Stalin's Speech Tightens Bonds of Unity with Fighting Allies" (16 November 1942, pp. 34, 36).
110. *New York Times*, 7 November 1942, p. 6.
111. Ibid.
112. Ibid.
113. Ibid., 8 November 1942, p. 1.
114. The importance of legitimate access to power was recognized by Adolf Hitler, who often pointed out that he had come to power by constitutional means.
115. On this point see Burns, *Roosevelt: Soldier of Freedom*, p. 319.

Notes to Chapter 5

1. Exceedingly complex concerns like these form the cornerstone of chapters 5 and 6. The basic reason why these concerns are so complex is because the discussion cannot be based on first-hand knowledge of any of the 140 million Americans living at this time, most of whom surely had very personal reasons for their attitudes on many subjects, including Russia. Because the student of attitudes is one step further removed from those who held the attitudes than the student of behavior (such as voting) is from those who acted in one way rather than another, description and analysis of attitudes probably involve even more generalization than most historical writing. On this point see Melvin Small, "Historians Look at Public Opinion," in Small, *Public Opinion and Historians*, pp. 13–32; and Peter G. Filene, *Americans and the Soviet Experiment 1917–1933*, pp. 1–2.

2. Harold J. Laski, *Reflections on the Revolution of Our Time*, p. ii.

3. William Z. Foster, *The USA and the USSR*, pp. 3–4.

4. *New York Times*, 7 November 1942, p. 14.

5. Ibid., 25 September 1942, p. 9.

6. Ibid.

7. Ibid., 8 November 1942, p. 1.

8. *New York PM*, 8 November 1942, p. 19.

9. Ibid.

10. National Council of American-Soviet Friendship, *Salute to Our Russian Ally*, p. 95.

11. Ibid., p. 110.

12. Ibid., p. 111.

13. Ibid.

14. Ibid., p. 114.

15. Ibid., pp. 116–17.

16. Ibid., p. 107.

17. Quoted in Elliott Roosevelt, *FDR: His Personal Letters*, 2:1365–66.

18. Sumner Welles, *The World of the Four Freedoms*, p. 85.

19. "Call to Brave Men," *Saturday Evening Post*, 28 October 1942, p. 108.

20. *New York PM*, 29 October 1942, p. 8.

21. Maurice Hindus, "Report on Russia," pp. 90–92.

22. *Department of State Bulletin* 7 (21 November 1942):943.

23. W. Averell Harriman, "Freedom Is a Fighting Word," pp. 26–29.

24. "Man of the Year," *Time*, 4 January 1943, pp. 21–24.

25. "Three-Star Classic," ibid., 21 December 1942, p. 45.

26. *New York Times*, 24 February 1943, p. 20.

27. *Christian Science Monitor*, 12 February 1943, p. 12.

28. *New York Times*, 23 February 1943, p. 3.

29. Henry Wallace, *Democracy Reborn*, p. 224. A recent critical biography of Wallace during these years is Norman D. Markowitz, *The Rise and Fall of the People's Century*. For private expressions of Wallace's concern in the spring of 1943 about possible American imperialism and anti-Russian attitudes after the war, see John Morton Blum, *The Price of Vision*, pp. 200–202.

30. CBS Tape 2412, "The World Today," 8 March 1943, Phonoarchive. For an analysis of the Standley incident basically complementary to the one presented here, see George C. Herring, Jr., *Aid to Russia 1941–1946*, pp. 91–97. Standley's own views are presented in William H. Standley and Arthur A. Ageton, *Admiral Ambassador to Russia*, pp. 340–41.

31. Wallace, *Democracy Reborn*, p. 223.

32. *Boston Globe*, 9 March 1943, p. 14.

33. *Christian Science Monitor*, 9 March 1943, p. 18.

34. *Philadelphia Inquirer*, 10 March 1943, p. 16.

35. *Detroit Free Press*, 10 March 1943, p. 6.

36. *Milwaukee Journal*, 10 March 1943, p. 14. The reference is to the Letts, Lithuanians, and Estonians.

37. *Chicago Tribune*, 11 March 1943, p. 14.

38. Ibid., 10 March 1943, p. 14.
39. *New York Times*, 12 March 1943, p. 16.
40. *Newark News*, 10 March 1943, p. 8.
41. *Philadelphia Bulletin*, 9 March 1943, p. 10.
42. *San Francisco Examiner*, 11 March 1943, p. 19.
43. *Wall Street Journal*, 11 March 1943, p. 6.
44. *St. Louis Post-Dispatch*, 10 March 1943, p. 12.
45. *Pittsburgh Press*, 10 March 1943, p. 14.
46. *Atlanta Constitution*, 10 March 1943, p. 6.
47. CBS Tape 2412, "The World Today," 8 March 1943, Phonoarchive.
48. NBC Disc 10276, "World News Roundup," 10 March 1943, NBC Recording Library.
49. *Department of State Bulletin* 8 (13 March 1943): 217.
50. *Baltimore Sun*, 10 March 1943, p. 1.
51. U.S. Congress, Senate, *Congressional Record*, 78th Cong., 1st sess., 1943, 89, pt. 2:1700.
52. *Baltimore Sun*, 10 March 1943, p. 1.
53. Quoted in Robert A. Divine, *Second Chance*, p. 93.
54. U.S. Congress, House, *Congressional Record*, 78th Cong., 1st sess., 1943, 89, pt. 9:A1109.
55. "Twohey Analysis of Newspaper Opinion," 1 May 1943, p. 7.
56. CBS Tape 2575, "World News Today," 2 May 1943, Phonoarchive.
57. *Washington Star*, 2 May 1943.
58. *Buffalo News*, 24 May 1943, p. 28.
59. *Chicago Daily News*, 25 May 1943, p. 12.
60. *Detroit Free Press*, 24 May 1943, p. 6.
61. *Minneapolis Star-Journal*, 24 May 1943, p. 10.
62. CBS Tape 2599, "The World Today," 23 May 1943, Phonoarchive.
63. Ibid.
64. Wendell L. Willkie, *One World*, p. 85. As with Reston's book I have cited the more widely circulated paperback edition.
65. "These convictions are not mere humanitarian hopes, they are not just idealistic and vague dreams," Willkie wrote in the introduction to *One World*. "They are based on things I saw and learned at first hand and upon the views of men and women, important and anonymous, whose heroism and sacrifices give meaning and life to their beliefs" (Ibid., p. 1).
66. Ibid., pp. 35–36.
67. Ibid., p. 22.
68. Ibid., p. 23.
69. Ibid., pp. 25–31.
70. Ibid., p. 34.
71. "Lend-Lease to Russia," *Life*, 29 March 1943, p. 13.
72. "The USSR," ibid., p. 20.
73. "The Father of Modern Russia," ibid., p. 29.
74. When had *Life* lavished such praise on Roosevelt and other administration officials!
75. Joseph E. Davies, "The Soviets and the Post-War," ibid., p. 49.
76. Ibid.
77. *Department of State Bulletin* 9 (4 September 1943): 154.
78. *Houston Post*, 1 September 1943, p. 1.
79. I. F. Stone, "V For Vituperation," p. 286.
80. Eddie Rickenbacker, "The War Is Not Over," p. 5.
81. Ibid., p. 6.
82. The Moscow Conference was a series of meetings held in the Soviet capital at the end of October 1943 among the foreign ministers of the three great Allied powers. The Moscow Declaration, the joint communiqué made public at the conclusion of the meetings,

pledged the three powers to complete unity until the unconditional surrender of all the Axis powers and promised continued cooperation in the postwar world. The most detailed discussion of the series of inter-Allied conferences in the fall of 1943 is in Robert Beitzell, *The Uneasy Alliance*, pp. 153–384.

83. Cantril to Roosevelt, 14 February 1944, File 857, Franklin Delano Roosevelt Papers, Roosevelt Library, Hyde Park, N.Y. (hereafter cited as the Roosevelt Papers). The results of the Gallup poll, which was conducted between 12 and 16 November, were somewhat different from Cantril's results. On the question of trust, 47 percent answered yes, 27 percent said no, and 26 percent had no opinion. The differences between the Cantril and Gallup results can be explained on the grounds that (1) the samples obviously were composed of different individuals; and (2) the Gallup polling was done nearly two weeks after the conference, when the initial exuberance had disappeared (Gallup release, 26 November 1943, Gallup organization files).

84. Ibid.

85. *Chicago Tribune*, 1 November 1943, p. 18.

86. "Twohey Analysis of Newspaper Opinion," 6 November 1943, p. 5.

87. *Asheville Citizen*, 2 November 1943, p. 4.

88. *New York Times*, 6 November 1943, p. 12.

89. *Wall Street Journal*, 4 November 1943, p. 6.

90. Raymond Clapper, *Watching the World, 1931–1944*, p. 343.

91. Text of radio address, 1 November 1943, Box 22, Raymond Gram Swing Papers, Library of Congress.

92. *New York PM*, 2 November 1943, p. 2.

93. Howard Brubaker, "Of All Things," *New Yorker*, 6 November 1943, p. 44.

94. "Talk of the Town," ibid., 13 November 1943, p. 8.

95. "Roosevelt-Stalin-Churchill Declaration," *International Conciliation*, no. 397 (February 1944): 120.

96. *Chicago Tribune*, 3 December 1943, p. 16.

97. *San Francisco Examiner*, 8 December 1943, p. 22.

98. David Lardner, "The Current Cinema," *New Yorker*, 20 November 1943, p. 88. Jack Warner revealed in his memoir that *Mission to Moscow* was filmed at President Roosevelt's request. This incident demonstrates that the president's influence as an opinion maker was even greater than most of his contemporaries realized (Warner, *My First Hundred Years in Hollywood*, pp. 290–94).

99. David E. Lilienthal, *The TVA Years*, p. 583.

100. *Moscow Strikes Back* may be viewed, along with many other films from this era, at the researcher's convenience in the National Archives.

101. National Council of American-Soviet Friendship, *Know the USSR*, cover.

102. Interview with Corliss Lamont, 7 March 1970. Much of the following discussion is based on this interview; the rest of it comes from miscellaneous literature from the period provided by the staff of the National Council.

103. "Russian War Relief Committees," *Soviet Russia Today*, June 1942, p. 23.

104. "With Our Allies in the Total War Effort," ibid., p. 5.

105. Jerome Bruner, *What America Thinks*, p. 159.

106. Gallup release, 30 April 1943, Gallup organization files.

107. "Do Americans Recognize Russia as an Equal?" *Opinion News*, 8 November 1943, p. 1.

108. Dixon Wecter, for example, noted that opinion polls consistently showed that youth were more favorably inclined toward New Deal programs and toward President Roosevelt than were their elders (*The Age of the Great Depression*, pp. 193–94).

109. Alfred O. Hero, Jr., *The Southerner and World Affairs*, p. 312. Although this quotation referred to southern women, it also applied generally to women outside of the South.

110. William Lydgate, *What America Thinks*, p. 116.

111. Ella Winter, "Our Allies, the Russians," p. 152. Of course, women as well as men received most of their information about foreign affairs not from women's magazines but from general-interest magazines, newspapers, and radio programs.

112. George Padmore, "Race Relations: Soviet and British," p. 345.

113. Ernest Johnson, "Democracy in Color," p. 345.

114. Warren B. Walsh, "What the American People Think of Russia," p. 520.

115. Reinhold Niebuhr, "Russia and the West," Part I, p. 83.

116. N. S. Timasheff, *Religion in Soviet Russia, 1917–1942*, p. 157.

117. Ralph Gorman, "Whitewashing the Kremlin," *Sign*, April 1942, p. 515.

118. Ignatius Kelly, "The Pope's Peace Plan," *Ecclesiastical Review*, July 1943, p. 18.

119. J. L. Benvenisti, "Russia and Brotherhood," p. 11.

120. "Russian Confidence," *Commonweal*, 14 April 1944, p. 635.

121. "The Meaning of It All," ibid., 4 June 1943, p. 159.

122. "Newsgram," *United States News*, 30 July 1943, p. 5.

123. "The Master's Voice," *American Hebrew*, 27 June 1941, p. 3.

124. William Zuckerman, "Soviet Jews Before and During the War," p. 16.

125. "Report of the Social Service Commission," *Annual of the Southern Baptist Convention*, p. 92. There were, of course, many Protestants more fundamentalist than most Southern Baptists, notably the myriad Holiness sects. But the Southern Baptists were by far the largest conservative Protestant group.

126. The term *social gospel* as used in this study does not refer specifically to the theological school of that name but rather to that grouping of Protestants who generally shared a profound and direct interest in bettering man's life on earth. It does, however, include Protestants who belonged to the social gospel school of theology as well as some who belonged to the neoorthodox school, notably Reinhold Niebuhr.

127. Eduard Heimann, "The Just War of Unjust Nations," p. 6.

128. John Foster Dulles, "Toward World Order," in Francis J. McConnell et al., *A Basis for the Peace to Come*, p. 47. Dulles's good friend John C. Bennett, in an interview with Princeton historian Richard D. Challener, said of Dulles's attitudes during the war, "I think that probably he was somewhat more open toward that [relations with Russia] than one would have guessed, reading back from a later position. . . . His book *War, Peace and Change* indicates the importance of a fluid kind of world" (John C. Bennett, Princeton Oral History Collection, Princeton University Library).

129. Reinhold Niebuhr, "Anglo-Saxon Destiny and Responsibility," p. 3.

130. Reinhold Niebuhr, "American Power and World Responsibility," p. 4.

131. "The Six 'Pillars of Peace,' " *Federal Council Bulletin*, April 1943, p. 11.

132. "Joint Catholic, Jewish, and Protestant Declaration on World Peace," *Christianity and Crisis*, 18 October 1943, p. 7.

133. "An 'Isolationist' Reaction?" *Fortune*, April 1943, p. 118.

134. "Government by Horse Sense: Selling the People on Russia," ibid., June 1943, p. 128.

135. Gallup release, 12 September 1943, Gallup organization files.

136. Gallup release, 26 November 1943, Gallup organization files.

137. Gallup release, 30 April 1943, Gallup organization files.

138. Ibid.

139. William A. Lydgate, *What America Thinks*, p. 45.

140. John Gunther, *Inside U.S.A.*, p. 462.

141. Herbert Gans, *The Urban Villagers*, passim.

142. Martin Kriesberg, "Dark Areas of Ignorance," in Lester Markel, *Public Opinion and Foreign Policy*, p. 50. Kriesberg extrapolated from the 1940 census as follows:

Persons in the U.S. 25 years of age or over	73,691,000
Persons who never completed one school year	2,800,000
Persons who completed grades 1 to 4	7,305,000
Persons who completed grades 5 and 6	8,515,000
Persons who completed grades 7 and 8	25,898,000
Persons who completed high school years 1 to 3	11,182,000
Persons who completed 4th year of high school	10,552,000

Persons who completed 1 to 3 years of college	3,407,000
Persons who completed 4 or more years of college	1,042,000
Median school years completed	8.4

143. Hero, *Southerner and World Affairs*, p. 248.

144. Ibid. These conclusions are from Hero's retabulations of results of a study of 10,000 college students made by the Bureau of Applied Social Research of Columbia University shortly after the war.

145. *Opinion News*, 8 November 1943, p. 1.

146. Ibid., 22 February 1944, p. 2.

147. *NORC Bulletin*, 3 April 1945, p. 3.

148. "Fortune Survey," *Fortune*, June 1942, p. 22.

149. Ibid.

150. Ibid.

151. Ibid.

152. For a recent assessment of Stalin's private position in regard to a separate peace with Germany, see Vojtech Mastny, "Stalin and the Prospects of a Separate Peace in World War II," pp. 1365–88.

153. George H. Gallup, *The Gallup Poll, 1935–1971*, p. 419, gives all the results listed except for the breakdown of the 30 percent who had neither heard nor read about the Moscow Conference. These results were extrapolated from the other data.

Notes to Chapter 6

1. Henry P. Van Dusen, "Allied Peace Plans," *Christianity and Crisis*, 26 January 1942, p. 8.

2. Max Eastman, "We Must Face the Facts About Russia," p. 1.

3. Ibid., p. 2.

4. Ibid., p. 7.

5. Ibid., p. 3 (italics in original).

6. Ibid., p. 7.

7. Ibid., p. 14.

8. "Public Opinion and Foreign Policy," *Fortune*, November 1943, p. 134.

9. Reinhold Niebuhr, "We Are in Peril," *Christianity and Crisis*, 18 October 1943, p. 2.

10. CBS Tape 890, FDR Christmas message, 24 December 1943, Phonoarchive.

11. "In the Afterglow," *Time*, 4 January 1944, p. 31.

12. Wendell L. Willkie, "Don't Stir Distrust of Russia," p. 4.

13. *New York Times*, 9 January 1944, p. D1.

14. Ibid., 2 February 1944, p. 1.

15. Ibid., p. 11.

16. *Asheville Citizen*, 7 February 1944, p. 4.

17. *New York Times*, 26 February 1944, p. 6; and 10 April 1944, p. 3.

18. *San Francisco Examiner*, 2 February 1944, p. 1.

19. *Minneapolis Star-Journal*, 2 February 1944, p. 14.

20. *Kansas City Star*, 4 February 1944, p. 22.

21. "The President's Week," *Time*, 3 April 1944, p. 3.

22. Ibid.

23. *New York Times*, 19 May 1944, p. 1.

24. Quoted in Edward J. Rozek, *Allied Wartime Diplomacy*, p. 133.

25. *New York PM*, 3 May 1942, p. 13.

26. Quote in Rozek, *Allied Wartime Diplomacy*, p. 149.

27. Ibid., p. 149.

28. Ibid., p. 175.

29. Ibid., p. 174.

30. *Washington Post*, 24 November 1943, p. 12.

31. R. M. MacIver, *Towards an Abiding Peace*, p. 65.

32. *New York Herald Tribune*, 6 January 1944, p. 18.

33. Irving Brant, *Road to Peace and Freedom*, p. 187.

34. "Twohey Analysis of Newspaper Opinion," 8 January 1944, p. 5.

35. CBS Tape 2915, "The World Today," 15 February 1944, Phonoarchive.

36. Henry R. Luce, "America's War and America's Peace," p. 85 and 91.

37. Henry Wallace, *Democracy Reborn*, p. 193.

38. J. O. Downey, "America in the Post-War World," p. 331.

39. U.S. Congress, Senate, *Congressional Record*, 77th Cong., 2nd sess., 1942, 88, pt. 10: A4324.

40. Raymond Moley, "You Can Do Business with Stalin," p. 112.

41. Congress of America-Soviet Friendship, *American Industry Commemorates the 10th Anniversary of American-Soviet Diplomatic Relations, 1933–1943*, n.p.

42. "Harriman's Broom," *Newsweek*, 15 November 1943, p. 24.

43. Donald M. Nelson, "What I Saw in Russia," p. 11.

44. Harland Allen, "Looking Ahead with Russia," p. 25 (italics in original).

45. "Stalin's Challenge to American Business," *Business Week*, 4 December 1943, p. 112.

46. Junius B. Wood, "Russia—Customer and Competitor," p. 30.

47. Junius B. Wood, "How Russia Goes at a Job," p. 29.

48. Eric Johnston, "A Business View of Russia," p. 21. On the 26 June 1944 meeting with Stalin, see Eric Johnston, "My Talk with Joseph Stalin," pp. 1–10. A summary of the meeting is in John Lewis Gaddis, *United States and the Origins of the Cold War*, pp. 185–86.

49. Eric Johnston, "A Business View of Russia," p. 210.

50. Johnston mentioned these products and others in a speech he delivered to an official Moscow reception for him during his visit. "I would like to see brisk exchanges of these commodities between us," Johnston concluded (Ibid.).

51. Robert A. Divine, *Second Chance*, pp. 52–58, 160–71, 314–17.

52. Henry C. Cassidy, *Moscow Dateline*, p. 361.

53. Ibid., p. 352.

54. Walter Graebner, *Round Trip to Russia*, p. 185.

55. Bernard Newman, *The New Europe*, p. 544.

56. Hiram Motherwell, *The Peace We Fight For*, p. 166.

57. Basil Mathews, *United We Stand*, p. 51.

58. Denna F. Fleming, *Can We Win the Peace?*, p. 105.

59. Ibid., p. 104.

60. Ibid., p. 27.

61. Luce's article was discussed in some detail earlier in this chapter. Parts of *The Problems of Lasting Peace* were reprinted in other books and in magazines throughout the war.

62. William Henry Chamberlin, *The Russian Enigma*, p. 307. For a more detailed and more sympathetic analysis of Chamberlin's wartime thinking about Soviet-American relations, see Gaddis, *United States and the Origins of the Cold War*, pp. 42–43. Gaddis's discussion apparently is based solely on Chamberlin's magazine articles.

63. Joseph M. Jones, *A Modern Foreign Policy for the United States*, p. 13.

64. Ibid., pp. 19–20.

65. Ibid., p. 21.

66. Neil MacNeil, *An American Peace*, p. 199.

67. Ibid.

68. Ibid., p. 215.

69. Ibid., p. 264.

70. David J. Dallin, *Russian and Postwar Europe*, p. 142.

71. Ibid., p. 177.

72. Ibid., p. 196.

73. Ibid., p. 191.

74. Joachim Joesten, *What Russia Wants*, p. 3.

75. Ibid., p. 9.

76. Ibid., p. 26.
77. Carl L. Becker, *How New Will the Better World Be?* p. 74.
78. Ibid., p. 95.
79. Ibid., p. 96.
80. Ibid., p. 192.
81. Ibid., pp. 192–93.
82. William T. R. Fox, *The Super-Powers*, p. 3.
83. Ibid., p. 119.
84. Walter Lippmann, *US War Aims*, pp. 132 and 135.
85. Ibid., pp. 136–37.
86. Ibid., pp. 133 and 158.

Notes to Chapter 7

1. Robert A. Divine, *Foreign Policy and US Presidential Elections*, pp. x–xi.
2. *Washington Star*, 1 May 1943, p. 9.
3. *Opinion News*, 27 September 1943, p. 1. More detail on the campaign of 1944 can be found in James MacGregor Burns, *Roosevelt: Soldier of Freedom*, pp. 497–531; in Divine, *Foreign Policy*, pp. 91–164; and in Leon Friedman, "Election of 1944," in Arthur M. Schlesinger, Jr., *History of American Presidential Elections*, 4:3009–38. In my study the emphasis will be on the domestic climate of opinion and on those aspects of the campaign which might well have affected American attitudes toward Russia.
4. Earl Warren, "Victory, Lasting Peace, Jobs for All: Republican Keynote Address," p. 591.
5. Samuel I. Rosenman, *The Public Papers and Addresses of Franklin D. Roosevelt*, 13:202.
6. *New York Herald Tribune*, 17 August 1944, p. 1. During August and September 1944, Allied officials held a series of meetings at Dumbarton Oaks (an estate in Washington, D.C.), which dealt primarily with international organization and related postwar security questions. The meetings revealed differences of opinion among the Allies, notably on the question of whether the great powers should have a veto over matters affecting them directly. The Russian delegate, Andrei Gromyko, successfully insisted that they should.
7. *New York Herald Tribune*, 18 August 1944, p. 16.
8. "Enter Dulles, Willkie," *Newsweek*, 28 August 1944, p. 38.
9. Ibid.
10. Herbert Brownell, Princeton Oral History Project, Princeton University Library. The question was posed by Princeton historian Richard D. Challener.
11. John W. Bricker, "Free Representative Government: Acceptance Speech," p. 710.
12. "Getting Wise to Russia," *Catholic World*, October 1944, p. 1.
13. "A Day of Ideals," *Farm Journal and Farmer's Wife*, October 1944, p. 27.
14. Thomas E. Dewey, "Corporate State Not an American System," p. 14.
15. Nathan Ausübel, *Voices of History, 1944–1945*, p. 534.
16. Rosenman, *Public Papers*, 13:403–4.
17. Ibid.
18. Gallup release, 11 March 1945, Gallup organization files.
19. Roosevelt's success in keeping the votes of most Polish-Americans in the Democratic column despite concern over the fate of Poland is discussed in adequate detail in Divine, *Foreign Policy*, pp. 138–43; and in John Lewis Gaddis, *The United States and the Origins of the Cold War*, pp. 143–49. Gaddis contends that Roosevelt's concern about the Polish-American vote was "one reason why he felt unable to prepare the American people for postwar developments in Eastern Europe." Another reason was fear of losing the support of important senators for the new international organization (p. 149).
20. "Talk of the Town," *New Yorker*, 5 August 1944, p. 6.
21. William C. Bullitt, "The World from Rome," *Life*, 4 September 1944, pp. 94–96.
22. The details of this episode were derived from John Gunther, *Inside USA*, pp. 205–6.
23. *Talks*, January 1945, pp. 2–4.
24. Alvarez Del Vayo, "Leadership in Europe," p. 689.

25. "Communists Ride Europe's Wave," *Life*, 11 December 1944, p. 21.

26. *New York Times*, 16 November 1944, p. 22.

27. CBS Tape 3271, "The World Today," 11 December 1944, Phonoarchive.

28. "Stalin Can't Ignore Storm Signals," *Saturday Evening Post*, 11 November 1944, p. 108.

29. William Green, "The Free and Not Free," p. 25.

30. *New York Times*, 17 November 1944, p. 8.

31. Ibid., 20 December 1944, p. 16.

32. Reinhold Niebuhr, "Russia and the Peace," p. 2.

33. Ibid.

34. Ibid.

35. Robert A. Divine, *Second Chance*, p. 261.

36. Quoted in ibid., p. 94.

37. *New York Times*, 7 January 1945, p. 32.

38. Ibid.

39. Quoted in Divine, *Second Chance*, p. 261.

40. Ibid.

41. U.S. Congress, Senate, *Congressional Record*, 79th Cong., 1st sess., 1945, 91, pt. 1: 164–67.

42. Ibid.

43. Ibid.

44. Ibid.

45. "Historic Force," *Time*, 5 February 1945, pp. 32, 38.

46. "Poland, Russia and America," *New Republic*, 8 January 1945, p. 3.

47. Vera Micheles Dean, "What Do We Want in Europe?" pp. 141–42.

48. *Department of State Bulletin* 12 (18 February 1945): 215.

49. "Twohey Analysis of Newspaper Opinion," 17 February 1945, p. 1.

50. *Boston Globe*, 13 February 1945, p. 6.

51. *Daily Worker*, 14 February 1945, p. 6.

52. *Asheville Citizen*, 13 February 1945, p. 4.

53. *Providence Journal*, 13 February 1945, p. 11.

54. *Philadelphia Bulletin*, 14 February 1945, p. 8.

55. *Milwaukee Journal*, 13 February 1945, p. 18.

56. *Detroit News*, 13 February 1945, p. 10.

57. *Chicago Tribune*, 14 February 1945, p. 4.

58. *Christian Science Monitor*, 15 February 1945, p. 18.

59. *Cleveland Plain Dealer*, 13 February 1945, p. 4.

60. *Casper Tribune-Herald*, 14 February 1945, p. 4.

61. *Baltimore Sun*, 13 February 1945, p. 8.

62. *Chicago Tribune*, 14 February 1945, p. 1.

63. *New York Mirror*, 16 February 1945, p. 14.

64. *Cleveland Plain Dealer*, 13 February 1945, p. 4.

65. *New York Journal-American*, 14 February 1945, p. 1.

66. *Casper Tribune-Herald*, 12 March 1945, p. 6.

67. *Wall Street Journal*, 15 February 1945, p. 6.

68. Ibid., 16 February 1945, p. 6.

69. CBS Tape 3336, "The World Today," 13 February 1945, Phonoarchive.

70. Draft of radio broadcast, Box 14, Raymond Gram Swing Papers, Library of Congress, Washington, D.C.

71. Disc 62618, "Richard Harkness in Washington," 13 February 1945, NBC Recording Library.

72. Consult, for example, Lowell Thomas on Disc 62615 and H. V. Kaltenborn on Disc 62650, NBC Recording Library.

73. Tom Connally, "Agreement at Yalta," p. 25.

74. Burton K. Wheeler, "Agreement at Yalta," p. 27.

75. "Moment in History," *Time*, 19 February 1945, p. 15.

76. "Second Thoughts," ibid., 26 February 1945, p. 24.

77. "After Yalta," *Life*, 26 February 1945, p. 24.

78. "The Big Three Take Their Stand," *Business Week*, 17 February 1945, p. 15.

79. "The Crimea Conference," *New Republic*, 19 February 1945, p. 243.

80. Rosenman, *Public Papers*, 13:586.

81. Ibid. As an example of his willingness to deceive earlier in the war, Roosevelt told Secretary of the Treasury Henry Morgenthau, "I am perfectly willing to mislead and tell untruths if it will help win the war" (John M. Blum, *From the Morgenthau Diaries*, p. 197).

82. For a brief definition of "Four Policemen," see Burns, *Roosevelt: Soldier of Freedom*, p. 409. For a lucid discussion of Roosevelt's foreign policies, including the concept of the "Four Policemen" as the cornerstone of his thinking about the postwar world, see Robert A. Divine, *Roosevelt and World War II*.

83. This speech, Roosevelt's major foreign policy address of the 1944 campaign, was basically a review of previous administration policies. It contained no specific information about developments in Europe nor about American foreign policy in the postwar world.

84. Quoted in *Opinion News*, 7 November 1944, p. 6.

85. Ibid., 3 April 1945, p. 4.

86. Ibid., 6 February 1945, p. 1.

87. *NORC Reports*, 6 March 1945, p. 1.

88. Gallup release, 11 March 1945, Gallup organization files.

89. Ibid.

90. Ibid.

91. Burns, *Roosevelt: Soldier of Freedom*, p. 583.

92. Bernard Asbell, *When F.D.R. Died*, p. 40.

93. *Atlanta Constitution*, 11 April 1945, p. 6.

94. *St Louis Post-Dispatch*, 24 April 1945, p. 8.

95. *Washington Post*, 28 April 1945, p. 7.

96. CBS Tape 3464, 27 April 1945, Phonoarchive.

97. CBS Tape 3483, 2 May 1945, Phonoarchive.

98. CBS Tape 912, 10 March 1945, Phonoarchive.

99. *San Francisco Examiner*, 4 April 1945, p. 1.

100. Herbert Hoover, *Addresses upon the American Road, 1941–1945*, p. 125.

101. "Russia Needs Honest American News," *Saturday Evening Post*, 24 March 1945, p. 100.

102. Eugene Lyons, "Appeasement in Yalta," pp. 465 and 468.

103. *Christian Science Monitor,* 3 April 1945, p. 18.

104. "Goings-on-in-Washington," *Farm Journal and Farmer's Wife*, May 1945, p. 11.

105. *San Francisco Examiner*, 5 April 1945, p. 14.

106. *Washington Post*, 7 April 1945, in Box 84, Joseph Davies Papers, Library of Congress, Washington, D.C.

107. For Cantril results see U.S. Department of State, "Fortnightly Survey of Public Opinion About International Affairs," no. 22, 7 March 1945; and no. 28, 19 June 1945. For Gallup results see Gallup, *The Gallup Poll, 1935–1971*, pp. 492, 508.

108. U.S. Department of State, "Fortnightly Survey of Public Opinion on International Affairs," no. 22, 7 March 1945; and no. 28, 9 June 1945.

109. Ibid., 23 May 1945.

110. *Trenton Times*, 25 April 1945, p. 10.

111. *Department of State Bulletin* 12 (18 February 1945): 215.

112. Ibid.

113. President Roosevelt visited with his son Elliott in Cairo on 5 December 1943, a few days after the Teheran conference, and warned him of the danger of an American-British alliance against Russia. "'The biggest thing,' Father commented, 'was in making clear to Stalin that the United States and Great Britain were not allied in one common bloc against the Soviet Union. I think we've got rid of that idea, once and for all. I hope so. The

one thing that could upset the applecart, after the war, is if the world is divided again, Russia against England and us. That's our big job now, and it'll be our big job tomorrow, too: making sure that we continue to act as referee, as intermediary between Russia and England.' And in doing that, it was clear, the United States had become world leader"(Elliott Roosevelt, *As He Saw It*, pp. 206–7).

Notes to Chapter 8

1. Actually, most of chapter 1 dealt with the theory of opinion circulation, which is but one facet of public-opinion theory. A related facet is the theory of opinion change. When we ask, How did American attitudes toward Russia change during World War II? we are obviously dealing with changes in opinions as well as with their circulation.

2. There is a pronounced need for historical studies of the opinion-making process and of opinion change with much narrower scopes than this one in terms of time covered and the number of opinion makers and the size of the public involved. But this study does suggest the value of adopting a dynamic, time-oriented, descriptive approach rather than an essentially static, analytic one to the study of attitudes.

3. James N. Rosenau, for example, argues that the mass public's "response to foreign policy matters is less one of intellect and more one of emotion, less one of opinion and more one of mood, of generalized, superficial, and undisciplined feelings which easily fluctuate from one extreme to the other" (*Public Opinion and Foreign Policy*, p. 35). Another summation of much research is this comment by Bernard Berelson: "In most campaigns, whether political or informational, the people best informed on the issue are the ones least likely to change their minds" ("Democratic Theory and Public Opinion," in Bernard Berelson and Morris Janowitz, *Reader in Public Opinion and Communication*, p. 493).

4. These adjectives applied generally to attitudes toward China thirty years later. See comments and reference in chapter 1.

5. Leon Festinger, *A Theory of Cognitive Dissonance*, esp. pp. 1–31. For a discussion of the very substantial amount of research and writing stimulated by Festinger's theory, see John J. Sherwood, James W. Barron, and H. Gordon Fitch, "Cognitive Dissonance: Theory and Research," in Richard V. Wagner and John J. Sherwood, *The Study of Attitude Change*, pp. 56–86.

6. On the sharp increase in negative attitudes toward Russia in early 1946, which occurred in conjunction with "a fundamental reorientation of policy toward the Soviet Union," see John Lewis Gaddis, *United States and the Origins of the Cold War*, pp. 281–315 (the quotation in this note is from page 281).

7. See, for example, Gaddis, *United States and the Origins of the Cold War*, pp. 356–57, passim; George C. Herring, Jr., *Aid to Russia 1941–1946*, pp. 287–88; and Arthur Schlesinger, Jr., "Origins of the Cold War," p. 38. Despite their highly questionable assumption that American leaders were more nearly followers than formulators of public attitudes and pressures, Gaddis's work is easily the finest single study of the diplomatic and decision-making aspects of the origins of the Cold War, Herring's is an excellent monograph, and Schlesinger's is among the most important articles on the coming of the Cold War.

8. "After the Yalta Conference in 1945," Robert Beitzell has written, "Roosevelt and Churchill declared themselves in favor of the new home for Poland. They further said Poland would be free, independent, and democratic. Roosevelt did not really anticipate an independent Poland, nor did he mention the Asian concessions to Russia which were also agreed to at Yalta. He deceived Cordell Hull and his fellow countrymen. He permitted, even encouraged, a gap to open between what the American and other Allied people thought would be the nature of the peace settlement and an already arranged and far different actuality" (*Uneasy Alliance*, p. 382). James MacGregor Burns argues that "the higher he [Roosevelt] set his goals and the lower he pitched his practical improvisations, the more he widened the gap between the existing and the ideal and raised men's expectations while failing to fulfill them" (*Roosevelt: Soldier of Freedom*, p. 550). Criticizing Roosevelt's leadership and candor at one of several points, John Lewis Gaddis concludes in regard to wartime east

European policy that "the President by his actions had led the American people to expect free elections in Eastern Europe, while at the same time leading the Russians to expect a free hand" (*United States and the Origins of the Cold War*, p. 173). And Lloyd C. Gardner faults Roosevelt for failing "to prepare the public for diplomatic adjustments" (*Architects of Illusion*, p. 40).

9. From an interview with George F. Kennan in Princeton, New Jersey, 24 March 1970.

10. Because of the markedly less open nature of the political process in the Soviet Union, it obviously made much less difference whether or not the Russian public was prepared for the probable structure of the postwar world order.

11. The sagacious Stimson told an aide shortly after Truman's accession to power, "Some Americans are anxious to hang on to exaggerated views of the Monroe Doctrine and at the same time butt into every question that comes up in Eastern Europe" (quoted in Lloyd C. Gardner, *Economic Aspects of New Deal Diplomacy*, p. 308). For evidence of widespread anti-Russian attitudes in the Truman administration by May 1945, see John Morton Blum, *The Price of Vision*, pp. 439–55.

~~Bibliography

Manuscripts
Hyde Park, N.Y. Franklin D. Roosevelt Library.
  Francis Biddle Papers
  Harry Hopkins Papers
  Franklin D. Roosevelt Papers
  Elbert D. Thomas Papers
New York, N.Y. Columbia University Library. Columbia Oral History Collection.
  Interview with H. V. Kaltenborn
  Interview with Norman Thomas
Princeton, N.J. University Library. Archives.
  Bernard Baruch Papers
  Harry Dexter White Papers
Princeton, N.J. University Library. John Foster Dulles Oral History Collection.
  Interview with Elliott V. Bell
  Interview with John C. Bennett
  Interview with Herbert Brownell
  Interview with Allen Dulles
  Interview with James Reston
Washington, D.C. Library of Congress.
  Raymond Clapper Papers
  Tom Connally Papers
  Joseph Davies Papers
  George Gallup Papers
  Raymond Gram Swing Papers
  Henry Wallace Papers

Official Documents
U.S. Congress. *Congressional Record*. 76th through 79th Congresses.
U.S. Office of War Information. *Facts About the United Nations*. Washington, D.C., 1943.
———. *Toward New Horizons: The World Beyond the War*. Washington, D.C., 1942.
———. *The United Nations Fight for the Four Freedoms*. Washington, D.C., n.d.

_____ . *U.S. Government War Information Films*. Washington, D.C. 1945.

U.S. Department of State. *Department of State Bulletin*. Vols. 1–12 (1939–1945).

_____ . "Fortnightly Survey of American Opinion," 1944–1945. Office of Policy Guidance, Bureau of Public Affairs, Department of State.

U.S. War Relief Control Board. *Voluntary War Relief During World War II*. Washington, D.C., 1946.

Interviews

George F. Kennan, 24 March 1970

Corliss Lamont, 7 March 1970

Robert Mumford, 3 March 1970

Unidentified Seattle businessman, 28 January 1970

Films

Mission to Moscow. Warner Brothers, 1943.

Moscow Strikes Back. Republic, 1942.

One Day of War–Russia 1943. Time, 1943.

Report from Russia. Office of War Information, 1943.

The True Glory. Army Signal Corps, 1945.

Yalta. U. S. War Department, 1945.

Miscellaneous newsreels from Paramount and United Artists

Radio Recordings

CBS Broadcasts. I listened to approximately two hundred tape recordings of Columbia Broadcasting System programs in the Phonoarchive of the School of Communications of the University of Washington, Seattle, Washington. The contents of these tapes are outlined in Milo Ryan's *History in Sound: A Descriptive Listing of the KIRO–CBS Collection of Broadcasts of the World War II Years and After, in the Phonoarchive of the University of Washington*. Seattle: University of Washington Press, 1963.

NBC Broadcasts. I listened to approximately one hundred disc recordings of National Broadcasting System programs in the Recording Library of NBC in New York City. There is no guide to the contents of these recordings.

Public Opinion Polls

I collected American Institute of Public Opinion, National Opinion Research Center, Office of Public Opinion Research, and Roper "Fortune" polls from one or more of the following sources:

American Institute of Public Opinion, Princeton, New Jersey.

Fortune, 1939–1945.

NORC Reports, 1943–1945.

New York Times, 1938–1945.

Opinion News, 1942–1945.

Public Opinion Quarterly, 1939–1945.

Roper Public Opinion Research Center, Williams College, Williamstown, Mass.

Newspapers

Asheville Citizen, 1939–1945

Atlanta Constitution, 1939–1945

Baltimore Sun, 1939–1945

Boston Globe, 1939–1945

Buffalo News, 1939–1945
Casper Tribune-Herald, 1939–1945
Chicago Daily News, 1939–1945
Chicago Defender, 1943–1945
Chicago Tribune, 1939–1945
Christian Science Monitor, 1939–1945
Cincinnati Enquirer, 1939–1945
Cleveland Plain Dealer, 1939–1945
Denver Post, 1939
Detroit Free Press, 1939–1945
Detroit News, 1939–1945
Houston Post, 1939–1945
Kansas City Star, 1939–1945
Los Angeles Examiner, 1941–1943
Los Angeles Times, 1939–1945
Milwaukee Journal, 1939–1945
Minneapolis Star-Journal, 1939–1945
Newark News, 1941–1943
New Orleans Times-Picayune,
 1939–1942
New York Daily News, 1939–1945
New York Daily Worker, 1943–1945
New York Herald Tribune, 1939–1945

New York Journal-American, 1939–1945
New York Mirror, 1939–1945
New York PM, 1941–1945
New York Post, 1939–1945
New York Times, 1939–1945
New York World-Telegram, 1939–1945
Philadelphia Bulletin, 1939–1945
Philadelphia Inquirer, 1939–1945
Pittsburgh Courier, 1939–1945
Pittsburgh Press, 1939–1945
Providence Journal, 1942–1945
St. Louis Post-Dispatch, 1939–1945
San Francisco Examiner, 1939–1945
Seattle Times, 1939–1945
The Targum (Rutgers University),
 1939–1945
Trenton Times, 1939–1945
University of Washington Daily,
 1939–1945
Wall Street Journal, 1941–1945
Washington Post, 1939–1945
Washington Star, 1939–1945
Washington Times-Herald, 1939–1945

Periodicals
America
American Ecclesiastical Review
American Economic Review
American Federationist
American Hebrew
American Historical Review
American Journal of Sociology
American Legion Magazine
American Library Association Bulletin
American Magazine
American Mercury
American Review of the Soviet Union
Antioch Review
Atlantic Monthly
Business Week
Catholic World
Christendom
Christian Century
Christianity and Crisis
CIO News
Collier's
Commonweal
Congress Weekly
Crisis

Current History
Farm Journal and Farmer's Wife
Federal Council Bulletin
Foreign Affairs
Fortune
Harper's
International Conciliation
International Teamster
Ladies' Home Journal
Life
Nation
National Education Association Journal
National Geographic
National Parent-Teacher
Nation's Business
New Republic
Newsweek
New Yorker
New York Times Magazine
Polish Jew
Reader's Digest
Rotarian
Russian Review
Saturday Evening Post
Saturday Review of Literature

Time
"Twohey Analysis of Newspaper Opinion"
United States News
Vital Speeches
Yale Review

Senior Scholastic
Sign
Soviet Russia Today
Survey Graphic
Talks

Signed Articles

Adey, Alvin. "For Better Relations with Russia." *Current History*, April 1943, pp. 106–9.

Adler, Les K., and Paterson, Thomas G. "Red Fascism: The Merger of Nazi Germany and Soviet Russia in the American Image of Totalitarianism, 1930's–1950's." *American Historical Review* 75 (1970): 1046–64.

Allen, Harland H. "Looking Ahead with Russia." *Rotarian*, February 1944, pp. 25–26.

Barach, Mitzi. "Education in the Soviet Union." *NEA Journal*, February 1945, pp. 40–41.

Bates, Ralph. "Need We Fear Russia?" *Nation*, 17 January 1942, pp. 60–62.

———. "Issues and Moscow."*Nation*, 23 October 1943, pp. 471–73.

Beaverbrook, Lord. "Opportunity to Win War in 1942: A Second Front in Europe to Aid Russia." *Vital Speeches*, 15 May 1942, pp. 458–60.

Bennett, John C. "The New Hope and the New Unity." *Christianity and Crisis*, 29 November 1943, pp. 1–2.

———. "Establish World Organization Now." *Christianity and Crisis*, 12 June 1944, p. 1.

———. "The Conference of the 'Big Three.'" *Christianity and Crisis*, 5 March 1945, pp. 1–2.

Benvenisti, J. L. "Russia and Brotherhood." *Commonweal*, 23 October 1942, pp. 8–11.

Bess, Demaree. "Stalin over Europe," *Saturday Evening Post*, 14 October 1939, p. 5.

———. "What Does Russia Want?" *Saturday Evening Post*, 20 March 1943, p. 19.

———. "Will Europe Go Communist after the War?" *Saturday Evening Post*, 22 January 1944, p. 15.

———. "Can We Live with Russia?" *Saturday Evening Post*, 7 July 1945, pp. 9–10.

Black, C. E. "Russia and Her Allies." *Current History*, April 1942, pp. 122–26.

———. "War Changes in Russia." *Current History*, June 1942, pp. 283–86.

Bliven, Bruce. "Russia's Morale—and Ours." *New Republic*, 1 September 1941, pp. 273–75.

———. "Emporia Goes to Moscow." *New Republic*, 19 March 1945, pp. 391–92.

Brailsford, H. N. "Locating the Enemy." *New Republic*, 15 January 1940, p. 76.

Bricker, John W. "Free Representative Government: Acceptance Speech." *Vital Speeches*, 15 September 1944, pp. 709–11.

Brubaker, Howard. "Of All Things." *New Yorker* 6, November 1943, p. 44.

———. "Of All Things." *New Yorker*, 13 November 1943, p. 75.

———. "Of All Things." *New Yorker*, 6 January 1945, p. 39.

———. "Of All Things." *New Yorker*, 27 January 1945, p. 51.

Buell, Raymond. "Poland: Key to Europe." *Reader's Digest*, July 1939, pp. 99–102.

Burnham, Philip. "Russia as an Ally." *Commonweal*, 6 February 1942, pp. 381–83.

Cantril, Hadley. "Educational and Economic Composition of Religious Groups: An Analysis of Poll Data." *American Journal of Sociology* 47: (1943): 574–79.

————. "What We Don't Know Is Likely to Hurt Us." *New York Times Magazine*, 14 May 1944, p. 9.

Chamberlin, William Henry. "Letter to Editor." *American Mercury*, November 1939, pp. 380–81.

————. "Russia: An American Problem." *Atlantic Monthly*, February 1942, pp. 148–56.

————. "Meet the Real Litvinoff." *American Mercury*, March 1942, pp. 273–83.

————. "Our Russian Ally." *Christian Century*, 12 August 1942, pp. 976–78.

————. "Russia as a Partner in War and Peace." *Saturday Evening Post*, 14 November 1942, p. 124.

————. "Russia and the Postwar World." *Russian Review* 2 (Autumn 1942): 3–9.

————. "American-Russian Cooperation." *Russian Review* 3 (Autumn 1943): 3–9.

————. "Can Stalin's Russia Go Democratic? No." *American Mercury*, February 1944, pp. 142–48.

————. "Will Stalin Dictate an Eastern Munich?" *American Mercury*, March 1944, pp. 263–74.

————. "Information, Please, about Russia." *Harper's*, April 1944, pp. 405–12.

Chase, Stuart. "The Twilight of Communism in the USA." *Reader's Digest*, September 1941, pp. 25–28.

Coffin, Henry Sloane. "Better Relations between Government and Church in Soviet Russia." *Christianity and Crisis*, 3 May 1943, pp. 5–7.

Connally, Tom. "Agreement at Yalta." *Talks*, April 1945, pp. 23–35.

Cot, Pierre. "Russia's Resurrection." *Nation*, 7 October 1944, pp. 408–10.

Counts, George S. "Democracy as a Great Social Faith." *National Parent-Teacher*, September 1941, pp. 24–26.

Cowley, Malcolm. "Russian Turnabout." *New Republic*, 14 June 1943, pp. 800–801.

Crawford, Kenneth. "Stalin's Boost to Mr. Dies." *Nation*, 28 October 1939, pp. 461–70.

Dallin, David. "Russia's Aims in Europe." *American Mercury*, October 1943, pp. 391–402.

Davies, Joseph E. "How Russia Blasted Hitler's Spy Machine." *American Magazine*, December 1941, pp. 80–81.

————. "Moscow Notebook—An Ambassador's Report." *New York Times Magazine*, 14 December 1941, pp. 12–13.

————. "What We Didn't Know about Russia." *Reader's Digest*, March 1942, pp. 45–50.

————. "Is Communism a Menace to US?" *New York Times Magazine*, 12 April 1942, p. 3.

————. "The Soviets and the Postwar." *Life*, 29 March 1943, pp. 49–55.

————. "Russia Today." *Vital Speeches*, 1 August 1943, pp. 638–40.

————. "Russia Will Hold This Summer." *Saturday Evening Post*, 20 June 1944, pp. 16–17.

Davis, Jerome. "Religion in the USSR." *New Republic*, 5 March 1945, pp. 330–31.

Davis, Kenneth. "Have We Been Wrong about Stalin?" *Current History*, September 1941, pp. 6–11.

Dean, Vera Micheles. "What Do We Want in Europe?" *New Republic*, 15 January 1945, pp. 141–42.

Del Vayo, Alvarez. "Leadership in Europe." *Nation*, 2 December 1944, pp. 688–90.

De Voto, Bernard. "The Easy Chair." *Harper's*, October 1944, pp. 426–29.

———. "Corporate State Not an American System." *Vital Speeches*, 15 October 1944, pp. 14–16.

———. "We Must Have Unity for Peace." *Vital Speeches*, 1 November 1944, pp. 38–40.

Dewey, Thomas E. "The Sixth Pillar." *Christianity and Crisis*, 12 July 1943, pp. 6–7.

Downey, J. O. "America in the Post-War World." *Current History*, July 1942, pp. 328–35.

Drucker, Peter. "Russia Surrenders Economic Isolation." *Saturday Evening Post*, 28 October 1944, p. 20.

Dubrowsky, D. H. "How Stalin Steals Our Money." *Collier's*, 20 April 1940, pp. 22–25.

Dunayerskaya, Raya. "A New Revision of Marxian Economics." *American Economic Review* 34 (1944): 531–37.

Duranty, Walter. "Is the Russian Revolution Over?" *New York Times Magazine*, 30 July 1944, p. 12.

Durr, C. J. "How Free is Radio?" *NEA Journal*, October 1944, pp. 167–68.

Eastman, Max. "Stalin's American Power." *American Mercury*, December 1941, pp. 671–80.

———. "We Must Face the Facts about Russia." *Reader's Digest*, July 1943, pp. 1–14.

Eddy, Sherwood. "Russia in the World Crisis." *Christianity and Crisis*, 28 July 1941, pp. 2–6.

Eulau, Heinz. "As the Big Three Meet." *New Republic*, 5 February 1945, pp. 168–70.

———. "Kremlin and Vatican," *New Republic*, 12 March 1945, pp. 416–17.

Fay, Sidney. "The Meaning of the Moscow Conference." *Current History*, December 1943, pp. 289–94.

———. "Russia's Western Border Lands." *Current History*, July 1943, pp. 289–300.

———. "What Does Stalin Want?" *Current History*, November 1943, pp. 199–208.

———. "The Russo-Polish Dispute." *Current History*, March 1944, pp. 193–200.

Fedotov, George P. "The Prospects of Christianity in Russia." *Christianity and Crisis*, 6 April 1942, pp. 3–6.

Fenton, Joseph Clifford. "Catholic Missions and Communist Tactic." *American Ecclesiastical Review*, March 1945, pp. 215–19.

Fischer, Louis. "Russia Goes West." *Nation*, 23 September 1939, pp. 310–16.

———. "What Russia Really Wants," *American Magazine*, December 1943, pp. 28–29.

Florinsky, Michael. "Stalin and Marxian Theory." *Current History*, April 1945, pp. 289–93.

Fox, Thomas A. "The Plight of the Liberals." *American Ecclesiastical Review*, May 1940, pp. 385–95.

Fuqua, Stephen. "Stalingrad—A Lesson in Fighting." *Newsweek*, 21 September 1942, p. 20.

———. "Russia Is Still the Main Battle Front." *Newsweek*, 26 October 1942, p. 28.

Gassner, John. "The Russians on Broadway." *Current History*, February 1943, pp. 548–51.

Gilkey, Charles W. "Some Soils and Seeds of Isolationism." *Christianity and Crisis*, 14 June 1943, pp. 2–6.

Gilmore, Eddy. "I Learn about the Russians." *National Geographic*, November 1943, pp. 619–40.

———. "Liberated Ukraine." *National Geographic*, May 1944, pp. 513–36.

Gloyn, Cyril K. "Christianity and the Influence of the Soviet Union." *Christendom* 9 (Spring 1944): 153–71.

Green, William. "Our Immediate Obligation." *American Federationist*, July 1941, pp. 20–21.

———. "The Free and Not Free." *American Federationist*, December 1944, p. 25.

———. "International Labor Policy." *American Federationist*, May 1945, pp. 16–17.

Gurian, Waldemar. "Russia—Pro and Con." *Commonweal*, 11 August 1944, pp. 390–92.

Harriman, W. Averell. "Freedom Is a Fighting Word." *Talks*, January 1943, pp. 26–29.

Heimann, Edward. "The Just War of Unjust Nations." *Christianity and Crisis*, 8 February 1943, pp. 2–6.

Hillman, Sidney. Speech of 31 December 1942. *CIO News*, 4 January 1943, p. 6.

Hindus, Maurice. "Report on Russia." *Reader's Digest*, November 1942, pp. 90–92.

———. "The Price that Russia Is Paying." *Reader's Digest*, April 1943, pp. 47–50.

———. "The Russian Slogan: 'Work, Study and Learn,'" *Reader's Digest*, February 1944, pp. 59–60.

Holmes, John Haynes. "If Russia Wins." *Christian Century*, 30 July 1941, pp. 954–56.

Hoover, Calvin. "Capitalism and Socialism, a New Soviet Appraisal." *Foreign Affairs* 22 (1944): 532–42.

Hoover, Herbert. "Russian Misadventure; Why We Should Recall Our Ambassador to the USSR." *Collier's*, 27 April 1940, pp. 21–22.

Hopper, Bruce. "The War for Eastern Europe." *Foreign Affairs* 20 (October 1941): 18–29.

Howe, Quincy. "American Foreign Policy and Public Opinion." *Yale Review* 31 (1942): 315–33.

Iswolski, Helen. "Russia at War." *Commonweal*, 25 July 1941, pp. 318–20.

Johnson, Ernest. "Democracy in Color." *Christianity and Crisis*, 23 March 1942, p. 1.

Johnston, Eric. "To Bridge the Gulf between the US and Russia." *Reader's Digest*, August 1944, pp. 33–36.

———. "A Business View of Russia." *Nation's Business*, October 1944, pp. 21–22.

———. "My Talk with Joseph Stalin." *Reader's Digest*, October 1944, pp. 1–10.

Kerensky, Alexander. "Russia is Ripe for Freedom." *American Mercury*, July 1943, pp. 158–65.

Kirchwey, Freda. "Congress and Russia." *Nation*, 18 October 1941, pp. 361–62.

———. "Russia and the Future." *Nation*, 20 June 1942, p. 701.

———. "Unfinished Business." *Nation*, 27 November 1943, p. 600.

Krivitsky, W. G. "When Stalin Counterfeited Dollars." *Saturday Evening Post*, 30 September 1939, pp. 8–9.

Kusiw, Basil. "Tragedy of the Ukrainian Evangelicals." *Federal Council Bulletin*, December 1939, p. 12.

Landon, Alfred. "Emancipators—True and False." *Vital Speeches*, 1 March 1940, pp. 308–10.

Lardner, David. "The Current Cinema." *New Yorker*, 13 November 1943, p. 77.

———. "The Current Cinema." *New Yorker*, 20 November 1943, p. 88.

Lattimore, Owen. "New Road to Russia." *National Geographic*, December 1944, pp. 641–76.

Lawrence, David. "Russia—Partner or Rival?" *United States News*, 20 August 1943, pp. 28–29.

Lerner, Max. "Russia and the War of Ideas." *New Republic*, 7 July 1941, pp. 17–19.

———. "Russia and the Future." *Atlantic Monthly*, November 1942, pp. 79–87.

Lindeman, Eduard. "Trouble at the Grass Roots." *Survey Graphic*, June 1944, pp. 280–82.

Lindley, Ernest. "How Russia Fits into United Nations Picture." *Newsweek*, 12 January 1942, p. 20.

———. "Russia: Partner in War and Peace." *Newsweek*, 8 June 1942, p. 31.

———. "Relations with Russia." *Newsweek*, 29 March 1943, p. 26.

———. "Big Three Are Edging Closer on Political and Military Fronts." *Newsweek*, 4 October 1943, pp. 19–20.

Lippmann, Walter. "Can We Have Peace after This War?" *Ladies' Home Journal*, August 1943, pp. 25–31.

———. "Can We Win the Peace?" *Ladies' Home Journal*, January 1944, pp. 22–23.

Litvinoff, Maxim. "More Fronts to Win the War Now." *Vital Speeches*, 15 March 1942, pp. 325–26.

———. "Russia's Contributions: We Are All Partners." *Vital Speeches*, 1 April 1942, pp. 358–60.

Luce, Henry R. "The American Century." *Life*, 17 February 1941, pp. 61–65.

———. "America's War and America's Peace." *Life*, 16 February 1942, pp. 82–91.

Lydgate, William. "What Our People Think." *Reader's Digest*, November 1944, pp. 1–8.

Lyons, Eugene. "The End of Joseph Stalin." *American Mercury*, August 1941, pp. 135–43.

———. "Cooperating with Russia." *American Mercury*, May 1943, pp. 536–45.

———. "The Progress of Stalin-Worship." *American Mercury*, June 1943, pp. 693–97.

———. "Appeasement in Yalta." *American Mercury*, April 1945, pp. 461–68.

McCulloch, Rhoda. "Shall We Lose the Peace?" *Christianity and Crisis*, 4 October 1943, pp. 1–2.

McManus, R. C. "Communist Beachhead in Agriculture." *Farm Journal and Farmer's Wife*, October 1944, p. 23.

McMillen, Wheeler. "All of Us." *Farm Journal and Farmer's Wife*, April 1944, p. 6.

Magidoff, Nila. "Americans and Russians Are *So* Alike." *American Magazine*, December 1944, p. 17.

Mastny, Vojtech. "Stalin and the Prospects of a Separate Peace in World War II." *American Historical Review* 77 (1972):1365–88.

Moley, Raymond. "Perspective." *Newsweek*, 4 September 1939, p. 48.

———. "Perspective." *Newsweek*, 11 September 1939, p. 60.

———. "Perspective: The Balkan Time Bomb." *Newsweek*, 8 November 1943, p. 112.

———. "Perspective: Hyphenated Votes." *Newsweek*, 20 December 1943, p. 104.

———. "Perspective: On Being Sorry for Finland." *Newsweek*, 6 September 1943, p. 112.

———. "Perspective: The Polish Problem." *Newsweek*, 11 October 1943, p. 112.

———. "Perspective: You Can Do Business with Stalin." *Newsweek*, 18 October 1943, p. 112.

———. "Perspective: The Polish Crisis." *Newsweek*, 1 January 1945, p. 80.

———. "Perspective: What Capitalism Learned at Yalta." *Newsweek*, 26 February 1945, p. 108.

———. "Perspective: In the Sweat of Their Brows." *Newsweek*, 26 March 1945, p. 116.

Morgan, Joy Elmer. "The Outlook for America." *NEA Journal*, March 1945, p. 49.

———. "The United Peoples of the World." *NEA Journal*, December 1942, p. 261.

Mort, Paul R. and Carnell, F. G. "A Poll of Parent Opinion." *National Parent-Teacher*, October 1939, pp. 27–30.

Mosely, Philip E. "The Small Nations and European Reconstruction." *Christianity and Crisis*, 1 June 1942, pp. 2–5.

Nelson, Donald M. "What I Saw in Russia." *Collier's*, 29 January 1944, p. 11.

Niebuhr, Reinhold. "The Russians and Our Interdependence." *Christianity and Crisis*, 24 August 1941, pp. 1–2.

———. "The Anglo-Russian Pact." *Christianity and Crisis*, 29 June 1942, pp. 2–3.

———. "Plans for World Reorganization." *Christianity and Crisis*, 19 October 1942, pp. 3–6.

———. "Russia and the West, Part I." *Nation*, 16 January 1943, pp. 82–84.

———. "Russia and the West, Part II." *Nation*, 23 January 1943, pp. 124–25.

———. "The United Nations and World Organization." *Christianity and Crisis*, 25 January 1943, pp. 1–2.

———. "American Power and World Responsibility." *Christianity and Crisis*, 5 April 1943, pp. 2–4.

———. "Educational and Religious Barrenness." *Christianity and Crisis*, 9 August 1943, pp. 1–2.

———. "Anglo-Saxon Destiny and Responsibility." *Christianity and Crisis*, 4 October 1943, pp. 2–4.

———. "Is Peace Being Made?" *Christianity and Crisis*, 27 December 1943, p. 2.

———. "Airplanes Are Not Enough." *Christianity and Crisis*, 7 February 1944, pp. 1–2.

———. "Stones from a Glass House." *Christianity and Crisis*, 16 October 1944, pp. 1–2.

———. "Russia and the Peace." *Christianity and Crisis*, 13 November 1944, pp. 2–4.

_____. "The Widow's Mite." *Christianity and Crisis*, 5 February 1945, pp. 1–2.

O'Brien, John A. "Communism and Religion, a Struggle unto Death." *American Ecclesiastical Review*, May 1940, pp. 396–404.

Owen, Russell. "Fifty below Zero." *New York Times Magazine*, 11 January 1942, p. 13.

Padmore, George. "Race Relations: Soviet and British." *Crisis*, November 1942, pp. 345–48.

_____. "Industrialized Soviet Backs Red Army." *Crisis*, June 1943, pp. 173–74.

Pares, Bernard. "On the Fear of Russia." *New Republic*, 19 April 1943, pp. 498–502.

_____. "Siberia—Russia's Middle West." *Rotarian*, February 1944, pp. 21–24.

Parker, Ralph. "Moscow Ski Classes." *New York Times Magazine*, 1 February 1942, p. 19.

_____. "Retreat from Moscow." *New York Times Magazine*, 22 February 1942, p. 35.

Pegler, Westbrook. "What Strange Bedfellows!" *American Legion Magazine*, April 1939, pp. 10–11.

Perry, Ralph Barton. "American-Soviet Friendship, an Invitation to Agreement." *New Republic*, 5 April 1943, pp. 433–47.

Peterson, Olga M. "So You're Celebrating Russia Book Week." *ALA Bulletin*, April 1944, pp. 152–54.

Planyi, Karl. "Why Make Russia Run Amok?" *Harper's*, March 1943, pp. 404–10.

Pope, Arthur. "Can Stalin's Russia Go Democratic? Yes." *American Mercury*, February 1944, pp. 135–42.

Rayburn, Sam. "We Must Have Unity." *Vital Speeches*, 1 February 1944, pp. 229–30.

Reston, James. "The Outspoken Mr. Litvinoff." *New York Times Magazine*, 18 January 1942, p. 15.

_____. "Washington (Indiana) Looks at Washington (D.C.)." *New York Times Magazine*, 18 April 1943, pp. 29–31.

Reynolds, Grant. "What the Negro Soldier Thinks about This War." *Crisis*, September 1944, pp. 289–91.

Richards, Bernard, "Millions Facing Certain Death." *Polish Jew*, October-November 1942, pp. 3–4.

Rickenbacker, Eddie. "The War Is Not Over." *Talks*, October 1943, p. 5.

Rylski, Marcin. "Poland and Russia." *Nation*, 9 October 1943, pp. 408–10.

Salisbury, Harrison. "Russia Beckons Big Business." *Collier's*, 2 September 1944, p. 11.

Schlesinger, Arthur M., Jr. "Origins of the Cold War." *Foreign Affairs* 46 (October 1967): 22–52.

Schuman, Frederick. "The Soviet Union and the Future of Europe." *Current History*, June 1944, pp. 465–72.

Scott, John. "Stalin's Ural Stronghold." *Reader's Digest*, February 1942, pp. 29–34.

_____. "Valiant Russia's Industrial Might." *National Geographic*, May 1943, pp. 525–56.

Small, Melvin. "How We Learned to Love the Russians: American Media and the Soviet Union During World War II." *Historian* 36 (1974): 455–78.

Snow, Edgar. "These Are the People of Russia." *Saturday Evening Post*, 15 December 1942, pp. 14–15.

———. "How Fast Can Russia Rebuild?" *Saturday Evening Post*, 12 February 1944, pp. 20–21.

———. "Eastern Europe Swings Left." *Saturday Evening Post*, 11 November 1944, pp. 9–11.

———. "Strong Men around Stalin." *Saturday Evening Post*, 24 March 1945, pp. 12–13.

Solow, Herbert. "Stalin's Great American Hoax, The League for Peace and Democracy." *American Mercury*, December 1939, pp. 394–402.

Standley, William. "Russia in the Postwar World." *Vital Speeches*, 1 January 1945, pp. 174–78.

Stolberg, Benjamin. "Communist Wreckers in American Labor." *Saturday Evening Post*, 2 September 1939, pp. 5–6.

Stone, I. F. "Chamberlain's Russo-German Pact." *Nation*, 23 September 1939, pp. 313–16.

———. "V For Vituperation." *Nation*, 11 September 1943, p. 286.

Stowe, Leland. "Living with the Russians." *Rotarian*, May 1943, pp. 11–13.

Strakhovsky, Leonid. "America, the Savior of Red Tyranny." *Catholic World*, November 1941, pp. 644–46.

Strong, Anna Louise. "Russia Rebuilds." *Atlantic Monthly*, December 1944, pp. 92–96.

Sullivan, Frank. "See It with Someone You Love!" *New Yorker*, 15 July 1944, p. 25.

Sullivan, Mark. "Uproot the Seeds of Totalitarianism." *Reader's Digest*, October 1939, pp. 5–6.

Sulzberger, C. L. "Sergei, Red Fighter." *New York Times Magazine*, 4 January 1942, p. 4.

———. "Report on Russia and the Russians." *New York Times Magazine*, 29 March 1942, pp. 3–4.

———. "The Russian Battle Front." *Life*, 20 July 1942, pp. 78–88.

———. "What Does Russia Want?" *New York Times Magazine*, 31 October 1943, p. 10.

Thompson, Dorothy. "America's Three Choices." *Ladies' Home Journal*, April 1943, p. 6.

Thompson, Paul. "The Nazis' Own Appraisal of the Russian Soldier." *Reader's Digest*, June 1943, pp. 15–18.

Tigner, Hugh S. "The Fall of the Soviet Star." *Christian Century*, 14 February 1940, pp. 215–18.

Timasheff, N. W. "Religion in Russia." *Christianity and Crisis*, 22 March 1943, pp. 2–5.

———. "Religion in Russia." *Current History*, February 1945, pp. 105–110.

Tobin, Daniel J. "Churchill! Stalin! dewey?" *International Teamster*, May 1944, pp. 7–8.

Utley, Freda. "The Great Russian Illusion." *Atlantic Monthly*, April 1941, pp. 470–77.

———. "The Limits of Russian Resistance." *American Mercury*, September 1941, pp. 292–300.

Van Dusen, Henry P. "The Deeper Issues." *Christianity and Crisis*, 27 July 1942, pp. 1–2.

Walsh, Warren B. "What the American People Think of Russia." *Public Opinion Quarterly* 8 (1944–45): 513–22.

————. "American Attitudes toward Russia." *Antioch Review* 7 (June 1947): 183–90.

Ward, Harry. "Is Russia Forsaking Communism?" *Christian Century*, 28 October 1942, pp. 1314–16.

Warren, Earl. "Victory, Lasting Peace, Jobs for All: Republican Keynote Address." *Vital Speeches*, 15 July 1944, pp. 591–93.

Welles, Sumner. "What Russia Wants." *Reader's Digest*, November 1944, pp. 20–24.

Wesson, Charles M. "Administering Lend-Lease for the Soviets." *American Review of the Soviet Union* 6 (November 1944):3–10.

Wheeler, Burton K. "Agreement at Yalta." *Talks*, April 1945, pp. 25–27.

White, William Allen. "Emporia in Wartime." *New Republic*, 13 April 1942, pp. 490–92.

Wieman, Henry Nelson. "Join Russia in the War!" *Christian Century*, 13 August 1941, pp. 1002–4.

Willen, Paul. "Who 'Collaborated' with Russia?" *Antioch Review* 14 (September 1954): 259–83.

Willkie, Wendell L. "Let's Look Ahead." *New York Times Magazine*, 15 February 1942, p. 5.

————. "We Must Work with Russia." *New York Times Magazine*, 17 January 1943, p. 5.

————. "Life on the Russian Frontier." *Reader's Digest*, March 1943, pp. 1–7.

————. "Don't Stir Distrust of Russia," *New York Times Magazine*, 2 January 1944, pp. 3–4.

Winter, Ella. "Our Allies, the Russians." *Ladies' Home Journal*, February 1943, p. 37.

Wolfe, Bertram. "The Silent Soviet Revolution." *Reader's Digest*, July 1941, pp. 87–90.

Wolfe, Henry C. "Keep an Eye on Russia." *Harper's*, April 1941, pp. 533–41.

Wood, Junius B. "Russia—Customer and Competitor." *Nation's Business*, March 1944, pp. 28–30.

————. "How Russia Goes at a Job." *Nation's Business*, July 1944, p. 29.

————. "A New Europe in the Making." *Nation's Business*, January 1945, p. 25.

————. "How Russia Trades with Us," *Nation's Business*, March 1945, p. 42.

Zuckerman, William. "Soviet Jews before and during the War." *American Hebrew*, 16 April 1943, pp. 16–18.

Books and Pamphlets

Adams, Henry H. *1942: The Year That Doomed the Axis*. New York: David McKay Co., 1967.

Agar, Herbert. *A Time for Greatness*. Boston: Little, Brown & Co., 1942.

Almedingen, E. M. *Tomorrow Will Come*. Boston: Little, Brown & Co., 1941.

Almond, Gabriel A. *The American People and Foreign Policy*. New York: Harcourt, Brace, & Co., 1950.

Alperovitz, Gar. *Atomic Diplomacy: Hiroshima and Potsdam*. New York: Simon & Schuster, 1965.

American Council on Soviet Relations. *The Slavic Peoples Against Hitler*. New York: American Council on Soviet Relations, n.d.

American Friends of Polish Democracy. *Unconquered Poland*. New York: American Friends of Polish Democracy, 1943.

Anderson, Paul B. *People, Church and State in Modern Russia*. New York: Macmillan, 1944.

Annual of the Southern Baptist Convention. Nashville: Broadman Press, 1939–1945.

Anshen, Ruth N., ed. *Beyond Victory*. New York: Harcourt, Brace & Co., 1943.

Asbell, Bernard. *When FDR Died*. New York: Holt, Rinehart, & Winston, 1961.

Ausübel, Nathan, ed. *Voices of History, 1944–1945*. New York: Phoenix Press, 1945.

Bailey, Thomas A. *The Man in the Street*. New York: Macmillan, 1948.

———. *America Faces Russia: Russian-American Relations from Early Times to Our Own Day*. Ithaca: Cornell University Press, 1950.

Baird, A. Craig, ed. *Representative American Speeches, 1942–1943*. New York: H. W. Wilson Co., 1943.

Barnard, Ellsworth. *Wendell Willkie: Fighter for Freedom*. Marquette, Mich.: Northern Michigan College Press, 1966.

Barnes, Joseph. *Willkie*. New York: Simon & Schuster, 1952.

Barnouw, Erik. *The Golden Web: A History of Broadcasting in the United States, 1933–1953*. New York: Oxford University Press, 1968.

Basseches, Nikolaus. *The Unknown Army: The Nature and History of the Russian Military Forces*. New York: Viking Press, 1943.

Beard, Charles A. *President Roosevelt and the Coming of War, 1941*. New Haven: Yale University Press, 1948.

Becker, Carl L. *How New Will the Better World Be?* New York: Alfred A. Knopf, 1944.

Beitzell, Robert. *The Uneasy Alliance: America, Britain, and Russia, 1941–1943*. New York: Alfred A. Knopf, 1972.

Berchin, Michel, and Ben-Horin, Eliahu. *The Red Army*. New York: George J. McLeod, 1942.

Berelson, Bernard. *Content Analysis in Communication Research*. Glencoe, Ill.: Free Press, 1952.

Berelson, Bernard, and Steiner, Gary A. *Human Behavior: An Inventory of Scientific Findings*. 2d ed. rev. New York: Harcourt, Brace & World, 1967.

Berelson, Bernard, and Janowitz, Morris, eds. *Reader in Public Opinion and Communication*. 2d ed. rev. New York: Free Press, 1966.

Best, Harry. *The Soviet Experiment*. New York: Richard R. Smith, 1941.

Best, James F. *Public Opinion: Micro and Macro*. Homewood, Ill.: Dorsey Press, 1973.

Bilmanis, Alfred. *Baltic States in Postwar Europe*. Washington, D.C.: Press Bureau of the Latvian Legation, 1943.

Blum, John Morton. *From the Morgenthau Diaries: Years of War, 1941–1945*. Boston: Houghton Mifflin Co., 1967.

———, ed. *The Price of Vision: The Diary of Henry A. Wallace 1942–1946*. Boston: Houghton Mifflin Co., 1973.

Bourke-White, Margaret. *Shooting the Russian War*. New York: Simon & Schuster, 1942.

Brant, Irving. *Road to Peace and Freedom*. Cornwall, N.Y.: McClelland & Stewart, 1943.

Browder, Earl. *Victory—and After*. New York: International Publishers Co., 1942.

———. *Teheran: Our Path in War and Peace*. New York: Progress Books, 1944.

Brown, James E. *Russia Fights*. New York: Charles Scribner's Sons, 1943.

Bruner, Jerome. *Mandate from the People*. New York: Duell, Sloan, & Pearce, 1944.

Buchanan, William, and Cantril, Hadley. *How Nations See Each Other: A Study in Public Opinion*. Urbana, Ill.: University of Illinois Press, 1953.

Buck, Pearl S. *Talk about Russia*. New York: John Day Co., 1945.

Burns, James MacGregor. *Roosevelt: The Soldier of Freedom*. New York: Harcourt Brace Jovanovich, 1970.

Bush, Merrill E. *Citizen, Plan for Peace!* New York: Harper & Bros., 1944.

Byrnes, James F. *Speaking Frankly*. New York: Harper & Bros.,1947.

————. *All in One Lifetime*. New York: Harper & Bros., 1958.

Caldwell, Erskine. *All-out on the Road to Smolensk*. New York: Duell, Sloan & Pearce, 1942.

Callender, Harold. *A Preface to Peace*. New York: Alfred A. Knopf, 1944.

Cardwell, Ann Su. *Poland and Russia: The Last Quarter Century*. New York: Sheed & Ward, 1944.

Carroll, Wallace. *We're in This with Russia*. Cambridge, Mass.: Houghton Mifflin Co., 1942.

Cassidy, Henry C. *Moscow Dateline, 1941–1943*. Boston: Houghton Mifflin Co., 1943.

Chadwin, Mark L. *The Hawks of World War II*. Chapel Hill: University of North Carolina Press, 1968.

Chamberlin, William H. *The Russian Enigma: An Interpretation*. New York: Charles Scribner's Sons, 1943.

————. *America: Partner in World Rule*. New York: Vanguard Press, 1945.

————. *America's Second Crusade*. Chicago: Henry Regnery Co., 1950.

Chandler, Albert D., ed. *The Papers of Dwight David Eisenhower: The War Years*. 5 vols. Baltimore: Johns Hopkins Press, 1970.

Childs, John L., and Counts, George S. *America, Russia and the Communist Party in the Postwar World*. New York: John Day Co., 1943.

Clapper, Raymond. *Watching the World, 1931–1944*. New York: McGraw-Hill Book Co., 1944.

Clemens, Diane Shaver. *Yalta*. New York: Oxford University Press, 1970.

Ciliga, Anton. *The Russian Enigma*. New York: George Routledge & Sons, 1940.

Cohen, Bernard. *The Press and Foreign Policy*. Princeton: Princeton University Press, 1963.

Cole, Margaret, ed., *Our Soviet Ally: Essays*. New York: Webb Publishing Co., 1943.

Cole, Wayne S. *America First*. Madison: University of Wisconsin Press, 1953.

————. *Charles A. Lindbergh and the Battle against American Intervention in World War II*. New York: Harcourt, Brace, Jovanovich, 1974.

Communist Party, USA. *Party Building: A Handbook for Branch Officers*. New York: Workers Library Publishers, 1943.

Cowles, Virginia. *Looking for Trouble*. New York: Harper & Bros., 1941.

Cressey, George B. *The Basis of Soviet Strength*. New York: McGraw-Hill, 1945.

Crocker, George N. *Roosevelt's Road to Russia*. Chicago: Henry Regnery Co., 1959.

Curti, Merle. *American Philanthropy Abroad: A History*. New Brunswick: Rutgers University Press, 1963.

Dallin, David J. *Soviet Russia's Foreign Policy, 1939–1942*. New Haven: Yale University Press, 1942.

————. *Russia and Postwar Europe*. New Haven: Yale University Press, 1943.

————. *The Real Soviet Russia*. New Haven: Yale University Press, 1944.

———. *The Big Three: The United States, Britain, Russia*. New Haven: Yale University Press, 1945.

Davies, Joseph E. *Mission to Moscow*. New York: Simon & Schuster, 1941.

———. *Our Soviet Ally in War and Peace*. New York: National Council of American-Soviet Friendship, 1944.

Davis, Kenneth S. *Experience of War: The United States in World War II*. Garden City, N.Y.: Doubleday & Co., 1965.

Dawson, Raymond H. *The Decision to Aid Russia, 1941*. Chapel Hill: University of North Carolina Press, 1959.

Deane, John R. *The Strange Alliance*. New York: The Viking Press, 1947.

De Huszar, George B., ed. *New Perspectives on Peace*. Chicago: University of Chicago Press, 1944.

Divine, Robert A. *The Reluctant Belligerent: America's Entry into World War II*. New York: John Wiley & Sons, 1965.

———. *Second Chance: The Triumph of Internationalism in America During World War II*. New York: Atheneum, 1967.

———. *Roosevelt and World War II*. Baltimore: Johns Hopkins Press, 1969.

———, ed. *Causes and Consequences of World War II*. Chicago: Quadrangle, 1969.

———. *Foreign Policy and U.S. Presidential Elections, 1940–1948*. New York: New Viewpoints, 1974.

Dulles, Foster R. *The Road to Teheran: The Story of Russia and America, 1781–1943*. Princeton: Princeton University Press, 1944.

Duranty, Walter. *The Kremlin and the People*. New York: Reynal & Hitchcock, 1941.

———. *USSR: The Story of Soviet Russia*. Philadelphia: J.B. Lippincott Co., 1944.

Eastman, Max. *Stalin's Russia and the Crisis in Socialism*. New York: W.W. Norton, 1940.

Efron, Andrew. *The New Russian Empire*. New Haven: Tuttle, Morehouse & Taylor, 1941.

Ehrenburg, Ilya. *Russia at War*. London: Hamish Hamilton, 1943.

———. *The Tempering of Russia*. New York: Alfred A. Knopf, 1944.

Eliot, George Fielding. *Hour of Triumph*. New York: McClelland & Stewart, 1944.

Farnsworth, Beatrice. *William C. Bullitt and the Soviet Union*. Bloomington: Indiana University Press, 1967.

Feis, Herbert. *The Road to Pearl Harbor: The Coming of the War between the United States and Japan*. Princeton: Princeton University Press, 1950.

———. *Churchill, Roosevelt, Stalin: The War They Waged and the Peace They Sought*. Princeton: Princeton University Press, 1957.

———. *Between War and Peace: The Potsdam Conference*. Princeton: Princeton University Press, 1960.

Festinger, Leon. *A Theory of Cognitive Dissonance*. Stanford: Stanford University Press, 1957.

Fields, J. *Behind the War Headlines*. New York: Workers Library Publishers, 1939.

Filene, Peter G. *Americans and the Soviet Experiment, 1917–1933*. Cambridge: Harvard University Press, 1967.

———, ed. *American Views of Soviet Russia, 1917–1965*. Homewood, Ill.: Dorsey Press, 1968.

Fischer, Ernst. *Is This a War for Freedom?* New York: Workers Library Publishers, 1940.

Fischer, Louis. *Men and Politics: An Autobiography.* New York: Duell, Sloan & Pearce, 1941.

————. *Empire.* New York: Duell, Sloan & Pearce, 1943.

Fischer, Markoosha. *My Lives in Russia.* New York: Harper & Bros., 1944.

Fleming, Denna F. *Can We Win the Peace?* Nashville: Broadman Press, 1943.

Flynn, Edward J. *You're the Boss.* New York: Viking Press, 1947.

Flynn, Elizabeth Gurley. *I Didn't Raise My Boy to Be a Soldier for Wall Street.* New York: Workers Library Publishers, 1940.

Foster, William Z. *From Defense to Attack.* New York: Workers Library Publishers, 1942.

————. *The USA and the USSR: War Allies and Friends.* New York: Workers Library Publishers, 1942.

Fox, William T.R. *The Super-Powers.* New York: Harcourt, Brace & Co., 1944.

Free, Lloyd A., and Cantril, Hadley. *The Political Beliefs of Americans; A Study of Public Opinion.* New Brunswick, N.J.: Rutgers University Press, 1968.

Gaddis, John Lewis. *The United States and the Origins of the Cold War, 1941–1947.* New York: Columbia University Press, 1972.

Gallup, George H. *Public Opinion in a Democracy.* Princeton: Princeton University, 1939.

————. *The Gallup Poll, 1935–1971.* New York: Random House, 1972.

Gans, Herbert J. *The Urban Villagers; Group and Class in the Life of Italian-Americans.* New York: Free Press, 1962.

Gardner, Lloyd C. *Economic Aspects of New Deal Diplomacy.* Madison: University of Wisconsin Press, 1964.

————. *Architects of Illusion: Men and Ideas in American Foreign Policy, 1941–1949.* Chicago: Quadrangle, 1970.

Goodman, Jack, ed. *While You Were Gone: A Report on Wartime Life in the United States.* New York: Simon & Schuster, 1946.

Graebner, Norman A., ed. *An Uncertain Tradition: American Secretaries of State in the Twentieth Century.* New York: McGraw-Hill, 1961.

Graebner, Walter. *Round Trip to Russia.* Philadelphia: J.B. Lippincott, 1943.

Gunther, John. *Inside USA* New York: Harper & Bros., 1947.

Guyol, Philip N. *Democracy Fights: A History of New Hampshire in World War II.* Hanover: Dartmouth Publications, 1951.

Hackett, Alice Payne. *Fifty Years of Best Sellers, 1895–1945.* New York: R.R. Bowker Co., 1945.

Hanc, Joseph. *Eastern Europe and the United States.* Boston: World Peace Foundation, 1942.

Harper, Paul V., ed. *The Russia I Believe in: The Memoirs of Samuel N. Harper, 1902–1941.* Chicago: University of Chicago Press, 1945.

Hart, Scott. *Washington at War.* Englewood Cliffs, N.J.: Prentice Hall, 1970.

Hassett, William D. *Off the Record with FDR, 1942–1945.* New Brunswick, N.J.: Rutgers University Press, 1958.

Hayek, Friedrich A. *The Road to Serfdom.* Chicago: University of Chicago Press, 1944.

Hero, Alfred O., Jr. *The Southerner and World Affairs.* Baton Rouge: Lousiana State University Press, 1965.

Herring, George C., Jr. *Aid to Russia 1941–1946. Strategy, Diplomacy and the Origins of the Cold War.* New York: Columbia University Press, 1973.

Herz, Martin F. *Beginnings of the Cold War.* Bloomington: Indiana University Press, 1966.

Hindus, Maurice. *Mother Russia*. Garden City, N.Y.: Doubleday & Co., 1943.

Hinshaw, David. *Home Front, USA*. New York: G.P. Putnam's Sons, 1943.

Hoehling, A. A. *Home Front, USA*. New York: Thomas Y. Crowell, 1966.

Hoover, Herbert. *Addresses upon the American Road, 1941–1945*. New York: Charles Scribner's Sons, 1946.

Hoover, Herbert, and Gibson, Hugh. *The Problems of Lasting Peace*. Garden City, N.Y.: McClelland & Stewart, 1942.

Hovland, Carl; Janis, Irving; and Kelley, Harold. *Communication and Persuasion: Psychological Studies of Opinion Change*. New Haven: Yale University Press, 1953.

Howe, Irving, and Coser, Lewis. *The American Communist Party: A Critical History, 1919–1957*. Boston: Beacon Press, 1957.

Hughes, Emmet John. *The Living Presidency*. New York: Coward, McCann, & Geoghegan, 1973.

Hull, Cordell. *The Memoirs of Cordell Hull*. Vol. 2. New York: Macmillan, 1948.

Israel, Fred L., ed. *The War Diaries of Breckinridge Long*. Lincoln: University of Nebraska Press, 1966.

Joesten, Joachim. *What Russia Wants*. Binghamton, N.Y.: Duell, Sloan & Pearce, 1944.

Johnson, Hewlett. *The Soviet Power*. New York: Modern Age Books, 1944.

Johnson, Walter. *The Battle against Isolation*. Chicago: University of Chicago Press, 1944.

Johnston, Eric. *America Unlimited*. Garden City, N.Y.: Doubleday & Co., 1944.

Jones, Joseph M. *A Modern Foreign Policy for the United States*. New York: Macmillan, 1944.

Jones, Robert H. *The Road to Russia: US Lend-Lease to the Soviet Union*. Norman: University of Oklahoma Press, 1969.

Josephson, Matthew. *Sidney Hillman: Statesman of American Labor*. New York: Doubleday & Co., 1952.

Kaltenborn, H. V. *Kaltenborn Edits the War News*. New York: E. P. Dutton, 1942.

──────. *Fifty Fabulous Years, 1900–1950*. New York: G. P. Putnam's Sons, 1950.

Kamp, Joseph P. *Vote CIO and Get a Soviet America*. New York: Constitutional Educational League, 1944.

Katz, Elihu, and Lazarsfeld, Paul. *Personal Influence: The Part Played by People in the Flow of Mass Communications*. Glencoe, Ill.: Free Press, 1955.

Kennan, George F. *Russia and the West under Lenin and Stalin*. Boston: Little, Brown, & Co., 1960.

──────. *Memoirs: 1925–1950*. Boston: Little, Brown & Co., 1967.

Kernan, W. F. *Defense Will Not Win the War*. Boston: Little, Brown & Co., 1942.

Kerr, Walter. *The Russian Army*. New York: Alfred A. Knopf, 1944.

Kleinberg, Otto. *Tensions Affecting International Understanding: A Survey of Research*. New York: Social Science Research Council, 1950.

Kolko, Gabriel. *The Politics of War: The World and United States Foreign Policy, 1943–1945*. New York: Random House, 1968.

Kournakoff, Sergei N. *Russia's Fighting Forces*. New York: Duell, Sloan and Pearce, 1942.

Lamont, Corliss. *Soviet Russia versus Nazi Germany*. New York: American Council on Soviet Relations, 1941.

──────. *America and Russia*. New York: National Council of American-Soviet Friendship, 1943.

————. *Soviet Russia and the Postwar World*. New York: National Council of American-Soviet Friendship, 1943.

Lasch, Christopher. *The American Liberals and the Russian Revolution*. New York: Columbia University Press, 1962.

Laserson, Max M. *Russia and the Western World*. New York: Macmillan, 1945.

Laski, Harold J. *Reflections on the Revolution of Our Time*. London: Viking Press, 1943.

Lauterbach, Richard E. *These Are the Russians*. New York: Harper & Bros., 1944.

Lazarsfeld, Paul F.; Berelson, Bernard; and Gaudet, Hazel. *The People's Choice: How the Voter Makes up His Mind in a Presidential Election*. New York: Duell, Sloan and Pearce, 1944.

Lazarsfeld, Paul F., and Kendall, Patricia. *Radio Listening in America*. Chapel Hill : University of North Carolina Press, 1948.

Lazarsfeld, Paul F., and Stanton, Frank N. *Communications Research, 1948–1949*. New York: Harper & Bros., 1949.

Lerner, Max. *Public Journal*. New York: Viking Press, 1945.

Lesueur, Larry. *Twelve Months that Changed the World*. New York: Alfred A. Knopf, 1943.

Lilienthal, David E. *The TVA Years, 1939–1945*. New York: Harper & Row, 1964.

Lippmann, Walter. *U. S. Foreign Policy*. Boston: Little, Brown & Co., 1943.

————. *U. S. War Aims*. Boston: Little, Brown & Co., 1944.

————. *The Cold War*. New York: Harper & Bros., 1947.

Lorwin, Lewis L. *Postwar Plans of the United Nations*. New York: Twentieth Century Fund, 1943.

Lovenstein, Meno. *American Opinion of Soviet Russia*. Washington, D. C. :American Council on Public Affairs, 1941.

Ludwig, Emil. *Stalin*. New York: G. P. Putnam's Sons, 1942.

Lutz, Francis E. *Richmond in World War II*. Richmond: Dietz Press, 1951.

Lydgate, William A. *What America Thinks*. New York: Thomas Y. Crowell, 1944.

Lynd, Robert, and Lynd, Helen. *Middletown in Transition: A Study in Cultural Conflicts*. New York: Harcourt, Brace & Co., 1937.

Lyons, Eugene. *Assignment in Utopia*. New York: Harcourt, Brace & Co., 1937.

————. *Stalin: Czar of All the Russians*. Philadelphia: J. B. Lippincott, 1940.

————. *The Red Decade: The Stalinist Penetration of America*. New York: Bobbs-Merrill, 1941.

————. *Herbert Hoover: A Biography*. Garden City, N. Y. : Doubleday & Co., 1964.

McConnell, Francis J., et al. *A Basis for the Peace to Come: The Merrick-McDowell Lectures for 1942*. New York: Abingdon-Cokesbury Press, 1942.

McCormick, Robert R. *Addresses and Editorials, 1941–1944*. Chicago: Chicago Tribune, 1944.

MacIver, R. M. *Towards an Abiding Peace*. New York: Macmillan, 1943.

MacNeil, Neil. *An American Peace*. New York: Charles Scribner's Sons, 1944.

McNeill, William H. *America, Britain, and Russia: Their Cooperation and Conflict, 1941–1946*. New York: Oxford University Press, 1953.

Markel, Lester, ed. *Public Opinion and Foreign Policy*. New York: Harper & Bros., 1949.

Markowitz, Norman D. *The Rise and Fall of the People's Century: Henry A. Wallace and American Liberalism, 1941–1948*. New York: Free Press, 1973.

Maryland Historical Society. *Maryland in World War II*. Vol. 1. Baltimore: Maryland Historical Society, 1950.

Mathews, Basil. *United We Stand*. Boston: Little, Brown & Co., 1943.

May, Ernest R. *American Imperialism: A Speculative Essay*. New York: Atheneum, 1968.

Mayer, Arno J. *Political Origins of the New Diplomacy*. New Haven: Yale University Press, 1959.

————. *The Politics and Diplomacy of Peacemaking*. New York: Alfred A. Knopf, 1967.

Menefee, Selden. *Assignment: USA*. New York: Reynal & Hitchcock, 1943.

Merton, Robert K. *Social Theory and Social Structure*. 3d ed. rev. New York: Free Press, 1968.

Mikhailov, Nicholas. *The Russian Story: The Coming of Age of a Great People*. New York: Sheridan House, 1945.

Millis, Walter, ed. *The Forrestal Diaries*. New York: Viking Press, 1951.

Motherwell, Hiram. *The Peace We Fight For*. New York: Harper & Bros., 1943.

National Council of American-Soviet Friendship. *Salute to Our Russian Ally*. New York: National Council of American-Soviet Friendship, 1942.

————. *American Industry Commemorates the Tenth Anniversary of American-Soviet Friendship, 1933–1943*. New York: National Council of American-Soviet Friendship, 1944.

————. *Know the USSR: Readings on the Soviet Union*. New York: National Council of American-Soviet Friendship, n.d.

National Municipal League. *People Must Think*. New York: National Municipal League, 1939.

Naughton, James W., ed. *Pius XII on World Problems*. New York: America Press, 1943.

Nazaroff, Alexander. *The Land of the Russian People*. Philadelphia: National Council of American-Soviet Friendship, 1944.

Neumann, William L. *After Victory: Churchill, Roosevelt, Stalin and the Making of the Peace*. New York: Harper & Row, 1967.

Newman, Bernard. *The New Europe*. New York: Macmillan, 1943.

Pares, Bernard. *Russia*. New York: Penguin Books, 1940.

————. *A History of Russia*. 4th ed. rev. New York: Alfred A. Knopf, 1944.

————. *Russia and the Peace*. New York: Macmillan, 1944.

Paterson, Thomas G. *Soviet-American Confrontation: United States Economic Diplomacy and the Origins of the Cold War*. Baltimore: Johns Hopkins Press, 1973.

Pells, Richard H. *Radical Visions and American Dreams: Culture and Social Thought in the Depression Years*. New York: Harper & Row, 1973.

Perrett, Geoffrey. *Days of Sadness, Years of Triumph: The American People, 1939–1945*. New York: Coward, McCann, & Geoghegan, 1973.

Polenberg, Richard. *War and Society: The United States, 1941–1945*. Philadelphia: J. B. Lippincott, 1972.

Ponomarev, B. *The Peoples of Europe versus Hitler*. Moscow: Foreign Languages Publishing House, 1943.

Pope, Arthur U. *Maxim Litvinoff*. New York: Martin, Secker & Warburg, 1943.

Range, Willard. *Franklin D. Roosevelt's World Order*. Athens: University of Georgia Press, 1959.

Reston, James B. *Prelude to Victory*. New York: Alfred A. Knopf, 1942.

Reynolds, Quentin, *Only the Stars Are Neutral*. New York: Random House, 1942.

Rokeach, Milton. *The Open and Closed Mind*. New York: Basic Books, 1960.

Roosevelt, Eleanor. *This I Remember*. New York: Harper & Bros., 1949.

Roosevelt, Elliott. *As He Saw It*. New York: Duell, Sloan & Pearce, 1946.

———, ed. *FDR: His Personal Letters, 1928–1945*. 2 vols. New York: Duell, Sloan & Pearce, 1950.

Rose, Lisle. *After Yalta*. New York: Charles Scribner's Sons, 1972.

Rosenau, James N. *Public Opinion and Foreign Policy*. New York: Random House, 1961.

———, ed. *Domestic Sources of Foreign Policy*. New York: Oxford University Press, 1967.

Rosenman, Samuel I., ed. *The Public Papers and Addresses of Franklin D. Roosevelt*. Vols. 9–13. New York: Random House, 1941–50.

———. *Working with Roosevelt*. New York: Harper & Bros., 1952.

Rozek, Edward J. *Allied Wartime Diplomacy: A Pattern in Poland*. New York: John Wiley & Sons, 1958.

Rugg, Harold. *Now Is the Moment*. New York: Duell, Sloan & Pearce, 1943.

Sales, Raoul de Roussy de. *The Making of Yesterday*. New York: Reynal & Hitchcock, 1947.

Sandburg, Carl. *Home Front Memo*. New York: Harcourt, Brace & Co., 1943.

Schlesinger, Arthur M., Jr., ed. *History of American Presidential Elections*. Vol. 4. New York: Chelsea Publishing Co., 1971.

Schramm, Wilbur, ed. *The Process and Effects of Mass Communication*. Urbana: University of Illinois Press, 1954.

Schwartz, Andrew J. *America and the Russo-Finnish War*. Washington, D. C. : Public Affairs Press, 1960.

Schwarzschild, Leopold. *Primer of the Coming World*. New York: Alfred A. Knopf, 1944.

Scott, John. *Behind the Urals: An American Worker in Russia's City of Steel*. Cambridge, Mass.: Houghton Mifflin Co, 1942.

Sheen, Fulton J. *Philosophies at War*. New York: Charles Scribner's Sons, 1943.

Sherwood, Robert E. *Roosevelt and Hopkins: An Intimate History*. New York: Harper & Bros., 1948.

Shotwell, James T. *The Great Decision*. New York: Macmillan, 1944.

Small, Melvin, ed. *Public Opinion and Historians: Interdisciplinary Perspectives*. Detroit: Wayne State University Press, 1970.

Smith, Bruce Lannes, and Smith, Chitra M. *International Communication and Political Opinion*. Princeton: Princeton University Press, 1956.

Smith, Bruce Lannes; Lasswell, Harold; and Carey, Ralph. *Propaganda, Communication, and Public Opinion*. Princeton: Princeton University Press, 1946.

Smith, Gaddis. *American Diplomacy during the Second World War, 1941–1945*. New York: Wiley & Sons, 1965.

Smith, M. Brewster; Bruner, Jerome S; and White, Robert S. *Opinions and Personality*. New York: John Wiley & Sons, 1956.

Snow, Edgar. *The Pattern of Soviet Power*. New York: Random House, 1945.

Sobel, Robert. *The Origins of Interventionism: The United States and the Russo-Finnish War*. New York: Bookman Associates, 1960.

Sorokin, Pitirim. *Russia and the United States*. New York: E. P. Dutton & Co., 1944.

Spykman, Nicholas John. *America's Strategy in World Politics*. New York: Harcourt, Brace & Co., 1942.

_____ . *The Geography of Peace*. New York: Harcourt, Brace, & Co., 1944.

Standley, William H., and Ageton, Arthur A. *Admiral Ambassador to Russia*. Chicago: Henry Regnery Co., 1955.

Steele, Richard W. *The First Offensive, 1942: Roosevelt, Marshall, and the Making of American Strategy*. Bloomington, Ind.: Indiana University Press, 1973.

Stettinius, Edward R., Jr. *Lend-Lease: Weapon for Victory*. New York: Macmillan, 1944.

_____ . *Roosevelt and the Russians*. Garden City, N. Y.: Doubleday & Co., 1949.

Stevens, Edmund. *Russia Is No Riddle*. New York: Greenberg, 1945.

Stimson, Henry L., and Bundy, McGeorge. *On Active Service in Peace and War*. New York: Harper & Bros., 1947.

Strausz-Hupé, Robert. *The Russian-German Riddle: Rivals or Partners?* Philadelphia: University of Pennsylvania Press, 1940.

Streit, Clarence K. *Union Now: A Proposal for a Federal Union of the Democracies of the North Atlantic*. New York: Harper & Bros., 1939.

Strong, Anna Louise. *The Soviets Expected It*. New York: Dial Press, 1941.

Sussmann, Leila A. *Dear FDR: A Study of Political Letter-Writing*. Totowa, N.J.: Bedminster Press, 1963.

Swing, Raymond Gram. *Preview of History*. Garden City, N. Y.: Doubleday & Co., 1943.

_____ . *"Good Evening!" A Professional Memoir*. New York: Harcourt, Brace & World, 1964.

Taft, Philip. *The AF of L from the Death of Gompers to the Merger*. New York: Harper & Bros., 1959.

Taracouzio, T. A. *War and Peace in Soviet Diplomacy*. New York: Macmillan, 1940.

Taylor, Myron C., ed. *Wartime Correspondence between President Roosevelt and Pope Pius XII*. New York: Macmillan, 1947.

Thomas, Evan W. *The Way to Freedom*. New York: War Resisters League, 1943.

Timasheff, N. S. *Religion in Soviet Russia, 1917–1942*. New York: Sheed & Ward, 1942.

Treviranus, G. R. *Revolutions in Russia: Their Lessons for the Western World*. New York: Harper & Bros., 1944.

Tully, Grace. *FDR My Boss*. New York: Charles Scribner's Sons, 1949.

Universities Committee on Postwar International Problems. *Problem XIV: Post-War Relations with the Soviet Union*. Boston: Universities Committee on Postwar International Problems, n.d.

USSR Society for Cultural Relations with Foreign Countries. *In Defense of Civilization against Fascist Barbarism: Statements, Letters, and Telegrams from Prominent People*. Moscow: Foreign Languages Publishing House, 1941.

Utley, Freda. *The Dream We Lost: Soviet Russia Then and Now*. New York: John Day Co., 1940.

Vandenberg, Arthur H., Jr., ed. *The Private Papers of Senator Vandenberg*. Boston: Houghton Mifflin Co., 1952.

Visson, André. *The Coming Struggle for Peace*. New York: Viking, 1944.

Voyetkhow, Boris. *The Last Days of Sevastopol*. New York: Alfred A. Knopf, 1943.

Wagner, Richard V., and Sherwood, John J., eds. *The Study of Attitude Change*. Belmont, Calif.: Wadsworth Publishing Co., 1969.

Wallace, Henry. *The Century of the Common Man*. Washington, D.C.: Office of War Information, 1942.

———. *Democracy Reborn*. New York: Reynal & Hitchcock, 1944.

Ward, Harry F. *The Soviet Spirit*. New York: International Publishers Co., 1945.

Warner, Jack. *My First Hundred Years in Hollywood*. New York: Random House, 1965.

Warren, Frank A., III. *Liberals and Communism: The "Red Decade" Revisited*. Bloomington, Ind.: Indiana University Press, 1966.

Webb, Sidney, and Webb, Beatrice. *The Truth about Soviet Russia*. New York: Longmans, Green & Co., 1942.

Wecter, Dixon. *The Age of the Great Depression, 1929–1941*. New York: Macmillan, 1948.

Welch, William. *American Images of Soviet Foreign Policy*. New Haven: Yale University Press, 1970.

Welles, Sumner. *The Rights of People to Their Freedom*. Washington, D.C.: Office of War Information, 1943.

———. *The World of the Four Freedoms*. New York: Columbia University Press, 1943.

———. *Time for Decision*. New York: Harper & Bros., 1944.

———, ed. *An Intelligent American's Guide to the Peace*. New York: Dryden Press, 1945.

Werth, Alexander. *Moscow '41*. New York: John Hamilton, 1942.

———. *The Year of Stalingrad*. New York: Alfred A. Knopf, 1943.

———. *Leningrad*. New York: Ryerson Press, 1944.

———. *Russia at War, 1941–1945*. New York: E. P. Dutton & Co., 1964.

Westerfield, H. Bradford. *Foreign Policy and Party Politics: Pearl Harbor to Korea*. New Haven: Yale University Press, 1955.

White, William L. *Report on the Russians*. New York: Harcourt, Brace & Co., 1945.

Whitton, John B., ed. *The Second Chance: America and the Peace*. Princeton: Princeton University Press, 1944.

Williams, Albert Rhys. *The Russians: The Land, the People, and Why They Fight*. New York: Harcourt, Brace & Co., 1943.

Willkie, Wendell L. *One World*. New York: Simon & Schuster, 1943.

———. *An American Program*. New York: Simon & Schuster, 1944.

Wriston, Henry M. *Strategy of Peace*. Boston: World Peace Foundation, 1944.

Young, Roland. *Congressional Politics in the Second World War*. New York: Columbia University Press, 1956.

Zaslavksy, David. *The Face of Hitler's Army*. Moscow: Foreign Languages Publishing House, 1943.

Ziff, William B. *The Gentlemen Talk of Peace*. New York: Prentice-Hall, 1944.

Index